Educational Communications and Technology: Issues and Innovations

This book series, published collaboratively between the AECT (Association for Educational Communications and Technology) and Springer, represents the best and most cutting edge research in the field of educational communications and technology. The mission of the series is to document scholarship and best practices in the creation, use, and management of technologies for effective teaching and learning in a wide range of settings. The publication goal is the rapid dissemination of the latest and best research and development findings in the broad area of educational information science and technology. As such, the volumes will be representative of the latest research findings and developments in the field. Volumes will be published on a variety of topics, including:

- Learning Analytics
- Distance Education
- Mobile Learning Technologies
- Formative Feedback for Complex Learning
- Personalized Learning and Instruction
- Instructional Design
- Virtual tutoring

Additionally, the series will publish the bi-annual AECT symposium volumes, the Educational Media and Technology Yearbooks, and the extremely prestigious and well known, Handbook of Research on Educational Communications and Technology. Currently in its 4th volume, this large and well respected Handbook will serve as an anchor for the series and a completely updated version is anticipated to publish once every 5 years.

The intended audience for Educational Communications and Technology: Issues and Innovations is researchers, graduate students and professional practitioners working in the general area of educational information science and technology; this includes but is not limited to academics in colleges of education and information studies, educational researchers, instructional designers, media specialists, teachers, technology coordinators and integrators, and training professionals.

More information about this series at https://link.springer.com/bookseries/11824

Mark V. Albert • Lin Lin
Michael J. Spector • Lemoyne S. Dunn
Editors

Bridging Human Intelligence and Artificial Intelligence

Springer

AECT
ASSOCIATION FOR EDUCATIONAL COMMUNICATIONS & TECHNOLOGY

Editors
Mark V. Albert
Computer Science and Engineering
University of North Texas
Denton, TX, USA

Lin Lin
Department of Learning Technologies
University of North Texas
Denton, TX, USA

Michael J. Spector
Department of Learning Technologies
University of North Texas
Denton, TX, USA

Lemoyne S. Dunn
Department of Learning Technologies
University of North Texas
Denton, TX, USA

ISSN 2625-0004 ISSN 2625-0012 (electronic)
Educational Communications and Technology: Issues and Innovations
ISBN 978-3-030-84728-9 ISBN 978-3-030-84729-6 (eBook)
https://doi.org/10.1007/978-3-030-84729-6

This Springer imprint is published by the registered company Springer Nature Switzerland AG
The registered company address is: Gewerbestrasse 11, 6330 Cham, Switzerland

Foreword

Neuroscience and artificial intelligence (AI) have an exciting history with periods where AI and biological intelligence strongly inform one another, interrupted by periods where AI focuses on other issues and views neuroscience as a distraction. In the early 2000s, AI, or more specifically machine learning (ML), was furthest from neuroscience, focusing on statistical learning theory and Bayesian statistics, branches of AI that are powerful in their ability to describe *everything* but that are, in their generality, hard to link to neuroscience. That changed in 2012 when Alexnet,[1] with inspiration from neuroscience, managed to beat the entire competition at recognizing objects in images. This, along with a rebranding as *deep learning,* has sparked a renewed interest in artificial neural networks, and currently is the dominating branch of ML. This is a timely book as we are in a phase where ML/AI and neuroscience are somewhat aligned, opening the doors to a fruitful exchange of ideas.

Like many, if not most, neuroscientists, my personal journey into the intersection of biological and artificial intelligence started with an interest in how we think. I quickly got the feeling that we cannot understand one without the other. As such, my entire career happened between studies attempting to understand biological intelligence, with its rich inspiration from animals and brains, and studies attempting to understand artificial intelligence, with its rich framework of mathematics and computational intuition. I used experiments with humans to ask how people deal with uncertainty. I used implementations, for example, in brain machine interfaces, to ask how we can build well-working systems. I used theories to understand how AI systems work. But above all, I tried to keep alive the communication between these communities. I found the biological intelligence and the artificial intelligence communities speak fundamentally different languages, with much of what they can contribute to one another's progress being lost in translation, highlighting the need for a book like this.

[1] Krizhavsky A, Sutskever I, Hinton GE (2012) Imagenet classification with deep convolutional neural networks. Advances in neural information processing systems 25, 1097–1105.

One bridge between these communities is through mutual understanding how AI has been developing. And modern methods from ML have been moving very quickly. An accumulating literature helps us understand why artificial neural networks function so well. And the first part of the book nicely and digestibly gets across in broad strokes what we know about the developments in the ML field itself and how these developments relate to human learning. To me, this conceptual understanding of where ML is has always been a necessary factor to make ML useful to the human intelligence community.

A second bridge is the use of AI to improve human intelligence. The traditional model of teaching suffers from many shortcomings. As a professor, I was able to observe this firsthand. Students have huge trouble following lectures and learning how to use the concepts at a much later point of time in homework. People are lonely, lacking ways to connect with one another. Tests are slow and time consuming. And the COVID pandemic brought on a host of new problems. AI now promises to help with all this. We can use it to scale and democratize education. For example, I am involved with Neuromatch Academy, a nonprofit organization bringing AI-powered learning to thousands of students. The role of universities will, arguably, be to incorporate insights from AI to improve its many processes. And that will probably require most instructors to have a level of understanding of artificial as well as human intelligence.

Models of the brain can also inform the AI community. Machine learning techniques are often used as model of the brain – people argue that because brains solve similar problems to ML systems that they must share properties. For example, many aspects of the visual system of mammals are well described by assuming similar representations between brains and artificial neural networks. In fact, I remember well my first exposure to this idea. I had long looked at the properties of neurons in the visual system. A really elegant paper by Bruno Olshausen showed that ML systems applied to understanding natural scenes can lead to system behaviors similar to neurons in the early visual system.[2] Evolution matters for human intelligence, but the ML field is also performing a kind of evolution: we only ever get to see the algorithms that work best. As such, there may be a lot that people interested in human intelligence can learn from artificial intelligence and vice versa. This book is highlighting a range of these similarities.

AI is starting to have a profound effect on us humans. AI systems are being built into just about all human endeavors, ranging from the mundane, such as recognizing spoken words, to the socially involved, such as deciding if a criminal is likely to re-offend and should thus remain incarcerated. So we really need to understand AI to build a better world. Where do our biases come from? Are the biases in the algorithm, the data, or their combination? How do AI systems relate to human creativity? When it comes to the application of AI, the sky is not the limit. As AI systems give us new powers, we need to make sure we use them responsibly.

---

[2] Olshausen, B., Field, D. Emergence of simple-cell receptive field properties by learning a sparse code for natural images. *Nature* **381,** 607–609 (1996). https://doi.org/10.1038/381607a0

Human and artificial intelligence have experienced crosspollination since AI systems existed. Both AI and the study of human intelligence have made massive progress over the last couple of decades, with many great advances made through shared concepts, tools, and especially people. However, there is still much work to be done, and this decade in particular is an exciting time of convergence between AI and human intelligence. This book builds that connection in a way that brings communities together for the benefit of all.

Konrad Körding Penn Integrated Knowledge Professor
University of Pennsylvania
Philadelphia, PA, USA, CIFAR Member
Toronto, Canada, Neuromatch Cofounder
Philadelphia, PA, USA

Preface

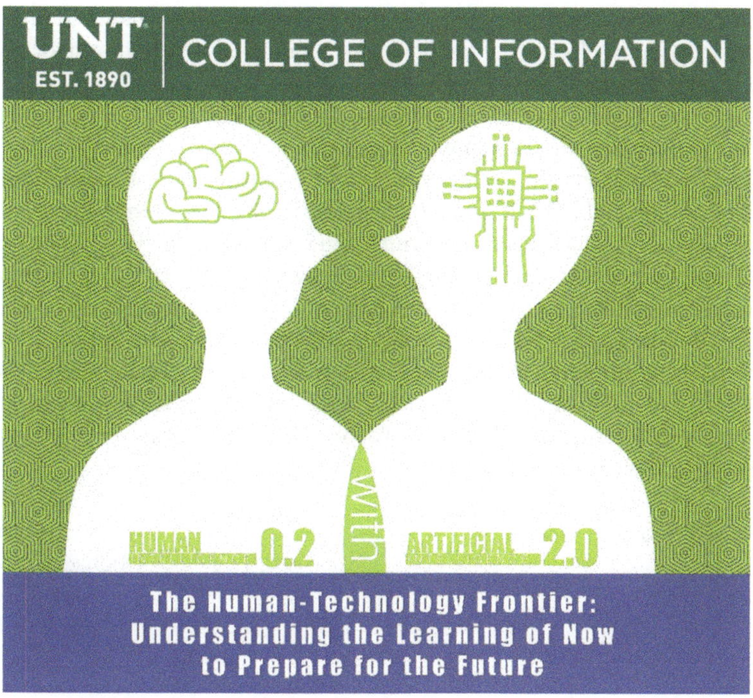

Fig. 1 Poster of the "Human-Technology Frontier" credit to Dr. Xue Yang

The concept of this edited book started with the two-and-a-half-day symposium sponsored by the Association for Educational Communications and Technology (AECT) and hosted by the Texas Center for Educational Technology at the University of North Texas in 2018. We are deeply grateful for the support of Dr. Phillip Harris, the executive director of AECT (https://www.aect.org/), and for the support of Dr. Kinshuk, dean of the College of Information at the University of North Texas (https://ci.unt.edu/).

The theme of the symposium was "The Human-Technology Frontier: Understanding the Learning of Now to Prepare for the Future" (See Fig. 1 for the symposium poster). The symposium was successful, and was well attended by over 15 distinguished speakers and over 80 participants from multiple institutions, countries, and professional contexts. The participants engaged in discussions on a range of topics such as human and holistic learning as informed by new research in neuroscience, creativity, critical thinking, self-directed learning, artificial intelligence, learning analytics, and measurements.

The original idea was to have the symposium presenters contribute chapters to the book. Yet, the book has since evolved to include much younger authors thanks to Dr. Mark Albert, who joined the editors' team in 2019. Dr. Albert introduced the book idea to the students at the Texas Academy of Math and Sciences (TAMS), who are in fact junior and senior high school students. As a result, we created a mentorship mechanism, where the TAMS high-school students would work with graduate students, who would be mentored by the faculty members to co-author the chapters. Consequently, most chapters of the book are co-authored by a high-school student, a graduate student, and a faculty member.

We are very pleased with the outcomes of the book. The book followed the original vision, which would: (1) be multidisciplinary and transdisciplinary; (2) provide a forward-thinking perspective likely to lead to significant and sustained improvement in learning; and (3) embrace an integrative approach to designing and implementing advanced technologies in learning and instruction. In addition, the process created an apprenticeship and mentorship model which provided the opportunity for the younger students (high-school students) to learn the methods of conducting research, to engage in intellectual dialogues on the interactions between human intelligence and artificial intelligence, and for the younger students to establish scholarship and interdisciplinary inquiries. We would like to acknowledge the hard work by our chapter authors and we look forward to further conversations on this important topic with our readers.

Denton, TX, USA

Lin Lin
Michael J. Spector
Mark V. Albert
Lemoyne Dunn

Contents

About the Editors

Mark V. Albert's professional goal in life is to leverage machine learning to automate the collection and inference of clinically useful health information to improve clinical research. His projects in wearable sensor analytics have improved the measurement of health outcomes for individuals with Parkinson's disease, stroke, and transfemoral amputations with a variety of additional populations and contexts including children with cerebral palsy as well as healthy toddler activity tracking. Current projects include video-based activity tracking and mobile robotic platforms, all in an effort to improve measures of clinical outcomes to justify therapeutic interventions.

Lin Lin is a Professor of Learning Technologies at the University of North Texas. Lin received her doctoral degree at Teachers College, Columbia University. Lin's research focuses on human-technology interactions, and life-long learning with innovative pedagogies and technologies. Specifically, she has published research in media multitasking, cognitive off-loading, multimedia design, executive functions, and (AI, VR) technology-supported STEM and STEM-enabling skills. Currently, Lin serves as the director of Texas Center for Educational Technology (TCET, https://tcet.unt.edu/). She also serves as the editor-in-chief of one of the top-tier journals, *Educational Technology Research and Development* (ETR&D Development Section, http://www.springer.com/11423).

Michael J. Spector is professor at UNT and was previously Professor of Educational Psychology at the University of Georgia; Associate Director of the Learning Systems Institute at Florida State University; Chair of Instructional Design, Development and Evaluation at Syracuse University; and Director of the Educational Information Science and Technology Research Program at the University of Bergen. He earned a Ph.D. from The University of Texas. He is a visiting research professor at Beijing Normal University, at East China Normal University, and the Indian Institute of Technology-Kharagpur. His research focuses on assessing learning in complex domains, inquiry and critical thinking skills, and program evaluation. He was executive director of the International Board of

Standards for Training, Performance and Instruction and a past president of the Association for Educational and Communications Technology. He is Editor Emeritus of Educational Technology Research & Development; he edited two editions of the *Handbook of Research on Educational Communications and Technology* and the *SAGE Encyclopedia of Educational Technology* and has more than 150 publications to his credit.

Lemoyne S. Dunn is an adjunct graduate faculty member at UNT who previously served as Director of a Title III Grant and as a Project Director for the Intel Teach to the Future program, training over 22,000 educators in north and west Texas. She also served as a lead evaluator for three of the seven TARGET grants evaluated by the Texas Center for Educational Technology. She earned her Ph.D. from UNT, as well as two master's degrees and multiple certificates and endorsements. Her B.S. is from Texas A&M University. Her areas of interest include educational technology, cognitive science, and gifted education.

Part I
Trajectory of AI. From Statistics and Machine Learning to Deep Learning

Understanding Machine Learning Through Data-Oriented and Human Learning Approaches

Sahar Behpour and Avi Udash

Introduction

Artificial intelligence (AI) has consistently strived to mimic human intelligence to independently perform tasks such as feature recognition, decision making, and anomaly detection (Turing, 1950). In order for an intelligent system to complete these tasks, the system must learn autonomously. Efforts in achieving such a self-learning capability in machines have introduced the subfield of machine learning (ML), which explores computers' ability to perform numerous tasks, such as pattern detection and classification, without being programmed with explicit instructions to do so. Therefore, Ml offers systems with human-like intelligence capable of independently identifying patterns in data such that problems can be solved with increased accuracy and efficiency while eliminating the need for explicitly written algorithms (Boutaba et al., 2018).

The study and simulation of different types of human learning processes through ML are still the most challenging and exciting goals of AI. Since the invention of computers, numerous research studies have aimed to mimic such capabilities with computers; for instance, in 2019 Dmitry Krotov and John Hopfield developed a backpropagation algorithm to simulate a biologically plausible learning model (Krotov & Hopfield, 2019). Also, brain inspired models, such as artificial neural networks, which are state of the art in many ML tasks, are inspired by biological neural networks that humans and animals use (McCulloch & Pitts, 1990). For instance, a direct correspondence between the hierarchy of the human visual areas,

S. Behpour (✉)
Department of Information Science, University of North Texas, Denton, TX, USA
e-mail: Sahar.behpour@unt.edu

A. Udash
Texas Academy of Math and Science, Sandford University, California, CA, USA

M. V. Albert et al. (eds.), *Bridging Human Intelligence and Artificial Intelligence*, Educational Communications and Technology: Issues and Innovations, https://doi.org/10.1007/978-3-030-84729-6_1

especially the primary visual cortex (V1), and the layers of convolutional neural networks (CNN) trained on visual object recognition (Lindsay, 2020). The primary visual cortex consists of two types of cells, simple cells with local receptive fields and complex ones which receive input from many different cells and have invariant responses. Transforming these findings of Hubel and Wiesel, in 1979, a novel multilayered neural network model named the "neurocognition," was proposed by Fukushima suggesting a hierarchical, multilayered architecture. This model, which was the precursor to CNN, could make a network with the ability to recognize a simple input pattern, regardless of a shift in the position, or significant distortion in the shape of the input pattern (Fukushima, 1979). Therefore, enabling computer systems to learn by achieving a complete understanding of the nature of the learning process is a common objective of AI and ML (Ramasubramanian & Singh, 2017).

Similarly, understanding different types of ML models through the human learning concepts is beneficial for creating effective automated systems. The learning and the learning processes are defined in many different ways. The most common definition of learning describes a relatively continuous change in behavior as a result of experience or practice (Lachman, 1997). It is stated that ML learning is a complex phenomenon that involves gaining and organizing new knowledge into general, efficient representations, as well as discovering new facts and theories by observation and examination (Carbonell et al, 1983). By implementing this approach of learning into an ML system, the system's ability to solve problems generally improves, as a system capable of learning can independently adjust itself to achieve better performance in future tasks. For example, a common optimization technique can be utilized to improve classification algorithms, yielding accuracies over 90% for a variety of datasets, including the IRIS flower dataset (Rehman & Nawi, 2011). So, machines capable of autonomously learning can provide a significant advantage in executing various tasks and problems. Therefore, researchers continue to pursue and improve ML models that replicate the features of the human learning process.

Further, with the huge amount of data that is produced by both humans and machines, there is a crucial need to explore ML models and their effectiveness from a data-driven perspective (Sagar, 2021).

The adaptation of a data-driven approach can result in creating various predictive and descriptive models with high accuracy and low computational costs. This can also lead to more evidence-based decision-making processes among various aspects of life including education, financial modeling, healthcare, marketing, and policing. Moreover, as the cost of data storage devices and developments and advancements of computational technologies reduce, understanding and investigating ML while utilizing data-driven models seem promising approaches for creating advanced learning tasks (Brownlee, 2014).

While algorithms can only be applied to specific, predetermined cases, ML can be used to build models with more general applications. Elementary coding classes often cite the example of algorithms being akin to giving a computer instruction to make a peanut butter jelly sandwich; in that vein, machine learning is akin to sending a computer to culinary school. Thus, with Ml's far-reaching real-world applications, this area of research has already turned into one of the most demanding and practical fields worldwide. In healthcare, machine learning helps doctors provide earlier and more accurate diagnoses, identify potential treatments and cures, and predict health risks in patients (Sumana De & Chakraborty, 2020). In e-commerce businesses such as Amazon, machine learning is implemented in product recommendation systems to improve the relevance of recommended items. In music, recommendation engines like Spotify, one of the most common ML/AI applications for consumer tech, cloud-based, AI-driven music composition platforms like Amper, systems, like Pandora, capable of automatically understanding the musicological content of an audio signal, are a few examples of the ML applications. In banking industries, machine learning is used to detect fraud, trade stocks algorithmically, and manage individual portfolios. Furthermore, by implementing and improving modern machine learning models and techniques, it is possible to significantly advance the understanding and development of other fields. For instance, various ML tools and techniques are being used to create automatic trend detections in scientific literature and conference papers. In that regard, a temporal automatic trend detection system can capture trending topics in the field of finance using several ML algorithms such as dimensionality reductions in the preprocessing and clustering for building the system. The method can also be easily amenable to other fields to provide information about trending areas of researchers for funding agencies and academic programs (Behpour et al., 2021).

Therefore, as ML techniques continue to develop, their applications and influence continue to spread, improving both the accuracy and efficiency of complex tasks that are being applied in various areas in academic, business and marketing, environment, legal, healthcare, and medicine.

Why Machine Learning?

A large distinction between humans and machines is that humans have the ability to learn from their experiences, while machines do not. Before machine learning, programmers had to write specific algorithms for every problem. Programmers would have already needed to find a solution for each problem, and computers would only have been used to do computational tasks. However, as problems get increasingly difficult and the volume of data approaches many terabytes or even petabytes, as seen in many modern applications of machine learning such as recommendation systems and fraud detection, manually sifting through these data and programming specific algorithms becomes completely unfeasible and sometimes impossible to do. Furthermore, for many complex tasks, it is difficult to algorithmically define the features and criteria of the problem in a concrete and simple manner. With machine learning, this challenge can be circumvented by permitting the computer to independently identify specific patterns from the data and apply these learned patterns to future datasets (Japkowicz, 2006). For instance, it is difficult to precisely define the conditions that distinguish cancerous tissue from healthy tissue, so humans are often unable to accurately identify cancerous cells manually. However, as demonstrated by Google's breast cancer detection deep learning network, machines have the capability to more accurately and efficiently locate cancerous tissues after autonomously learning to identify affected cells; Google's network achieved an accuracy of 89%, which greatly succeeded the 73% score of human pathologists (McKinney et al., 2020). Computers' learning ability thus provides a significant advantage in feature extraction and other non-algorithmically defined tasks, making machine learning a valuable tool in various fields.

Moreover, computers are highly effective at examining data and finding patterns within that data. For example, Microsoft's deep residual network achieved a 3.75% error rate in categorizing the ImageNet test set at the 2015 ImageNet Large Scale Visual Recognition Challenge (ILSVRC), highlighting machine learning's significant ability to classify and detect a variety of objects, scenes, and shapes (He et al., 2016). As machines identify patterns in data such as images, they "learn" and create models to represent these patterns. These computer-generated models can then be applied to multiple similar problems, eliminating the need for programmers to write specific algorithms with limited scopes.

Machine Learning Problems and Methods

While machine learning can be used to solve many different types of problems, it excels at regression and classification problems. Regression-type problems involve finding a function to predict future outcomes given a set of data. For example, a computer could be given x and y value points and be asked to find a formula in the form of $y = mx + b$. Then, when any x value is given, a corresponding y value could be predicted by simply plugging in the x value into the equation. This would be an example of linear regression (Seal, 1968) or finding the line of best fit.

On the other hand, classification problems involve finding patterns to separate the data into distinct groups or classes. For example, a computer could be given an email with the goal of classifying it as spam or not. A more complicated example would involve the computer being able to classify an unknown animal in a given image.

To solve these problems, machines can use a variety of different learning methods. Popular learning methods include supervised learning, unsupervised learning, semi-supervised learning, and reinforcement learning. In all instances, having a large amount of data is one possible, though not the only, key to create an effective model.

Supervised Learning

The primary objective of supervised learning models is to uncover a relationship between the input points, or features, and the output points, or labels, of the given labeled data (Van Houwelingen, 2004). Labeled data is defined to come in pairs of features and labels, where features are the independent variables that influence the labels (the dependent variables). In the case of a basic linear regression model, the labeled data is composed of pairs of x and y values, with the x-value being the feature and the y-value being the label. While each pair in the data of this simple model is limited to a single numerical x and a single numerical y value, complex data can consist of intricate webs of multiple features and multiple labels all intertwined. In any case, supervised learning models aim to find the relationships that tie the features to labels, with the overarching goal of predicting the most accurate label on future data (Zhu & Goldberg, 2009).

Depending on the domain of the labels, supervised learning problems are further divided into two categories: classification and regression. Classification problems involve a finite number of possible discrete label values, with the goal of categorizing future input data to fit into one of these label values. Each label in a categorization problem can be thought of as a group, and the supervised learning model will attempt to place future input data into one of these groups. In categorization, each label may be given a numerical value (typically positive integers starting from 1), though this numbering method is often arbitrary and does not suggest structure (Zhu & Goldberg, 2009). For example, a label with a value of 1 does not necessarily contain features that are closer to a label with a value of 2 compared to a label with a value of 3. These numerical labels are entirely representational; therefore, no amount of math can be done on these labels.

A human example of a supervised classification problem is when children are shown different colors and given names for each color so that they can identify the colors later on. In this case, the labels are the names of the colors, and the features are the visual representation of the colors. After the children can map the visual identity of each color to its respective name, they will successfully be able to identify distinctive colors. Since the children are only taught a few basic colors, the number of possible labels is limited, thus making this an example of a classification problem. If this problem was to be modeled for a computer, it might be described in the following way: the color hues could be represented by RGB values while each label, or color name, could be given a discrete number (for example, red is 1, blue is 2, yellow is 3, and green is 4). The classification algorithm could then take the training data, attempt to make connections between each RGB value and its corresponding color name, and be able to recognize color names. An example of a pattern the computer might recognize is that an RGB code with a high red value and low green and blue values has an increased possibility of being classified into group 1.

On the other hand, regression models aim to approximate a function f using labeled training data, with the objective of predicting a numerical value for the label y given some future data x (Fernández-Delgado et al., 2019). Often, this label y is a quantity, such as the predicted market value for a home. The features of the house—such as the year it was built, its square footage, the market value of surrounding houses, and the number of bedrooms and bathrooms—are represented by multiple x-values (Nghiep & Al, 2001). In this example, the regression model will take in the features of the house and attempt to learn a function that can map the features of the house to the market value of the house. This function can then be utilized to predict

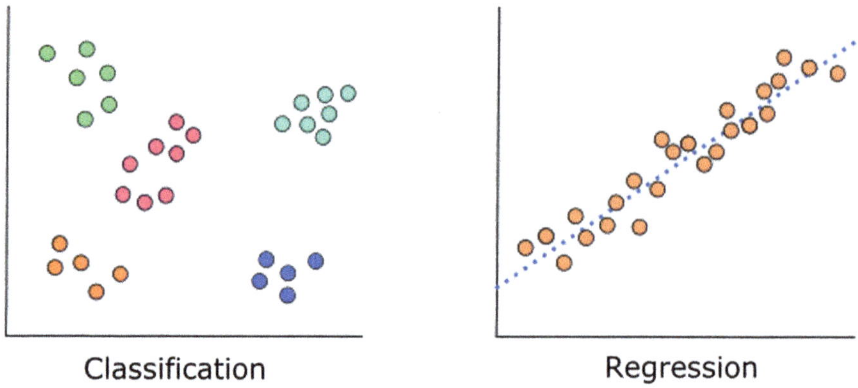

Fig. 1 *Classification vs. regression.* Classification problems require sorting data into different groups or buckets. Regression problems require finding the curve of best fit to predict the outcome given some amount of data

or estimate the market values for any house, given the features of that house. Figure 1 depicts a visual distinction between classification and regression problems.

Classification and regression problems require the implementation of different algorithms to train the model. Two commonly used classification algorithms are the K-Nearest Neighbor (KNN) and logistic regression algorithms. The KNN algorithm operates on the presumption that data points with the same labels will be near each other since they generally have similar properties (Kotsiantis et al., 2006). Given this assumption, when a new data point is provided to the model, the KNN algorithm will find the data point's k nearest neighbors (training data points with similar properties). Then, the algorithm classifies this new data point by identifying the most frequent label that appears on its nearest neighbors. For example, if k is designated to be 5, the algorithm searches for the five closest neighbors. If four of those neighbors have a label of 1 and only a single neighbor has a label of 2, the KNN algorithm will classify the new data point with 1.

Regression problems, as stated earlier, require approximating a function through training with given data. A simple, yet important method of solving a regression problem is the linear regression model. Some of the most common algorithms used for supervised learning include linear regression, logistic regression, and decision trees. Figure 1 from earlier in the section provides an example of linear regression, while Fig. 2 provides the general form of a decision tree as a regression problem. Decision trees consist of three types of nodes: the root node, the internal node, and the leaf node. The root node is the main question/problem that the algorithm is trying to solve, the internal nodes are branches of the root node, and the leaf nodes are the final conclusion.

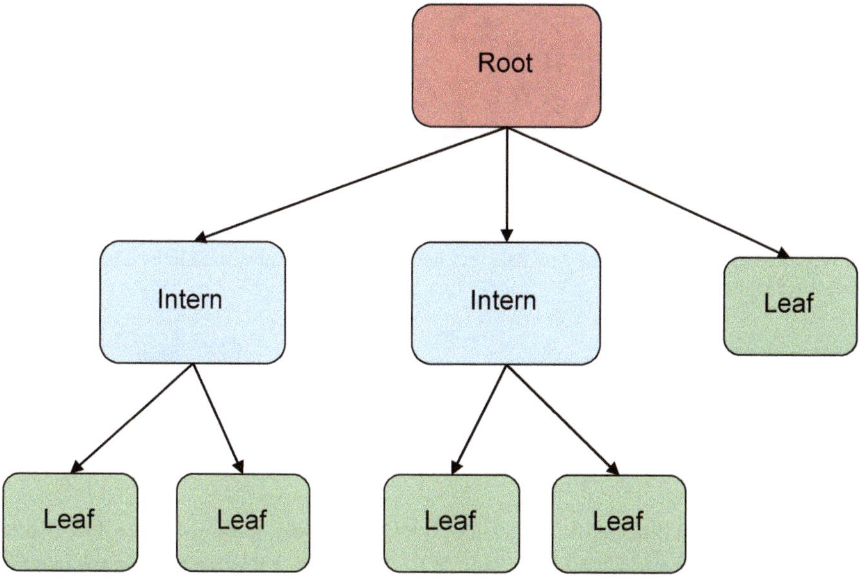

Fig. 2 *Decision trees*. A supervised regression model with a root node (the first red box) refers to the problem that the model will solve. The internal nodes (blue boxes) are branches of the root node, and the leaf nodes are the conclusion

Fig. 3 *K-means clustering*. K-means clustering, as a centroid-based model, can categorize samples into globular shapes. Clusters are shaped based on the distance from the centroid, shown as a red circle. Some samples are out of the clusters and resemble outliers

Unsupervised Learning

In unsupervised learning, as suggested by its name, the dataset utilized by the machine is not labeled. While supervised learning models are trained on both the input and the output, unsupervised learning models are only exposed to the input data. Therefore, rather than identifying the data, the model attempts to categorize it into distinct arbitrary groups. Clustering, a subset of classification problems whose dataset is not labeled, and dimensionality reduction problems are commonly solved using unsupervised learning (Ghahramani, 2004). K-means clustering (Fig. 3), DBSCAN clustering (Fig. 4), Hierarchical clustering, Hidden Markov Model

Fig. 4 *DBSCAN clustering*. DBSCAN clustering, as a density-based clustering algorithm, can classify data into any shape of clusters in a dataset. Sparse areas are borders between clusters that are required to separate clusters. Any data that lies in this area is considered to be a broader point corrupted by noise

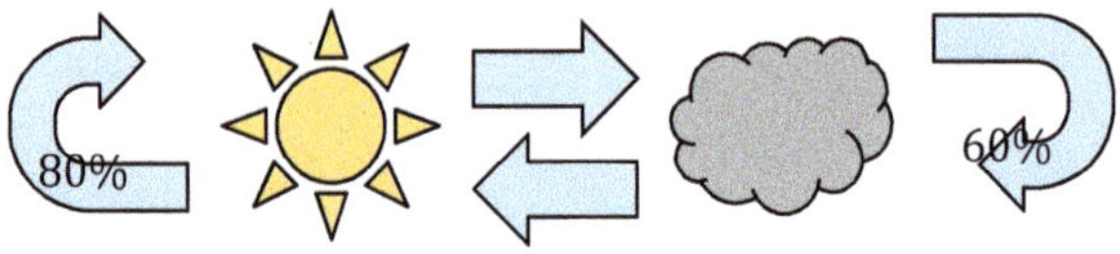

Fig. 5 *Hidden Markov Model*. As an example, if it is sunny today, tomorrow has an 80% chance of being sunny and a 20% chance of being cloudy. Note that this model does not consider yesterday's weather in order to make its forecast for tomorrow

(HMM) (Fig. 5), and association rules are some popular algorithms used to create unsupervised learning models. A common use for clustering is in customer segmentation. To better target marketing campaigns at the right people and reduce waste in marketing campaigns, marketing teams must group customers based on age, income, recent purchases, behavior, or other attributes. By using a K-means clustering algorithm, the customer data will be classified based on the specified number of segments. If you get a new customer, the model will be able to help determine which segment the customer belongs to and display products that are associated with that segment.

Hierarchical Clustering

Hierarchical clustering, or connectivity-based clustering, is another commonly used clustering technique in unsupervised learning. In contrast to k-means clustering, this method does not require the number of clusters to be predetermined. In hierarchical clustering, data is sorted into a hierarchy of clusters in which clusters that are more closely related are grouped closer together. This is represented through a dendrogram, a tree diagram that illustrates the relationship between data values based on the specified linkage criteria, which determines the distance between two clusters. There are two forms of hierarchical clustering: the first, agglomerative clustering, works bottom-up by first assuming each data point is an independent cluster. It then repeatedly combines the two most similar clusters into a new cluster until only one cluster remains; this cluster becomes the root of the dendrogram. The second, divisive clustering, works in a manner opposite to that of agglomerative clustering.

In this method, all data values are initially placed in a single cluster. The algorithm then repeatedly divides each cluster into two unique clusters until each data point is its own cluster. Hierarchical clustering has diverse applications in various fields; for instance, as demonstrated by Nicholas Heard et al., Bayesian hierarchical clustering (a form of agglomerative clustering) can be used to identify groups of similar gene expression profiles in malaria-infected mosquitoes with greater efficiency and effectiveness as compared to other techniques (Heard et al., 2006). By using hierarchical clustering, the relationships between various clusters can be more easily observed; thus, this technique is a valuable tool for ML data analysis methods.

Hidden Markov model

With certain time-series data, one can choose to model them as Markov chains. A Markov chain is a model that describes a sequence in which the state of an event depends solely on the state of the previous event (Fig. 4).

When a computer develops a model for a process, it has to determine the nature of the relations between subsequent events. A hidden Markov model assumes that the process being modeled is an unobservable Markov chain *X*. It then assumes that there is an observable process *Y* that is dependent on *X*. By observing *Y*, the computer is tasked with learning about *X*. For example, assume that we give a computer a weather report for the previous 10 days as follows:

$$\{\text{sunny,sunny,sunny,sunny,sunny,sunny,sunny,cloudy,cloudy,sunny}\}$$

Our computer would then be tasked with determining probabilities for the next day's forecast given the current day's weather. Due to its deterministic nature, hidden Markov models have been used in fields such as thermodynamics, economics, and gesture recognition (Rabiner, 1990).

Association Rule Learning

In certain databases, one can assume that there are rules predicting how certain variables are associated with each other. If this is the case, one can apply association rule learning, which is a rule-based machine learning method in which a computer discovers statistically significant relations (or "association rules") between the presence of variables in a large database. The method was popularized in a study by Agrawal et al. (1993) that offered the context of a supermarket owner trying to determine optimal product. In this context, a computer would look for association rules in a database of consumer purchases. One such rule might be given as

$$\{\text{soda,chips,plastic plates} \Rightarrow \text{plastic cups}\}$$

indicating that a consumer who had purchased soda, chips, and plastic plates would also be likely to purchase plastic cups. A similar approach can also be used in other consumer industries like e-commerce (Dai et al., 2016). In order to discover meaningful association rules, one needs to consider several constraints, such as support, confidence, and lift.

Support is defined as the proportion of associations in a dataset that contains the variables of interest. Returning to the supermarket example, a hypothetical

$$\{\text{milk} \Rightarrow \text{eggs}\}$$

The relationship might be defined as more insignificant if a high proportion of purchases contain eggs, on the grounds that purchasing milk does not singularly predict purchasing eggs.

Confidence indicates how often an association rule is found to be true, is defined as

$$\text{confidence}(X \Rightarrow Y) = \frac{\text{support}(X \cup Y)}{\text{support}(X)}.$$

A hypothetical association rule with low confidence can be dismissed on the grounds that it does not accurately predict the occurrence of variables.

Finally, a lift is used to determine whether the probabilities of two variables occurring are independent of each other or not. It is defined as

$$\text{lift}(X \Rightarrow Y) = \frac{\text{support}(X \cap Y)}{\text{support}(X)\text{support}(Y)}.$$

If an association rule has a lift = 1, its variables occur independently of each other. If a rule has a lift > 1, its variables are positively correlated with each other. If a rule has a lift < 1, its variables are negatively correlated with each other (Dai et al., 2016; Hahsler et al., 2005).

Semi-Supervised Learning

Semi-supervised learning (Zhu, 2005) aims to combine supervised and unsupervised learning methods by using a mix of both labeled and unlabeled data to train models. Semi-supervised learning can be especially useful when there is a limited amount of labeled data but a large amount of unlabeled data to train with. A common application of semi-supervised learning is in speech transcription since manual speech transcription is tedious and time-consuming work (Zhu & Goldberg, 2009). Although it is more difficult to find labeled speech data (since it requires human annotators), unlabeled speech data is quite easy to obtain. Semi-supervised learning

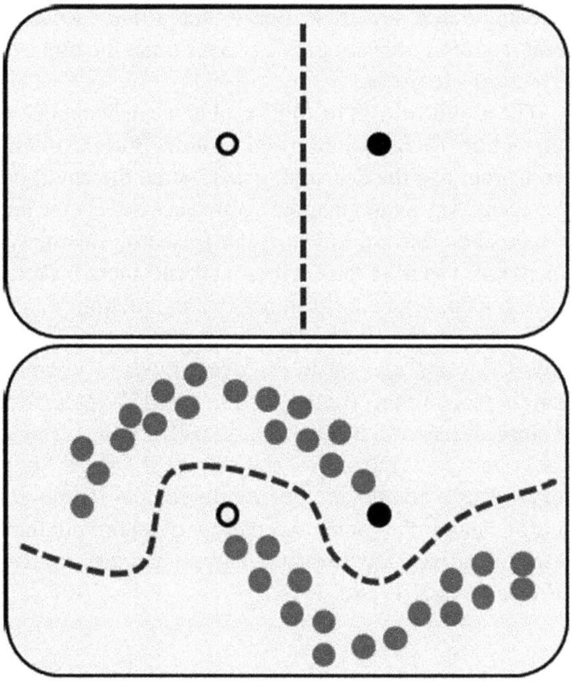

Fig. 6 *Classification in semi-supervised learning.* The top panel shows an example of classification based on only two labeled examples (white and black circles). The bottom panel shows classification based on those examples plus unlabeled data points (gray circles)—graphic by Techerin, distributed under a CC BY-SA 4.0 license via Wikimedia Commons

can utilize the combination of both labeled and unlabeled speech data to create models that can automatically transcribe audio. Figure 6 shows the impact of using semi-supervised learning to combine labeled and unlabeled data.

Semi-supervised learning can be further differentiated into two slightly different categories: transductive learning and inductive learning. In the case of supervised learning, the singular goal is to predict future outcomes since all the data is labeled. However, semi-supervised learning trains with both labeled and unlabeled data, thus resulting in two different goals: one to classify future test cases and the other to provide labels to the existing unlabeled data. The former is called transductive learning, while the latter is known as inductive learning (van Engelen & Hoos, 2020).

Reinforcement Learning

The final type of machine learning covered here is reinforcement learning (Sutton & Barto, 2018). Unlike the previously discussed types of learning, reinforcement learning trains a model to make a series of decisions. The computer is placed in a game-like environment and has to make decisions that impact this game, often randomly and through trial and error. Then, the computer gets a reward or a penalty, depending on how good of a decision it made. The main goal of the computer is to maximize the rewards it receives. Reinforcement learning can be compared to teaching a dog new trick. Every time a dog successfully does the desired trick, a treat is given to reward the dog. Over time, the dog learns that doing the trick properly results in treats.

The reinforcement learning problem can be modeled using an agent-environment interaction. Richard Sutton and Andrew Barto explain that in a system, the agent is the learner and the decision-maker, while the environment is everything outside of the agent. Any action that the agent takes affects the environment, which sends back a state and a reward to the agent. Based on this new state and the reward that the agent receives from the environment, the agent makes another decision thus restarting the loop. Figure 6 illustrates this interaction.

Reinforcement learning is immensely successful in interactive scenarios, as opposed to the previously discussed types of learning that focused on "statistical pattern recognition" (Sutton & Barto, 2018). Interactive scenarios refer to tasks that require decision-making, such as self-driving vehicles, robotics, and games like chess and go. AlphaZero—the strongest Chess, Shogi, and Go AI player in history—uses a combination of reinforcement learning and neural networks to train itself to master the games. According to Deepmind (the company behind AlphaZero), AlphaZero beat the strongest current engines crafted for Chess, Shogi, and Go (Silver et al., 2018).

Creating Effective Models

In order to build effective machine learning models that can generalize well on new data, one needs various considerations across the whole data lifecycle, from data generation and collection to interpretation and reporting. In other words, to build a high-quality machine learning model, an appropriate selection and interpretation of assessment criteria are required. This section discusses data quality, model bias, and validation strategies that need to be addressed when building any machine learning model.

Data Quality

Today's corporations are increasingly data-driven and ML-based; thus, they are tasked with ensuring data quality. Data quality, i.e., the degree to which the data characteristics meet the expectation of the users (Ge & Helfert, 2007; "Website," n.d.), is proven to have a tremendous impact on ML algorithms, especially those used in data analysis and text mining processes, to support automated decision-making tasks (Ge & Helfert, 2007). Data quality characteristics, issues, and frameworks have been discussed and defined from various perspectives over the last 50 years (Bicevska et al., 2018). One way to define data quality is through its characteristics that are categorized from diverse perspectives; though the most common ones in the literature ("Data Quality Assessment," n.d.; Maydanchik, 2007) are as follows:

- Accessibility: Can be accessed in a specific context (including its suitability for representation in a model)?
- Accuracy: Do the data's attributes correctly represent the right value of the intended object?
- Completeness: Do entities have values for all expected attributes and some other related entity instances?
- Consistency: Is the information object presented in the same format, being compatible with similar information objects?
- Currency: The extent to which data holds attributes of the right age.

Major resources on data quality define and measure the value of these characteristics informally. In other words, though these characteristics are commonly used, the mechanisms that specify them have not yet been formalized. Recently, a new data quality management approach has been proposed that presents three different Domain Specific Language (DSL) groups (Bicevskis et al., 2018). The first group uses the concept of data objects to analyze data quality, the second group concerns data quality requirements, and the third group describes the quality management process.

In general, data-quality problems can be divided into two major categories; schema-level and instance-level (Barateiro & Galhardas, 2005). The first type, schema-level, does not depend on the actual content of the data. Therefore, they can be improved with a schema design, transition, and/or integration. The following are some examples of the data-quality problems that can be improved with a schema-level strategy: missing data, wrong data type, wrong data value, dangling data, exact duplicate data, generic domain constraints, wrong categorical data, outdated temporal data, inconsistent spatial data, name conflicts (the same field name is used for different objects or different names are used for the same object), and structural conflicts (different schema representations of the same object in different tables or databases).

On the other hand, instance-level data-quality problems cannot be solved with an improved schema design because the schema definition languages or characteristics cannot specify all the constraints of the data content. These data-quality problems, errors, are not visible or solvable in the schema level, and they are divided into two major parts: single-record and multiple-record problems. In a single-record data problem, only one entity is considered, and the rest of the attributes or entities are not related to the information stored in the data. Missing data in a not null field, erroneous data, misspellings, embedded values, misfielded values, and ambiguous data are such examples of single record data quality problems.

Multiple-record data problems cannot be detected by considering each record separately as the data problem concerns more than one record. Notice that multiple record problems can occur among records belonging to the same entity set (or table) or to different entity sets (corresponding to different tables or even to different databases). In other words, there are some interconnections between the entities and their data problems. These problems include duplicate records, records with no contradictory information but the same real entity, contradicting records, records with contradicting information from the same entity, non-standardized data, and different representations of data.

There are many data quality tools that aim to detect and solve these problems and improve the accuracy and efficiency of a machine learning or artificial intelligence task. Depending on the type of data quality process (Olson, 2003), the tools are categorized into six different types as follows: data profiling, data analysis, data transformation, data cleaning, duplicate elimination, and data enrichment (Sadiq, 2013).

Bias in the ML Models

The professional world and our daily life are now experiencing a new paradigm of automated AI decision-making applications. However, there is still the critical question of how to avoid discrimination and bias against a specific population or minority when using ML algorithms to build such automated decision-making models. There are many forms of bias in data and models that, in some cases, can lead to unfairness in machine learning tasks. Several studies have proposed categorizations and descriptions of different kinds of biases corresponding to each part of the data lifecycle from data source, generation, collection, and pre-processing to modeling, validation, and visualization. For instance, Gordon and Desjardins (1995) describe that machine learning biases can be categorized into forms such as procedural bias and representational bias ("Feature Selection and Evaluation," 2012; Gordon & Desjardins, 1995). Herein, we summarize some of the examples and categorizations in order to highlight the significant possibility of introducing bias into the data lifecycle while aiming to implement a machine learning task.

Types of Bias Inaccurate assumptions made by machine learning algorithms often result in significant bias errors in the model, resulting in an inability to identify trends in the data. Various forms of bias exist, including (but not limited to) sampling bias, in which the training data does not realistically represent the environment in which the model will eventually be implemented; exclusion bias, in which variables or data that are assumed to be unnecessary are removed; and observer bias, in which programmers' expectations of trends in the data influence their assessment of results produced by the models. These biases can significantly impact the performance of ML models applied in the real world; for instance, gender bias in word embeddings trained on sources such as Google News can exacerbate existing gender stereotypes, emphasizing the need to develop algorithms to minimize these biases (Bolukbasi et al., 2016). However, while it is important to minimize some forms of bias, having no bias at all generally results in overfitting; when the model is unable to make assumptions regarding the data, it can only fit the training data and is unable to generalize, as described by Mitchell (2002). Thus, in developing an ML model, it is important to be aware of potential biases in order to avoid overfitting and overgeneralization, both of which are described below.

Overfitting and Overgeneralization In training a supervised machine learning model, programmers must pay careful attention to generalization—a model's ability to adapt to previously unseen data. Specifically, programmers need to ensure that neither overfitting nor overgeneralization, both of which significantly hinder a model's predictive accuracy, occurs. Overfitting occurs when the model becomes overly adapted to the training data as a result of low bias and high variance; in this case, the model begins to merely "memorize" the data and is unable to identify general trends, thus causing poor performance on testing datasets (Fig. 9). In contrast, overgeneralization, or underfitting, occurs when the model is unable to adequately capture the features and patterns in the data as a result of high bias and low variance, thus producing inaccurate results on both training and testing datasets (Fig. 8).

Thus, in training learning models, it is ideal to find a balanced fit in bias and variance in order to minimize an algorithm's generalization error (Fig. 9). Various approaches can be utilized to minimize errors resulting from overfitting and overgeneralization, such as the Homogeneity-Based Algorithm and Convexity-Based Algorithm (Pham & Triantaphyllou, 2008). In general, overfitting and overgeneralization can be prevented by using cross-validation techniques, training with different volumes of data, and modifying models' complexity in order to improve their ability to generalize.

Fairness in the ML Models

In response to notable examples of bias in ML models, such as gender bias in job-related ads (Watzenig & Horn, 2016), racial bias in evaluating names on resumes (Caliskan et al., 2017), and racial bias in predicting criminal recidivism (Kirchner claims may wrong-foot Macri), the importance and the volume of research

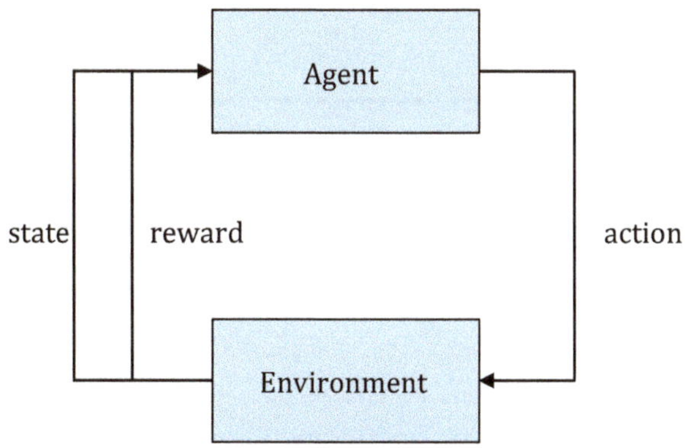

Fig. 7 *Agent Environment Model.* The model shows how the *agent* and the *environment* interact with each other. The agent takes an action on the environment which then sends a state and a reward to the agent

Fig. 8. *Overgeneralization.* This type of bias cannot capture the underlying trend of the data by underestimating the data. A linear function in the figure is used to perform the model; however, the model is unable to fit the training data well enough to learn with a good performance

Fig. 9 *Overfitting.* In this example, overfitting is created by using a quadratic function that fires too well on the training data and noise. There are few samples that are not covered in the quadratic function. Thus the model does not categorize the data correctly because of too many details and noise

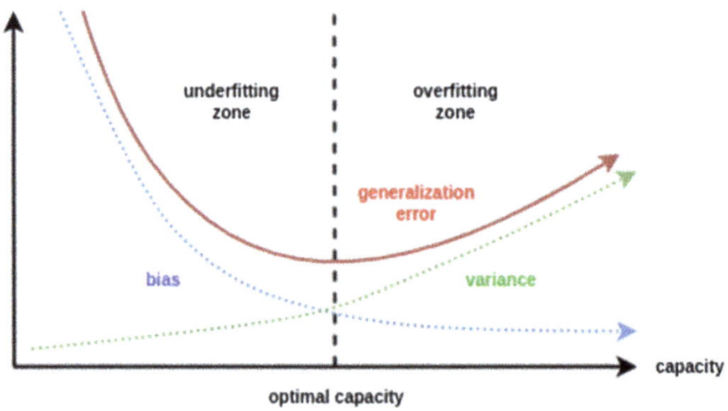

Fig. 10 *Balanced Fit.* In high-bias and low-variance models, underfitting occurs, resulting in significant generalization errors. Similarly, in low-bias and high-variance instances, overfitting reduces a model's ability to generalize and make accurate predictions. To prevent this, models should ideally be trained at an optimal capacity at which generalization error is minimized. License via Wikimedia

regarding algorithmic fairness utilizing different metrics and approaches have grown in the past few years.

Validation Strategies

A challenge that ML researchers face is ensuring that their models are able to make accurate predictions. Choosing only to train a model on a dataset can lead to issues such as overgeneralization or overfitting, as explained above. In order to improve the accuracy of their models, some researchers opt to use validation, which helps estimate a model's prediction error so that the best model can be chosen. This is done before moving into testing.

To train a model on a dataset, researchers split the dataset into two subsets: one for training and one for final testing. The training subset is split into two further subsets in a validation strategy, with one being used for validation. Several validation strategies have been developed. This section examines the train/test split, K-fold cross-validation (K-fold), Leave-P-Out cross-validation (LPO), nested cross-validation, and time-series cross-validation. The information in this section is from Van Houwelingen (2004) unless otherwise noted (Van Houwelingen, 2004).

Train/Test Split

This is the simplest validation strategy. In this method, one splits a training dataset into two subsets. The model is trained on the first subset, and its estimated prediction error is determined using the second. For example, one could set aside one-third of a large dataset for validation, leaving the other two-thirds for training.

This approach is appropriate in data-rich environments. However, when researchers are dealing with limited datasets, cross-validation (CV) techniques may be more useful.

K-Fold Cross-Validation

In this method, the training dataset is split into k groups (or folds). One of the folds is used to validate the model, while the remaining k – 1 folds are used as training data. After the initial split, this process is repeated a total of k times: a new model is generated on the Kth iteration, and the Kth fold serves as the validation subset. Notably, this method is non-exhaustive, meaning that it does not compute all possible ways of splitting the initial training dataset. For example, one could perform threefold CV (K-fold with K = 3) on a sample training dataset. In the first iteration, a model would be generated, and the first fold would be used to validate. In the second iteration, another model would be generated, and the second fold would be used to validate. The process iterates once more for the third fold.

As demonstrated by Kim (2009), K-fold cross-validation often performs better than bootstrap and holdout validation methods in classifying training samples, as it generally experiences fewer bias issues with various sample sizes (Kim, 2009). Similarly, tenfold CV outperforms techniques such as leave-one-out, holdout, and bootstrap validation in various simulations (Borra & Di Ciaccio, 2010). In general, k-fold cross-validation is an effective method, particularly for smaller datasets in which train/test split is not feasible, to produce a minimally biased model; as a result, it is a popular CV technique and is often used to identify potential overfitting in machine learning models.

Leave-P-Out Cross-Validation

In each iteration of this method performed on a training dataset with n members, p members are used to validate the model while the remaining n – p members are used to train the model. This is repeated for each possible iteration of the data for a total of n-choose-p times; therefore, the method is exhaustive. For example, in L2O (LPO with $p = 2$), with $n = 5$, two members would be chosen as a validation subset, and the remaining three would be chosen to train. A model would be created and would be trained and validated using each subset. This process would repeat 5-choose-2 times, or 10 times in total. This method may be more effective than K-fold in applications such as risk estimation (Celisse & Robin, 2008). An LPO risk estimator with some p applied on a set of size n should behave similarly to a k-fold risk estimator with $K = n/p$ applied on the same set. However, when a simulation was performed with each method, the estimates made with k-fold were significantly less uniform than those made with LPO.

Leave-one-out cross-validation (LOO) is a specific case of LPO where $p = 1$. It can be described as a form of k-fold where $K = n$. In some cases, it runs faster than LPO, with only n iterations. However, it is still computationally expensive when working with large datasets (Celisse & Robin, 2008; Molinaro et al., 2005). Additionally, LOO performs poorly in model selection compared to k-fold in some cases (Breiman & Spector, 1992). In their simulation, LOO performed better at estimating error across dimensions, but k-fold typically selected models with lower errors.

Nested Cross-Validation

Nested cross-validation (nested CV) operates differently from other CV techniques. While the previous methods discussed separate a training dataset into further subsets for training and validation, this method separates an entire dataset into training, validation, and testing subsets. To do so, it uses an outer and an inner loop. The outer loop iterates through the dataset, splitting it into a training dataset and a testing subset. The inner loop then iterates through the training dataset, splitting it into validation and training subsets.

Nested CV can be visualized as two k-folds iterating in tandem (Raschka, 2018). Varma and Simon, who proposed the method, find that nested CV can reduce bias compared to k-fold and LOO (Varma & Simon, 2006). After running random datasets through shrunken centroids and Support Vector Machine classifiers, they used different CV methods to predict each model's true error. Due to the random nature of the data, a "perfect" method would have estimated a 50% average error rate. LOO and k-fold with k = 10 underestimated the error rate by 12.2% and 8.3%, respectively. Nested CV overestimated the error rate by only 4.2%. However, Wainer and Cawley argue that nested CV is overzealous for many practical applications. They note that there are other, less computationally expensive methods that provide similarly effective model selection, proposing an alternative called "flat cross-validation" (Wainer & Cawley, 2018).

Time-Series Cross-Validation

The previous methods work under the assumption that each member in a dataset is statistically independent of all other members in the dataset. As a result, these methods will not work for time-series data. For example, a meteorologist trying to predict the next day's weather would be unable to use k-fold or LPO, as the state of each day's weather relies on those of previous days.

Instead, when working with time-series data, one can use time-series cross-validation. In this method, a dataset consists of observations taken in chronological order. A series of validation sets is taken, each consisting of one observation. Each training set includes only observations made before the validation set. For example, on a dataset with 5 days' worth of observations, the process would iterate four times. In the first iteration, day 1's observation would be the training data, and day 2's would be the validation data. In the second iteration, the observations for days 1 and 2 would be the training data, and day 3's observation would be the validation data. The process would iterate two more times accordingly. The model's forecast accuracy is computed by taking the average of the test sets (Hyndman & Athanasopoulos, 2018).

Advancements in the Field

Machine learning has evolved tremendously and is continuing to do so at a steady pace. Stanford's HAI (Human-centered Artificial Intelligence) lab published an AI Index report in 2019 that stated that "the volume of peer-reviewed AI papers has grown by more than 300%."

Machine learning is dependent on access to large amounts of data. Without a lot of data, it becomes difficult to test models for accuracy without reducing the scope of their training sets. With the rise of big data, many of these issues cease to be concerned as researchers have access to ever-increasing amounts of data. In 2012, there were an estimated 2.72 zettabytes of data in existence (Sagiroglu & Sinanc, 2013).

Deep learning, a subset of machine learning that focuses on creating algorithms modeled after the human brain, has also surged in popularity in recent years. According to the same AI Index report, the number of deep learning papers on arXiv—an archive of scholarly articles in the field of physics, math, and computer science—has more than tripled in North America and more than quadrupled in Europe, Central Asia, East Asia, and the Pacific since 2015 (Benaich & Hogarth, 2020).

In many fields, such as speech recognition and computer vision, raw data often has high dimensionality. Working in high-dimensional spaces poses issues, as analyzing these raw data can be computationally intractable. This is where autoencoders come in. By converting high-dimensional datasets into low-dimensional embeddings, one can reduce the processing power needed to analyze a dataset while keeping some meaningful properties of the original data (Khodr & Younes, 2011).

As was mentioned in the introduction, the primary advantage of machine learning over algorithm development lies in the fact that machine learning can be used in more general situations than algorithms. Transfer learning takes this one step further. In this case, the knowledge gained while solving one problem can then be used on another related problem. We give the example of a model trained to recognize different types of trees applying its knowledge to recognize different types of bushes. With transfer learning, more extensive models can be built (Karimpanal & Bouffanais, 2019).

With new advancements in facial recognition and autonomous vehicles being made, computer vision has become more important in recent years. Computer vision deals with teaching computers to understand photos and videos. In 2015, a model was created that was able to surpass human-level performance on the ImageNet 2012 classification dataset (He et al., 2015).

As much of the world's data includes written text in the form of emails and texts, it is important to train computers to recognize the semantics of the human language. This is where natural language processing comes in. Every year, the Visual Question Answering competition is hosted, in which programs are tasked with answering natural language queries about images. According to the aforementioned AI Index report, accuracy in the 2019 competition increased from 2.85% to 75.28% overall.

Big Data

As the world becomes increasingly technological, the volume of data created, transferred, and stored has grown astronomically as well. For instance, humans generate an estimated four petabytes through the social media platform Facebook and send around 306 billion emails on a daily basis (Marr, 2018). Large volumes of data such as these are known as big data. Through analysis of big data, organizations can utilize digitally stored information to improve various aspects of their products and work. This can be observed in various governments' efforts to integrate big data into their decision-making processes regarding domestic issues such as terrorism and unemployment (Kim et al., 2014). Similarly, in the healthcare industry, big data is utilized to improve patient treatments, enhance predictive analytics, and refine early disease detection. For instance, through analysis of extensive amounts of previous patient data, Harvard Medical School physicians diagnosed patients with Type I and Type II diabetes (Wullianallur Raghupathi, 2014). Thus, big data can greatly facilitate the analysis of human and machine-generated information to improve various industries and their efforts in coming years.

Deep Learning

Big data comes in various forms, including structured, unstructured, and semi-structured data. In the analysis of complex or unstructured data, such as images, deep learning can greatly facilitate the process of data classification. This automatic feature detection enables deep learning machines to perform complex tasks, such as speech recognition and natural language processing, particularly on large volumes of data. As recent work in the field demonstrates, the various applications and techniques of deep learning continue to advance. For instance, using discriminative deep association learning with both labeled and unlabeled data, researchers have been able to significantly improve facial expression recognition (Wullianallur Raghupathi, 2014). Researchers have also applied deep learning to DNA–protein binding; by using DeepSite, DNA–protein binding sites could be predicted with an improved 89.19% accuracy (Zhang et al., 2020). As deep learning continues to evolve, its potential for the future continues to grow as well; deep learning remains a powerful and effective technique for feature learning and recognition with big data.

Autoencoders and Embeddings

In processing data, dimensionality is an important property to consider. Perhaps counterintuitively, increasing the dimensionality of a dataset decreases the network's predictive capabilities. A higher-dimensional data generally increases the likelihood of severe overfitting in pattern recognition and feature extraction (Liu & Gillies, 2016). Thus, in the analysis of high-dimensionality data, it becomes critical to reduce the number of features associated with the data. This can be done using autoencoders, which are unsupervised networks that implement dimensionality reduction such that high-dimensional data can be converted into a low-dimensional form while retaining critical properties of the original data and filtering out noise. In doing so, autoencoders transform, or encode, their input into a relatively low-dimensional embedding that can later be decoded into a form as close to the original input as possible. This capability is valuable for data analysis in various fields; for instance, Kyunghyun Cho demonstrated that sparse autoencoders could be used to significantly improve the denoising of noisy images (Cho, 2013). Furthermore, Shaunak De et al. found that autoencoders can assist in the prediction of the popularity of Instagram posts, providing valuable insight into marketing and outreach strategies (Shaunak De et al., 2017). As they advance, autoencoding techniques continue to boost high-dimensional data analysis and noise reduction, yielding greater efficiency in machine-learning guided feature extraction methods across various fields.

Transfer Learning

Training a deep learning network often requires extensive amounts of time, data, and resources; thus, it can be convenient to extend the knowledge gained in one network to a similar field rather than training multiple networks to perform similar tasks. Transfer learning is a technique in which a model that has been previously trained is then adapted to solve a different but related problem. Using this method, already trained neural networks can be applied to new tasks using significantly less training data. Since its introduction, transfer learning has rapidly become a popular technique. Its broad applications include many in the medical fields, such as the enhancing of genetic algorithms (Koçer & Arslan, 2010) and improving the classification of breast cancers (Khan et al., 2019). As Chuong Do and Andrew Ng demonstrated, transfer learning can also be used to develop text classification algorithms that perform significantly better than traditional classification methods (Raina et al., 2006). As machine learning continues to expand into different fields and problems, transfer learning can be used to more efficiently develop networks that complete similar tasks.

Computer Vision

Computer vision is an intricate field centered on how machines can detect, interpret, and classify the physical world. By using computer vision, many technologies, such as facial recognition programs and autonomous vehicles, have been made possible. Like transfer learning, computer vision has quickly grown into a popular field. Some of its modern applications include cell classification; for example, deep learning and computer vision can be utilized to accurately distinguish colon cancer cells from T-lymphocytes and algal cells (Chen et al., 2016). As more sophisticated methods develop, computer science and machine learning have significant potential to enhance medical diagnoses, improve augmented/mixed reality programs, and assist in the development of efficient manufacturing techniques.

Natural Language Processing

Though machines can understand text in the form of code, comprehending natural languages such as English is a much more difficult task. However, this capability is highly desirable for its various applications, such as speech recognition, text extraction, and chatbot development. Giving rise to the intricate field of Natural Language Processing (NLP), an interdisciplinary field involving both linguistics and artificial intelligence centered around machine interpretation of natural languages. Though the first NLP-based speech recognition devices, such as the IBM Shoebox developed in the 1960s, could recognize less than 20 spoken words ("IBM Archives: IBM Shoebox," 2003), today NLP has given rise to significantly more sophisticated technologies, such as virtual assistants and online translators. In recent years, NLP techniques have also facilitated sentiment analysis in languages such as Arabic, allowing for accuracies up to 0.9568 for certain datasets (Alayba et al., 2018). In coming years, NLP has the potential to yield sophisticated systems that can more accurately interpret natural languages and realistically perform speech synthesis, thus improving the quality of many voice user interfaces that have become ubiquitous today.

References

Agrawal, R., Imieliński, T., & Swami, A. (1993). Mining association rules between sets of items in large databases. In *Proceedings of the 1993 ACM SIGMOD International conference on management of data – SIGMOD '93*. Retrieved from https://doi.org/10.1145/170035.170072.

Alayba, A. M., Palade, V., England, M., & Iqbal, R. (2018). A combined CNN and LSTM model for Arabic sentiment analysis. *Lecture Notes in Computer Science*. Retrieved from https://doi.org/10.1007/978-3-319-99740-7_12.

Barateiro, J., & Galhardas, H. (2005). A survey of data quality tools. Datenbank-Spektrum, 14(15–21), 48. – Bing. (n.d.). Retrieved 9 May 2021, from https://www.bing.com/search?q=Barateiro%2C+J.%2C+%26+Galhardas%2C+H.+(2005).+A+survey+of+data+quality+tools.+Datenbank-Spektrum%2C+14(15-21)%2C+48.&cvid=dbe10d81049b453cb2e0d5a8bce31ccc&aqs=edge..69i57.556j0j1&pglt=547&FORM=ANNAB1&PC=U531

Behpour, S., Mohammadi, M., Albert, M. V., Alam, Z. S., Wang, L., & Xiao, T. (2021). Automatic trend detection: Time-biased document clustering. *Knowledge-Based Systems*. Retrieved from https://doi.org/10.1016/j.knosys.2021.106907.

Benaich, N., & Hogarth, I. (2020). *State of AI Report 2020*. Retrieved from https://www.stateof.ai/

Bicevska, Z., Bicevskis, J., & Oditis, I. (2018). Models of data quality. *Information Technology for Management. Ongoing Research and Development*. Retrieved from https://doi.org/10.1007/978-3-319-77721-4_11.

Bicevskis, J., Bicevska, Z., Nikiforova, A., & Oditis, I. (2018). Data quality evaluation: A comparative analysis of company registers' open data in four European countries. In *FedCSIS (Communication Papers)* (pp. 197–204).

Bolukbasi, T., Chang, K.-W., Zou, J., Saligrama, V., & Kalai, A. (2016, July 21). *Man is to Computer Programmer as Woman is to Homemaker? Debiasing Word Embeddings. arXiv [cs. CL]*. Retrieved from http://arxiv.org/abs/1607.06520

Borra, S., & Di Ciaccio, A. (2010). Measuring the prediction error. A comparison of cross-validation, bootstrap and covariance penalty methods. *Computational Statistics & Data Analysis*. Retrieved from https://doi.org/10.1016/j.csda.2010.03.004.

Boutaba, R., Salahuddin, M. A., Limam, N., Ayoubi, S., Shahriar, N., Estrada-Solano, F., & Caicedo, O. M. (2018). A comprehensive survey on machine learning for networking: Evolution, applications and research opportunities. *Journal of Internet Services and Applications, 9*(1), 1–99. Retrieved 8 May 2021 from.

Breiman, L., & Spector, P. (1992). Submodel Selection and Evaluation in Regression. The X-Random Case. *International Statistical Review / Revue Internationale de Statistique*. Retrieved from https://doi.org/10.2307/1403680.

Brownlee, J. (2014). A data-driven approach to choosing machine learning algorithms. Retrieved 20 May 2021, from https://machinelearningmastery.com/a-data-driven-approach-to-machine-learning/

Caliskan, A., Bryson, J. J., & Narayanan, A. (2017). Semantics derived automatically from language corpora contain human-like biases. *Science, 356*(6334), 183–186.

Carbonell, J. G., Michalski, R. S., & Mitchell, T. M. (1983). An overview of machine learning. *Machine Learning*. Retrieved from https://doi.org/10.1007/978-3-662-12405-5_1.

Celisse, A., & Robin, S. (2008). Nonparametric density estimation by exact leave–out cross-validation. *Computational Statistics & Data Analysis*. Retrieved from https://doi.org/10.1016/j.csda.2007.10.002.

Chen, C. L., Mahjoubfar, A., Tai, L.-C., Blaby, I. K., Huang, A., Niazi, K. R., & Jalali, B. (2016). Deep Learning in Label-free Cell Classification. *Scientific Reports*. Retrieved from https://doi.org/10.1038/srep21471.

Cho, K. (2013). Simple Sparsification Improves Sparse Denoising Autoencoders in Denoising Highly Corrupted Images. In *International conference on machine learning* (pp. 432–440). PMLR. Retrieved 9 May 2021 from https://proceedings.mlr.press/v28/cho13.pdf

Dai, J., University of British Columbia, Canada, & Zeng, B. (2016). An Association Rule Algorithm for Online e-Commerce Recommendation Service. *Journal of Economics, Business and Management*. Retrieved from https://doi.org/10.18178/joebm.2016.4.10.454.

Data Quality Assessment. (n.d.). *SpringerReference*. Retrieved from https://doi.org/10.1007/springerreference_63252.

De, S., & Chakraborty, B. (2020). Disease detection system (DDS) using machine learning technique. *Learning and Analytics in Intelligent Systems*. Retrieved from https://doi.org/10.1007/978-3-030-40850-3_6.

De, S., Maity, A., Goel, V., Shitole, S., & Bhattacharya, A. (2017). Predicting the popularity of instagram posts for a lifestyle magazine using deep learning. In *2017 2nd international conference on communication systems, computing and IT applications (CSCITA)*. Retrieved from https://doi.org/10.1109/cscita.2017.8066548.

Feature Selection and Evaluation. (2012). *Machine Learning in Image Steganalysis*. Retrieved from https://doi.org/10.1002/9781118437957.ch13.

Fernández-Delgado, M., Sirsat, M. S., Cernadas, E., Alawadi, S., Barro, S., & Febrero-Bande, M. (2019). An extensive experimental survey of regression methods. *Neural Networks: The Official Journal of the International Neural Network Society, 111*, 11–34.

Fukushima, K. (1979). Neural Network Model for a Mechanism of Pattern Recognition Unaffected by Shift in Position-Neocognitron. *IEICE Technical Report, A, 62*(10), 658–665. Retrieved 19 May 2021 from.

Ge, M., & Helfert, M. (2007). A review of information quality assessment. In *China-Ireland International Conference on Information and Communications Technologies (CIICT 2007)*. Retrieved from https://doi.org/10.1049/cp:20070800.

Ghahramani, Z. (2004). Unsupervised Learning. *Advanced Lectures on Machine Learning*. Retrieved from https://doi.org/10.1007/978-3-540-28650-9_5.

Gordon, D. F., & Desjardins, M. (1995). Evaluation and selection of biases in machine learning. *Machine Learning*. Retrieved from https://doi.org/10.1007/bf00993472.

Hahsler, M., Grün, B., & Hornik, K. (2005). Arules- A Computational Environment for Mining Association Rules and Frequent Item Sets. *Journal of Statistical Software*. Retrieved from https://doi.org/10.18637/jss.v014.i15.

He, K., Zhang, X., Ren, S., & Sun, J. (2015). Delving deep into rectifiers: Surpassing human-level performance on ImageNet classification. In *2015 IEEE international conference on computer vision (ICCV)*. Retrieved from https://doi.org/10.1109/iccv.2015.123.

He, K., Zhang, X., Ren, S., & Sun, J. (2016). Deep residual learning for image recognition. In *2016 IEEE conference on computer vision and pattern recognition (CVPR)*. Retrieved from https://doi.org/10.1109/cvpr.2016.90.

Heard, N. A., Holmes, C. C., & Stephens, D. A. (2006). A quantitative study of gene regulation involved in the immune response of Anopheline mosquitoes. *Journal of the American Statistical Association*. Retrieved from https://doi.org/10.1198/016214505000000187.

Hyndman, R. J., & Athanasopoulos, G. (2018). *Forecasting: Principles and practice*. OTexts.

IBM Archives: IBM Shoebox. (2003). Retrieved 7 May 2021, from https://www.ibm.com/ibm/history/exhibits/specialprod1/specialprod1_7.html

Japkowicz, N. (2006). Why question machine learning evaluation methods. In *AAAI workshop on evaluation methods for machine learning* (pp. 6–11).

Karimpanal, T. G., & Bouffanais, R. (2019). Self-organizing maps for storage and transfer of knowledge in reinforcement learning. *Adaptive Behavior*. Retrieved from https://doi.org/10.1177/1059712318818568.

Khan, S., Islam, N., Jan, Z., Din, I. U., & Rodrigues, J. J. P. (2019). A novel deep learning based framework for the detection and classification of breast cancer using transfer learning. *Pattern Recognition Letters*. Retrieved from https://doi.org/10.1016/j.patrec.2019.03.022.

Khodr, J., & Younes, R. (2011). Dimensionality reduction on hyperspectral images: A comparative review based on artificial datas. In *2011 4th international congress on image and signal processing*. Retrieved from https://doi.org/10.1109/cisp.2011.6100531.

Kim, J.-H. (2009). Estimating classification error rate: Repeated cross-validation, repeated hold-out and bootstrap. *Computational Statistics & Data Analysis*. Retrieved from https://doi.org/10.1016/j.csda.2009.04.009.

Kim, G.-H., Trimi, S., & Chung, J.-H. (2014). Big data applications in the government sector: A comparative analysis among leading countries. *Communications of the ACM, 57*(3), 78–85. Retrieved 7 May 2021 from.

Koçer, B., & Arslan, A. (2010). Genetic transfer learning. *Expert Systems with Applications*. Retrieved from https://doi.org/10.1016/j.eswa.2010.03.019.

Kotsiantis, S. B., Zaharakis, I. D., & Pintelas, P. E. (2006). Machine learning: A review of classification and combining techniques. *Artificial Intelligence Review*. Retrieved from https://doi.org/10.1007/s10462-007-9052-3.

Krotov, D., & Hopfield, J. J. (2019). Unsupervised learning by competing hidden units. *Proceedings of the National Academy of Sciences of the United States of America, 116*(16), 7723–7731.

Lachman, S. J. (1997). Learning is a process: Toward an improved definition of learning. *The Journal of Psychology, 131*(5), 477–480.

Lindsay, G. W. (2020). Convolutional neural networks as a model of the visual system: Past, present, and future. *Journal of Cognitive Neuroscience*, 1–15.

Liu, R., & Gillies, D. F. (2016). Overfitting in linear feature extraction for classification of high-dimensional image data. *Pattern Recognition*. Retrieved from https://doi.org/10.1016/j.patcog.2015.11.015.

Marr, B. (2018). *How much data do we create every day? The mind-blowing stats everyone should read*. Retrieved 9 May 2021, from https://www.forbes.com/sites/bernardmarr/2018/05/21/how-much-data-do-we-create-every-day-the-mind-blowing-stats-everyone-should-read/

Maydanchik, A. (2007). *Data quality assessment*. Technics Publications.

McCulloch, W. S., & Pitts, W. (1990). A logical calculus of the ideas immanent in nervous activity. 1943. *Bulletin of Mathematical Biology, 52*(1-2), 99–115; discussion 73–97.

McKinney, S. M., Sieniek, M., Godbole, V., Godwin, J., Antropova, N., Ashrafian, H., et al. (2020). International evaluation of an AI system for breast cancer screening. *Nature, 577*(7788), 89–94.

Mitchell, T. M. (2002). *The need for Biases in learning generalizations*. Retrieved 9 May 2021 from http://www.cs.cmu.edu/~tom/pubs/NeedForBias_1980.pdf

Molinaro, A. M., Simon, R., & Pfeiffer, R. M. (2005). Prediction error estimation: A comparison of resampling methods. *Bioinformatics, 21*(15), 3301–3307.

Nghiep, N., & Al, C. (2001). Predicting housing value: A comparison of multiple regression analysis and artificial neural networks. *Journal of Real Estate Research*. Retrieved from https://doi.org/10.1080/10835547.2001.12091068.

Olson, J. E. (2003). *Data quality: The accuracy dimension*. Elsevier.

Pham, H. N. A., & Triantaphyllou, E. (2008). The impact of overfitting and overgeneralization on the classification accuracy in data mining. *Soft Computing for Knowledge Discovery and Data Mining*. Retrieved from https://doi.org/10.1007/978-0-387-69935-6_16.

Rabiner, L. R. (1990). A tutorial on hidden Markov models and selected applications in speech recognition. *Readings in Speech Recognition*. Retrieved from https://doi.org/10.1016/b978-0-08-051584-7.50027-9.

Raina, R., Ng, A. Y., & Koller, D. (2006). Constructing informative priors using transfer learning. *Proceedings of the 23rd international conference on machine learning – ICML '06*. Retrieved from https://doi.org/10.1145/1143844.1143934.

Ramasubramanian, K., & Singh, A. (2017). Machine learning theory and practices. *Machine Learning Using R*. Retrieved from https://doi.org/10.1007/978-1-4842-2334-5_6.

Raschka, S. (2018, November 13). *Model evaluation, model selection, and algorithm selection in machine learning. arXiv [cs.LG]*. Retrieved from http://arxiv.org/abs/1811.12808

Rehman, M. Z., & Nawi, N. M. (2011). Improving the accuracy of gradient Descent Back propagation Algorithm (GDAM) on classification problems. *International Journal of New Computer Architectures and Their Applications, 4*(4), 861–870. Retrieved 9 May 2021 from.

Sadiq, S. (2013). *Handbook of data quality: Research and practice*. Springer.

Sagar, R. (2021). *Andrew Ng urges ML Community to be more data-centric*. Retrieved 9 May 2021, from https://analyticsindiamag.com/big-data-to-good-data-andrew-ng-urges-ml-community-to-be-more-data-centric-and-less-model-centric/

Sagiroglu, S., & Sinanc, D. (2013). Big data: A review. *2013 International Conference on Collaboration Technologies and Systems (CTS)*. Retrieved from https://doi.org/10.1109/cts.2013.6567202.

Seal, H. L. (1968). *The Historical Development of the Gauss Linear Model*. Yale University.

Silver, D., Hubert, T., Schrittwieser, J., Antonoglou, I., Lai, M., Guez, A., et al. (2018). A general reinforcement learning algorithm that masters chess, shogi, and Go through self-play. *Science, 362*(6419), 1140–1144.

Sutton, R. S., & Barto, A. G. (2018). *Reinforcement Learning, second edition: An Introduction*. MIT Press.

Turing, A. M. (1950). I.—Computing machinery and Intelligence. *Mind*. Retrieved from https://doi.org/10.1093/mind/lix.236.433.

van Engelen, J. E., & Hoos, H. H. (2020). A survey on semi-supervised learning. *Machine Learning*. Retrieved from https://doi.org/10.1007/s10994-019-05855-6.

Van Houwelingen, H. C. (2004). *The elements of statistical learning, data mining, inference, and prediction*. Trevor Hastie, Robert Tibshirani and Jerome Friedman, Springer, 2001. No. of pages: xvi 533. ISBN 0-387-95284-5. *Statistics in Medicine*. Retrieved from https://doi.org/10.1002/sim.1616

Varma, S., & Simon, R. (2006). Bias in error estimation when using cross-validation for model selection. *BMC Bioinformatics, 7*(1), 1–8. Retrieved 9 May 2021 from.

Wainer, J., & Cawley, G. (2018, September 25). *Nested cross-validation when selecting classifiers is overzealous for most practical applications*. Retrieved 8 May 2021 from http://arxiv.org/abs/1809.09446

Watzenig, D., & Horn, M. (2016). *Automated driving: Safer and more efficient future driving*. Springer.

Website. (n.d.). Retrieved 13 December 2020, from H. Baldwin, 'Drilling Into the Value of Data.' [Online]. Available: http://www.forbes.com/sites/howardbaldwin/2015/03/23/drilling-into-the-value-of-data/

Wullianallur Raghupathi, V. R. (2014). Big data analytics in healthcare: Promise and potential. *Health Information Science and Systems*, 2. Retrieved 7 May 2021 from https://doi.org/10.1186/2047-2501-2-3.

Zhang, Y., Qiao, S., Ji, S., & Li, Y. (2020). DeepSite: Bidirectional LSTM and CNN models for predicting DNA–protein binding. *International Journal of Machine Learning and Cybernetics*. Retrieved from https://doi.org/10.1007/s13042-019-00990-x.

Zhu, X. (jerry). (2005). *Semi-supervised learning literature survey*. Retrieved 20 May 2021 from https://minds.wisconsin.edu/handle/1793/60444

Zhu, X., & Goldberg, A. B. (2009). Introduction to semi-supervised learning. *Synthesis Lectures on Artificial Intelligence and Machine Learning*. Retrieved from https://doi.org/10.2200/s00196ed1v01y200906aim006.

Sahar Behpour is a data science Ph.D. candidate, a teaching fellow in the College of Information, Department of Information Science, University of North Texas. Her primary research interests include machine learning, artificial intelligence, and data mining. Her papers are published in various journals including the Knowledge-Based System, Artificial Intelligence Review, and the Frontier in Physiology. Her research papers have been accepted for presentation at the American Physical Society, Association for Library and Information Science, International Conference of Knowledge Management, and ACM Richard Tapia Celebration of Diversity in Computing.

Avi Udash is a current Undergraduate Student in the Vice Provost for Undergraduate Education department, Standford University. His interests include machine learning, artificial intelligence, and human–computer interaction. He was accepted into the computer science program at Stanford University as a QuestBridge National College Match Scholarship Recipient and will be attending Stanford.

Deep Learning: Why Neural Networks Are State of the Art

Arvind Ganesh and Namratha Urs

Introduction

While vastly different in their application, media recommendation algorithms, translation apps, and smart home assistants all have one thing in common: the use of deep learning (Edu et al., 2019; Wu et al., 2016; Zhang et al., 2019b). Unlike humans, computers generally exceed at tasks that are algorithmic or computational in nature. For instance, a computer can easily perform 10-digit multiplication or parse a file of one million objects since the tasks are logically well defined, and thus easy to code.

However, when faced with tasks that are less well defined and more intuition based, it becomes largely infeasible for humans to apply traditional programming practices. For example, in a translation app, it is possible to create a dictionary of words with the same meaning across languages. But since language is highly contextual and often varies in structure, a programmer would not be able to add contextual processing with traditional rule-based instruction because they would have to impossibly define every contextual scenario in code.

One possible approach is to apply traditional machine learning algorithms to the problem (discussed in chapter A1). However, traditional machine learning techniques would still require humans to explicitly define contextual rules (Deng & Yu, 2014). Consequently, a traditional machine learning (ML) approach would still be infeasible, necessitating an alternative. A deep learning approach would use a neural

A. Ganesh (✉)
Texas Academy of Mathematics and Science, University of North Texas, Plano, TX, USA

N. Urs
Department of Computer Science and Engineering, University of North Texas, Plano, TX, USA
e-mail: namrathaurs@my.unt.edu

M. V. Albert et al. (eds.), *Bridging Human Intelligence and Artificial Intelligence*, Educational Communications and Technology: Issues and Innovations, https://doi.org/10.1007/978-3-030-84729-6_2

network (Wu et al., 2016), which would, through the review of a prepared dataset of language, learn to translate with the inclusion of context. Importantly, the use of deep learning would remove humans from the process of defining contextual rules, leading to a more robust translation algorithm.

In general, deep learning algorithms are superior to traditional algorithmic approaches when "the rules" for a problem are difficult to define and when potential scenarios are highly unpredictable – for example, weather prediction (Salman et al., 2015) or the diagnosis of cancer (Litjens et al., 2016). Neural networks are the foundation of deep learning, and therefore, it is crucial to understand their fundamentals.

What Is a Neural Network?

The power of the human brain comes from its ability to define abstract traits about an observation without explicit external instruction (Pulvermüller, 2013). For example, suppose a child is learning about animals in school and sees a picture of a horse. The child didn't identify the horse using its special hooves or tail but could subconsciously recognize it after seeing horses. The child just "knew" what it looked like – something which can be attributed to the brain's ability to identify unique patterns and break down concepts.

Like the brain, a neural network is an algorithm designed to recognize defining patterns or "features" in data (Goodfellow et al., 2016). Neural networks are unique in computing because of their ability to learn features from a dataset without external intervention. If a neural network was trained to identify horses, like the human brain, it wouldn't need explicit instruction about the special type of hooves or tail that a horse has. After seeing many training examples of a horse, a neural network will automatically begin to associate characteristics like slender legs and a long neck with being a horse. Furthermore, when applied to even more complex problems, neural networks truly begin to shine as they are able to computationally identify features that are too abstract for humans to grasp, allowing them to be applied in situations where human cognition cannot.

As seen in Fig. 1, broadly speaking, all neural networks have an input layer, hidden layer(s), and an output layer (Goodfellow et al., 2016). Rudimentary neural networks often only have an input layer, a single hidden layer, and an output layer. The input layer is where a neural network receives the input, like an image of a horse. In the hidden layer, a neural network processes the input and determines features. In the identification of a horse, the hidden layer may recognize its slender legs or the shape of its neck. The output layer evaluates these features and determines whether they are characteristic of a horse.

Under the hood, neural networks are fundamentally interconnected networks of neurons governed by their weights and biases. The weights and biases of a network are responsible for the strength of the connections between the neurons; they control how reinforced certain ways of "thinking" are within the network (Goodfellow

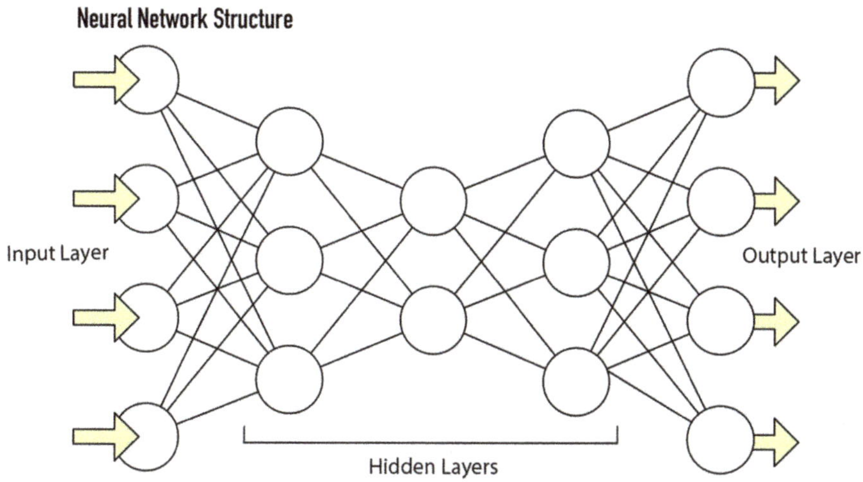

Fig. 1 Neural networks receive their inputs in the input layer. From there, computation occurs in the hidden layers. Finally, the result of the computation is displayed in the output layer

et al., 2016). Training a neural network involves iteratively tuning its weights and biases in order to produce desired outputs based on a given input for supervised learning tasks.

When training a neural network to identify horses, the network could eventually learn to look for a horse's long neck and will strengthen the neural pathways (tune the weights and biases) where the presence of a horse-like neck and the output prediction of "horse" are strongly correlated. After training, when the horse-identification network sees an animal with the unique neck of a horse, it will be more likely to think that the new animal is indeed a horse as the corresponding neural pathways were reinforced during training (further detail in the section "How Do Neural Networks Improve?").

Basic neural networks with a single hidden layer perform well in most situations, but when tasks get more and more complex, the performance of simpler neural networks begins to falter. One way to address this complexity is to add hidden layers to a neural network, allowing the network to model more intricate relationships between input and output data. The field of neural networks with multiple hidden layers is known as deep learning (LeCun et al., 2015). In recent years, deep learning has rapidly revolutionized many fields including self-driving cars, computer vision, entertainment, and health care. Through their ability to recognize increasingly abstract patterns in data, deep neural networks have become indispensable tools that can be applied to many complex scenarios.

How Do Neural Networks Improve?

In the previous example about the horse, there needed to be some way to systematically calibrate the neural network to incrementally improve its detection capabilities. With humans, a possible approach to learning might include studying from flashcards, with extra focus on incorrectly tested material. Remarkably, neural network training takes a very similar approach.

As seen in Fig. 2, humans are able to determine mistakes in learning by comparing their incorrect answers to the expected answers. From there, humans can learn from mistakes subconsciously. Similarly, to determine mistakes and minimize them, neural networks focus on decreasing or minimizing a cost function – a function whose output is a numerical representation of how "wrong" a neural network is given a configuration of weights and biases (Goodfellow et al., 2016). One common example of a cost function, as illustrated in Fig. 3, is the mean squared error (Zhang et al., 2019a). (Note that decreasing cost or error is directly correlated with increasing accuracy.)

For each possible input into a neural network, we have a predicted output and an expected output. As seen in Fig. 3, the output from a neural network, based on a certain set of weights and biases, is compared to the expected output through the cost function. The cost function is simply the average of the square of the differences between the predicted and expected outputs. The lower the value of the cost function, the better the network performs (Goodfellow et al., 2016).

To minimize this cost function, an optimization algorithm known as "gradient descent" can be used. Gradient descent is an algorithm used to find local minimums for a given differentiable function (Curry, 1944). Suppose our cost function resembles the function depicted in Fig. 4.

Consider the following analogy. Suppose we pick a point on a given cost function and place a ball there. Intuitively, the ball will roll downwards on the steepest path till it reaches the locally lowest point. Gradient descent is a mathematical way to compute the path that this ball would take to converge to a local minimum. Figure 5 illustrates the algorithm in more detail.

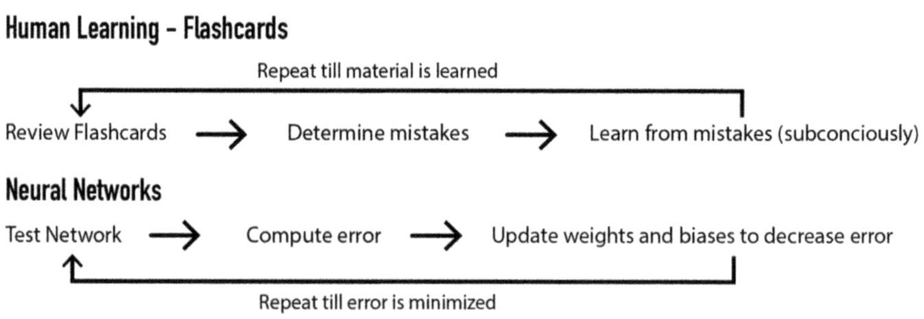

Fig. 2 Humans and neural networks learn in a similar fashion. With each iteration of training, neural networks, like humans, try to minimize their error (Goodfellow et al., 2016)

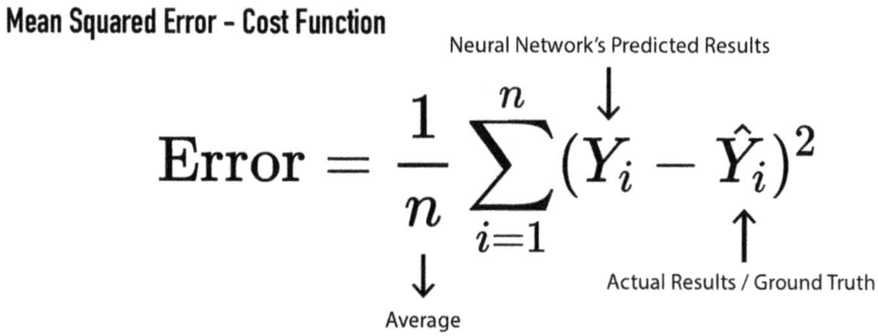

Fig. 3 Mean squared error (MSE) is a commonly used cost function found in numerous statistical and machine learning applications. Minimizing the cost function by calibrating the weights and biases of a neural network is the goal of the training process

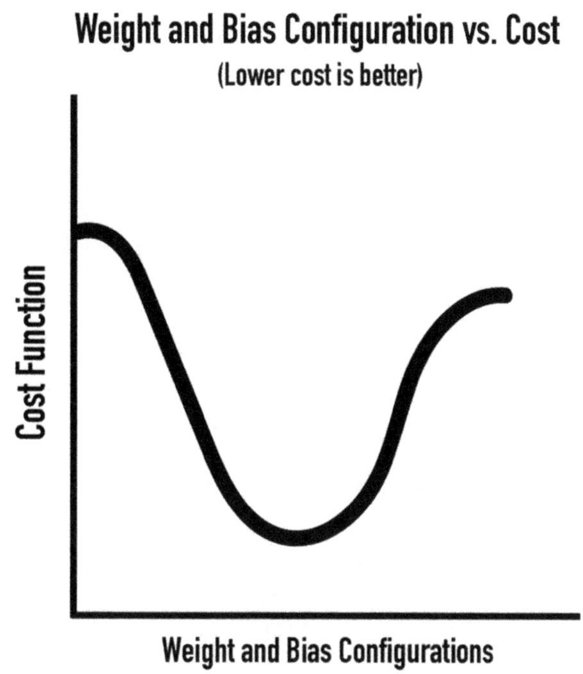

Fig. 4 Represents the error of the neural network with respect to various configurations of weights and biases. The goal of training is to minimize the value of this function. Note that the diagram is in 2D, but in practice, cost functions for neural networks tend to be in thousands if not millions of dimensions depending on the complexity of the network they model

First, we initialize our weights and biases to some random configuration. We compute the "steepest" direction from that point mathematically (usually done with differentiation). Next, we update the weights and biases to nudge the cost function in that direction through an algorithm known as backpropagation (outside the scope of this chapter) (Goodfellow et al., 2016). Finally, we repeatedly move in the calculated steepest direction until we have configured the weights and biases to produce a minimum of the cost function. At this point, the neural network has been trained.

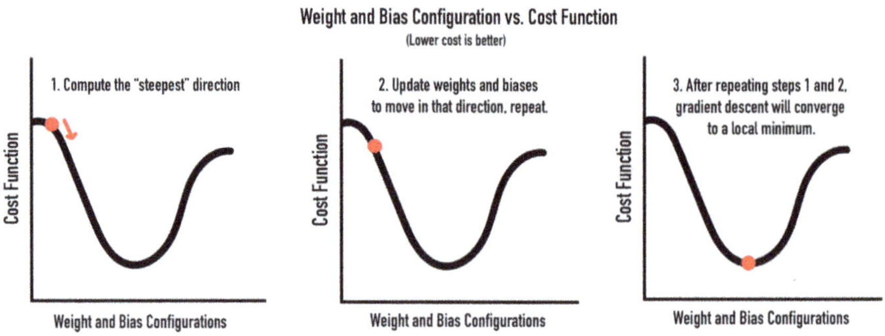

Fig. 5 Illustrates the process of gradient descent in order to find a local minimum of the cost function

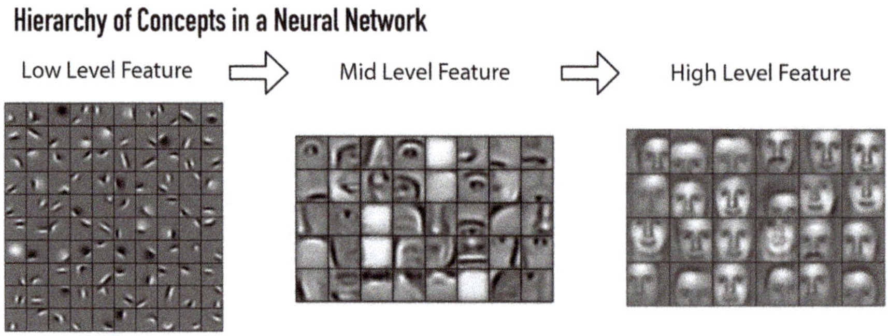

Fig. 6 An illustration depicting how the layers of a neural network hierarchically learn features, going from simple to complex (Lee et al., 2009). The image depicts the feature extraction process for a convolutional neural network which is applied to images, making visualization of the process easier. However, the general idea is thought to hold true for all neural networks (Bengio, 2012)

What Sets Deep Learning Apart?

As technology has rapidly progressed over the years, so has the collection of data. In web browsers, websites collect cookies, storing information about how a given user interacts with a site. When using search engines, companies collect data about users' search histories. Additionally, social media companies collect data about the preferences of users in order to tailor the content served on their apps. In order to match the complexity and magnitude of available datasets, optimal methods of analysis generally favor the use of deep learning because of an idea known as the "hierarchy of concepts" (Bengio, 2012) (Fig. 6).

Essentially, deep neural networks learn simple concepts in data and use them to learn more complicated concepts (Bengio, 2012). Figure 4 shows a possible set of features extracted for a convolutional neural network (CNN) meant to detect faces. In the first layer, the neural network detects the types of edges that make up a given picture. In the second layer, the neural network takes the edges detected in the first layer and detects the types of structures that could be made from them: the eyes, the nose, the mouth, and so on. Finally, in the third layer, the neural network can now find a face as it is a combination of the facial structures detected in the second layer. It is important to note that deep neural networks may not extract features in a way that is clearly interpretable by humans (Erhan et al., 2009), but they still utilize a hierarchy of concepts to learn more complicated ideas by building off of simpler ones. The hierarchy of concepts allows deep learning algorithms to extract features without human involvement, making them superior to alternative modeling approaches.

To illustrate the power of automatic feature extraction, we will look at one of the primary image classification benchmarks, the ImageNet Challenge. The ImageNet Challenge is a competition meant to evaluate and compare object detection and recognition algorithms (Russakovsky et al., 2015). The dataset includes more than 1000 different categories with 1.2 million images in total. In the ImageNet Challenge, competitors are tasked with creating models to identify objects in images. Figure 7 shows the output of VGG (a convolutional neural network), the winner of the ImageNet challenge in 2014 on a picture of a dog.

Prior to the use of deep neural networks in the ImageNet Challenge, support vector machines (SVMs) were one of the best performing types of algorithms used. Lin et al. (2011) achieved a classification accuracy of 52.9% using SVMs – state of the art performance at the time. However, their approach employed a complex feature extraction algorithm which required significant human effort to develop.

In 2012, Alex Krizhevsky designed AlexNet, a convolutional neural network (CNN) for the ImageNet challenge (Krizhevsky et al., 2017). In contrast to other competitors, AlexNet did not employ a vastly complicated manual feature extraction algorithm. Due to the fact that it was a CNN, a deep learning model that can automatically perform feature extraction, AlexNet crushed the competition by achieving a top-5 error rate of 15.3%, more than 10% less than the nearest competitor. AlexNet revolutionized the field of deep learning by demonstrating how

Fig. 7 VGG, the ImageNet Challenge winner in 2014 (Simonyan & Zisserman, 2014) classifies the image as "German Shepherd"

valuable automatic feature extraction could be. Since then, deep learning algorithms have dominated the ImageNet Challenge and improve each year (Simonyan & Zisserman, 2014; Szegedy et al., 2015; Zeiler & Fergus, 2014).

Various Types of Deep Neural Networks

The human brain has a variety of structures to accommodate its numerous functions. Over time, humans have evolved to become proficient at a number of different types of tasks. Interestingly, all of these tasks can be performed by one central unit. Deep learning algorithms, however, are not so widely applicable. Depending on the task, certain structures of deep neural networks perform better than others. These neural network structures are known as architectures (Liu et al., 2017). This section will provide a brief overview of common deep learning architectures and their applications (Fig. 8).

Convolutional Neural Networks

Convolutional neural networks (CNN) are one of the most prominent neural network architectures due to their applications in image processing and computer vision (Albawi et al., 2017). Their main advantage is that they are able to model spatial relationships within an image due to their use of convolutions (which are briefly discussed below). Figure 9 depicts the standard architecture for a CNN.

Using a feed forward neural network for image classification would require the processing of an image, pixel by pixel (Goodfellow et al., 2016). Pixel-by-pixel processing is inefficient because as the resolution grows, the number of pixels would grow quadratically. Convolutions allow CNNs to "slide" over an image and look at an image block-by-block rather than pixel-by-pixel (the feedforward neural network approach). Importantly, this convolution-based approach drastically reduces computational requirements. The use of convolutions also helps CNNs extract key features from an image since convolutions represent sections of an image (as opposed to pictures). For example, as illustrated in "Convolution Layer 1" in Fig. 10, the use of convolutions allows LeNet (a convolutional neural network trained to recognize handwritten digits) to recognize the edges corresponding to the loops that comprise an "8" (Lecun et al., 1998). After recognizing the parts of the loop, in the following "Pooling Layer 1," the network learns a more complex feature: the entire loop. It can then use these learned features to recognize the defining characteristics of a handwritten eight through the "Fully Connected" layers. CNNs are discussed in more detail in Chapter A5.

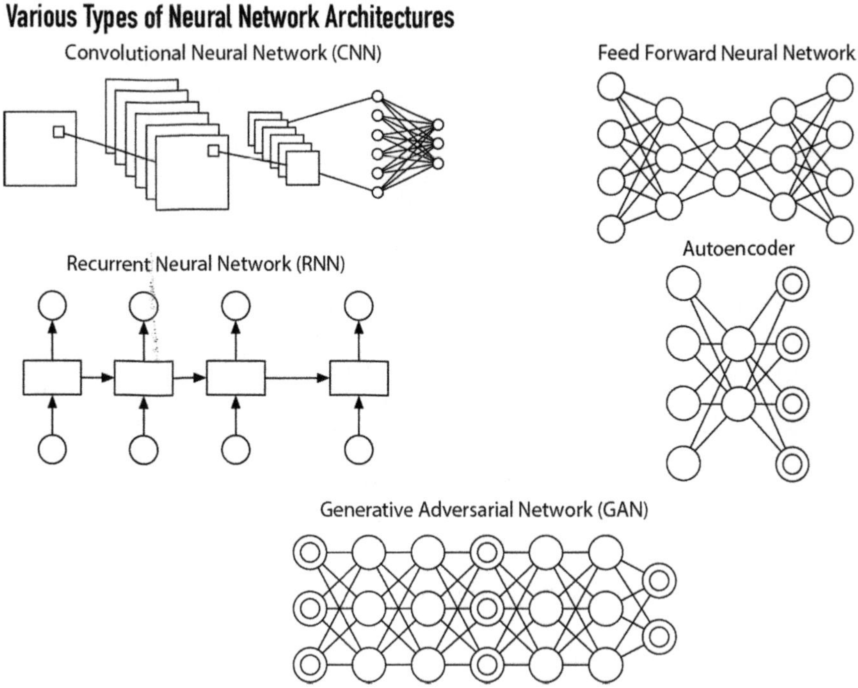

Fig. 8 Many different types of neural network architectures exist, each with their own unique purpose. Additionally, it is possible to create hybrid architectures by combining aspects of other well-known architectures

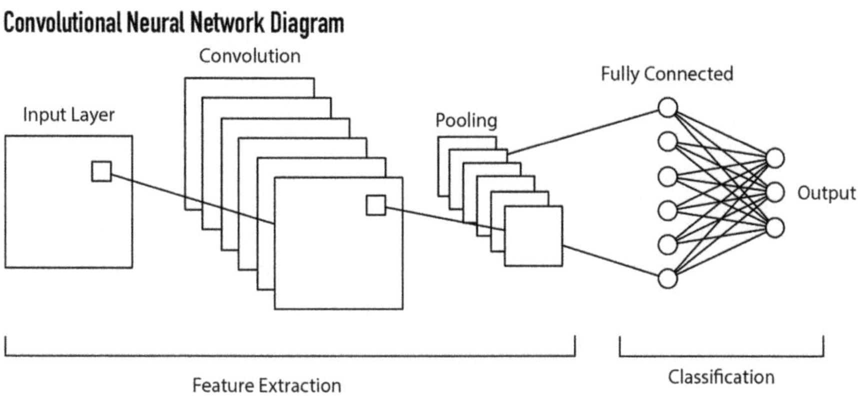

Fig. 9 Standard architecture of a convolutional neural network (CNN)

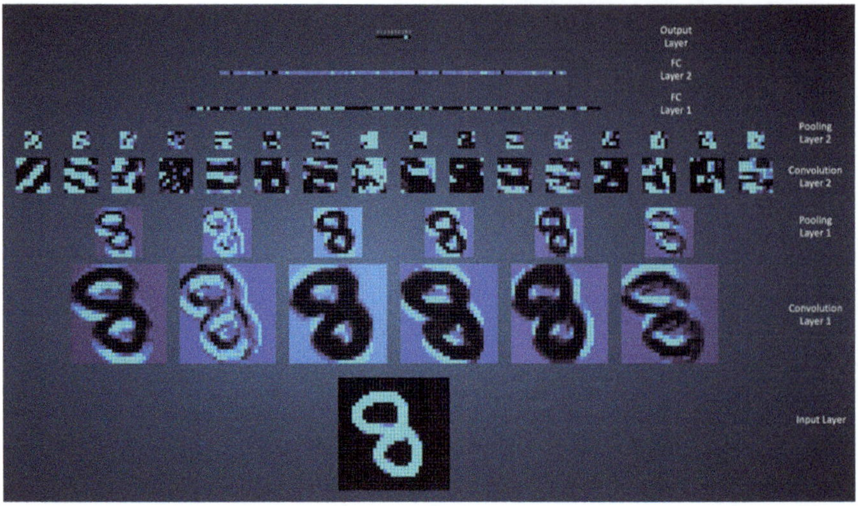

Fig. 10 A layer-by-layer breakdown of a convolutional neural network trained to recognize handwritten digits (Harley, 2015). As we go deeper into the network, the initial image is processed into simpler chunks before the number "8" is outputted

Recurrent Neural Networks

In addition to CNNs, recurrent neural networks (RNNs) are another extremely popular type of neural network. Uniquely, RNNs have the ability to comprehend time and other sequential relationships. As a result, RNNs are widely applied in tasks that require contextual understanding like auto-completion or video captioning (Sutskever et al., 2011; Yu et al., 2016). For example, if we wanted to predict the last word in the sentence "It is fall, the leaves are _____", an RNN would look through the sentence and see the word "fall," and understand that by the context, the last word is most likely "brown." Recurrent neural networks allow contextual information to "recur" and be used when making a prediction on an input (Goodfellow et al., 2016).

In Fig. 11, the circles labeled x_0 through x_t represent the inputs to the network, and h_0 through h_t represent its outputs. From the previous example, x_0 through x_t would represent the words "it," "is," "fall," etc. The box labeled A represents the RNN cells. The lateral arrows connecting A represent the moving of contextual information between predictions on an input. These lateral arrows are the core part of what makes an RNN "recurrent." These cells will take information and perform calculations on them. One of the most commonly used cells is called an LSTM (Long Short-Term Memory) cell (Hochreiter & Schmidhuber, 1997). Standard RNN cells tend to struggle with predictions for large inputs. LSTM cells were invented to fix the shortcomings with standard RNNs and vastly increased the potential applications of the RNN.

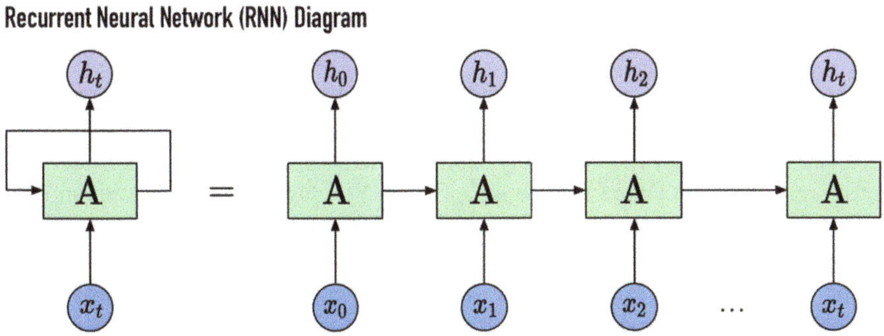

Fig. 11 Diagram of the architecture of an RNN performing a prediction. Note that the lateral arrows represent the recurrence of information

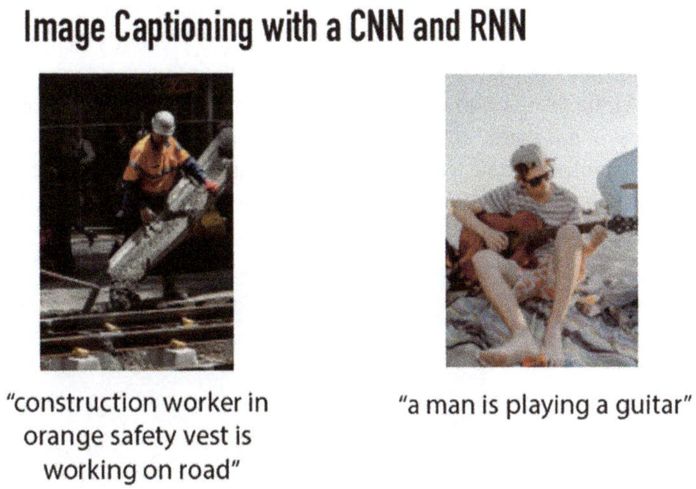

Fig. 12 The images were captioned using a combination of the CNN and RNN architectures. The CNN was used to decompose the image into its defining features which the RNN then used in order to caption the image (Based off of Karpathy & Fei-Fei, 2015, CS 231n at Stanford)

The captions in Fig. 12 were generated as follows. First, the images were fed to a CNN to utilize its ability to efficiently generate features from a given image. From there, these features were fed to LSTM cells, which then generated the captions seen above. Using a CNN and an RNN for their own special properties and then combining them yielded the results seen above. This highlights the power of different neural network architectures.

This section only highlighted a fraction of the numerous neural network architectures used today. In addition to the architectures described above, it is important to mention that Gated Recurrent Units (GRUs, a part of RNNs), Generative Adversarial Networks (GANs), autoencoders (discussed in A3), transformers, and several others are prominent in the field (Liu et al., 2017).

Success of Deep Neural Networks

In recent years, deep learning has been successfully applied in a vast number of diverse fields, constantly pushing the boundaries of what was thought to be possible.

Deep learning has been extremely successful in computer vision. One instance of its success is YOLO (You Only Look Once) v4. YOLOv4 is the newest iteration of one of the most advanced object detectors ever created. It has the ability to look at a frame once (hence the name) and detect many of the objects present within the frame. What makes YOLOv4 unique is that it can now be used in real time and is fast enough to be used on video that is shot at approximately 65 frames per second! YOLO v4 applies convolutional neural networks (Bochkovskiy et al., 2020). Figure 13 shows an example prediction of YOLO v4 for a given image. The boxes surrounding the objects, bounding boxes, are outputted by the algorithm.

Deep learning models are beginning to surpass humans in many complex games. A deep learning-based chess player named "AlphaZero" recently beat the world's best chess computer "Stockfish" (Stockfish is better than the world's best humans). Furthermore, AlphaZero is also one of the world's best players of the games Go and Shogi (Japanese board game, similar to chess). AlphaZero was trained using a concept known as reinforcement learning (discussed further in Chapter C5). In addition, AlphaZero applied convolutional neural networks (Silver et al., 2018).

Fig. 13 Shows YOLO v4, a state-of-the-art object detector (Bochkovskiy et al., 2020)

In 2019, OpenAI Five, a team of five neural networks, convincingly beat the world champion DOTA2 team (five humans) (Berner et al., 2019). What makes this victory so special is the coordination required to play team games like DOTA2. A player must be able to predict the best course of action for not only itself, but the team. They did so using *Deep Reinforcement Learning*, a combination of the ideas discussed here and another sub-field of machine learning, reinforcement learning.

Additionally, an autonomous vehicle may employ deep learning in order to detect obstructions and important objects on roads such as pedestrians, signs, and other cars (Chen et al., 2015). Due to the fact that driving is such an unpredictable task, models will require significant amounts of data in order to safely navigate roads. This makes deep learning algorithms prime candidates for autonomous vehicles as they thrive on vast datasets.

Limitations of Deep Learning

While deep learning models have proven to be very successful in numerous fields, they possess certain shortcomings which can make them unsuitable for certain use cases.

One place where deep learning models fall short is their computational expense. Deep learning models require vast amounts of computational power due to the algorithms used to iteratively tune hyperparameters. One of the fastest ways to train a deep learning model is with Graphics Processing Units (GPUs). GPUs are capable of handling the significant computation required to train deep learning models but are very expensive. Even while using the best GPUs, training complex deep learning models can require weeks to months of processing time, making them time-consuming and costly to develop.

Deep learning models are applied in various fields for numerous types of tasks. However, despite their widespread application, their inner workings are very difficult to explain. This is known as the black box problem (Castelvecchi, 2016). In deep learning, the processes of neuron activation and learning are well understood, but oftentimes when we want to explain why a neural network performs a certain way or explain anomalies in performance, we struggle due to the fact that many parts of deep neural networks (like specific features extracted or layers) are intangible to humans. To overcome this, it is possible to "probe" a deep learning model and look at what it is doing in each layer and each node, but as explained earlier, it would be difficult to decipher.

In addition to the black box problem, due to the fact that deep learning is data driven, deep neural networks can very easily adopt biases in datasets. In 2015, Amazon developed a deep learning-based tool to automatically rank resumes (Dastin, 2018). However, they realized that the tool was not performing in a gender-neutral way, prioritizing male applicants over female applicants. This bias was found because Amazon trained its neural networks over previous resumes submitted to the company, with most resumes coming from men. To minimize such biases, it is important to utilize more general datasets and thorough data analysis to find biases and handle them accordingly (Tommasi et al., 2017). However, as bias is inherently a part of human nature, datasets will always contain bias, so identifying and removing biases are important aspects of applying deep learning that must be addressed (Buss, 2015).

Conclusions

In recent years, deep learning has taken the world by storm and has truly begun to rival and surpass human intelligence and cognition in many places. Through its extensive application by companies like Google, Facebook, Microsoft, Snap, Tesla, and numerous others, deep learning has become increasingly integral to our daily lives. Furthermore, it has become prominent in many active areas of research including but not limited to neuroscience (Marblestone et al., 2016), genomics (Eraslan et al., 2019), and medicine (Shah et al., 2019). It is clear that deep learning will continue to change the world for years to come.

Acknowledgments We extend our sincere thanks to Sridhar Nandigam, Avi Udash, Sahar Behpour, and Dr. Mark V. Albert for their help with the editing and reviewing of this chapter.

References

Albawi, S., Mohammed, T. A., & Al-Zawi, S. (2017). Understanding of a convolutional neural network. In *2017 international conference on engineering and technology (ICET)* (pp. 1–6).

Bengio, Y. (2012). Deep learning of representations for unsupervised and transfer learning. In *Proceedings of ICML workshop on unsupervised and transfer learning* (pp. 17–36).

Berner, C., Brockman, G., Chan, B., Cheung, V., Dębiak, P., Dennison, C., … & Zhang, S. (2019). *Dota 2 with large scale deep reinforcement learning*. arXiv preprint arXiv:1912.06680.

Bochkovskiy, A., Wang, C.-Y., & Liao, H.-Y. M. (2020). *YOLOv4: Optimal Speed and Accuracy of Object Detection. arXiv [cs.CV]*. Retrieved from http://arxiv.org/abs/2004.10934

Buss, D. M. (Ed.). (2015). The evolution of cognitive bias. In *The handbook of evolutionary psychology* (Vol. 42, pp. 1–20). Hoboken: Wiley.

Castelvecchi, D. (2016). Can we open the black box of AI? *Nature, 538*(7623), 20–23.

Chen, C., Seff, A., Kornhauser, A., & Xiao, J. (2015). Deepdriving: Learning affordance for direct perception in autonomous driving. In *Proceedings of the IEEE international conference on computer vision* (pp. 2722–2730).

Curry, H. B. (1944). The method of steepest descent for non-linear minimization problems. *Quarterly of Applied Mathematics, 2*(3), 258–261.

Dastin, J. (2018). Amazon scraps secret AI recruiting tool that showed bias against women. *San Francisco, CA: Reuters. Retrieved on October*, 9, 2018.

Deng, L., & Yu, D. (2014). Deep learning: Methods and applications. *Foundations and Trends in Signal Processing, 7*(3–4), 197–387.

Edu, J., Such, J. M., & Suarez-Tangil, G. (2019). *Smart home personal assistants: A security and privacy review. arXiv [cs.CR]*. Retrieved from http://arxiv.org/abs/1903.05593

Eraslan, G., Avsec, Ž., Gagneur, J., & Theis, F. J. (2019). Deep learning: New computational modelling techniques for genomics. *Nature Reviews Genetics, 20*(7), 389–403.
Erhan, D., Bengio, Y., Courville, A., & Vincent, P. (2009). Visualizing higher-layer features of a deep network. *University of Montreal, 1341*(3), 1.
Goodfellow, I., Bengio, Y., & Courville, A. (2016). Deep learning book. *MIT Press, 521*(7553), 800.
Harley, A. W. (2015). An interactive node-link visualization of convolutional neural networks. In *Advances in visual computing* (pp. 867–877). New York: Springer International Publishing.
Hochreiter, S., & Schmidhuber, J. (1997). Long short-term memory. *Neural Computation, 9*(8), 1735–1780.
Karpathy, A., & Fei-Fei, L. (2015). Deep visual-semantic alignments for generating image descriptions. In *Proceedings of the IEEE conference on computer vision and pattern recognition* (pp. 3128–3137).
Krizhevsky, A., Sutskever, I., & Hinton, G. E. (2017). ImageNet classification with deep convolutional neural networks. *Communications of the ACM, 60*(6), 84–90.
Lecun, Y., Bottou, L., Bengio, Y., & Haffner, P. (1998). Gradient-based learning applied to document recognition. *Proceedings of the IEEE, 86*(11), 2278–2324.
LeCun, Y., Bengio, Y., & Hinton, G. (2015). Deep learning. *Nature, 521*(7553), 436–444.
Lee, H., Grosse, R., Ranganath, R., & Ng, A. Y. (2009). Convolutional deep belief networks for scalable unsupervised learning of hierarchical representations. In *Proceedings of the 26th annual international conference on machine learning* (pp. 609–616). New York: Association for Computing Machinery. Retrieved 10 May 2021 from.
Lin, Y., Lv, F., Zhu, S., Yang, M., Cour, T., Yu, K., … Huang, T. (2011). Large-scale image classification: Fast feature extraction and SVM training. In *CVPR 2011* (pp. 1689–1696).
Litjens, G., Sánchez, C. I., Timofeeva, N., Hermsen, M., Nagtegaal, I., Kovacs, I., … van der Laak, J. (2016). Deep learning as a tool for increased accuracy and efficiency of histopathological diagnosis. *Scientific Reports, 6*, 26286.
Liu, W., Wang, Z., Liu, X., Zeng, N., Liu, Y., & Alsaadi, F. E. (2017). A survey of deep neural network architectures and their applications. *Neurocomputing, 234*, 11–26.
Marblestone, A. H., Wayne, G., & Kording, K. P. (2016). Toward an integration of deep learning and neuroscience. *Frontiers in Computational Neuroscience, 10*, 94.
Pulvermüller, F. (2013). How neurons make meaning: Brain mechanisms for embodied and abstract-symbolic semantics. *Trends in Cognitive Sciences, 17*(9), 458–470.
Russakovsky, O., Deng, J., Su, H., Krause, J., Satheesh, S., Ma, S., … Fei-Fei, L. (2015). ImageNet large scale visual recognition challenge. *International Journal of Computer Vision, 115*(3), 211–252.
Salman, A. G., Kanigoro, B., & Heryadi, Y. (2015). Weather forecasting using deep learning techniques. In *2015 international conference on advanced computer science and information systems (ICACSIS)* (pp. 281–285).
Shah, P., Kendall, F., Khozin, S., Goosen, R., Hu, J., Laramie, J., … Schork, N. (2019). Artificial intelligence and machine learning in clinical development: a translational perspective. *Npj Digital Medicine*. Retrieved from https://doi.org/10.1038/s41746-019-0148-3.
Silver, D., Hubert, T., Schrittwieser, J., Antonoglou, I., Lai, M., Guez, A., … Hassabis, D. (2018). A general reinforcement learning algorithm that masters chess, shogi, and Go through self-play. *Science, 362*(6419), 1140–1144.
Simonyan, K., & Zisserman, A. (2014). *Very deep convolutional networks for large-scale image recognition. arXiv [cs.CV]*. Retrieved from http://arxiv.org/abs/1409.1556
Sutskever, I., Martens, J., & Hinton, G. E. (2011). *Generating text with recurrent neural networks*. Retrieved 13 December 2020 from https://openreview.net/pdf?id=SyEoB2-dZH
Szegedy, C., Liu, W., Jia, Y., Sermanet, P., Reed, S., Anguelov, D., … Rabinovich, A. (2015). Going deeper with convolutions. In *Proceedings of the IEEE conference on computer vision and pattern recognition* (pp. 1–9).

Tommasi, T., Patricia, N., Caputo, B., & Tuytelaars, T. (2017). A Deeper Look at Dataset Bias. In G. Csurka (Ed.), *Domain adaptation in computer vision applications* (pp. 37–55). Cham: Springer International Publishing.

Wu, Y., Schuster, M., Chen, Z., Le, Q. V., Norouzi, M., Macherey, W., ... Dean, J. (2016). *Google's Neural Machine Translation System: Bridging the Gap between Human and Machine Translation. arXiv [cs.CL].* Retrieved from http://arxiv.org/abs/1609.08144

Yu, H., Wang, J., Huang, Z., Yang, Y., & Xu, W. (2016). Video paragraph captioning using hierarchical recurrent neural networks. In *Proceedings of the IEEE conference on computer vision and pattern recognition* (pp. 4584–4593).

Zeiler, M. D., & Fergus, R. (2014). Visualizing and understanding convolutional networks. In *Computer vision – ECCV 2014* (pp. 818–833). Springer International Publishing.

Zhang, N., Shen, S., Zhou, A., & Xu, Y. (2019a). Investigation on performance of neural networks using quadratic relative error cost function. *IEEE Access, 7*, 106642–106652.

Zhang, S., Yao, L., Sun, A., & Tay, Y. (2019b). Deep learning based recommender system: A survey and new perspectives. *ACM Computing Surveys, 52*(1), 1–38.

Arvind Ganesh is an undergraduate researcher passionate about deep learning, open-source software, and bio-medical applications of AI. Currently, he is focusing on the project FallCatcher, developing a fall-detection algorithm for stroke victims. In summer 2020, he presented FallCatcher at the UNT Artificial Intelligence Summer Research Conference and received the Best Presentation Award. In his free time, he enjoys playing violin, lifting weights, and talking to friends.

Namratha Urs is a PhD candidate in computer science at the University of North Texas (UNT), specializing in natural language processing and applied machine learning. She is a member of the Human Intelligence and Language Technologies Lab and the Biomedical AI Lab at UNT. Her primary research is in the investigation of deep learning techniques to identify conversational styles in dialogue. She has also worked on applying machine learning techniques to understand neural processing by simulating computational neuroscience principles. She has presented at the Society of Neuroscience and ACM Richard Tapia Celebration of Diversity in Computing. She has also served as the President of the UNT Women in Computing group (2020–2021).

Autoencoders and Embeddings: How Unsupervised Structural Learning Enables Fast and Efficient Goal-Directed Learning

Sridhar Nandigam, Thasina Tabashum, and Ting Xiao

Introduction to Unsupervised Learning

The world is full of data and, with each advancement in technology, we become better at collecting this data. It can take the form of tweets, texts, security footage, fitness trackers, and customer reviews. In order to make the most of this raw data, we must make it suitable for analysis and data science algorithms. There are multiple methods to make unstructured data fit for usage; traditional factor analysis and unsupervised deep learning. With traditional factor analysis, the data scientist must manually analyze the data points and how they relate to each other. However, this process requires prior knowledge of the domain and a significant amount of time which is less than ideal when dealing with a large dataset.

In the previous chapter, we discussed the forms of supervised deep learning models such as convolutional neural networks and recurrent neural networks. These models are capable of learning how to predict a certain output by using a given input. However, the real world is filled with raw unstructured data. This means that certain correlations or relationships between this data can be invisible to the human eye. If we cannot understand the structure of the input data, we cannot properly construct a neural network that can process it. Unsupervised deep learning, as the name suggests, lets the network figure out for itself which parts of the input data are significant by creating representations of data and capturing nonlinearity. By doing so, the learned representations can further be utilized in decision making or for making prediction tasks (Mendelson & Smola, 2003). For example, training data might contain a sequence of sound wavelengths and no indication of preferred target

S. Nandigam (✉) · T. Tabashum · T. Xiao
Department of Computer Science and Engineering, University of North Texas, Denton, TX, USA
e-mail: SridharNandigam@my.unt.edu; thasinatabashum@my.unt.edu; tingxiao@unt.edu

M. V. Albert et al. (eds.), *Bridging Human Intelligence and Artificial Intelligence*, Educational Communications and Technology: Issues and Innovations, https://doi.org/10.1007/978-3-030-84729-6_3

values. An unsupervised model would be able to discover patterns from the data and detect similar groups of data to identify and distinguish speakers. A deep layered architecture can learn complexity of data more efficiently than shallow techniques (Larochelle et al., 2009).

The complexity of data is a common challenge in tasks. Data quantity, data quality, and data explainability are empirically core determinants of the performance of models. These unusual patterns can significantly affect the overall performance of a neural network architecture. The first step to dealing with these challenges is dimensionality reduction.

Reducing Dimensionality

In order to make algorithms and machine learning models that can start understanding raw data from the real world, we have to deal with the curse of dimensionality. The curse of dimensionality means that the input data simply has too many features and details. A machine learning model and even a seasoned data scientist may have trouble figuring out which features are most relevant to achieving a specific outcome. With the problem of too much input data, the obvious logical solution is to reduce the amount of features of the input data. Dimensionality reduction techniques are able to scrub out all of the "noisy" data that may distract an algorithm from using the relevant data.

A good example of the curse of dimensionality can be found in a library. Let's suppose that we want to organize all the books by fiction or nonfiction. A human can easily sort them by analyzing various elements of science fiction, mystery, fantasy, biography, etc. just to sort it into two categories. Now if we gave these details to a machine learning model to train with and ask it to organize them in a similar manner, we run the risk of confusing the model or overfitting. With so much input data and potential outcomes, the program starts believing that these points are equally similar, thus defeating the purpose of algorithms like clustering. To solve this, we can simply reduce the dimensionality of the data by only including details about the book that can classify it as fiction or nonfiction. However, most of the real-world data is usually high dimensional and needs to be transformed into a meaningful manner. In the following sections, we will cover the traditional linear technique PCA and then nonlinear techniques to deal with complex data in order to get a general idea of how dimensionality reduction works.

Principal Component Analysis (PCA)

To properly understand the concepts behind dimensionality reduction and its advantages, let us take a look at one of the most prominent techniques of factor analysis. Principal component analysis (PCA) is a popular dimensionality reduction technique that uses an orthogonal transformation to condense the data into principal components (Gewers et al., 2018). The number of these components is limited and retains a large amount of the variance from the dataset. By capturing underlying factors, this method is able to identify latent factors in highly correlated datasets.

The first step in PCA is standardization. Standardizing the data is a common first step for most data science related tasks ("Data Standardization," n.d.). In this step, we make sure that all the data is reduced to a reasonable scale without a large variety of ranges. Outliers that fall in a much larger range can warp the algorithm's understanding of the data.

Once we have properly processed our data, we can begin to understand the correlations within the data. This is accomplished with a covariance matrix, which essentially sums up the relationship between every single pair of data points. Next, linear algebra is used to construct the principal components. The principal components are uncorrelated new variables with as much information retained in each one as possible. In this process, the first component represents the most information out of all the other components following it. Then, the second component does the same, although it is slightly less than the first component. This process continues until we have components that are hardly relevant in our understanding of the data. The principal components are crucial because they represent the amount of variance, which is the dispersion of the data points along a certain direction (Fig. 1). A higher variance therefore indicates that we have more information about the dataset. Now that we have condensed the information into its principal components, we must actually start reducing dimensions. We do this by choosing which principal

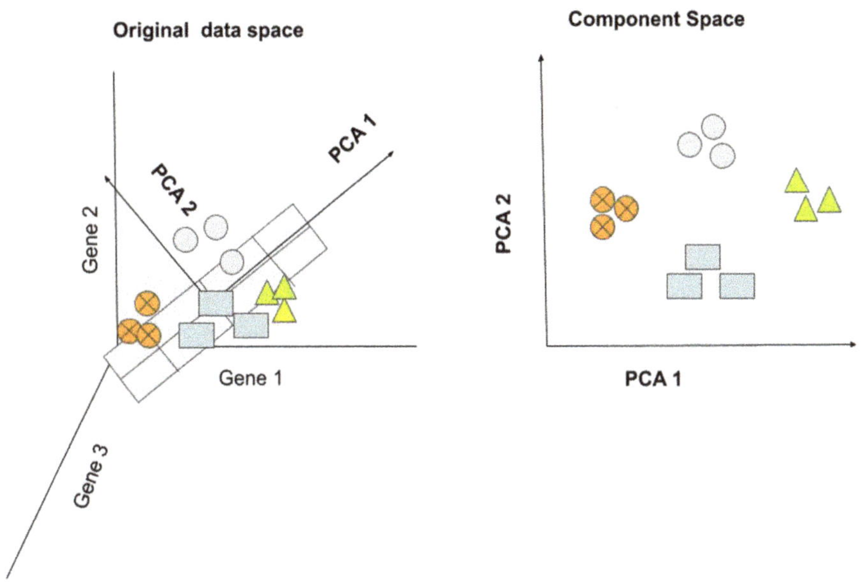

Fig. 1 Scholz (n.d.) demonstrated three-dimensional gene expression reduced to two dimensions capturing the highest variance that allows visualizing the qualitative information optimally

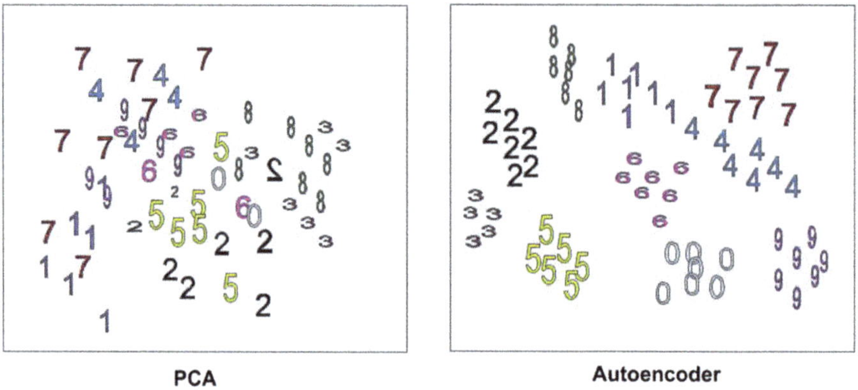

Fig. 2 Hinton and Salakhutdinov (2006) illustrated the difference between PCA and autoencoder dimensionality reduction of MNIST dataset

components have the most variance of data in a certain direction. As stated earlier, there will be some that we have generated that give us little information about the data and do not need to be used for the sake of simplicity.

Principal component analysis is relatively simple but it is incapable of capturing nonlinearity in data and forces orthogonality between projections (Shlens, 2014)). In these scenarios, we introduce algorithms such as the autoencoder, a powerful model which captures nonlinear relationships between the data points and ensures minimum reconstruction error. Such a model can learn better representation in a reduced dimensional space and overcome some of the shortcomings of PCA. Hinton and Salakhutdinov (2006) trained autoencoder on handwritten digits ("MNIST handwritten digit database, Yann LeCun, Corinna Cortes and Chris Burges," n.d.-a) dataset and demonstrated the produced reconstructions of images are much better than PCA (Fig. 2).

For the last two decades, it is apparent that deep autoencoders are effective and faster in handling complex data compared to nonparametric methods.

Autoencoders

Autoencoders are unsupervised machine learning methods that can learn complex statistical relationships and useful features of data through a series of neural network layers (Yu & Príncipe, 2019). In order to do so, the model deconstructs and reconstructs the original input. It is trained to predict its input itself like a self-supervised learning model (Murphy, 2012). This form of machine learning is called representation learning since the ultimate goal is to create a compressed version of the input data that can serve as a good representation of the original data. The main advantage of autoencoders lies in the fact that we can use layers that have nonlinear activation functions, thus allowing us to recognize nonlinear relationships. This means that autoencoders are an ideal method for feature extraction. There are various types of autoencoders: standard autoencoder, stacked autoencoder, denoising autoencoder, sparse autoencoder, and variational autoencoder.

Standard Autoencoder

The architecture of a standard autoencoder consists of three parts: the encoder, code, and decoder. The encoder compresses the original data into a latent space representation. The goal of this layer is to reduce the dimensionality of the data points while retaining important features. The code layer simply serves as the representation of the compressed data, also known as a latent space representation. In Fig. 3, it is shown as the compressed feature vector. The decoder takes the summary representation and attempts to reconstruct the original input. The decoded output from this layer has the same dimensions as the input data but fewer features. This process is meant to serve as a "bottleneck." After training the autoencoder with the decoder and encoder, the code component can be used as an input sequence for another model.

Stacked Autoencoder

A standard autoencoder generally has an encoding layer, the bottleneck, and the decoding layer. However, it is possible to introduce several hidden layers between the encoding and decoding layers. This is similar to how a deep neural network has

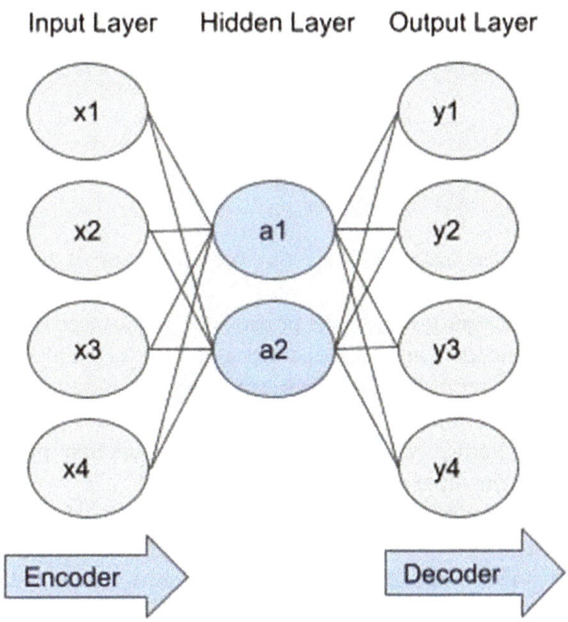

Fig. 3 Standard autoencoder: encoder consists of four inputs (left), two encoded representation (middle), and decoder with four outputs (right)

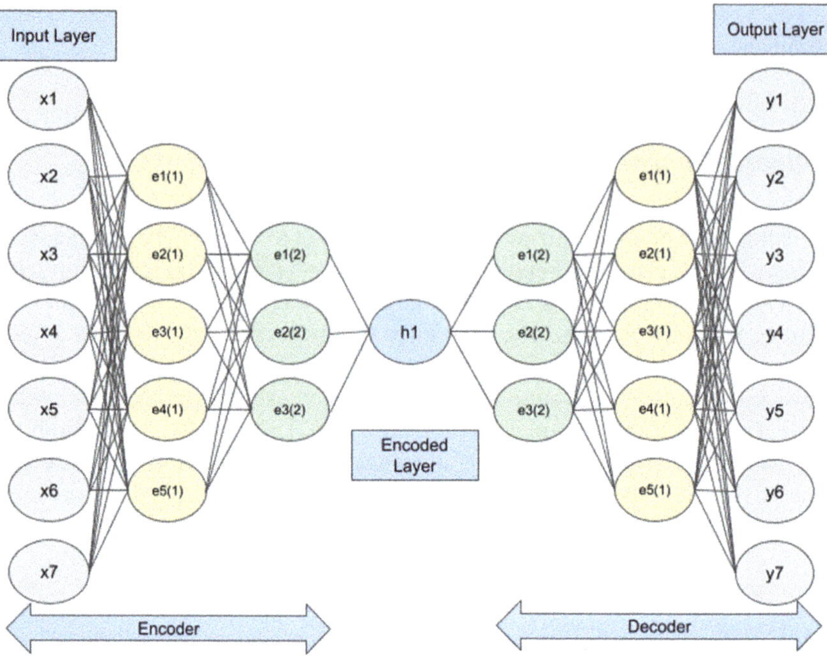

Fig. 4 Stacked autoencoder: three layered encoder (left), one encoded representation (middle), and three layered decoder (right)

multiple hidden layers in order to train more accurately. Stacked autoencoders also have each layer train on the input data and pass on the learned data to the next layer (Fig. 4). Then, backpropagation is used to fine-tune the weights and biases to reduce the cost function. This architecture allows for much more accurate feature extraction.

Denoising Autoencoder

Denoising autoencoders are a simple variation of the standard autoencoder architecture and a good starting point to better understand how different variations can serve different purposes. In the previous section, we observed the structure of a standard autoencoder and how it encodes and decodes the input data in order to create a compressed representation. However, a regular autoencoder often runs the risk of simply spitting out the exact same input data with no significant changes in the output. In other words, we end up with an identity function that will tell us nothing important about the input data (Vincent et al., 2010).

A standard example of MINST (Jordan, 2018; "MNIST handwritten digit database, Yann LeCun, Corinna Cortes and Chris Burges," n.d.-b) dataset that compresses an image and the model learns to reconstruct input as possible. The

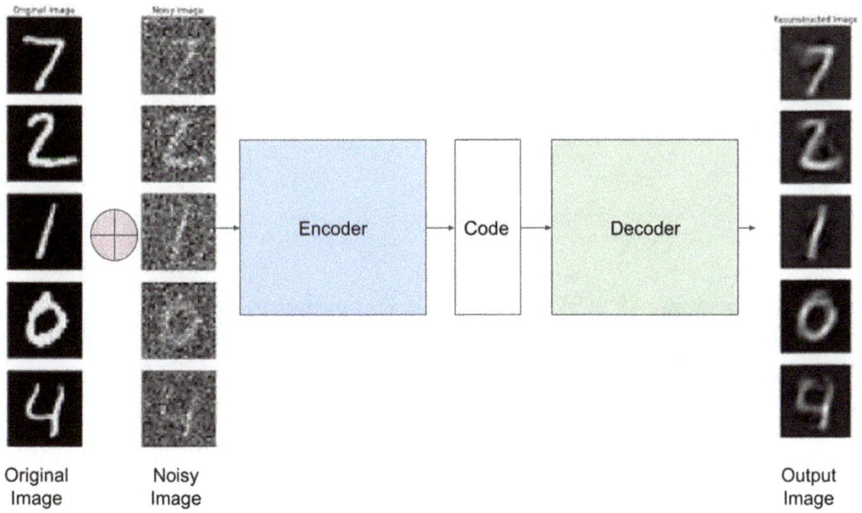

Fig. 5 Denoising autoencoder: noise is added to original images and then autoencoder is trained on that noisy dataset

autoencoder tries to create an output similar to input ("Unsupervised Feature Learning and Deep Learning Tutorial," n.d.). In Fig. 5, the image pixel intensity values from 28*28 images (784), but the compressed representation is a lot less than 784. The encoder is forced to find patterns in the compressed representation. The decoder takes the compressed representation and reconstructs the values to closely match the original input.

To avoid this common shortcoming, we can make a tweak to the architecture by simply adding noise. Denoising autoencoders can overcome the above-mentioned limitation by corrupting the original input data by intentionally introducing noise. With this method, we are guaranteed to avoid getting a perfect copy of the input.

As observed in the previous Fig. 5, the noise is added to the original image before feeding it into the encoder. The outputs are clearly recognizable as it should be. However, they are not the exact same as the input and it is far less detailed, while retaining the original shape. Therefore, the denoising autoencoder achieved its purpose in giving us a compact and more simple representation of the input data.

Contractive Autoencoder

Denoising autoencoders are trained by corrupting training points to reconstruct the original input. On the other hand, contractive autoencoders are improved autoencoders that learn robust features by introducing local penalties to the original cost function. The architecture of contractive autoencoders is built with the purpose of extracting robust features for the sake of a more concrete representation of the input

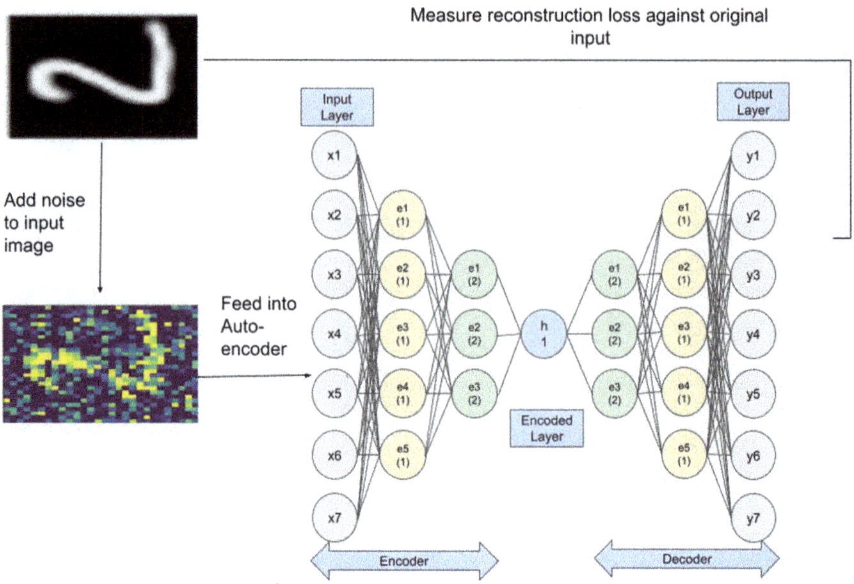

Fig. 6 Contractive autoencoder: noise is added to the data, fed into the autoencoder, and the reconstruction loss is calculated and used to minimize it for the next feedforward run

data. In order to achieve this, the autoencoder must be less sensitive to small variations within the input data (Rifai et al., 2011).

Robust features can be identified by the contraction of the input space when projected into the feature space (Rifai et al., 2011). The contraction of the data occurs due to the penalty term that is added to the cost function in order to minimize it. As shown in the figure above, we can also introduce small perturbations or noise to the input data to encourage the contractive autoencoder to be less sensitive to these small changes (Fig. 6). This architecture allows the contractive autoencoder to outperform denoising autoencoders when it comes to feature extraction as it not only avoids giving us an identity function, but it manages to identify important robust features that help us understand the data.

Sparse Autoencoder

Sparse autoencoders are a special variation that uses sparsity penalty rather than simple bottlenecking in order to better learn the depth of input data. The difference in architecture lies in the fact that there are generally more hidden nodes than input nodes. However, only a few of these hidden nodes will be activated in the feedforward process (Fig. 7). This form of autoencoder derives its name from the fact that only the largest activated nodes will be used to reconstruct the input while the rest of the hidden nodes will be set to zero in order to prevent too many nodes from

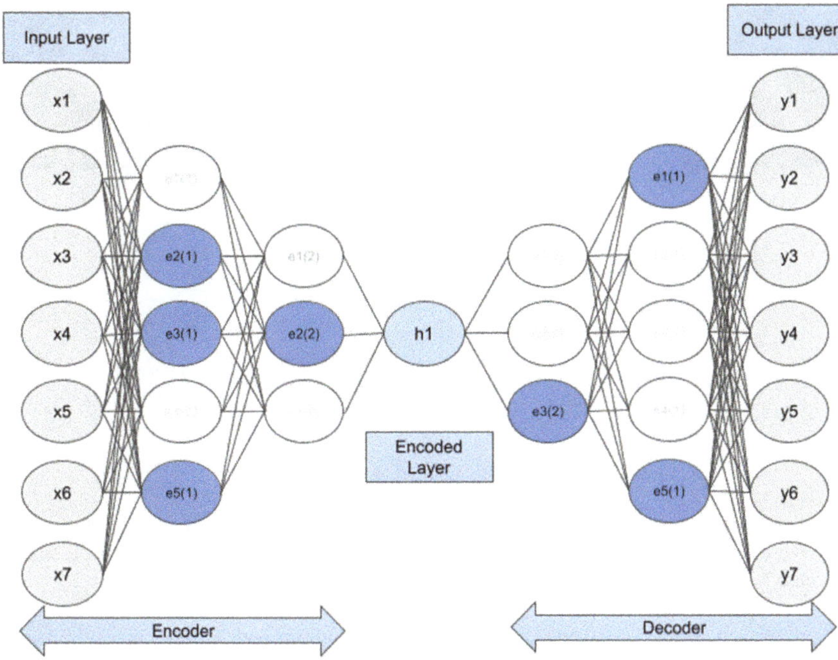

Fig. 7 Sparse autoencoder: Three layered encoder with four in-active nodes (left) and three layered decoder with five inactive nodes (right)

being active (Makhzani & Frey, 2013). In doing so, we force the network to focus on specific features that are useful in understanding the data. Sparse autoencoders also implement a sparsity penalty that is enacted each time a hidden node is activated. This penalty prevents too many hidden nodes from being activated for each input and with this, we can push the network into recognizing detailed patterns in our data. By constructing the loss function in this manner, we prevent traditional drawbacks to machine learning models and autoencoders such as overfitting.

Convolutional Autoencoders

In the previous chapter, we introduced convolutional neural networks (CNNs) that are typically used for image labeling applications. As a brief summary, CNN uses convolutions to assess images by each section and extract key features. Convolutional autoencoders also implement convolutional layers, but within an autoencoder architecture.

Using convolutional layers to better analyze an image allows convolutional autoencoders to surpass traditional autoencoders when it comes to 2D image processing. Convolutional autoencoders are able to identify localized image features and retain

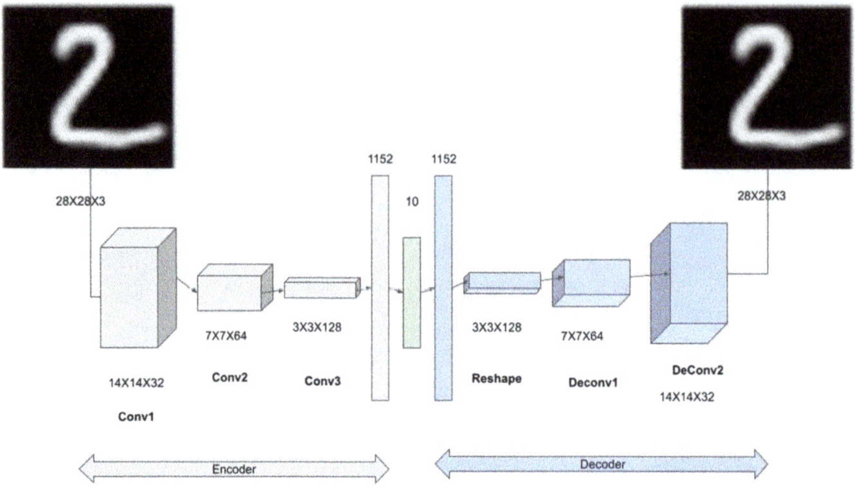

Fig. 8 Guo et al. (2017) proposed a deep CNN autoencoder for the MNIST dataset, the encoder has three CNN layers, the embedded layers has 10 fully connected neurons, and the decoder is transpose layers

spatial information about the image (Masci et al., 2011). In Fig. 8, the convolutional layers extract the original 2D image into cubics. In the middle is the real autoencoder with the encoding, hidden, and decoding layers. After the decoding layer, the data is then reshaped into a 2D image with deconvolutional layers. This process makes convolutional autoencoders extremely effective in image denoising as shown in Fig. 8 where the output image appears much "cleaner" than the original.

Variational Autoencoders

Variational autoencoders are an incredibly powerful form of autoencoders that are widely used in the field of image processing. As stated previously, we generally use autoencoders to create compact representations of data and for denoising data. Variational autoencoders open up new possibilities for data generation.

In order to understand variational autoencoders, we must first explore the field of generative modeling. Simply put, generative modeling is a field of machine learning that is able to generate new instances of data (Doersch, 2016). Machine learning models discussed in previous chapters are classified as discriminative models that have the simple task of figuring out the probability that a certain label applies to a certain data point. In order to better understand this, let us look at a case where we are given a dataset of cat pictures. A generative model is able to find the correlations between each data point within a picture of a cat. For example, it observes that cats tend to have two ears that are positioned above the eyes. It notices that there is a

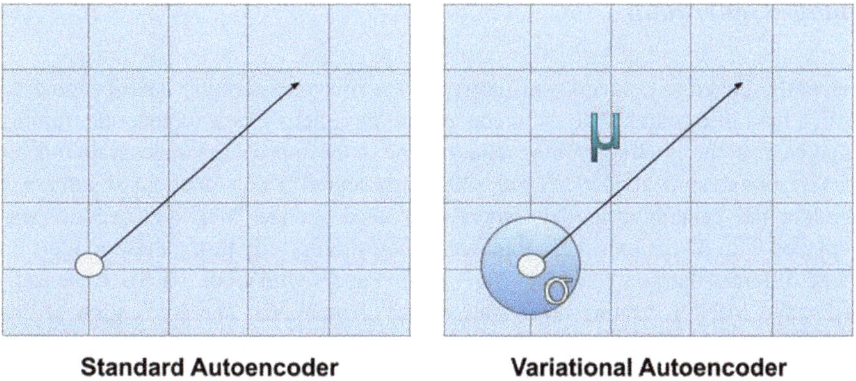

Fig. 9 Encoded representation of standard autoencoder (left) and encoded space generated by the variational autoencoder

certain probability that the nose will be a certain distance above the mouth. Given these observations, a generative model will be able to create new variations of the input data. In this case, it would be able to generate new pictures of cats that are essentially variations of the input images.

Variational autoencoders are a form of generative modeling that so happen to resemble the structure of a standard autoencoder. The difference between variational autoencoders and regular autoencoders lies in their ability to observe latent distributions in the data. Standard autoencoders are able to create a specific and direct encoding within a latent space for a specific input data point, as illustrated in the image above (Fig. 9). With a large amount of input data, there will be several encodings within that latent space that will be clumped into clusters. This works just fine when we are simply trying to recreate a more compact version of the input data. However, if we want to generate new data, we want variations of the input data. In order to do so, we need to identify the "area" around the encoding that is viable for the encoder to choose from. Without this, the encoder will still pick any random point within the latent space, but will not know how to implement it when generating new data.

Applications of Autoencoders

Apart from their use in dimensionality reduction and feature extraction, we have already shown how autoencoders have various applications in image processing, audio processing, and other fields that tend to have a large amount of noisy data. Similar to noise reduction, other notable applications of autoencoders are image generation, sequence to sequence prediction, recommendation systems, and anomaly detection.

Image Generation

Recently, generative adversarial networks for image generation have become an active field of research. The main concept of these networks is to generate training images from the existing training dataset. One of the approaches to generate images is variational autoencoders. Sagar (2020) presented a combination of inference models and generative models where they used encoder VAE and decoder was replaced with discriminator. In this work, they successfully tested these models on three different datasets ("celeb_a_hq," n.d.; "Papers with Code – LSUN Dataset," n.d.), and MINST, beating other state of the art methods. The application of this kind of network can reduce the shortage of imaging datasets, specifically benefiting the biomedical imaging field the most. A more interesting application lies in the entertainment industry, such as generating anime characters.

Sequence to Sequence Prediction

The general purpose of sequence to sequence prediction is to predict the next item from an input sequence. A few examples include predicting the next frame of the videos, speech recognition, and caption generation. It is significantly challenging as the input length can be varied, requiring extraction features from the temporal ordering of observation and in particular, the output itself will be a sequence. The LSTM autoencoder can be used to compress the representation of the sequences to feed another prediction model. Srivastava et al. (2015) utilized the LSTM autoencoder to learn video representations. They used learned representation in a classifier and found which composite model along with an encoder performed best in their experiments.

Recommendation Systems

Machine learning approaches are widely used in recommender systems more precisely personalized recommendation systems in e-commerce. Within the growing variety of popular recommendation systems, the autoencoder-based approaches are outperforming classical models. One of the earliest proposed novel autoencoder frameworks for collaborative filtering is "AutoRec" which outperforms biased matrix factorization and RBM-collaborative filtering (Sedhain et al., 2015). After that Kuchaiev and Ginsburg (2017) proposed a deeper and more generalized autoencoder for rating prediction tasks. However, to deal with such a huge volume, complex dataset, as well as dynamic information, the autoencoder-based approaches showed quality results in recommender systems in the past decade. Integrating autoencoders with recommendation systems will significantly improve the systems as the autoencoders are performing extremely well in feature extraction and data reconstruction (Zhang et al., 2020).

Anomaly Detection

Anomalies can be defined as outliers that are simply different from normal data. This is slightly different from noisy data since noise is corrupt and useless data that is recorded as a result of scenarios like system glitches. On the other hand, outliers come from rare or unexpected events. Anomalous data can be recorded as a result of faulty equipment, system errors, glitches, misprints, etc. As such, this data can prove useful when trying to root out issues with the system recording this data (Salgado et al., 2016). In machine learning, such anomalies can impact a model's ability to make the most of the important frequent data within a dataset. Deep autoencoders can be used in such scenarios to give us clean training data (Zhou & Paffenroth, 2017). Anomaly detection with autoencoders essentially gets rid of noisy data and detects potentially useful outliers.

Embeddings

An embedding takes a sequence of inputs such as words and maps them onto a continuous vector to gain an understanding of how its features compare to those of others. In this section, we will be discussing embeddings in a machine learning context where such vector representations are automatically learned. This process is also a form of dimensionality reduction since we can properly represent categories in a low dimensional space. Neural network embeddings are especially useful because machine learning models take vectors or arrays of numbers as input. With embeddings, we can essentially vectorize non-numerical values such as text and other objects.

The significance in embeddings lies in the fact that we can visualize all the points of data and their relations to their neighbors. With this ability, we can start clustering or grouping certain variables and recognize general patterns. If a human is unable to do this, we have at least made it easier for a neural network to do so. Previously, researchers used to deal with this conversion explicitly using word similarity statistics, but neural embeddings achieved significantly better performance (Turian et al., 2010). In the next few sections, we will briefly discuss some of the embeddings.

Word Embeddings

One of the most popular neural embeddings that have been utilized for the last few years is word2vec (Mikolov et al., 2013). Word embeddings are a type of representation that allows words with similar meanings to have a similar representation. Word2vec is a statistical representation of words as vectors that encodes correlated words in the same dimensional space. There are several approaches to word embedding such as Continues Bag-of-Words and Continues Skip-Gram. Figure 10 illustrates how word2vec clusters words in dimension space.

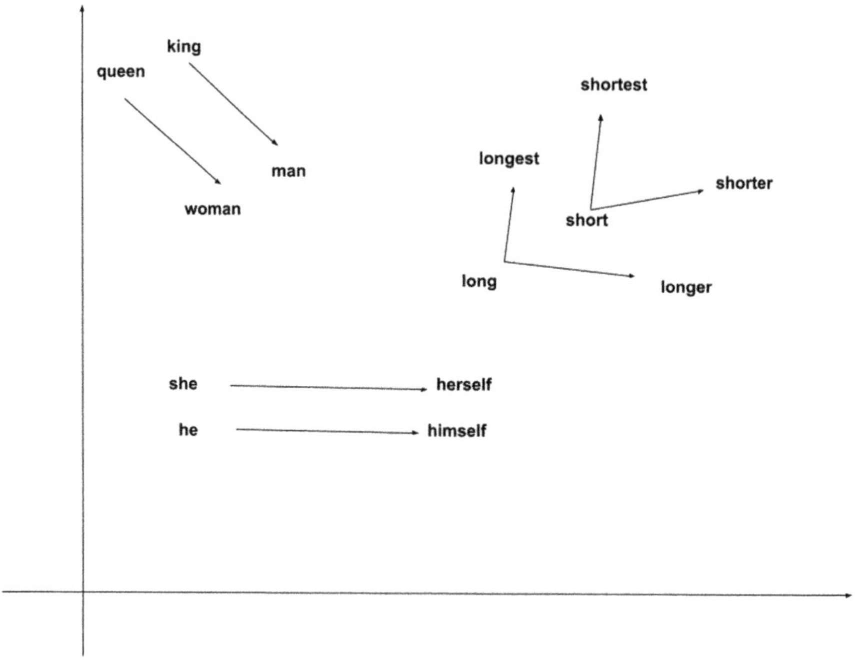

Fig. 10 Word embeddings: the pairs (king, man) and (queen, woman) are in the same dimensional space

Location Embeddings

Similar to word2vec, geospatial image data and map coordinates can be used to understand vector representations (Jean et al., 2019). Tile2Vec is a feature learning algorithm that learns semantically meaningful representations from image tiles. It is able to perform non-image task prediction and is capable of predicting country health indices, generalizing significantly well across data modalities. "Loc2Vec: Learning location embeddings with triplet-loss networks – Sentiance" (2018) introduced location embeddings that are able to learn metric space from similar image patches between different geographical location coordinates. These types of embedding spaces can be utilized for transport classifiers and venue mappers.

Graph Embeddings

Graph-structured data is a dominant field of machine learning research that is used in bioinformatics, social media, and cybersecurity. To obtain results, this domain also requires vectorial representations to accomplish tasks such as malware detection. Graph kernels evaluate the similarity between pairs and extract the substructure of graphs. Usually, the features are handcrafted, and when these features are used on large datasets of graphs that leads to poor generalization. Recently, embedding techniques have been explored to learn the representation of graphs such as nodes, paths, and sub-graphs. Graph2vec is mainly based on the idea of doc2vec where graphs are similar to documents and trained to maximize the probability of predicting sub-graphs (Narayanan et al., 2017).

The embeddings have made significant progress in recent years. Using the same methodology, there have been many feature representation work going on in a wide range of fields, for example, the stock market dataset (stock2vec) (Wang et al., 2020) and automobile sensor data drive2vec (Hallac et al., 2018). The data-driven approach of learning representation has revealed true potentials in recent years.

Conclusion

Deep learning models are quickly growing more complex and, as a result, are achieving incredible things in multiple domains. However, the deeper these networks get in order to accommodate a greater variety of data and continue performing well, the more bloated they become, wasting significant computational resources and time. Dimensionality reduction extends the quality and speed of the deep neural network models and allows data scientists to gain a better understanding of their own data as well. As such, embeddings and autoencoders are paving the way for the complete integration of artificial intelligence into our daily lives.

References

celeb_a_hq. (n.d.). Retrieved 24 April 2021, from https://www.tensorflow.org/datasets/catalog/celeb_a_hq

Data Standardization. (n.d.). Retrieved 22 April 2021, from https://www.sciencedirect.com/topics/computer-science/data-standardization

Doersch, C. (2016, June 19). *Tutorial on Variational Autoencoders. arXiv [stat.ML]*. Retrieved from http://arxiv.org/abs/1606.05908

Gewers, F. L., Ferreira, G. R., de Arruda, H. F., Silva, F. N., Comin, C. H., Amancio, D. R., & da Costa, F. L. (2018, April 7). *Principal component analysis: A natural approach to data exploration. arXiv [cs.CE]*. Retrieved from http://arxiv.org/abs/1804.02502

Guo, X., Liu, X., Zhu, E., & Yin, J. (2017). Deep clustering with convolutional autoencoders. In *Neural information processing* (pp. 373–382). Springer.

Hallac, D., Bhooshan, S., Chen, M., Abida, K., Sosic, R., & Leskovec, J. (2018, June 12). *Drive2Vec: Multiscale state-space embedding of vehicular sensor data. arXiv [cs.LG]*. Retrieved from http://arxiv.org/abs/1806.04795

Hinton, G. E., & Salakhutdinov, R. R. (2006). Reducing the dimensionality of data with neural networks. *Science, 313*(5786), 504–507.

Jean, N., Wang, S., Samar, A., Azzari, G., Lobell, D., & Ermon, S. (2019). Tile2Vec: Unsupervised representation learning for Spatially Distributed Data. *Proceedings of the AAAI Conference on Artificial Intelligence, 33*(01), 3967–3974. Retrieved 25 April 2021 from https://doi.org/10.1609/aaai.v33i01.33013967

Jordan, J. (2018). *Introduction to autoencoders*. Retrieved 22 April 2021, from https://www.jeremyjordan.me/autoencoders/

Kuchaiev, O., & Ginsburg, B. (2017, August 5). *Training Deep AutoEncoders for Collaborative Filtering. arXiv [stat.ML]*. Retrieved from http://arxiv.org/abs/1708.01715

Larochelle, H., Bengio, Y., Louradour, J., & Lamblin, P. (2009). Exploring strategies for training deep neural networks. *Journal of Machine Learning Research: JMLR, 10*(1). Retrieved from http://www.jmlr.org/papers/volume10/larochelle09a/larochelle09a.pdf.

Loc2Vec: Learning location embeddings with triplet-loss networks – Sentiance. (2018). Retrieved 25 April 2021, from https://www.sentiance.com/2018/05/03/venue-mapping/

Makhzani, A., & Frey, B. (2013, December 19). *k-Sparse Autoencoders. arXiv [cs.LG]*. Retrieved from http://arxiv.org/abs/1312.5663

Masci, J., Meier, U., Cireşan, D., & Schmidhuber, J. (2011). Stacked convolutional auto-encoders for hierarchical feature extraction. *Lecture Notes in Computer Science*. Retrieved from https://doi.org/10.1007/978-3-642-21735-7_7.

Mendelson, S., & Smola, A. J. (Eds.). (2003). *Advanced lectures on machine learning: Machine learning summer school 2002 Canberra, Australia, February 11–22, 2002 revised lectures*. Springer.

Mikolov, T., Yih, W.-T., & Zweig, G. (2013). Linguistic regularities in continuous space word representations. In *Proceedings of the 2013 conference of the North American chapter of the association for computational linguistics: Human language technologies* (pp. 746–751). Association for Computational Linguistics.

MNIST handwritten digit database, Yann LeCun, Corinna Cortes and Chris Burges. (n.d.-a). Retrieved 26 April 2021, from http://yann.lecun.com/exdb/mnist/

MNIST handwritten digit database, Yann LeCun, Corinna Cortes and Chris Burges. (n.d.-b). Retrieved November 2, 2020, from http://yann.lecun.com/exdb/mnist/index.html

Murphy, K. P. (2012). *Machine learning: A probabilistic perspective*. MIT Press.

Narayanan, A., Chandramohan, M., Venkatesan, R., Chen, L., Liu, Y., & Jaiswal, S. (2017, July 17). *graph2vec: Learning distributed representations of graphs. arXiv [cs.AI]*. Retrieved from http://arxiv.org/abs/1707.05005

Papers with Code – LSUN Dataset. (n.d.). Retrieved 24 April 2021, from https://paperswithcode.com/dataset/lsun

Rifai, S., Vincent, P., Muller, X., Glorot, X., & Bengio, Y. (2011, January 1). *Contractive auto-encoders: Explicit invariance during feature extraction*. Retrieved 22 April 2021 from https://openreview.net/pdf?id=HkZN5j-dZH

Sagar, A. (2020, August 12). *Generate High Resolution Images With Generative Variational Autoencoder. arXiv [eess.IV]*. Retrieved from http://arxiv.org/abs/2008.10399

Salgado, C. M., Azevedo, C., Proença, H., & Vieira, S. M. (2016). Noise versus outliers. In *Secondary analysis of electronic health records*. Springer.

Scholz, M. (n.d.). *PCA – Principal Component Analysis*. Retrieved 22 April 2021, from http://www.nlpca.org/pca_principal_component_analysis.html

Sedhain, S., Menon, A. K., Sanner, S., & Xie, L. (2015). AutoRec: Autoencoders meet collaborative filtering. In *Proceedings of the 24th international conference on world wide web* (pp. 111–112). Association for Computing Machinery. Retrieved 24 April 2021 from.

Shlens, J. (2014, April 3). *A Tutorial on Principal Component Analysis. arXiv [cs.LG]*. Retrieved from http://arxiv.org/abs/1404.1100

Srivastava, N., Mansimov, E., & Salakhudinov, R. (2015). Unsupervised learning of video representations using LSTMs. In F. Bach & D. Blei (Eds.), *Proceedings of the 32nd international conference on machine learning* (Vol. 37, pp. 843–852). PMLR.

Turian, J., Ratinov, L.-A., & Bengio, Y. (2010). Word representations: A simple and general method for semi-supervised learning. In *Proceedings of the 48th annual meeting of the association for computational linguistics* (pp. 384–394). Association for Computational Linguistics.

Unsupervised Feature Learning and Deep Learning Tutorial. (n.d.). Retrieved 2 November 2020, from http://ufldl.stanford.edu/tutorial/unsupervised/Autoencoders/

Vincent, P., Larochelle, H., Lajoie, I., Bengio, Y., Manzagol, P.-A., & Bottou, L. (2010). Stacked denoising autoencoders: Learning useful representations in a deep network with a local denoising criterion. *Journal of Machine Learning Research: JMLR, 11*(12) Retrieved from http://www.jmlr.org/papers/volume11/vincent10a/vincent10a.pdf?source=post_page

Wang, X., Wang, Y., Weng, B., & Vinel, A. (2020, September 29). *Stock2Vec: A Hybrid Deep Learning Framework for Stock Market Prediction with Representation Learning and Temporal Convolutional Network. arXiv [q-fin.ST].* Retrieved from http://arxiv.org/abs/2010.01197

Yu, S., & Príncipe, J. C. (2019). Understanding autoencoders with information theoretic concepts. *Neural Networks: The Official Journal of the International Neural Network Society, 117*, 104–123.

Zhang, G., Liu, Y., & Jin, X. (2020). A survey of autoencoder-based recommender systems. *Frontiers of Computer Science, 14*(2), 430–450.

Zhou, C., & Paffenroth, R. C. (2017). Anomaly detection with robust deep autoencoders. In *Proceedings of the 23rd ACM SIGKDD international conference on knowledge discovery and data mining* (pp. 665–674). Association for Computing Machinery. Retrieved 24 April 2021 from https://doi.org/10.1145/3097983.3098052

Sridhar Nandigam is a computer science student and a machine learning researcher. He has previously worked in the Biomedical AI Lab, training LSTM models to recognize hand gestures from accelerometer data. He is currently working as a machine learning intern and builds web applications in his spare time.

Thasina Tabashum is a PhD student in computer science and engineering at the University of North Texas since 2019. She has completed her undergraduate from American International University – Bangladesh (2018), and before joining UNT she worked as a full-time junior software engineer at Dynamic Solution Innovators Limited. She is currently working as a research assistant in Biomed AI Lab. Her research focus includes improving health outcomes and reducing treatment costs for individuals with transfemoral amputations, and building machine learning models to quantify surgical outcomes for children with cerebral palsy. She is currently working on a mobile phone application to automatically segment speakers in a conversation which was originally used to moderate group conversations, but she will use the tool to quantify speaking and social engagement for people undergoing therapy, including individuals with aphasia, to improve their ability to communicate.

Ting Xiao is an assistant professor of information science at the University of North Texas. She applies statistical and machine (deep) learning tools to extract meaningful information from large datasets including recent projects processing video, audio, and wearable sensors. Her deep learning approaches focus on distilling high-throughput data using a combination of unsupervised (autoencoders) and supervised (transfer learning) dimensionality reduction techniques. To fully utilize these results, she also creates the interfaces to interpret and visualize the resulting information. She specializes in developing models and software used by clinical collaborators with user testing, feedback, and the subsequent impact on human decision-making as all part of the approach.

Transfer Learning: Leveraging Trained Models on Novel Tasks

Riyad Bin Rafiq and Mark V. Albert

What Is Transfer Learning?

Humans have inherent ways to transfer knowledge from one task to another task. From previous learning experiences, we can acknowledge and apply related knowledge to new tasks. Learning new tasks will be more robust if the new task is more related to our previous experiences. However, traditional machine learning algorithms mostly care about isolated tasks. But transfer learning changes this idea by transferring knowledge between two tasks to make machine learning as powerful as human learning. With the advances in deep learning, the explosive growth of transfer learning has been seen in recent years. Transfer learning is a machine learning method that conveys knowledge from one domain to another domain to accomplish related tasks. In transfer learning, a model is trained on a specific task in the source domain, and then leveraging this knowledge, the model can be improved to generalize related tasks in the target domain (Fig. 1).

For example, the task of a sentiment classifier is to classify the reviews on a product, such as a brand of mobile phone, into positive and negative reviews. The dataset should consist of a large number of labeled reviews for this classification task and then a classifier would be trained based on that dataset. As the reviews among different types of products may vary, a huge number of labeled data should be collected to maintain a good classification performance. However, this data labeling task can be very expensive. To avoid this task, it would be helpful if a classification model adapted to some products learns to classify reviews for some other products. In this situation, transfer learning can help to save a notable amount of

R. B. Rafiq (✉) · M. V. Albert
Department of Computer Science and Engineering, University of North Texas, Denton, TX, USA
e-mail: RiyadBinRafiq@my.unt.edu; Mark.Albert@unt.edu

M. V. Albert et al. (eds.), *Bridging Human Intelligence and Artificial Intelligence*, Educational Communications and Technology: Issues and Innovations, https://doi.org/10.1007/978-3-030-84729-6_4

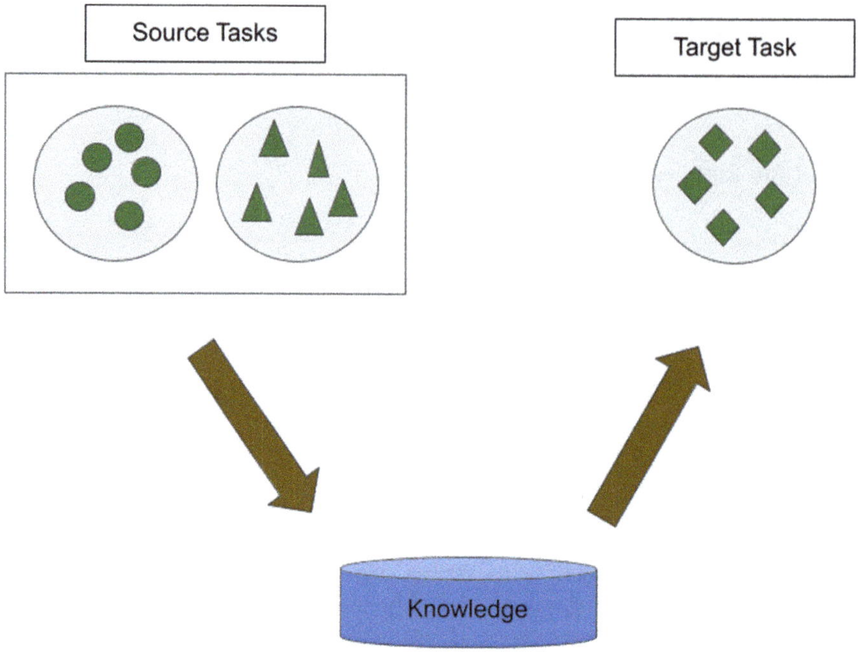

Fig. 1 Learning process of a transfer learning setting

labeling effort (Blitzer et al., 2007). Besides, transfer learning helps to speed up training and enhance the performance of a deep learning model.

History of Transfer Learning

Transfer learning research started in 1976 by Stevo Bozinovski and Ante Fulgosi when they explicitly stated transfer learning in neural networks training in a paper (Stevo Bozinovski, 2020). In 1981, Stevo Bozinovski demonstrated a work where both positive and negative transfer learning were presented in the application of transfer learning in training a neural network based on a dataset of images depicting letters of computer terminals (S. Bozinovski, 1981). However, Lorien Pratt published a paper in 1993 formulating the discriminability-based transfer (DBT) algorithm where he introduced transfer learning in a new way (Pratt, 1993). From 1995 transfer learning has been used by many different names such as learning to learn, life-long learning, knowledge transfer, inductive transfer, multitask learning, knowledge consolidation, context-sensitive learning, knowledge-based inductive bias, meta-learning, and incremental/cumulative learning (Thrun & Pratt, 2012). Among these, multitask learning is a closely related method to transfer learning (Caruana, 1997). Multitask learning attempts to learn either the same or different tasks simultaneously by uncovering the common features which can exploit each separate task. In 2005, the new idea of transfer learning emerged which was to apply knowledge and skills from a previously learned task to a novel task. So the contrast has been created between multitask learning and transfer learning as transfer learning now focuses most on the target task rather than learning all of the source and target tasks simultaneously.

Why Transfer Learning?

In recent years, we have been able to train more accurate models. The performance of the models reaches such a stage that they are the best at a specific task. For example, the residual networks show extraordinary performance at recognizing objects (Szegedy et al., 2017); Google's Smart Reply can automatically handle mobile responses (Kannan et al., 2016); error of speech recognition has been reduced more than before and it is now more accurate than typing (Ruan et al., 2016); Google's NMT system is utilized in production for more than ten language pairs (Wu et al., 2016), and there are more examples. These models are built on huge amounts of labeled data that have been collected over years. For instance, the ImageNet dataset has millions of images for different categories which were created by Stanford by years of hard work (Jia Deng et al., 2009). Most deep learning models are expertise in an individual domain or even a particular task. For this reason, it is difficult to obtain vast loads of labeled data for supervised learning and furthermore, it takes a considerable amount of time and effort to label each data point. Transfer learning can help in this situation by transferring the acquired knowledge from one domain to new tasks and domains.

Types of Transfer Learning Techniques

Different transfer learning techniques are based on task, domain, and availability of data. From the following figure, the categorization of transfer learning techniques can be explained (Fig. 2):

Inductive Transfer Learning

Though the source and the target domains are either same or not, the target task is different from the source task in inductive transfer learning. According to the availability of labeled and unlabeled data in the source domain, two case studies arise in the inductive transfer learning setting.

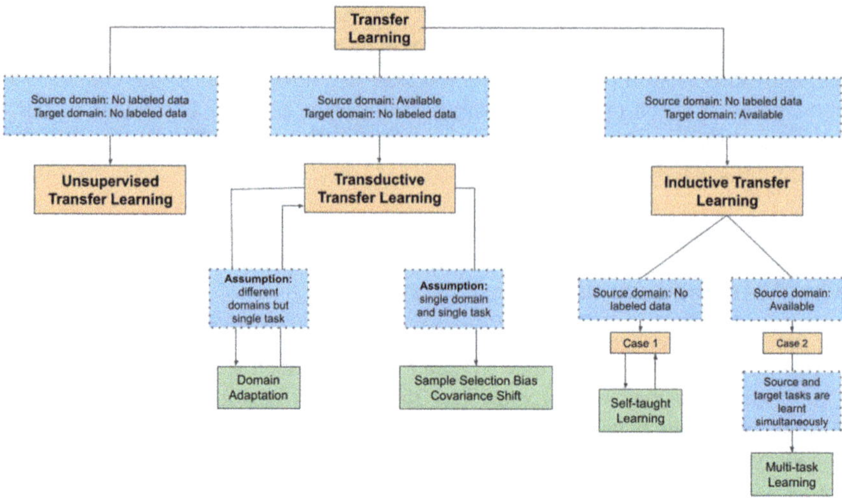

Fig. 2 An overview of different settings of transfer learning strategies (Pan & Yang, 2010)

Case 1 In this case, the source domain is unavailable for labeled data. So, the inductive transfer learning setting works like a self-taught learning setting, addressed by Raina et al. (2007). As the source domains and the target domains may not be the same in the self-taught learning setting, the source domain cannot be utilized directly.

Case 2 This case appears when there exists a lot of labeled data in the source domain. The inductive transfer learning setting works like the multitask learning setting in this case. Inductive transfer learning setting transfers knowledge from the source task to achieve high performance in the target task. On the other hand, the multitask learning setting learns the source task and the target task concurrently.

Transductive Transfer Learning

The source tasks and the target tasks are the same in the transductive transfer learning but the source and the target domains are different. In this setting, a lot of labeled data in the source domain are available. On the other hand, the target domain has no labeled data.

Unsupervised Transfer Learning

The unsupervised transfer learning setting is similar to the inductive transfer learning setting where the target task is different but related to the source task. However, unsupervised transfer learning tries to solve unsupervised learning tasks such as clustering, dimensionality reduction, and density reduction in the target domain. In this setting, labeled data is unavailable in both the source and the target domain.

Pre-trained Models in Transfer Learning

Transfer learning enables the use of pre-trained models from other people. A pre-trained model is a model which is usually developed for solving a similar task by someone else. To solve a similar problem, a pre-trained model based on another problem can be utilized instead of building a whole new model from scratch. For example, to build an image classifier, a new image classification model can be built from scratch by spending years. In this case, the inception model (a pre-trained model) based on ImageNet data built by Google can help to identify images. However, the pre-trained models can save huge effort and time at the starting point.

VGG-16

The VGG-16 was first developed by Karen Simonyan and Andrew Zisserman of the Visual Geometry Group Lab of Oxford University in 2014 (Simonyan & Zisserman, 2014). They proposed the model for an annual competition named ImageNet Large Scale Visual Recognition Challenge (ILSVRC). In the challenge, there are two tasks: one task is to detect objects within an image which is called object localization and another task is to classify images which are referred to as image classification. The VGG-16 model completed each task successfully and secured the first and second positions respectively. However, this model remains the best model to beat till now, and eventually, it has been utilized in the research and the industry for image classification tasks.

Inception

Google developed Inception v1 which also demonstrated its potential in ILSVRC (Szegedy et al., 2015). The model was much smaller than VGG and AlexNet and it has only 7 million parameters. There is one problem with the Inception v1 model as it uses 5x5 convolutions. This causes the model to decrease accuracy. The reason behind that if the input dimension reduces considerably, the Inception network can lose significant information. So, Inception v2 appears when two 3x3 convolutions replace the 5x5 convolution (Szegedy et al., 2016). However, Inception v3 is the third member of the Inception convolutional neural network family and this model has similar features of Inception v2 with some changes. In the research of Leukemia, Inception v3 has been successfully utilized (Milton-Barker, 2019).

With the prevalence of transfer learning in numerous fields, NLP adoption has also been increased in recent years. So many pre-trained state-of-the-art models emerge in this diversified field.

ULMFiT

ULMFiT stands for Universal Language Model Fine-Tuning which was first proposed by Jeremy Howard and Sebastian Ruder (Howard & Ruder, 2018). This is an effective technique for fine-tuning a language model which can be applied to any natural language processing task. NLP research mostly focuses on transductive learning (Blitzer et al., 2007). In the field of inductive transfer learning, word embedding is a method which only targets a model's first layer (Mikolov et al., 2013). Though word embeddings is a pre-trained model that has been significantly used in most state-of-the-art models, practically, it has some limitations. However, in the NLP domain, the inductive transfer has been unsuccessful (Mou et al., 2016). So, ULMFiT has been developed that outperforms the different state-of-the-art on six text classification tasks with significantly lower errors.

BERT

BERT stands for Bidirectional Encoder Representations from Transformers which was developed by Google. Unlike other pre-trained models, BERT is the first bidirectional, unsupervised pre-trained language model which was trained on only a plain text corpus (Devlin et al., 2018). As BERT builds on contextual representation, it understands the context in a sentence from both sides (left and right). However, with only one additional output layer modification, the pre-trained BERT can create state-of-the-art models for numerous tasks, such as question answering and a language inference system. Moreover, it achieves significant results on 11 natural language processing tasks.

Applications of Transfer Learning

Transfer learning has been applied in extensive amounts of different fields such as computer vision, audio/speech recognition, and natural language processing with great success.

Transfer learning has been quite successfully utilized using different convolutional neural network architectures for different computer vision tasks, such as object recognition and identification. In computer vision, features are transferable in deep neural networks (Yosinski et al., 2014) where lower layers act as conventional feature extractors, such as edge detectors, and the final layers of network function toward task-specific features. These findings have made some already existing models, such as VGG, AlexNet, and Inceptions work toward target tasks, such as style transfer and face detection. These existing models were trained for different tasks at first. In the field of facial recognition, a transfer learning approach is employed to transfer information of face image from one ethnic group to a different group for improving the performance of a classifier (Kan et al., 2014). Besides, transfer learning is also applied in the application of sign language recognition (Farhadi et al., 2007). In Xie et al. (2016), a convolutional neural network model using transfer learning was proposed to predict poverty mapping from night time light intensity which was initially anticipated by daytime imagery.

Machine learning and deep learning become challenging during working with text data. Word2vec and FastText have established embeddings that are trained using different datasets for different tasks. Now, these models are used in sentiment analysis and document classification by transferring the knowledge from their source tasks. In Dai et al., 2007a, b; Raina et al. (2006), transfer learning techniques were used to learn textual data across different domains. Moreover, in Ling et al. (2008), a transfer learning method was applied to translate webpages from English to Chinese. As it is a cross-language classification problem, there is enough labeled English text data in the source domain and only a small number of labeled Chinese data exist in the target domain. So transfer learning as a suitable mapping function is able to solve the problem between the two feature spaces. Besides, there are other newer models such as BERT and Universal Sentence Encoder which can be successfully utilized in the future.

In audio/speech recognition, transfer learning has been playing a vital role like other domains, natural language processing, and computer vision. For example, Automatic Speech Recognition (ASR) models developed for the English language have been efficiently used to enhance the performance of speech recognition systems for other languages, such as German. Besides, transfer learning has significantly assisted in automated speaker identification. Moreover, in the application of speech emotion recognition, multiple labeled speech sources transfer information to the target source using transfer learning (Jun Deng et al., 2013).

Negative Transfer

Recognizing the limitation of leveraging the power of transfer learning is a major issue. The concept of transfer learning is to enhance the performance of target learners by transferring knowledge of data from a related source domain to a target domain. But what happens if the source domain and the target domain are not well related? In this situation, the weak relation can cause a negative impact which is referred to as negative transfer. The area of negative transfer is huge but it has not been broadly explored. Some novel researches on transfer learning are described in the following papers.

In a study, the authors (Rosenstein et al., 2005) claimed that the source task needs to be reasonably related to the target task. If they are dissimilar, the transferred knowledge from the source task will have a negative effect on the target task. They demonstrated various cases of negative transfer in experiments using a hierarchical Naive Bayes classifier. An unique graph-based technique for knowledge transfer was proposed in a study by some authors (Eaton et al., n.d.). They proposed to build a target learner using a transferability measure from multiple related source domains. In this setting, the graph was constructed by mapping the problem. And then a function learned based on this graph transferred to the new learning task by controlling the parameters. The experiments were executed in document classification and alphabet classification. Current transfer learning mostly focuses on transferring knowledge from a source domain to a target domain but does not care about various source domains which can be unrelated and produce a negative transfer. In another research, the authors (Ge et al., 2014) also mentioned that knowledge transfer can be hindered because of irrelevant or unrelated source domains. Their model consists of multiple source domains with labeled data and a single target domain with limited labeled data. The demonstrations were executed in three application areas such as cardiac arrhythmia detection, spam email filtering, and intrusion detection.

Conclusion

Transfer learning has been integrated with many real-world applications and vast applications are in need of transferring knowledge to new tasks and new domains. If the source domain or task is not similar to the target domain or task, a negative transfer may happen and it will worsen the performance of the model to the target task. So there is a huge scope of research when the feature spaces between source and target are different. However, transfer learning will become a key factor in research and industry as many fields in it are yet to be explored.

References

Blitzer, J., Dredze, M., & Pereira, F. (2007). Biographies, Bollywood, boom-boxes and blenders: Domain adaptation for sentiment classification. In *Proceedings of the 45th annual meeting of the association of computational linguistics* (pp. 440–447). United States Association for Computational Linguistics.

Bozinovski, S. (1981). *Teaching space: A representation concept for adaptive pattern classification*. Retrieved from COINS Technical Report, University of Massachusetts at Amherst

Bozinovski, S. (2020). Reminder of the First Paper on Transfer Learning in Neural Networks, 1976. *Lithuanian Academy of Sciences. Informatica, 44*(3). Retrieved 28 April 2021 from. https://doi.org/10.31449/inf.v44i3.2828

Caruana, R. (1997). Multitask learning. *Machine Learning, 28*(1), 41–75.

Dai, W., Xue, G.-R., Yang, Q., & Yu, Y. (2007a). Co-clustering based classification for out-of-domain documents. In *Proceedings of the 13th ACM SIGKDD international conference on Knowledge discovery and data mining* (pp. 210–219). Association for Computing Machinery. Retrieved 29 April 2021 from https://doi.org/10.1145/1281192.1281218

Dai, W., Xue, G.-R., Yang, Q., & Yu, Y. (2007b). Transferring naive Bayes classifiers for text classification. In *AAAI* (Vol. 7, pp. 540–545).

Deng, J., Dong, W., Socher, R., Li, L.-J., Li, K., & Fei-Fei, L. (2009). ImageNet: A large-scale hierarchical image database. In *2009 IEEE conference on computer vision and pattern recognition* (pp. 248–255). IEEE.

Deng, J., Zhang, Z., Marchi, E., & Schuller, B. (2013). Sparse autoencoder-based feature transfer learning for speech emotion recognition. In *2013 Humaine association conference on affective computing and intelligent interaction* (pp. 511–516). IEEE.

Devlin, J., Chang, M. -W., Lee, K., & Toutanova, K. (2018, October 11). *BERT: Pre-training of deep bidirectional transformers for language understanding. arXiv [cs.CL].* Retrieved from http://arxiv.org/abs/1810.04805

Eaton, E., desJardins, M., & Lane, T. (n.d.). Modeling transfer relationships between learning tasks for improved inductive transfer. *Machine Learning and Knowledge Discovery in Databases.* Retrieved from https://doi.org/10.1007/978-3-540-87479-9_39.

Farhadi, A., Forsyth, D., & White, R. (2007). Transfer learning in sign language. In *2007 IEEE conference on computer vision and pattern recognition* (pp. 1–8). ieeexplore.ieee.org

Ge, L., Gao, J., Ngo, H., Li, K., & Zhang, A. (2014). On handling negative transfer and imbalanced distributions in multiple source transfer learning. *Statistical Analysis and Data Mining, 7*(4), 254–271.

Howard, J., & Ruder, S. (2018, January 18). *Universal language model fine-tuning for text classification. arXiv [cs.CL].* Retrieved from http://arxiv.org/abs/1801.06146

Kan, M., Wu, J., Shan, S., & Chen, X. (2014). Domain adaptation for face recognition: Targetize source domain bridged by common subspace. *International Journal of Computer Vision, 109*(1-2), 94–109.

Kannan, A., Kurach, K., Ravi, S., Kaufmann, T., Tomkins, A., Miklos, B., et al. (2016). Smart reply: Automated response suggestion for email. In *Proceedings of the 22nd ACM SIGKDD international conference on knowledge discovery and data mining* (pp. 955–964). Association for Computing Machinery. Retrieved 28 April 2021 from https://doi.org/10.1145/2939672.2939801

Ling, X., Xue, G.-R., Dai, W., Jiang, Y., Yang, Q., & Yu, Y. (2008). Can Chinese web pages be classified with English data source? In *Proceedings of the 17th international conference on World Wide Web* (pp. 969–978). Association for Computing Machinery. Retrieved 29 April 2021 from https://doi.org/10.1145/1367497.1367628

Mikolov, T., Sutskever, I., Chen, K., Corrado, G., & Dean, J. (2013, October 16). *Distributed representations of words and phrases and their compositionality. arXiv [cs.CL].* Retrieved from http://arxiv.org/abs/1310.4546

Milton-Barker, A. (2019). Inception V3 deep convolutional architecture For classifying acute Myeloid/Lymphoblastic Leukemia. Accessed on: February, 17.

Mou, L., Meng, Z., Yan, R., Li, G., Xu, Y., Zhang, L., & Jin, Z. (2016, March 19). *How transferable are neural networks in NLP applications? arXiv [cs.CL].* Retrieved from http://arxiv.org/abs/1603.06111

Pan, S. J., & Yang, Q. (2010). A survey on transfer learning. *IEEE Transactions on Knowledge and Data Engineering, 22*(10), 1345–1359.

Pratt, L. Y. (1993). Discriminability-based transfer between neural networks. *Advances in Neural Information Processing Systems*, 204–204.

Raina, R., Ng, A. Y., & Koller, D. (2006). Constructing informative priors using transfer learning. In *Proceedings of the 23rd international conference on Machine learning* (pp. 713–720). Association for Computing Machinery. Retrieved 29 April 2021 from https://doi.org/10.1145/1143844.1143934

Raina, R., Battle, A., Lee, H., Packer, B., & Ng, A. Y. (2007). Self-taught learning: Transfer learning from unlabeled data. In *Proceedings of the 24th international conference on Machine*

learning (pp. 759–766). Association for Computing Machinery. Retrieved 28 April 2021 from https://doi.org/10.1145/1273496.1273592
Rosenstein, M. T., Marx, Z., Kaelbling, L. P., & Dietterich, T. G. (2005). To transfer or not to transfer. In *NIPS 2005 workshop on transfer learning* (Vol. 898, pp. 1–4). engr.oregonstate.edu
Ruan, S., Wobbrock, J. O., Liou, K., Ng, A., & Landay, J. (2016). Speech is 3x faster than typing for english and mandarin text entry on mobile devices. *arXiv Preprint arXiv:1608. 07323.* Retrieved from https://hci.stanford.edu/research/speech/paper/speech_paper.pdf
Simonyan, K., & Zisserman, A. (2014, September 4). *Very deep convolutional networks for large-scale image recognition. arXiv [cs.CV].* Retrieved from http://arxiv.org/abs/1409.1556
Szegedy, C., Liu, W., Jia, Y., Sermanet, P., Reed, S., Anguelov, D., et al. (2015). Going deeper with convolutions. In *Proceedings of the IEEE conference on computer vision and pattern recognition* (pp. 1–9).
Szegedy, C., Vanhoucke, V., Ioffe, S., Shlens, J., & Wojna, Z. (2016). Rethinking the inception architecture for computer vision. In *Proceedings of the IEEE conference on computer vision and pattern recognition* (pp. 2818–2826).
Szegedy, C., Ioffe, S., Vanhoucke, V., & Alemi, A. (2017). Inception-v4, Inception-ResNet and the impact of residual connections on learning. *Proceedings of the AAAI Conference on Artificial Intelligence, 31*(1) Retrieved 28 April 2021 from https://ojs.aaai.org/index.php/AAAI/article/view/11231
Thrun, S., & Pratt, L. (2012). *Learning to learn.* Springer.
Wu, Y., Schuster, M., Chen, Z., Le, Q. V., Norouzi, M., Macherey, W., et al. (2016, September 26). *Google's neural Machine translation system: Bridging the gap between human and machine translation. arXiv [cs.CL].* Retrieved from http://arxiv.org/abs/1609.08144
Xie, M., Jean, N., Burke, M., Lobell, D., & Ermon, S. (2016). Transfer learning from deep features for remote sensing and poverty mapping. *Proceedings of the AAAI Conference on Artificial Intelligence, 30*(1). Retrieved 30 April 2021 from https://ojs.aaai.org/index.php/AAAI/article/view/9906
Yosinski, J., Clune, J., Bengio, Y., & Lipson, H. (2014, November 6). *How transferable are features in deep neural networks? arXiv [cs.LG].* Retrieved from http://arxiv.org/abs/1411.1792

Riyad Bin Rafiq is pursuing his PhD degree in Computer Science and Engineering at the University of North Texas. He is applying machine learning and deep learning in biomedical field and his focus is to develop a personalized gesture recognition system for the individuals unable to speak.

Dr. Mark V. Albert 's professional goal in life is to leverage machine learning to automate the collection and inference of clinically useful health information to improve clinical research. His projects in wearable sensor analytics have improved the measurement of health outcomes for individuals with Parkinson's disease, stroke, and transfemoral amputations with a variety of additional populations and contexts including children with cerebral palsy as well as healthy toddler activity tracking. Current projects include video-based activity tracking and mobile robotic platforms, all in an effort to improve measures of clinical outcomes to justify therapeutic interventions.

Progress in Computer Vision: Object Recognition

Himan Namdari, Devak Nanda, and Xiaohui Yuan

Brief History

Computer vision has been around since the 1970s. Researchers have been using computers to turn images into different datasets of ones and zeros. In the late 1980s, computer scientists were able to isolate the critical parts of an image. They achieved this by using image analysis techniques such as scale-space inference and edge detection. However, the dream of computers with vision capability like humans was still unachievable. Today we know that most image classification models yield close to 99% accuracy in recognizing the object and differentiating old objects from new ones (Jiao et al., 2019). This boom in computer vision happened around 2010, specifically in 2012, due to deep learning in computer vision classification models.

How Computer Vision Works

Computer vision works through three main steps: getting the image, processing the image, and then analyzing data. Computer vision models can use images through their graphical attributes like a 2D digital camera; however, other models can use 3D cameras, multi-camera arrays, and live video feeds. The second step is the hardest, choosing the type of model. When processing an image, the computer

H. Namdari (✉) · D. Nanda
Department of Computer Science, University of Illinois at Urbana-Champaign, Urbana, IL, USA
e-mail: Himan.namdari@unt.edu

X. Yuan
University of North Texas, Denton, TX, USA
e-mail: xiaohui.yuan@unt.edu; http://covis.cse.unt.edu

M. V. Albert et al. (eds.), *Bridging Human Intelligence and Artificial Intelligence*, Educational Communications and Technology: Issues and Innovations, https://doi.org/10.1007/978-3-030-84729-6_5

vision model is trying to find valuable data within the image. There are different image processing techniques, image segmentation, object detection, facial recognition, edge detection, image classification, feature matching, and many other models. After a model processes the image and gathers the data it deems sufficient, it then goes about reading that data and drawing a conclusion. To see it all in action, let us use the example of a picture of a dog. The computer vision model would first have to receive an image; then it will process the image looking for tail size, nose position, fur color, ears up or down. After this step, it will find the image in more detailed futures such as pointy ears, black and brown fur, black eyes, and a large body and conclude that the image of the dog is a German Shepherd dog.

Features

In the context of Computer Vision, a feature is a distinct piece of data commonly used in image classification or recognition (Mahony et al., 2019). These features can be points, edges, shadow lines, and light reflections (Fig. 4). As we discussed before, the first step for a Computer Vision algorithm is processing the image by extracting the main features of the image. This process includes going through the image in waves, extracting specific features, and creating layers of distinct features. Once the feature extraction is complete, the algorithm will then recombine all the layers to recreate the actual photo for the machine. In essence, the image is distilled into its core parts and then reanalyzed to be understood by the computer. To put it simply, imagine a book in Japanese, but you only have a translation book for Japanese to Korean, Korean to Latin, and Latin to English. Without knowing any of the languages, you would have to look for similar characters to distill the original Japanese word into English.

Feature Extraction

Feature extraction is a core component of the computer vision pipeline. The entire deep learning model works around extracting valuable features that clearly define the objects in the image. Feature extraction involves reducing the number of resources required to describe a large set of data. When performing complex data analysis, one of the major problems stems from the number of variables involved. Analysis with many variables generally requires a large amount of memory and computation power. Also, it may cause a classification algorithm to overfit the training examples and generalize poorly to new samples. Feature extraction is a general term for constructing combinations of the variables to get around these problems while still describing the data with sufficient accuracy (Fig. 1). Many machine learning practitioners believe that properly optimized feature extraction is the key to practical model construction (Sun et al., 2020).

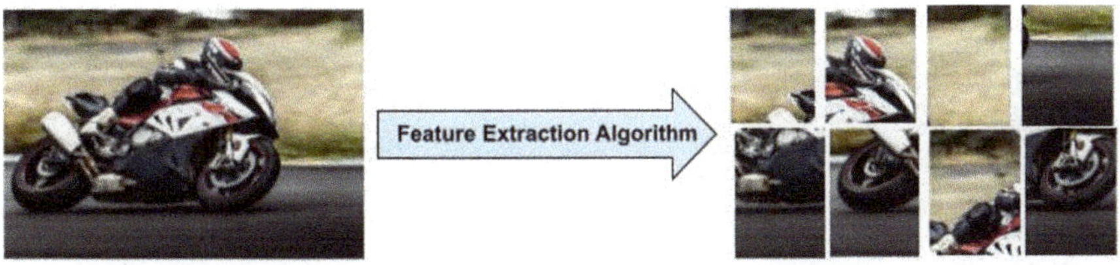

Fig. 1 This figure illustrates the feature extraction algorithm and its features

Deep Learning and Computer Vision

As stated previously, deep learning has led to an exponential increase in image classification by utilizing computer vision models. Deep learning uses the machine learning model that works by mimicking the human mind's inner workings. A combination of deep learning with computer vision algorithms can improve the learning rate and create more accurate results. (e.g., ImageNet classification challenge) In ImageNet Large Scale Visual Recognition Challenge 2011 (ILSVRC) utilizing deep learning algorithm, AlexNet error rate was about 25%, but in 2012 that error rate dropped to 16%, the last ILSVRC had an error rate of less than 5% (Alex et al., 2017). Going back to the dog example, if the model has been identifying only dogs and then fed by an image of a cat, using the deep learning technology, the image recognition model can differentiate between an image of a dog and a cat. The model would also recognize the distinct features of different breeds and classify them more accurately. Besides AlexNet, other deep learning models for computer vision, such as ZFNet, GoogleNet, ResNets, and DenseNet, have been utilized for large-scale computational deep learning models with huge computational advances.

Putting All Pieces Together: ConvNet

Convolutional Neural Networks (CNN or ConvNets) are a type of neural network that goes hand in hand with computer vision (Fig. 2). There are many different aspects of ConvNets. One of many is AlexNet which we discussed earlier. The first ConvNet made: LeNet's Architecture. Developed by Yann LeCun in 1988 (who continued development until the late 90s), LeNet was famous for character recognition. While LeNet might have been the first CNN, its architecture is the backbone of every other ConvNet; all known ConvNets use the same basic layout as LeNet, so by examining it, we can understand how every other ConvNet works at its fundamental level.

Figure 2 shows four primary operations: Convolution, Non-Linearity (ReLU), Pooling/Subsampling, and Classification. Every CNN uses these operators to some degree. The Convolutional in ConvNet comes from the convolutional operator, which is how the feature extraction happens. Every image is just a matrix of numbers to a computer.

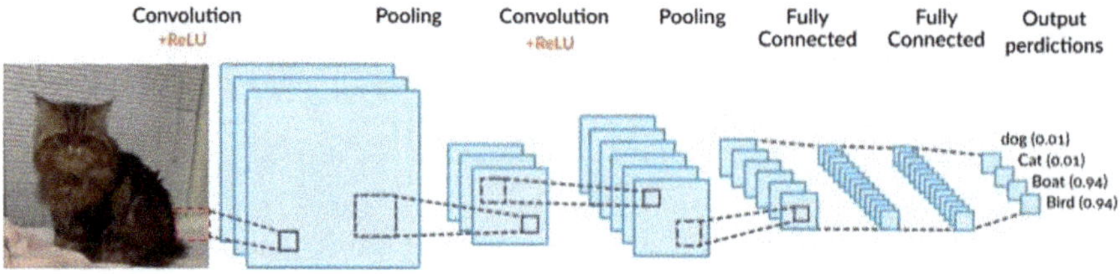

Fig. 2 This figure illustrates a convolutional model structure and its layers

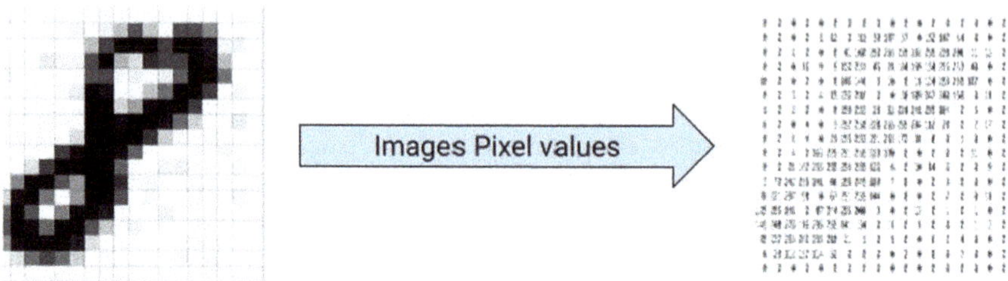

Fig. 3 Resembles the feature detection based on pixel values in image processing

A computer will use a *feature detector* to distinguish between the different values, another smaller matrix that slides across the original matrix of values performing matrix multiplication across "stride." In Fig. 2, the smaller square inside the larger square is our *feature detector*. The matrix of products produced by sliding ("strides" made by the feature detector) is called the *feature map*. Different kinds of feature detectors produce different feature maps. Below is a shortlist of a few (Figs. 3 and 4).

As can be seen in Fig. 5, different feature detectors can create different feature maps designed to search for a specific type of feature, like edges and point (Baker, 1998).

The final process of feature extraction is shown in the last column.

The next layer is called the Rectified Linear Unit (ReLU). ReLU aims to introduce nonlinearity into the CNN model due to the linear nature of convolution. Remember, convolution is just matrix multiplication and addition, meaning that there will be negative values. However, real-life imagery does not have "negative" values. There is no image of the sea with a negative value for the amount of blue. ReLU makes those negative values a zero or the black color value. ReLU is not the only way to introduce nonlinearity into a CNN; there are functions like tanh or sigmoid, but ReLU is the most common one used in CNN (Fig. 5).

Pooling operations, also called subsampling, are the next layer. It is straightforward but has an essential rule: it cuts out the fat from the feature map and only keeps the most critical data—the subsampling combines many different mathematical algorithms like Max Pooling, Average Pooling, or Sum Pooling to provide subsampled data. Looking back at the pooling step of Fig. 6, notice how pooling is applied to each map individually.

Fig. 4 Example of feature detector fining the edges

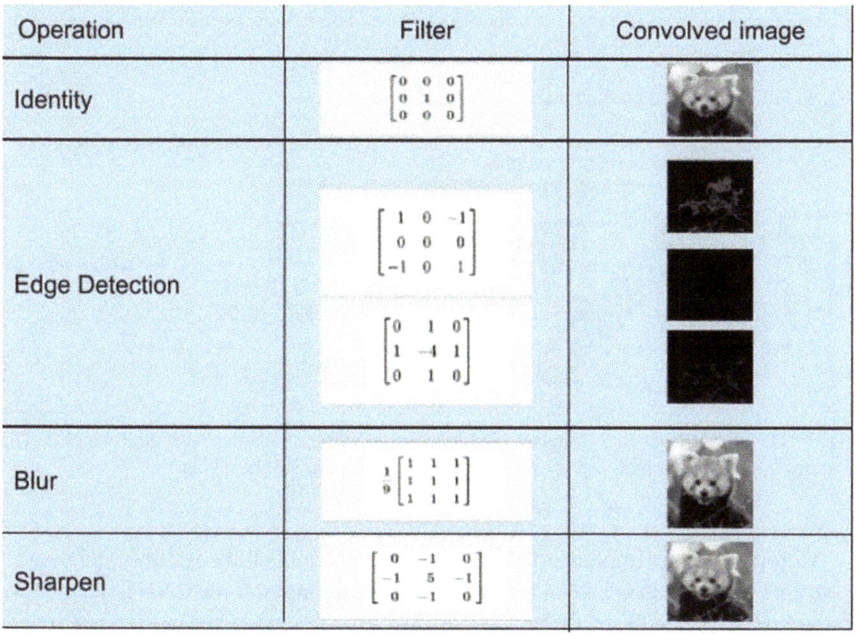

Fig. 5 This figure illustrates the operation and matrix filter used in convolutional layers and the result of the operation on the actual image

The importance of pooling layers is to reduce the spatial size of the input progressively while increasing the feature density of the output (Alzubaidi et al., 2021). The Convolutional Operator, Non-Linearity Operator, and Pooling Operator(s) are all used to provide the densest and valuable information to the Classification Operator. The purpose of the classification layer, also called the Fully Connected layer, is to give weight to different possible classes based on the features found in the previous steps. In Fig. 7, we can see that the ConvNet has four classes (dog, cat, boat, and bird). Based on the features fed to it, based on the results, "boat" is given the most considerable weightage for the image classification.

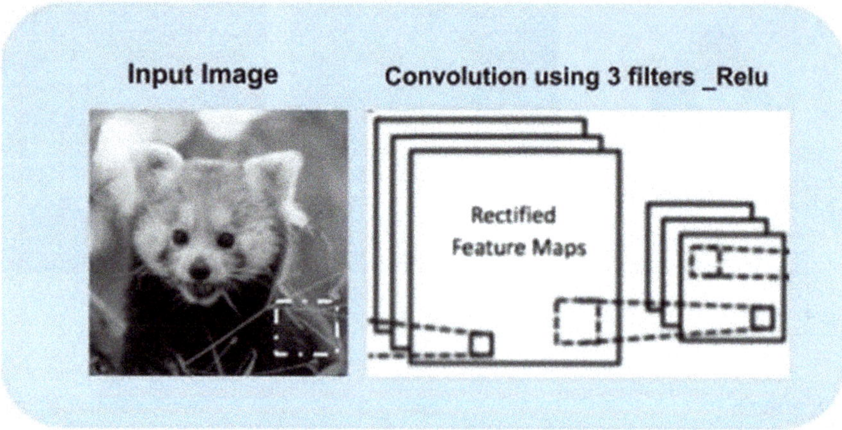

Fig. 6 Polling function on each map function and layers

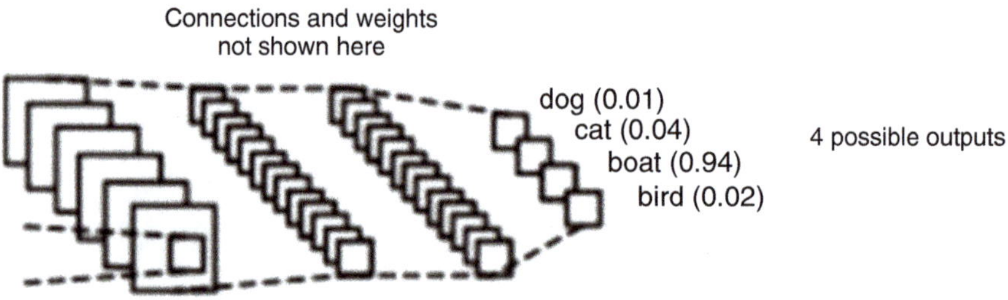

Fig. 7 The output layer in a ConvNet model, and four different classes with their weights. The boat has the highest weight, and the result of this classification will be a boat

All four steps are implemented to train the CNN, and all the weights and parameters are optimized in ConvNet to classify the right images. If the CNN is adequately trained, ConvNet will go through a forward propagation when an unseen image (outside of the training set) is being processed; the CNN will assign the highest weight to the right image.

Improvements of Computer Vision Over Time

Computer vision has lots of usages today; however, two specific examples are both special in their regard. First is the Tesla Autopilot technology. Onboard every Tesla vehicle that can drive itself, a computer vision/deep learning mind acts as the car's eyes. The Autopilot technology can account for road conditions, weather conditions, and atmospheric conditions as it scans the road for signs, other cars, people, road lines, and stoplights. This technology allows the car to recognize objects on the road and act accordingly quickly. The second technology is handwriting recognition used by the US Postal Service. Developed in 1997, it does not use Deep Learning but instead sets rules and algorithmic knowledge to log the letter's handwriting quickly. However, it is not confident, as some handwritings are unreadable and need to be sent to a human handwriting analyst and log their information.

Future Development

Whenever talking about bleeding-edge technologies such as AI, ML, DL, and Computer Vision, there is an understanding that these technologies are more like black boxes. While functionally, the inner workings of Computer Vision and CV-CNN are incomprehensible. However, unlike its flashy counterparts, the true nature of Computer Vision allows it to be better analyzed. While Computer Vision gets more efficient and competent, benefiting human lives through increased practical use (like in self-driving cars or facial recognition), the scientific advancements of the future of Computer Vision will more than likely be a proper understanding of its working. When combined with other technologies like DL and CNN, Computer Vision can mimic human vision by mimicking how humans see objects, classify them, and classify new objects based on previously understood objects. Computer Vision would most likely be the first technology involving self-teaching where a program could create an image of an object it has never seen before or learn to classify images like a human. While the future might be uncertain as a whole for the field, Computer Vision will be a mainstay.

Bibliography

Alex, K., Ilya, S., & Geoffrey, E. (2017). Hinton Communications of the ACM. 60(6):84–90. https://doi.org/10.1145/3065386

Alzubaidi, L., Zhang, J., & Humaidi, A. J. et al. (2021). Review of deep learning: concepts, CNN architectures, challenges, applications, future directions. *J Big Data* 8, 53. https://doi.org/10.1186/s40537-021-00444-8

Baker, S. (1998). *Design and evaluation of feature detectors*. http://citeseerx.ist.psu.edu/viewdoc/summary?doi=10.1.1.39.9490

Jiao, L., Zhang, F., Liu, F., Yang, S., Li, L., Feng, Z., & Qu, R. (2019). A Survey of Deep Learning-Based Object Detection. *IEEE Access*, 7, 128837–128868.

Mahony, N. O., Campbell, S., Carvalho, A., Harapanahalli, S., Velasco-Hernández, G.A., Krpalkova, L., Riordan, D., & Walsh, J. (2019). Deep Learning vs. Traditional Computer Vision. CVC.

Sun, S., Cao, Z., Zhu, H., & Zhao, J. (2020). A Survey of Optimization Methods From a Machine Learning Perspective. *IEEE Transactions on Cybernetics*, 50, 3668–3681.

Himan Namdari received a B.S. degree in software engineering from the Hamedan University of Technology, Iran, in 2012 and a master's degree in computer science from La Sapienza

University, Rome, Italy 2017. He is a Ph.D. student in computer science at the University of North Texas. His research interests include computer vision, artificial intelligence, data mining, and machine learning. He is a teacher assistant in the department of computer science. His recent paper "Tumor tracking using Template matching and Kalman filter" has been accepted at the BIBM conference. In 2020 he received the TAPIA scholarship for a poster titled "Using Machine Learning to predict the glass component."

Devak Nanda is currently pursuing a B.S. in Computer Science at the University of Illinois at Urbana-Champaign. He has authored two papers during his time at the Biomedical AI Lab – "Temporal Distance Map" and "Wearable Spasticity Estimation and Validation using Machine Learning" – as a researcher from the Texas Academy of Mathematics and Science (TAMS) at the University of North Texas (UNT). His hobbies include working out, coding, and talking with friends.

Xiaohui Yuan received a BS degree in electrical engineering from the Hefei University of Technology, China in 1996 and a PhD degree in computer science from the Tulane University in 2004. He is currently an associate professor at the University of North Texas. His research interests include computer vision, artificial intelligence, data mining, and machine learning. His research findings have been published in more than 180 peer-reviewed papers. He is the editor-in-chief of the *International Journal of Smart Sensor Technologies and Applications*, serves on the editorial board of several international journals, and as chair in several international conferences. He is a recipient of the Ralph E. Powe Junior Faculty Enhancement Award in 2008.

Progress in Natural Language Processing and Language Understanding

Phillip Nelson, Namratha V. Urs, and Taraka Rama Kasicheyanula

Introduction

Language is an inherent aspect of human personality and has been a prime channel of communication for human–human interactions. The digital era has swiftly enabled technology to become a quintessential aspect of our life, so much so that the increasing use of technology warrants our interactions with machines. Recently, language-oriented smart assistants have become features of most modern commercial goods and have become common in many households due to the convenience they offer. One can speak a command and the device will (almost always) respond accurately and instantaneously. Along with the convenience aspect, services offered by such smart assistants are valuable in industrial as well as commercial context. Therefore, human-to-machine communications continue to be of increased interest for both businesses and consumers.

With every search, click, swipe, and stream, massive amounts of data are generated every minute, especially with digital news platforms, in-app messaging, social media platforms, digital discussion forums, blogs, and the like. Despite these being fundamentally language-driven, use of language and its implications vary across streams

P. Nelson (✉)
Texas Academy of Mathematics and Science, University of North Texas, Denton, TX, USA
e-mail: phillipnelson@my.unt.edu

N. V. Urs
Department of Computer Science and Engineering, University of North Texas, Denton, TX, USA
e-mail: namrathaurs@my.unt.edu; https://www.github.com/namrathaurs

T. R. Kasicheyanula
Department of Linguistics, University of North Texas, Denton, TX, USA
e-mail: taraka.kasicheyanula@unt.edu; https://phylostar.github.io

M. V. Albert et al. (eds.), *Bridging Human Intelligence and Artificial Intelligence*, Educational Communications and Technology: Issues and Innovations, https://doi.org/10.1007/978-3-030-84729-6_6

which clearly reveal the absence of a definite structure in data. For instance, language used in social media is short, concise, uses hashtags, and occasional direct mentions which is typically not the case with other data streams. Additionally, language is diverse, complex, and ambiguous, all of which allow us to express ourselves in many ways (think of languages, dialects, regional accents, language-specific grammar, and so on!). These characteristics of human language together with the staggering magnitude of available data from an extremely unstructured data source make it difficult for any human being to comb through all the data tirelessly and consistently.

Analyzing large volumes of highly unstructured data can be valuable to companies, big or small, in terms of decision-making, strategic thinking, and maintaining client/partner relations (Deloitte, n.d.; Columbus, 2018). Such business impacting analyses are feasible with assistance beyond sheer manual effort, i.e., involving the use of computing systems to process language. However, a critical question to consider is whether a mere machine is capable of adequately interpreting the complexities of human language. Natural, human language may follow a set of rules, but the overwhelming amount of ambiguity, exceptions, and subjectivity that can affect a word's meaning presents a hard challenge for computers to accurately understand. Examples include contextual word meanings (such as *bank* which could mean a financial institution or the slope along the edge of a river), disambiguating pronoun reference using commonsense (*The ball would not fit in the bag because it was too small* versus *The ball would not fit in the bag because it was too big*), and defining words unambiguously (*family*, *love*, etc. which are concepts).

Natural language processing (NLP) is a branch of artificial intelligence pertaining to the design and production of computers that can interpret and process human language. NLP is interdisciplinary as the field intersects with linguistics, computer science, neuroscience, and psychology. NLP enables machines to address complex tasks such as language understanding (primarily disambiguation, commonsense reasoning among others), language generation (translation and summarization), speech recognition, information extraction, and question answering, which are crucial for most of the user-facing downstream applications. Tackling the ambiguity in language in a consistent manner, NLP adds structure to the naturally unstructured human language, but due to the richness and peculiarities of language, this becomes a herculean task. NLP has consistently witnessed significant milestones and through this chapter, our aim is to introduce the reader to some of the game-changing developments in the field, specifically from the perspective of language understanding. It is important to remember that the chapter is not an exhaustive list of everything that comprises NLP, but of a smaller subset that provides the reader a glimpse into the key contributions that serve as a starting point in furthering their understanding of the field.

Types of Tasks (Syntactic and Semantic)

Aspects of language such as form, meaning, and context along with certain environmental factors are critical to the analysis and comprehension of natural language. Computational techniques that formalize these aspects form the core of NLP and are categorized under phonetics, phonology, morphology, syntax, semantics, discourse, pragmatics, and so on. While there exists significant literature regarding each of these categories, this chapter provides a good first view into some of the achievements in the field specifically targeting syntax and semantics.

Syntax focuses on stating grammatical rules regarding sentence structure using words and other language units as well as the order in which words are organized. For example, in English language, the *subject + verb + direct object* as a grammatical rule results in a sentence such as "John saw a car." Additionally, the rule also implies that "Saw John a car" does not conform to a valid rule that comprises the syntax for the language. A typical example of a syntactic task is parsing where sentences are divided into their grammatical constituents.

On the other hand, semantics deals with the meaning of words, phrases, clauses, and sentences. Semantic tasks analyze the structure of sentences and how certain words may affect the meaning of others to derive meaning. Primary examples are translation between languages and sentiment analysis, where emotions are extracted from a given text. Subsequently, semantic analysis is typically more difficult than its syntactic counterpart because it is directly influenced by the ambiguity that language carries whereas syntactical analysis is only concerned with following rigid rules.

Completing an NLP task is not as simple as following rules or referencing a clear dictionary definition. As humans utilize context clues to interpret a word using the surrounding words, a computer will need to learn to consider the surrounding words and how the context affects the meaning of a given word to complete a semantic task. Both categories (syntax and semantics) are composed of hundreds of subtasks that each involve analyzing a unique aspect of the human language.

Evolutionary Stages of NLP

Although there are exceptions to grammatical rules, having clear guidelines for how to interpret syntax is what encouraged the development of rule-based systems, one of the earliest approaches to NLP. However, it was not until the 1980s that statistical inference models were developed to tackle other NLP tasks more efficiently. These two approaches laid the foundation for modern NLP. Following these, neural NLP was introduced where word representations and deep learning methods have been catalytic to the success of the field.

Rule-Based NLP

Artificial Intelligence (AI) models driven by rule-based algorithms incorporate specific user-defined rules in a *match-resolve-act* cycle, as illustrated in Fig. 1. The match-resolve-act cycle forms the core of most rule-based engines and, therefore, is not exclusive to NLP models. Using this concept, given a word or piece of text, the

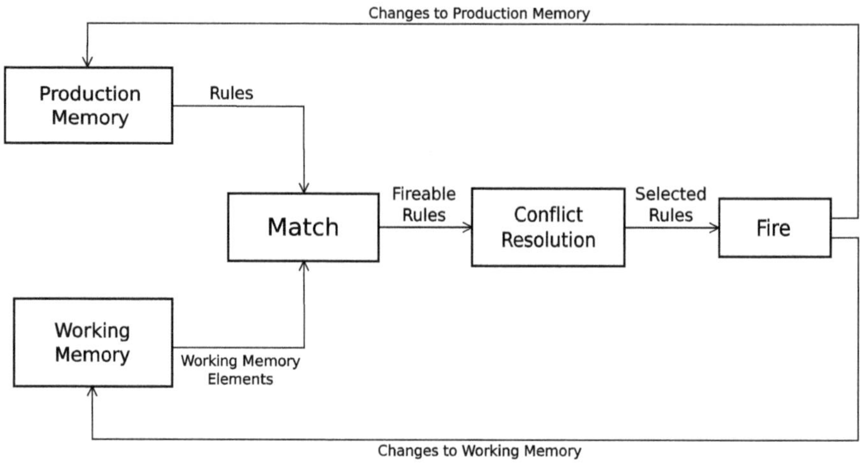

Fig. 1 The match-resolve-act cycle in rule-based systems to select and apply rules in NLP syntactic problems. Condition of the *condition-action* rule is matched against the working memory, collecting all the rules that match. Conflict resolution takes place when there are multiple matches. Once the conflict is resolved, the *action* is performed. The algorithm iterates until a stopping criterion is met, i.e. action is STOP or there are no conditions that match. Adapted from Wang et al. (2014) and Wilson (2012)

model finds all applicable rules by matching between the rule base in the production memory and the working memory and stores them in a conflict set. If no rules are applicable, then the cycle is terminated. If only one rule is applicable, the action corresponding to the matched rule is performed. However, if more than one rule is found to be applicable, a conflict resolution strategy is chosen, and the action is performed. If the problem is not solved upon performing this action, then the next rule in the conflict set is applied until the problem is resolved or there are no more applicable rules in the conflict set.

Since the model looks through every rule to select the optimal one, it is imperative that each rule is meticulously handwritten by a linguist to ensure that the system abides by grammatical rules. As a result, models motivated by a rule-based approach will achieve very high precision but will have a relatively low recall rate; recall being the model's ability to find all relevant cases in the data. For instance, assume a model that is to be used for identifying nouns in text. The rule-based approach becomes a hindrance for efficiently defining the set of all possible nouns in our model, which implies that a noun word that is not explicitly listed in the rules will be overlooked. Because of this, rule-based models scale poorly and may not be the optimal algorithm depending on the magnitude of the task at hand. Although capable of carrying out semantic tasks, creating specific rules to derive meaning from sentences with varying contexts becomes difficult. This shortcoming of rule-based engines led to the eventual development of statistical models in the late 1980s and mid-1990s.

Statistical NLP

Besides following a strict set of rules, the grammar of a language is also probabilistic by nature. Consider the simplest language processing task of predicting the next word in the text given previous words, commonly known as language modeling. For example, if a given word is preceded by an adjective, the probability of that word being a noun is relatively high. Instead of referring to the grammatical rules, one could instead make predictions, for instance to identify parts of speech, using probabilities. For example, if a word precedes a noun, it is more likely that the given word is an article or adjective rather than another noun. Using such probabilities, models can roughly abide by grammatical rules without explicitly knowing them. These statistical methods became more prevalent during the late 1980s to early 1990s as statistical models were found to be extremely capable and easier to train than pure rule-based models.

From a statistical formulation standpoint, the objective of a language model is to accurately learn the probability distribution $P(u)$ of various linguistic units in natural language (Rosenfeld, 2000); the simplest case being to estimate the frequency of a sequence of words as a sentence in that language. Mathematically, a statistical language model calculates the conditional probability of the next word given the previous words. Characteristics of language such as inherent word ordering and temporality of words in the sentence have been used to alleviate the difficulty when modeling natural language. n-grams (n = 1, 2, 3 ...) has been a classic approach of statistical language modeling where probability of the n-th word is computed with respect to combinations of previous $n-1$ words in the sequence.

Due to the strict dependence on frequently occurring, successive words in the corpus, the n-gram modeling strategy does not scale well when previously unseen combination of n words are encountered (typically during inference). Zero probabilities can be assigned in such cases but there is a reasonable chance that this new combination of words can be encountered in larger contexts. Instead smoothing or back-off techniques can be employed to help models reasonably generalize from observations in the corpus to unseen data (Katz, 1987). Empirically, tri-grams (n = 3) have resulted in state-of-the-art performance; however, a combination of strategies have also demonstrated considerable improvement (Goodman, 2001).

Neural NLP

Despite their practical significance, statistical language models suffer from the *curse of dimensionality*. The curse of dimensionality is typical with modeling high dimensional, discrete data, such as language, since the set of all possible word combinations is much larger than an observable, finite set of data (Bengio & Bengio, 2000). In other words, there is a good chance that a sequence of words encountered during testing has never been seen by the model during training. n-gram language models are restrictive in that they fail to make use of all the information that is available in the word sequence (only look as far as two previous words).

Further, the n-gram models also do not factor in the linguistic aspects that the words might be taking on. The ability to learn linguistic phenomena during training helps in better generalization. For example, "The cat is walking in the bedroom" helps the generalization of "A dog was running in a room" due to similar semantic and grammatical roles of corresponding words between these two sentences (Bengio et al., 2001, 2003). Starting in the year 2000, statistical NLP took a turn and began focusing on the use of neural networks and deep learning to create predictive models, like the statistical counterparts, and develop more advanced systems. The very first neural language model was the feed-forward neural network proposed by (Bengio et al., 2001, 2003), which was also the first to learn vector representations of words.

Word Embeddings A fundamental step toward processing language is that of data representation. One such approach views words, pertaining to a language, as a vector space model where words exist in a common vector space such that each word is represented as a set (vector) of numbers. Bag-of-Words (BoW) and Term Frequency-Inverse Document Frequency (TF-IDF) have been the long-standing schemes in NLP for deriving word vectors. Words are exceptionally complex because they are high-dimensional in nature. The traditional schemes yield sparse representations for words resulting in high-dimensional features that cannot easily be converted to lower-dimensional spaces that are simpler to interpret. Additionally, BoW and TF-IDF consider words to be atomic in nature and hence fail to capture any form of similarity between them. Researchers sought to circumvent these issues with the concept of word embeddings.

Word embeddings are distributional vectors that are used to create low-dimensional representations of higher-dimensional information. In 2013, two model architectures were proposed for learning dense, distributed vector representations of words using a vocabulary of millions of words (Mikolov et al., 2013): (1) Continuous Bag-of-Words model, and (2) Skip-Gram model. The resulting word vectors are now popularly known as Word2Vec embeddings. By predicting a word's meaning given the context, Word2Vec derives vector representations that store the word's meaning. Similar words will be located near each other in this vector space which makes it easier to see the relation between words. For instance, a word like "king" is similar (in terms of being related or in distance) to the word "man," as "queen" would be to "woman." Further, Word2Vec embeddings could retain the syntactic and semantic aspects of a word and capture certain relationships while simultaneously reducing them to a vector space that is easier to interpret (see Fig. 2). As a result, word embeddings became a common form of data representation in NLP and was one of the early techniques for deriving meaning from words efficiently.

Following word embeddings, NLP embraced neural network models such as recurrent neural networks (RNNs) that were capable of handling dynamic inputs, in terms of word sequence lengths. While vanilla RNNs (Elman, 1990) triggered the recurrence paradigm, long short-term memory networks (LSTMs) (Hochreiter &

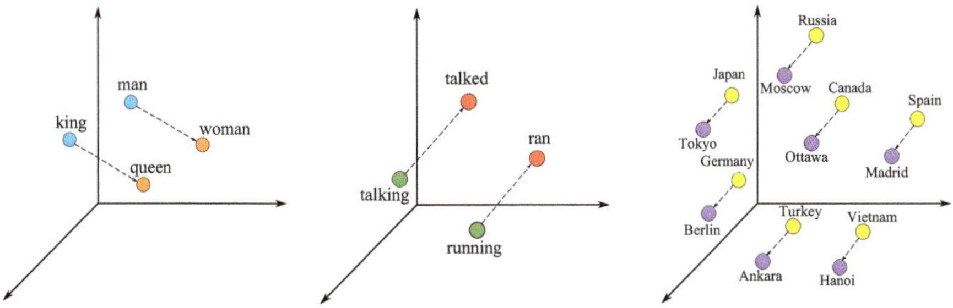

Fig. 2 Three-dimensional representations of word vectors illustrating linguistic aspects of verb tense (middle) and certain relationships such as gender (left) and country-capital (right) as derived from Word2Vec (Mikolov et al., 2013). Despite the low-dimensionality of the word representations, the relationships between words are still preserved as they would typically be in a higher-dimensional space

Schmidhuber, 1997) and gated recurrent units (GRUs) (Cho et al., 2014a, b) were later proposed as a means to address the exploding and vanishing gradient problems of their predecessor(s). Using LSTM networks, a learning framework that uses an encoder and decoder neural network for sequence-to-sequence (seq2seq) mapping was proposed (Sutskever et al., 2014).

The encoder network converts a source sequence, in this case a sentence, into a fixed size representation, commonly referred to as the *context vector*, which is used by the decoder in the generation of a target sequence (sentence). The squashing of information, from the source sentence, as a fixed-length vector was found to degrade the performance of the neural network with increasing sentence length (Cho et al., 2014a). Also, the requirement to remember the entire sentence did not align conceptually with how human beings process sentences. To address these issues, *attention* mechanism was introduced as an extension to the seq2seq networks (Bahdanau et al., 2014). The key idea behind attention is, for every target word being generated, the decoder learns to "attend" to parts of the source sentence depending on previously generated target words. A weighted combination of all the input states determines the target word being generated, as illustrated in Fig. 3.

Attention has been a significant game-changer in neural machine translation, with performance of neural MT surpassing classic phrase-based systems (Wu et al., 2016). Various attention mechanisms (Luong et al., 2015) have been used in constituency parsing (Vinyals et al., 2015), reading comprehension (Hermann et al., 2015), to name a few. Additionally, the flexibility of the sequence to sequence framework to allow different encoder and decoder models makes seq2seq networks useful in natural language generation tasks.

Pre-trained Language Models Slow hardware, minimal support for deep learning and efficiency led to word embedding vectors being a foundational representation technique in NLP. Despite the significance, word embeddings are *shallow* representations due to their "expressivity-efficiency" tradeoff, thereby failing to capture more useful, higher-level information needed for a machine to understand language (Ruder, 2018). NLP models initialized with such pre-trained word embeddings (at

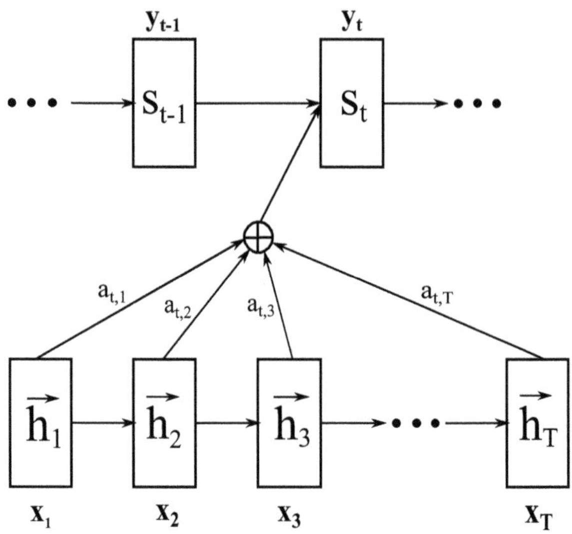

Fig. 3 Attention mechanism when generating the t-th target word y_t given a source sentence containing words $x_1, x_2, x_3, \ldots, x_T$. Each h_i (hidden state) contains information about the entire input sentence but a strong focus on parts surrounding the i-th word of the input sentence. Probability of a word is conditioned on a distinct context vector for each target word. The context vector is computed as the weighted sum of all the hidden states, h_i where $i = 1, 2, \ldots, T$ (Bahdanau et al., 2014)

only a single layer) still require training the entire neural network with a large set of task-specific data.

NLP witnessed major changes in 2018 with a series of new contenders: ELMo (Peters et al., 2018), ULMFiT (Howard & Ruder, 2018), and OpenAI transformer (Radford et al., 2018). The central aspect of these models is the pre-training of the entire model with hierarchical representations (Ruder, 2018), hence the name pre-trained language models. Because the entire model is being (pre)trained, as opposed to a single layer, models become capable of learning deep representations in a hierarchical sense, from low-level words to high-level semantic concepts. Therefore, pre-training (Dai & Le, 2015) and transfer learning paradigms have immensely steered modern-day NLP and are regarded as major milestones similar to how pre-training of ImageNet models was significant in computer vision.

Transformer Models Prior to the genesis of transformer models, sequence-to-sequence (Sutskever et al., 2014) and Long Short-Term Memory (LSTM) (Hochreiter & Schmidhuber, 1997) were the standard neural network architectures for NLP tasks. These models interpreted text from either left-to-right, right-to-left, or both and were subsequently dependent on the organization of the text. As each word in the input is read, the word was cross-referenced with other words in the sentence to determine how much importance the word carried. Models were required to abide by the limits of the sequence and the processing time was lengthy, thus affecting memory constraints and possible parallelization (batching) during training. Although computational efficiency and improved performance could be achieved with a few tricks (Kuchaiev & Ginsburg, 2017; Shazeer et al., 2017), the fundamental nature of sequential computation was still pervasive.

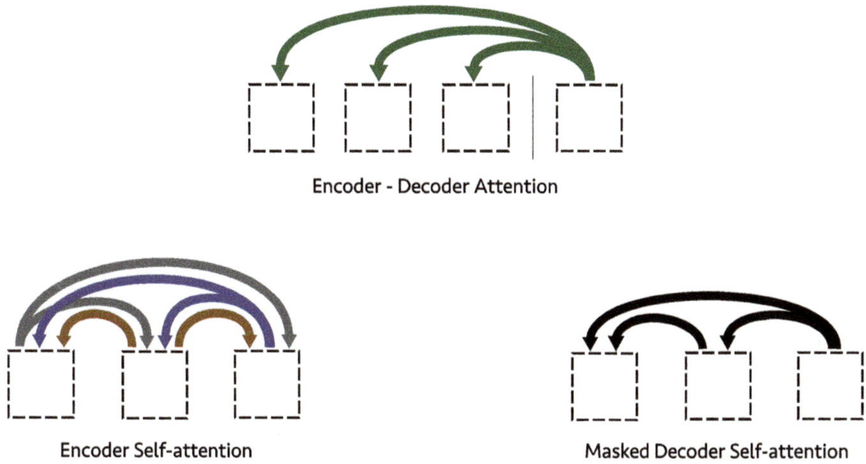

Fig. 4 Three ways of calculating attention in a transformer architecture (Vaswani et al., 2017). The encoder network uses self-attention, i.e., all word positions in the sequence attend to each other (bottom left, multi-colored arrows). The decoder's first self-attention layer is modified to avoid attending to subsequent positions which correspond to the words yet to be predicted (bottom right, black arrows). The second self-attention layer (top row, green arrows) enables the decoder to focus on relevant parts of the input sentence, like the standard attention mechanism in seq2seq models. Illustration inspiration and adaptation from Łukasz Kaiser's Masterclass at Pi School (2017)

The introduction of the transformer architecture eliminated the performance-inhibiting sequential dependence by removing recurrence. A striking feature of the transformer model is the *self-attention* mechanism (Vaswani et al., 2017) which models relationships between all words in a given sentence regardless of their positions. Self-attention looks at every other word in a sentence (instead of words within a window) to determine how much each word contributes to the next representation of a given word; the three ways of calculating attention is illustrated in Fig. 4. Not only do transformers work more effectively overall as models, but words can be processed simultaneously and in shorter steps. As a result, the transformer architecture has become a core part of all advanced modern NLP models, primarily due to the drastic reduction in training time.

Bidirectional Encoder Representations from Transformers The Bidirectional Encoder Representations from Transformers model (BERT) (Devlin et al., 2019) is one of the most recent groundbreaking models that applies bidirectional training of transformers to language modelling. This model was released by Google AI Language in 2018, and has since achieved top scores on benchmarks such as SQuAD (Rajpurkar et al., 2016), GLUE (Wang et al., 2018), and Situations With Adversarial Generations (SWAG) (Zellers et al., 2018). But how is this model able to achieve such state-of-the-art scores?

Previous models would read text from either left-to-right or right-to-left like a human would, but BERT reads an entire sequence of text at once. This allows the model to learn the context of a word given all its surroundings, resulting in a deeper contextual interpretation of a given sentence. When training language models, models typically predict the next word in a sequence, but this directional approach can limit context learning. The BERT model surmounts this problem by using two new training techniques: Masked Language Modeling (MLM) and Next Sentence Prediction (NSP).

MLM replaces 15% of the words in the given text with a masked token, i.e., [MASK], and the model attempts to predict the original value of each of the masked words using the context of surrounding non-masked words. The process of replacing so many words makes BERT implementation slower than other directional models, but this downside is offset by the increased contextual awareness. Further, for NSP, the text is split into pairs of sentences, and the model will predict whether the second sentence in the pair is subsequent to the original text (first sentence). Both techniques serve to gain a stronger interpretation of the language's context and minimize the strategies' combined loss function.

BERT was another breakthrough in NLP models, and models utilizing its training strategies still hold top spots on most benchmark leaderboards. The techniques of MLM and NSP have been witnessed in many subsequent models, thereby demonstrating the value of transformers as an architecture in NLP.

Generative Pre-trained Transformer-3 Released by OpenAI in August 2020, Generative Pre-trained Transformer-3 (GPT-3) (Brown et al., 2020) currently stands as the most significant language model ever. The model has been able to generate stories, imitate writing styles, and produce text of any type. It takes in 175 billion parameters, which is over 100 times more than its predecessor, GPT-2, which aids in its incredible accuracy. For context, the entirety of English Wikipedia is roughly six million articles which is only 0.6% of its training data. While still in its early stages, the value of this model comes from its base layer of training that can then be fine-tuned to perform downstream tasks, i.e., those supervised learning tasks that make use of the pre-trained component. Below is the text from a synthetic article as generated by the GPT-3 model regarding the split of the United Methodist Church (Brown et al., 2020):

```
"Title: United Methodists Agree to Historic Split
Subtitle: Those who oppose gay marriage will form their own
  denomination
Article: After two days of intense debate, the United Methodist
  Church has agreed to a historic split - one that is expected
  to end in the creation of a new denomination, one that will
  be "theologically and socially conservative," according to
  The Washington Post. The majority of delegates attending
  the church's annual General Conference in May voted to
  strengthen a ban on the ordination of LGBTQ clergy and to
  write new rules that will "discipline" clergy who officiate
  at same-sex weddings. But those who opposed these measures
  have a new plan: They say they will form a separate denomi-
  nation by 2020, calling their church the Christian Methodist
  denomination.
```

The Post notes that the denomination, which claims 12.5 million members, was in the early 20th century the "largest Protestant denomination in the U.S.," but that it has been shrinking in recent decades. The new split will be the second in the church's history. The first occurred in 1968, when roughly 10 percent of the denomination left to form the Evangelical United Brethren Church. The Post notes that the proposed split "comes at a critical time for the church, which has been losing members for years," which has been "pushed toward the brink of a schism over the role of LGBTQ people in the church." Gay marriage is not the only issue that has divided the church. In 2016, the denomination was split over ordination of transgender clergy, with the North Pacific regional conference voting to ban them from serving as clergy, and the South Pacific regional conference voting to allow them. " (Brown et al., 2020)

Benchmarks in Natural Language Processing

Evaluating a machine learning model is essential as well as critical to the performance of the model. Unlike other deep learning tasks, evaluating the model for an NLP task is difficult since there does not exist a predetermined solution. Because language is very subjective, there could be more than one solution that the model can be scored against which makes it difficult to calculate the model's error and loss. For example, if asked to describe an image of a skyline, there are many aspects of the picture that can be described. Describing a building as "big" or "very large" are both technically correct and a model should not be penalized for selecting one word over the other. Albeit simple, this example is representative of a larger issue which is variation in the ground truth as skills like language comprehension and usage differs across people. If a model cannot be evaluated accurately, it becomes impossible to assess the quality of the model which can inhibit further development. Depending on the task, numerous benchmarks have been introduced and are being widely used in the field of natural language processing. In many ways, the evolution of evaluation metrics and benchmarks has equally been responsible for the rapid development of NLP models in the past decade.

BiLingual Evaluation Understudy

Machine translation (MT), a popular area in NLP, deals with automatically converting text in a source language to text in a target language, different from the source. With regard to human evaluations, aspects of *adequacy*, *fidelity*, and *fluency* judgements of the translation have been some of the most common metrics (Hovy, 1999; White et al., 1994). However, human evaluations are expensive and time-consuming since there are many possible translations for a given source sentence.

The BiLingual Evaluation Understudy, commonly referred to as BLEU, is a well-known and widely adopted metric used in evaluating neural machine translation systems. BLEU (Papineni et al., 2002) is an automatic, language-independent evaluation method primarily proposed to circumvent the bottleneck with human evaluations. While BLEU is a quick and efficient substitute for human judges, it has also been the standard metric for assessing machine translation quality to this day.

With BLEU, translations generated by the system are scored by their similarity to a translation made by humans, so a BLEU score measures the difference between a human and machine translation output. Specifically, a machine translated sentence (candidate) is compared with a set of human translations (references) of the source data, assigning each word a "1" if it appears in a reference sentence and "0" if not. The scores are then averaged to provide a percentage indicating the accuracy of the translation. However, BLEU does not consider a word's meaning when scoring. The BLEU method evaluates all words equally, but some words convey more of a sentence's meaning and should subsequently have more weight in the scoring process. Additionally, sentence structure is not considered when scoring, so a high scoring machine translation may have improper syntax.

While not the most accurate, BLEU scoring measure was one of the first to provide a consistent metric to evaluate neural MT models. Further, string matching-based automatic evaluation metrics, such as NIST (Doddington, 2002) and METEOR (Banerjee & Lavie, 2005), have been proposed to address the limitations of BLEU. Despite the new metrics being developed for MT evaluation, BLEU continues to serve as the benchmark against which newly developed metrics are compared.

Stanford Question Answering Dataset

Machine reading comprehension, another popular task in NLP, entails reading a text passage and answering questions based on the given passage by the system. Question answering (QA) systems can be successful at machine comprehension when components of natural language understanding and world knowledge are unified. Despite the availability of several realistic datasets for evaluating QA systems (Berant et al., 2014; Hermann et al., 2015; Hill et al., 2015; Richardson et al., 2013), the need for a better dataset continued to thrive due to significant drawbacks in the realistic counterparts, such as size of the data and data being atypical of reading comprehension (RC) questions. To this end, the Stanford Question Answering Dataset was one of the newest datasets developed that improves on size as well as being characteristic of typical reading comprehension questions.

The Stanford Question Answering Dataset, or SQuAD (Rajpurkar et al., 2016), tests the machine's reading comprehension ability. SQuAD 1.1, the earliest version of the benchmark, consists of over 100,000 question–answer pairs from 500+ high quality Wikipedia articles spanning a broad spectrum of topics. Questions are created by crowdworkers[1] and answers to these questions are text spans (single word or multiple words) from the respective passage. Answers are selected from all possible spans within the passage subjecting the system to deal with a set of candidates rather than an answer from a list of choices. For system evaluation purposes, the SQuAD benchmark uses two metrics: (1) exact match and (2) f1-score. The *exact match* metric measures the percentage of system predictions that match any of the ground truth answers exactly, while the *f1-score* metric measures the average overlap between the system prediction and the ground truth answer (Rajpurkar et al., 2016).

Although models built on SQuAD 1.1 could locate the correct answer to a question, an analysis revealed that models based on type-matching heuristics coupled with contextual learning can also perform well on SQuAD (Weissenborn et al., 2017). Further, models that were successful on SQuAD failed on adversarial examples as the adversaries could easily fool the model during testing (Jia & Liang, 2017). Since SQuAD 1.1 focuses on the *existence* of a correct answer rather than the correct answer, the model may make an unreliable guess and select a span of text most related to the question even though the question does not have an answer. SQuAD 1.1 did provide an adequate metric for evaluation but the models discounted the bare essentials of relevance and existence of plausible answers (Rajpurkar et al., 2018).

To incorporate these essentials, SQuAD 2.0 (also known as SQuADRUn) (Rajpurkar et al., 2018) was released with over 50,000 additional unanswerable questions alongside the answerable questions from SQuAD 1.1. Along with being relevant to the context of the passage, the unanswerable questions were also required to have a likely answer that matches the type of the actual answer to the question being asked. Models were then expected to either answer questions correctly or determine if there was no answer that was supported by the given article. The increased difficulty would serve to evaluate models more accurately. Advanced neural systems that could achieve a score of 86% on v1.1 of the benchmark could only achieve a score of 66% on v2.0. This improved version of the benchmark became a standard measurement of a model's performance and has allowed developing NLP models to surpass human performance.

When originally released, SQuAD 1.1 exhibited a human performance F1-score of 86.8% which was significantly higher than the 51.0% score of an advanced logistic regression model. Four years later, tens of thousands of models have surpassed human performance, achieving F1-scores of up to 93.011 (see Fig. 5). Achievable F1-scores of models increased over 30%, hereby suggesting that the development of SQUaD was a primary catalyst to the growth and progress of NLP.

[1] The term *crowdworkers* refers to a large number of people who each contribute a small amount of labor to execute a given task (https://www.collinsdictionary.com/dictionary/english/crowdworking)

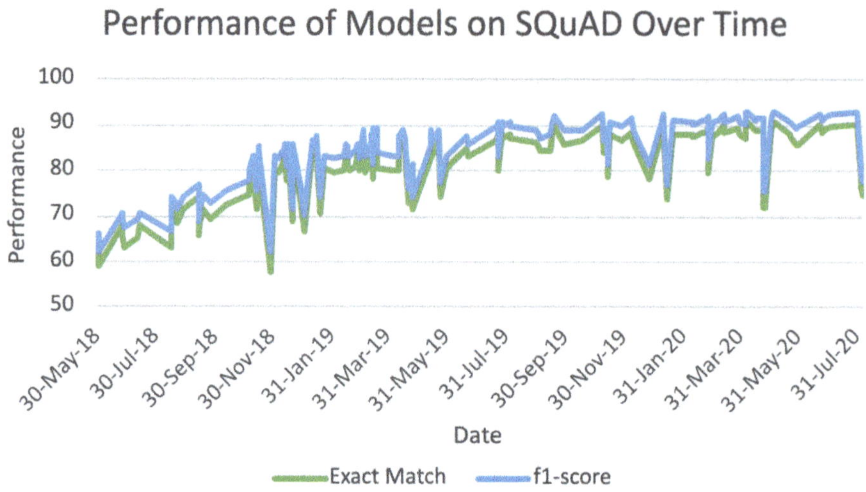

Fig. 5 Progression of model performance on the SQuAD 2.0 leaderboard over time. Two metrics, exact match and f1-score, were measured to determine the ranking between models. The scores achieved by models were posted on the SQuAD website against the human baseline for easy comparison

General Language Understanding Evaluation

Until 2018, all the primary benchmarks, specifically introduced to test the model's language understanding ability, were created for a single task. Despite their high-scoring nature, the models were not necessarily the best when it comes to generalization, robustness, and flexibility since they do not cope well with out-of-domain data. Since 2010, transfer learning has become a viable NLP technique where models are trained on large sets of unlabeled data from related tasks and domains such that all of the knowledge is combined and allows for easy adaptation (Ruder, 2019). Due to the nature of these models, an improvement in evaluation benchmarks was highly required to determine the effectiveness of knowledge transfer across a variety of NLP tasks. Catering to this need, the General Language Understanding Evaluation benchmark (GLUE) was created and has become the standard for training, probing, and evaluating models in various linguistic tasks across different domains.

As listed in Fig. 6, GLUE (Wang et al., 2018), a multi-task benchmark, is a collection of nine implicitly established, pre-existent datasets pertaining to English sentence understanding tasks of varying sizes, genres, and difficulties. Additionally, the benchmark also includes an expert-curated diagnostic dataset for investigating and analyzing whether trained models learn certain linguistic phenomena such as common sense and world knowledge, thereby enabling model robustness. Therefore, the analysis dataset together with the existing corpora allow for a more holistic assessment of the model. Further, due to the varying characteristics of the included

Dataset	Description	Data Example	Metric
CoLA	Is the sentence grammatical or ungrammatical?	"This building is than that one." = Ungrammatical	Matthews
SST-2	Is the movie review positive, negative, or neutral?	"The movie is funny , smart , visually inventive , and most of all , alive ." = .93056 (Very Positive)	Accuracy
MRPC	Is the sentence B a paraphrase of sentence A?	A) "Yesterday , Taiwan reported 35 new infections , bringing the total number of cases to 418 ." B) "The island reported another 35 probable cases yesterday , taking its total to 418 ." = A Paraphrase	Accuracy / F1
STS-B	How similar are sentences A and B?	A) "Elephants are walking down a trail." B) "A herd of elephants are walking along a trail." = 4.6 (Very Similar)	Pearson / Spearman
QQP	Are the two questions similar?	A) "How can I increase the speed of my internet connection while using a VPN?" B) "How can Internet speed be increased by hacking through DNS?" = Not Similar	Accuracy / F1
MNLI-mm	Does sentence A entail or contradict sentence B?	A) "Tourist Information offices can be very helpful." B) "Tourist Information offices are never of any help." = Contradiction	Accuracy
QNLI	Does sentence B contain the answer to the question in sentence A?	A) "What is essential for the mating of the elements that create radio waves?" B) "Antennas are required by any radio receiver or transmitter to couple its electrical connection to the electromagnetic field." = Answerable	Accuracy
RTE	Does sentence A entail sentence B?	A) "In 2003, Yunus brought the microcredit revolution to the streets of Bangladesh to support more than 50,000 beggars, whom the Grameen Bank respectfully calls Struggling Members." B) "Yunus supported more than 50,000 Struggling Members." = Entailed	Accuracy
WNLI	Sentence B replaces sentence A's ambiguous pronoun with one of the nouns - is this the correct noun?	A) "Lily spoke to Donna, breaking her concentration." B) "Lily spoke to Donna, breaking Lily's concentration." = Incorrect Referent	Accuracy

Fig. 6 A list of nine GLUE tasks and their evaluation metrics. Each task uses a different dataset to evaluate a unique NLP task with the overall objective of creating a well-rounded benchmark. Adapted from McCormick (2019)

datasets, GLUE encourages models that are capable of learning general linguistic knowledge that can be shared across tasks (Wang et al., 2018).

Additionally, an online evaluation platform and leaderboard (https://gluebenchmark.com/leaderboard) is also offered to publicly track model performances. The model-agnostic feature of this platform enables model evaluation, given that the model can process sentences and sentence pairs to make predictions using the benchmark. Human baselines are also included in this leaderboard, with scores for each of the various tasks. While human performance has been surpassed by several NLP models, results indicated that joint training on tasks can be helpful than single-task training for models that use attention (Vaswani et al., 2017) or ELMo embeddings (Peters et al., 2018). Due to the varied set of language tasks encompassed, GLUE benchmark has been a significant framework for model evaluation and has galvanized the use of transfer learning to be prominent in NLP.

GLUE benchmark has been a notable general-purpose evaluation toolkit in stimulating the progress of multi-task learning and transfer learning. However, outperforming human baselines on three of the nine tasks does not directly dictate the model's mastery over language. For instance, the Winograd Schema challenge (WNLI) (Levesque et al., 2012), a single binary question-based reading comprehension test, evaluates a model's understanding on the basis of worldly knowledge and typical commonsense reasoning abilities. Although humans can perform well on such commonsense reasoning tasks, a wide scope of improvement exists for machines to be capable of applying typical reasoning abilities as we do effortlessly.

This implied that the initial version of GLUE would be limited in terms of being an appropriate metric to quantify model performance.

Following the same design as GLUE, a more rigorous benchmark called SuperGLUE was introduced. SuperGLUE (Wang et al., 2019) includes a more diverse yet challenging set of seven language understanding tasks that are human-solvable but not by existing methods such as BERT. The 7-task set has retained the Recognizing Textual Entailment and Winograd Schema Challenge tasks from GLUE since the current best models still have not been able to – almost there but not yet – perform beyond the established human baseline. New tasks added help in evaluating question answering, coreference resolution, and commonsense reasoning abilities of a model. The current status of the leaderboard is available at https://super.gluebenchmark.com/leaderboard.

The Social Aspect of Natural Language Processing

Modern NLP methods for language understanding have been targeted for use in major downstream applications that have a direct impact on our lives: for example, personal voice assistants, product recommendation systems, applicant tracking systems, and the like. Addressing fairness and ethical concerns becomes extremely important when life-impacting technology is in the limelight. Technically a mere set of words, language is an instrument that is powerful enough to convey information in an implicit fashion. For instance, language used in social media has characteristics that may be useful to trace information pertaining to the author. Data being the fundamental driving force for machine learning brings in the possibility of certain risks associated when using language to build models; the most ubiquitous being bias.

Bias refers to the subjective thoughts and beliefs induced consciously or unconsciously that results in prejudices. Common forms of bias in language include societal biases such as gender bias, racial bias, and demographic bias. Numerically, NLP-dominated black-box models have demonstrated human-like performance on several language understanding tasks but the very same cannot be said when these models are evaluated in terms of reducing implicit biases. Examples of language bias investigations such as resume reviewing and rating system (now discontinued) revealed discrimination against female candidates since the data was biased with the then existing trends in the tech industry, word embeddings trained on news articles revealed human-like gender stereotyping to a significant extent (Bolukbasi et al., 2016), YouTube's automatic captioning system showed differences in performance across gender and dialect (Tatman, 2017), coreference resolution systems demonstrated that gendered pronouns favor pro-stereotypical entities than anti-stereotypical entities (Zhao et al., 2018), among many others.

With bias being implicit in the data, research in ethical AI has been at the forefront of advocating for fairness in intelligent systems. Techniques such as data augmentation (Zhao et al., 2018) and debiasing (Bolukbasi et al., 2016) have demonstrated that bias mitigation is possible without significantly affecting performance. Accounting for biases as part of the modeling process not only reduces the impact of language bias in models, but also enables more socially responsible and accountable AI systems.

Conclusion

Natural language processing has been a primary area of artificial intelligence research. With promising advancements and exponential evolution, models today have been successful in achieving high performance on a wide array of language understanding tasks. Despite the incredible success that language understanding has witnessed in the past decade, questions regarding the viability of the models still remain. A recent study claims that the success of GPT-3 is led by its 175 billion training parameters, 10x that of any other non-sparse language model but brings along a great deal of limitations (Brown et al., 2020). Scaling the model drastically improved the accuracy, placing the model competitively with other state-of-the-art models. However, the elementary question regarding the model's understanding being meaningful still needs to be addressed (Bender & Koller, 2020; Dunietz et al., 2020). Rather than throwing computing power at these models to improve results, making improvements that enable the model's ability to understand in a meaningful way would be more valuable. Since most of the models still perform pale in comparison with that of a human, studying the underlying behavior of these models will be resourceful. Nonetheless, these models continue to have a strong training requirement of a massively sized text corpora for a task that we, as humans, can master with minimal experience.

Regardless, the growth that NLP has experienced over the last two decades is indisputable given that languages are strange and ambiguous. Led by the advancement of unsupervised learning approaches and the development of benchmarks that create a clear metric for grading, NLP has risen to prominence in commercial and educational applications. Systems powered by conversational artificial intelligence and sentiment analysis have become trademarks of customer experience, while speech recognition, language understanding, and text translation have found applications in most modern smartphones. Despite the fluid structure of language, large- and small-scale state-of-the-art models have been successful in resolving ambiguity to a great extent. Thus, natural language processing methods and practices continue to look promising for language understanding while demonstrating a need for highly sophisticated and nuanced language processing systems.

Acknowledgments We would like to extend our sincere thanks to Sridhar Nandigam, Arvind Ganesh, and Thasina Tabashum for being the early reviewers and critiques of the chapter while the writing was in progress. Their timely feedback on the very first draft of this chapter provided valuable inputs and suggestions which constructively helped us in tailoring our chapter more specifically for the intended audience.

References

Bahdanau, D., Cho, K., & Bengio, Y. (2014). Neural machine translation by jointly learning to align and translate. *arXiv preprint arXiv*, 1409.0473.

Banerjee, S., & Lavie, A. (2005). METEOR: An automatic metric for MT evaluation with improved correlation with human judgments. In *Proceedings of the ACL workshop on intrinsic and extrinsic evaluation measures for machine translation and/or summarization* (pp. 65–72).

Bender, E. M., & Koller, A. (2020). Climbing towards NLU: On meaning, form, and understanding in the age of data. In *Proceedings of the 58th annual meeting of the association for computational linguistics* (pp. 5185–5198).

Bengio, S., & Bengio, Y. (2000). Taking on the curse of dimensionality in joint distributions using neural networks. *IEEE Transactions on Neural Networks, 11*, 550–557.

Bengio, Y., Ducharme, R., & Vincent, P. (2001). A neural probabilistic language model. In *Advances in neural information processing systems* (pp. 932–938).

Bengio, Y., Ducharme, R., Vincent, P., & Janvin, C. (2003). A neural probabilistic language model. *The Journal of Machine Learning Research, 3*, 1137–1155.

Berant, J., Srikumar, V., Chen, P.-C., Vander Linden, A., Harding, B., Huang, B., … Manning, C. D. (2014). Modeling biological processes for reading comprehension. In *Proceedings of the 2014 conference on empirical methods in natural language processing (EMNLP)* (pp. 1499–1510).

Bolukbasi, T., Chang, K.-W., Zou, J., Saligrama, V., & Kalai, A. (2016). Man is to computer programmer as woman is to homemaker? Debiasing word embeddings. *arXiv preprint arXiv*, 1607.06520.

Brown, T. B., Mann, B., Ryder, N., Subbiah, M., Kaplan, J., Dhariwal, P., … others. (2020). Language models are few-shot learners. *arXiv preprint arXiv*, 2005.14165.

Cho, K., van Merriënboer, B., Bahdanau, D., & Bengio, Y. (2014a). On the properties of neural machine translation: Encoder–decoder approaches. In *Proceedings of SSST-8, eighth workshop on syntax, semantics and structure in statistical translation* (pp. 103–111).

Cho, K., Van Merriënboer, B., Gulcehre, C., Bahdanau, D., Bougares, F., Schwenk, H., & Bengio, Y. (2014b). Learning phrase representations using RNN encoder-decoder for statistical machine translation. *arXiv preprint arXiv*, 1406.1078.

Columbus, L. (2018). Global state of enterprise analytics, 2018. *Global state of enterprise analytics, 2018*. Retrieved from https://www.forbes.com/sites/louiscolumbus/2018/08/08/global-state-of-enterprise-analytics-2018/?sh=528f58d76361

Dai, A. M., & Le, Q. V. (2015). Semi-supervised sequence learning. In *Proceedings of the 28th international conference on neural information processing systems-volume 2* (pp. 3079–3087).

Deloitte. (n.d.). The analytics advantage. In *The analytics advantage*. Retrieved from https://www2.deloitte.com/content/dam/Deloitte/global/Documents/Deloitte-Analytics/dttl-analytics-analytics-advantage-report-061913.pdf

Devlin, J., Chang, M.-W., Lee, K., & Toutanova, K. (2019). BERT: Pre-training of deep bidirectional transformers for language understanding. In *Proceedings of the 2019 conference of the north American chapter of the Association for Computational Linguistics: Human language technologies, volume 1 (long and short papers)* (pp. 4171–4186).

Doddington, G. (2002). Automatic evaluation of machine translation quality using n-gram co-occurrence statistics. In *Proceedings of the second international conference on human language technology research* (pp. 138–145).

Dunietz, J., Burnham, G., Bharadwaj, A., Rambow, O., Chu-Carroll, J., & Ferrucci, D. (2020). To test machine comprehension, start by defining comprehension. In *Proceedings of the 58th annual meeting of the association for computational linguistics* (pp. 7839–7859).

Elman, J. L. (1990). Finding structure in time. *Cognitive Science, 14*, 179–211.

Goodman, J. T. (2001). A bit of progress in language modeling. *Computer Speech & Language, 15*, 403–434.

Hermann, K. M., Kočiský, T., Grefenstette, E., Espeholt, L., Kay, W., Suleyman, M., & Blunsom, P. (2015). Teaching machines to read and comprehend. In *Proceedings of the 28th international conference on neural information processing systems-volume 1* (pp. 1693–1701).

Hill, F., Bordes, A., Chopra, S., & Weston, J. (2015). The goldilocks principle: Reading children's books with explicit memory representations. *arXiv preprint arXiv*, 1511.02301.

Hochreiter, S., & Schmidhuber, J. (1997). Long short-term memory. *Neural Computation, 9*, 1735–1780.

Hovy, E. H. (1999). Toward finely differentiated evaluation metrics for machine translation. In *Proceedings of the EAGLES workshop on standards and evaluation pisa, Italy, 1999.*

Howard, J., & Ruder, S. (2018). Universal language model fine-tuning for text classification. In *Proceedings of the 56th annual meeting of the association for computational Linguistics (volume 1: Long papers)* (pp. 328–339).

Jia, R., & Liang, P. (2017). Adversarial examples for evaluating Reading comprehension systems. In *Proceedings of the 2017 conference on empirical methods in natural language processing* (pp. 2021–2031).

Katz, S. (1987). Estimation of probabilities from sparse data for the language model component of a speech recognizer. *IEEE Transactions on Acoustics, Speech, and Signal Processing, 35*, 400–401.

Kuchaiev, O., & Ginsburg, B. (2017). Factorization tricks for LSTM networks. *arXiv preprint arXiv*, 1703.10722.

Levesque, H., Davis, E., & Morgenstern, L. (2012). The winograd schema challenge. In *Thirteenth international conference on the principles of knowledge representation and reasoning.*

Luong, M.-T., Pham, H., & Manning, C. D. (2015). Effective approaches to attention-based neural machine translation. Proceedings of the 2015 conference on empirical methods in natural language processing, (pp. 1412–11421).

McCormick, C. (2019). *GLUE explained: Understanding BERT through Benchmarks.* Retrieved from https://mccormickml.com/2019/11/05/GLUE/

Mikolov, T., Chen, K., Corrado, G., & Dean, J. (2013). Efficient estimation of word representations in vector space. *arXiv preprint arXiv*, 1301.3781.

Papineni, K., Roukos, S., Ward, T., & Zhu, W.-J. (2002). Bleu: A method for automatic evaluation of machine translation. In *Proceedings of the 40th annual meeting of the association for computational linguistics* (pp. 311–318).

Peters, M., Neumann, M., Iyyer, M., Gardner, M., Clark, C., Lee, K., & Zettlemoyer, L. (2018). Deep contextualized word representations. In *Proceedings of the 2018 conference of the North American chapter of the association for computational linguistics: Human language technologies, volume 1 (long papers)* (pp. 2227–2237).

Pi School x Łukasz Kaiser. (2017). Attention is all you need; Attentional Neural Network Models I Łukasz Kaiser I Masterclass. *Attention is all you need; Attentional Neural Network Models | Łukasz Kaiser | Masterclass.* Retrieved from https://www.youtube.com/watch?v=rBCqOTEfxvg&t=2466s&ab_channel=PiSchool

Radford, A., Narasimhan, K., Salimans, T., & Sutskever, I. (2018). *Improving language understanding by generative pre-training.* Retrieved from https://cdn.openai.com/research-covers/language-unsupervised/language_understanding_paper.pdf

Rajpurkar, P., Zhang, J., Lopyrev, K., & Liang, P. (2016). SQuAD: 100,000+ questions for machine comprehension of text. In *Proceedings of the 2016 conference on empirical methods in natural language processing* (pp. 2383–2392).

Rajpurkar, P., Jia, R., & Liang, P. (2018). Know what you Don't know: Unanswerable questions for SQuAD. In *Proceedings of the 56th annual meeting of the association for computational linguistics (volume 2: Short papers)* (pp. 784–789).

Richardson, M., Burges, C. J., & Renshaw, E. (2013). Mctest: A challenge dataset for the open-domain machine comprehension of text. In *Proceedings of the 2013 conference on empirical methods in natural language processing* (pp. 193–203).

Rosenfeld, R. (2000). Two decades of statistical language modeling: Where do we go from here? In *Proceedings of the IEEE, 88* (pp. 1270–1278).
Ruder, S. (2018). NLP's ImageNet moment has arrived. In *NLP's ImageNet moment has arrived.*
Ruder, S. (2019). *Neural Transfer Learning for Natural Language Processing.* Ph.D. dissertation, National University of Ireland, Galway.
Shazeer, N., Mirhoseini, A., Maziarz, K., Davis, A., Le, Q., Hinton, G., & Dean, J. (2017). Outrageously large neural networks: The sparsely-gated mixture-of-experts layer. *arXiv preprint arXiv*, 1701.06538.
Sutskever, I., Vinyals, O., & Le, Q. V. (2014). Sequence to sequence learning with neural networks. *Advances in Neural Information Processing Systems, 27*, 3104–3112.
Tatman, R. (2017). Gender and dialect bias in YouTube's automatic captions. In *Proceedings of the first ACL workshop on ethics in natural language processing* (pp. 53–59).
Vaswani, A., Shazeer, N., Parmar, N., Uszkoreit, J., Jones, L., Gomez, A. N., … Polosukhin, I. (2017). Attention is all you need. In *Proceedings of the 31st international conference on neural information processing systems* (pp. 6000–6010).
Vinyals, O., Kaiser, Ł., Koo, T., Petrov, S., Sutskever, I., & Hinton, G. (2015). Grammar as a foreign language. *Advances in Neural Information Processing Systems, 28*, 2773–2781.
Wang, J., Zhou, R., Li, J., & Wang, G. (2014). A distributed rule engine based on message-passing model to deal with big data. *Lecture Notes on Software Engineering, 2*, 275.
Wang, A., Singh, A., Michael, J., Hill, F., Levy, O., & Bowman, S. (2018). GLUE: A multi-task benchmark and analysis platform for natural language understanding. In *Proceedings of the 2018 EMNLP workshop BlackboxNLP: Analyzing and interpreting neural networks for NLP* (pp. 353–355).
Wang, A., Pruksachatkun, Y., Nangia, N., Singh, A., Michael, J., Hill, F., … Bowman, S. R. (2019). SuperGLUE: A stickier benchmark for general-purpose language understanding systems. *Advances in Neural Information Processing Systems, 32.*
Weissenborn, D., Wiese, G., & Seiffe, L. (2017). Making neural QA as simple as possible but not simpler. In *Proceedings of the 21st conference on computational natural language learning (CoNLL 2017)* (pp. 271–280).
White, J. S., O'Connell, T. A., & O'Mara, F. E. (1994). The ARPA MT evaluation methodologies: Evolution, lessons, and future approaches. In *Proceedings of the first conference of the association for machine translation in the Americas.*
Wilson, B. (2012, 6). The AI Dictionary. *The AI dictionary*. Retrieved from http://www.cse.unsw.edu.au/billw/dictionaries/aidict.html
Wu, Y., Schuster, M., Chen, Z., Le, Q. V., Norouzi, M., Macherey, W., … others. (2016). Google's neural machine translation system: Bridging the gap between human and machine translation. *arXiv preprint arXiv*, 1609.08144.
Zellers, R., Bisk, Y., Schwartz, R., & Choi, Y. (2018). SWAG: A large-scale adversarial dataset for grounded Commonsense inference. In *Proceedings of the 2018 conference on empirical methods in natural language processing* (pp. 93–104).
Zhao, J., Wang, T., Yatskar, M., Ordonez, V., & Chang, K.-W. (2018). Gender bias in Coreference resolution: Evaluation and debiasing methods. In *Proceedings of the 2018 conference of the north American chapter of the association for computational linguistics: Human language technologies, volume 2 (Short papers)* (pp. 15–20).

Phillip Nelson is a student at the Texas Academy of Mathematics and Science at the University of North Texas. His research interests lie in the application of machine learning techniques in business environments. His current contribution is for a research effort that concerns the utilization of word embeddings to infer organizational metrics for companies. He has also co-authored a poster titled "Multi-Agent Hierarchical Reinforcement Learning Strategy and Tactics in Competitive Play" and has been published in the Richard Tapia Celebration of Diversity in Computing Conference.

Namratha V. Urs is a Ph.D. candidate in computer science at the University of North Texas (UNT), specializing in natural language processing and applied machine learning. She is a member of the Human Intelligence and Language Technologies Lab and the Biomedical AI Lab at UNT. Her primary research is in the investigation of deep learning techniques to identify conversational styles in dialogue. She has also worked on applying machine learning techniques to understand neural processing by simulating computational neuroscience principles. She has presented at the Society of Neuroscience and ACM Richard Tapia Celebration of Diversity in Computing. She has also served as the President of the UNT Women in Computing group (2020–2021).

Dr. Taraka Rama Kasicheyanula 's research is in computational approaches to language evolution which includes application of Bayesian phylogenetic methods and neural networks. Dr. Rama has published in NLP venues such as *ACL, CONLL, and COLING and high impact venues such as PLOS ONE and Royal Society. His recent paper titled "Testing methods of linguistic homeland detection using synthetic data" has been published in "Philosophical Transactions of the Royal Society B: Biological Sciences" and evaluates the performance of different Bayesian phylogeographic methods at the task of homeland detection. In another paper, published in CONLL, Dr. Rama explores the use of neural alignment methods for predicting reflexes in modern Indo-Aryan languages. In another published work, Dr. Rama probed if multilingual BERT captures any typological or genetic signals.

Part II
Enhancing Human Intelligence Through AI

AI-Enhanced Education: Teaching and Learning Reimagined

Nanxi Meng, Tetyana K. Dhimolea, and Zain Ali

Why AI in Education

Artificial Intelligence (AI) is changing the essential relationship between technology and human beings. It is reshaping the ecosystem of education and growing to be a primary focus of multinational technological corporations, education departments, and governments of countries around the world. From 2016 to 2018, the government of the United States published three documents emphasizing the importance of AI and its standing in the development of the countries: *Preparing for the Future of Artificial Intelligence* (Bundy, 2017; United States, 2016), *A National Machine Intelligence Strategy for the United States* (Carter et al., 2018), and *The National Artificial Intelligence Research and Development Strategic Plan* (National Science and Technology Council, 2019). All three documents put emphasis on education being the core application of AI. In 2019 the Open University in UK released the *Innovative Pedagogy 2019* (Ferguson et al., 2019), which points out the importance of "learning with robots" (p. 12), in order to help teachers free their time for teaching. The *Innovative Pedagogy 2020* report (Kukulska-Hulme et al., 2020) starts with Artificial Intelligence in Education as the first chapter and provides a detailed description of a possible application of AI in teaching and learning, and projects the bright future of AI development in multiple scenarios in education. Moreover, UNESCO held the conference titled "Planning Education in the AI Era: Lead the Leap" in Beijing, China, in which ten essential topics including policy formulation, learning management, teaching, and teacher development were discussed. AI is the essential power promoting educational reform.

N. Meng (✉) · T. K. Dhimolea · Z. Ali
University of North Texas, Denton, TX, USA
e-mail: nanxi.meng@unt.edu; Tetyana.Kucher@unt.edu; zain.ali@unt.edu

M. V. Albert et al. (eds.), *Bridging Human Intelligence and Artificial Intelligence*, Educational Communications and Technology: Issues and Innovations, https://doi.org/10.1007/978-3-030-84729-6_7

The current education system is insufficient to address some typical acute questions: education inequality is increasing due to the unbalanced development of the technological advancements, socioeconomic concerns, and political upheaval in some regions and countries (Facer, 2011), which cause the limited accessibility to educational resources for learners in those disadvantaged areas. Even in the countries where education is under the spotlight of national development, issues like mal-supported instructors (Schmid & Hegelheimer, 2014), engaging proper technology-enhanced pedagogy to stimulate the greatest learner potential remain top concern for instructors and educational researchers. For learners who have difficulty learning in the standard environment, their learning quality cannot be guaranteed without further attention and intervention from the instructor or the teaching system. Technologies like learning analytics and machine learning have been utilized to acquire the data about the learning experiences from numerous learners. AI grants people opportunities and hope to make education more accessible, and to identify effective new learning patterns, models, and insights to understand learning, teaching, and the roles of people engaged in those processes.

With the resources we possess so far, education is the science and practice that prepares our young generation facing the uncertainty in the future. The responsibility of educators and educational researchers is to prepare students with essential twenty-first-century skills and life-long and life-wide learning capacity. In this chapter, we first look into the technologies that are applied in AI and how they enhance education. Then, we review the applications available to education administration, teachers, and learners, and how each role might be enhanced or redefined by the affordances of AI. Finally, yet importantly, we elaborate on some concerns for future AI applications in education.

Fundamental Technologies in Educational AI

Learning Analytics

Learning analytics is the intersection of multiple academic disciplines such as education, AI, and data science, among many others. Through collecting, analyzing, and reporting students' learning data, the essential function of learning analytics is to understand and improve learning to the optimum level. More operationally, Society for Learning Analytics Research (SoLAR) defines learning analytics as the measurement, collection, analysis, and reporting of data about learners and their contexts, for understanding purposes and optimizing learning and the environments in which it occurs. There are three major elements in learning analytics: data, analytics, and action plan (Chen et al., 2020). Data refers to collecting data that provide analytical insights about learners and their learning behavior; analytics entails applying research methodologies and algorithms to produce high quality and insightful analysis; action plans are the bridge between the analytics and the desired learning objectives, through applying the insights and models gained to attain the learning purpose. According to this study, in Fig. 1, we visualized the three elements.

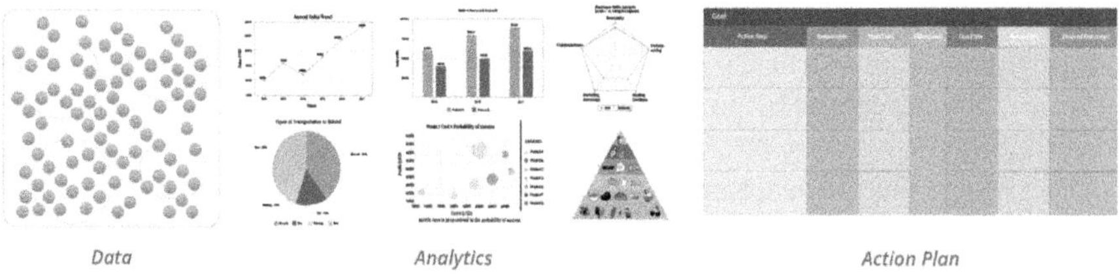

Fig. 1 Three major components of learning analytics

Levels of Learning Analytics			
Descriptive	**Diagnostic**	**Predictive**	**Perspective**
What has happened?	*Why did it happen?*	*What will happen?*	*What should I do?*
• Look at facts, figures and data to create a detailed picture. • Did the student fail a quiz? • What was mastered? • What was not mastered?	• Examining the descriptive to critically assess what really happened? • The student did ok in one area but not ok in another area? • What were the root causes such as time devoted, homework, class discussions, etc.?	• By looking at the past can we predict what will happen in the future? • If time devoted, homework, class discussions were levers such as A, B, C, then what is the impact of each lever on the future?	• How can specific outcomes be achieved by tweaking each one of the levers? • How can we apply Descriptive, Diagnostic and Predictive knowledge to achieve our learning outcomes?

Fig. 2 Four levels of learning analytics

Arroway et al. (2015) applied a hierarchy approach of understanding learning analytics, in which learning analytics could be divided into four levels: descriptive analytics, diagnostic analytics, predictive analytics, and prescriptive analytics. We create the table in Fig. 2 to help better understand these four levels.

Descriptive analytics focuses mainly on the historical data that is collected from multiple related resources to trace the previous learning behavior of learners. Diagnostic analytics intends to identify patterns and get insights into a specific learning problem. Predictive analytics builds on historical data to develop statistical models that can forecast the future possibilities for learners. It is the process of identifying probable difficulties and creating opportunities to provide targeted support to learners. Prescriptive analytics takes another step further to consider the possible forecasted outcomes and predict consequences for these outcomes, which provides the strategic plan to intervene in the learning process in order to improve the efficiency of learning. Compared to descriptive data solely focused on historical data received, predictive analytics and prescriptive analytics are the two most widely applied types in learning analytics. One example of representative predictive analytics applications is the Course Signal system developed by Purdue University. This system applies the data collected by instructional tools within the educational institution to determine which students might be at risk, partially indicated by their effort within a course. The Course Signal system offers them support and resources to help students succeed by predicting and providing early interventions (Arnold & Pistilli, 2012).

The wide usage of learning analytics brings more accurate prediction of students' learning behavior, which allows institutes to take intervention actions, but it also projects a challenge on solving course-specific and institute-specific contexts issues, especially the instructional conditional differences (the efficiency of Learning Management system, quality of instruction, etc.), as it brings challenges to structure the models for customized analytics. Example applications and products of learning analysis in education include student and learning behavior modeling (Holstein et al., 2018; Santamaría-Bonfil et al., 2020), learning performance prediction (Ifenthaler et al., 2019), AI-assisted learning self-reflection and awareness (Buckingham Shum & Crick, 2016; Viberg et al., 2020), and learning administrative management that monitors student retention and drop-out issues (Lacave et al., 2018; Mah, 2016).

Machine Learning

The strength of machine learning is its ability to make accurate predictions based on the input data (Mannila, 1996). It is different from traditional statistics that is often used for making connections among the variables and making inferences in order to find possible explanations from the data provided. The essential function of machine learning is knowledge and insights discovery (Chen et al., 2020) since it creates models with various degrees of interpretation. Machine learning applied in education benefits include machine learning, data mining, statistics, and data modeling. It provides solutions to the problems learners encounter through learning patterns discovery, prediction, and decision-making based on the input data sets. Combining the computational and statistical perspectives of data analysis, data collected from the educational devices and software provide valuable information about learners and insights into their learning behaviors. Machine learning can reflect the more personalized nature of the data and form more customized insights and solutions to learners in their unique learning contexts. The four applications and products of machine learning in education include: (1) education administration that frees teachers from tedious teaching management tasks (Amigud et al., 2017); (2) monitor students' learning progress (Gray & Perkins, 2019); (3) analytics of content (Lan et al., 2014), and (4) instruction improvement (Zhou et al., 2018). The application and products of machine learning in education are shown in Fig. 3.

Two essential fundamental mechanisms of machine learning application in education include *educational data mining* and *deep learning* (Hernández-Blanco et al., 2019). Educational data mining is a process that analyzes the unique types of raw data generated from educational settings. It develops the methods to help understand students and the settings in which they learn, and provides useful insights that

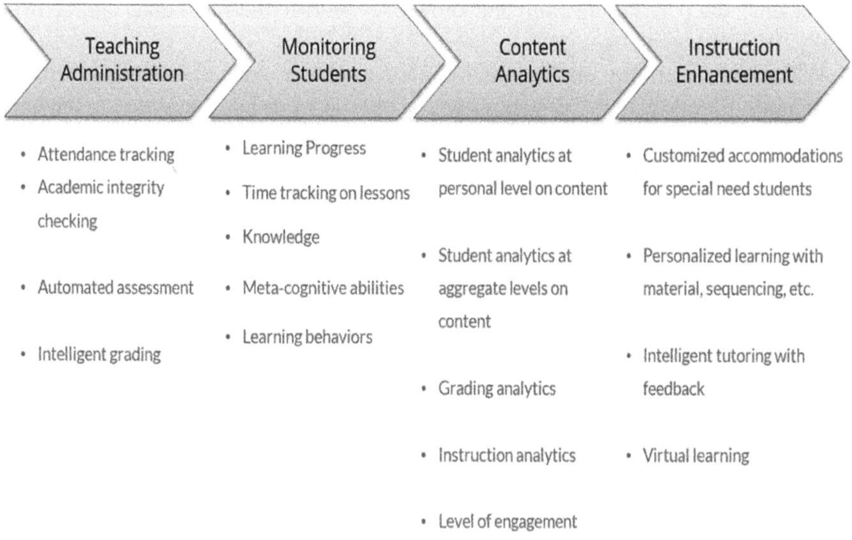

Fig. 3 Application and products of machine learning in education

could potentially be impactful on educational research and practice (Dutt et al., 2017; Romero & Ventura, 2010). In recent years, the trend of educational data mining applied as a new methodology to investigate educational research questions is observed widely (ElAtia et al., 2016).

Educational data mining is typically closely associated with specific learning objectives (Dutt et al., 2017). It is a powerful tool to improve the learning process and knowledge mastery for learners – learning pattern discovery and predictive modeling applied in extracting hidden knowledge in specific contexts. Educational data mining provides advantages such as laboratory experiments, in vivo experiments, and design research. The application and products of data mining in education include (1) analyzing student learning motivation, attitude, and behavior, i.e., performing erroneous actions, low motivation, cheating, and academic failure, (Mulwa et al., 2010); (2) understanding learning styles of students, i.e., student modeling (Sivakumar et al., 2016); (3) supporting diversified learning format and methods, i.e., personalized learning, e-learning, and collaborative learning (Dutt et al., 2017); and (4) learning outcome prediction (Mueen et al., 2016).

Deep learning is a machine learning method. Based on neural network architectures with multiple layers of processing units, it allows computational models to "learn representations of data with multiple levels of abstraction" (LeCun et al., 2015, p. 436). There are two key aspects of deep learning that allow it to outperform traditional machine learning with increased size of dataset: "(1) models consisting of multiple layers or stages of nonlinear information processing; and (2) methods for supervised or unsupervised learning of feature representation at successively higher, more abstract layers" (Deng & Yu, 2014, p. 201). Deep learning has made great progress in complex tasks like image recognition and natural language processing, and performing complete knowledge games like chess and "Go" (Fawaz et al., 2019; Nguyen et al., 2019).

With deep learning applied as the approach to educational data mining, Hernández-Blanco et al. (2019) summarized in total 13 tasks. In addition to the ones previously mentioned in the educational data mining subsection, deep learning enhanced data mining could also help with the following three aspects in education. First, it can be applied to social network analysis, which can show the various possible relationships among students and better understand their learning-related interactions. Second, it can provide feedback to students, which allows them to find and highlight the information related to course activities and student's usage information on course materials for instructors and course designers. Third, deep learning enhanced data mining can help develop concept maps of various aspects to help instructors define the process of education.

With a good understanding of the available techniques of AI in education, we present the applications and available products with the above-mentioned technologies as the foundation for three major agencies in education: education administration, teachers, and learners.

Agencies of AI in Education

Effective and appropriate application of AI offers opportunities to revolutionize education by assisting teachers with administrative tasks and teaching while subsequently impacting students' learning. In this section, we focus on specific applications of AI systems in the domains of education administration, instruction, and learning.

Education Administration

Traditionally, educational administrative tasks are primarily carried out by teachers at the classroom level, by educational administrators at the school and district level, and stakeholders at a wider and higher level. Introducing AI-enhanced education administration can free teachers from performing administrative work and allow more support and attention to go to the actual instruction. From the available AI-enhanced technology and applications, education administration can be facilitated at four different levels:

Level I: Substitution. At this level, AI applications free teachers from daily tedious manual/labor work by performing tasks like taking class attendance and grading objective questions. Substitution functions of AI are particularly beneficial for providing timely feedback and increase their effectiveness in classes with large numbers of students.

Level II: Intellectual augmentation. AI in this level collects and tracks students' learning data over an extended period of time, which provides comparable and more holistic information for teachers to see the learning development of students over a period of time, and reduces the impact of possible biases or subjective impressions the teacher formed based on individual learning performance. Examples could be seen in student profiling systems and learning performance-monitoring systems.

Level III: Revolution. Based on the AI characteristics of modeling and prediction, education administration systems nowadays can provide learning predictions and allow educational institutions to engage in student learning interventions. Representative examples are drop-out prevention systems and at-risk student identification systems.

Level IV: Holistic revolution. Some intellectual education administration systems have performed functions beyond learning management. The systems can support teaching in various formats and styles. Many educational establishments incorporate interactive learning environments (ILE), such as learning management systems (LMS), to assist teachers and professors with administrative tasks. ILE is a software system which sometimes includes specialized hardware designed to support teaching and learning in education (Psotka, 2012). It combines digital technologies, e-learning techniques, and interactive pedagogical approaches to maximize students' personalized learning (Chassignol, Khoroshavin, Klimova & Bilyatdinova Chassignol et al., 2018). The four levels are shown in Fig. 4. In the rest of this section, we introduce several representative education administration systems to help understand how AI supports teachers and administrators.

Artificially Intelligent Tutoring System (ITS) is a branch developed as a part of LMS evolution that uses AI systems to achieve the goal of interactive and personalized learning. ITSs are computer systems developed to improve teachers' effectiveness by offering instructions and guidance to and off-loading teachers' duties of providing assessments and feedback (Chassignol et al., 2018). As teachers are often guided by grading rubrics, similar techniques are used by automatized assessment technologies offered by the AI. A typical ITS includes four main components (Almasri et al., 2019):

1. The Domain Model
2. The Student Model
3. The Teaching Model
4. The Communication Model (Fig. 5).

The Knowledge Model represents the knowledge about the teaching material. The Student Model contains the knowledge about each student to respond to their individual skills and interests and promote effective learning. The Teaching Model helps select a suitable tutoring strategy and pedagogical actions (e.g., providing a hint, or feedback) based on the information from the Student Model and on student's interaction with the system (Almasri et al., 2019). The Teaching Model

Fig. 4 Four levels of AI-enabled education administration

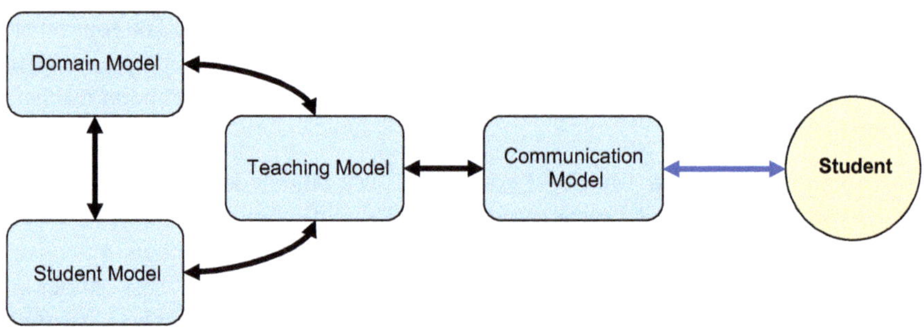

Fig. 5 Structure of a typical ITS. (Adapted from Almasri et al., 2019)

component can aid teachers in performing administrative tasks, and it has been used to assist teachers in providing feedback on mechanical rules. An important quality of ITS is that it receives information about students' intermediate steps of different tasks. Therefore, it can provide students feedback and hints on each step. The Communication Model ensures a successful interaction between the system and the user by means of graphic communication, speech recognition, and social intelligence.

Another important component in designing ITSs is *scaffolding*. Traditionally, scaffolding is defined as support offered by a teacher or a more competent peer which is adjusted to the student's level of understanding, and it is gradually removed when the necessary support is provided to transfer the responsibility back to the learner (van de Pol et al., 2010). By this definition, scaffolding strategies should be tailored to individual learners depending on their struggles and needs. In computer-based contexts, ITSs use students' prior knowledge to determine the level of fading needed to adapt to the individual learner (Booth et al., 2017). One example of an ITS called ASSISTment was developed to provide assessments on students' performance on a standardized state test preparation while providing them with instructional assistance when needed (Feng et al., 2006). Scaffolding helps break down problems by providing students with a brief tutoring session that gradually guides the student to the right answer. CAPIT is another ITS developed to teach students English grammar (Mayo et al., 2000). It provides students with short and specific feedback when their submitted solution contains errors and adds appropriate hints to scaffold student knowledge.

Teachers may take advantage of ITSs by using them as a tool for students to answer common questions about class assignments, course policies, or study schedules. In addition, ITSs may help identify gaps in students' knowledge (Chassignol et al., 2018). Based on a teacher's evaluations of students' past performance, the ITS can create a model which incorporates the same principles used by the teacher in their evaluations and implement this model to conduct assessments of other students.

ITSs are becoming frequently used to identify potential at-risk students and ways that can help them increase their performance using academic failure monitoring systems. Arnold and Pistilli (2012) describe Course Signals, a tool designed at Purdue University, which incorporated learning analytics to track students' progress and predict their academic success. Using the trace data collected by the LMS and the data from the institutional Student Information System, Course Signals implemented a data-mining algorithm to identify students at risk of academic failure in a course. In addition to identifying these students, the system also provided them with resources and recommendations that would help set students on the right track and improve their performance. The incorporation of this early alert algorithm and the student support system showed high levels of predictive accuracy and positively affected student retention and course pass rate when compared to students in courses where the Course Signals tool was not implemented (Fig. 6).

Feng et al. (2006) also investigated the predictive model of AI-based ITS. In their study, the ITS logged the number of assistance requests sent by students to perform different tasks and complete course assignments, such as the number of hints requested and the number of attempts made. The ITS was able to successfully predict students' test scores by taking into account the information on students' assistance requests.

Personalized learning ensures that the educational process is centered round students' needs and includes content sequencing, scaffolding, feedback, and assessment (Canales et al., 2007). The incorporation of Web-Based Educational Systems (WBES) requires not only meeting individual students' needs, but also creating solutions that include reusable content components for different communities of teachers and students (Wang & Qian, 2005).

Brusilovsky and Peylo (2003) emphasize the importance of WBES to be both intelligent and adaptive to students' needs. WBES supported by AI can provide high-quality support for its users by providing individual responses to specific students based on the information accumulated about them such as their goals and preferences.

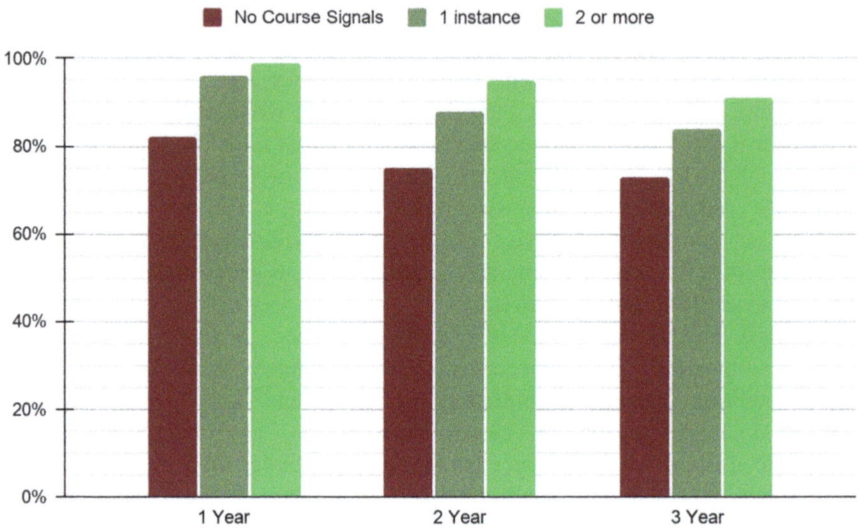

Fig. 6 Retention rates from the 2008 entering cohort among students who used and did not use Course Signals. (Created based on Arnold & Pistilli, 2012)

Additionally, AI enhanced education administration not only restricted its application in the interactions between the instructors, teaching management agencies, and the learners, it also extensively employed in monitoring the interactions between the learning environment and the learners. In some Chinese elementary schools, AI facial recognition is used to help capture the student attendance information. Classroom robots are used to collect and analyze the data of students' health and engagement level; the students' uniforms are designed with chips embedded to track the students' physical location and provide safety protection for students' in school and commuting (Panchal & Shaikh Mohammad, 2020).

Instruction

AI has facilitated the creation and deployment of systems, and these systems provide powerful pedagogical tools that can improve the quality of the instruction (Chen et al., 2020). The integration of AI in education combined with other technologies resulted in the development of advanced instructional tools. The adoption of AI systems in robotics for education leads to the development of robot teaching assistants that can help teachers during a class without disrupting the lesson. They can undertake tasks of different complexities that can foster effective instruction, such as providing assistance in reading and pronouncing certain words (Timms, 2016) as well as answering questions students commonly have about assignment requirements, policies, and information about instructional materials (Pokrivcakova, 2019; Sharma et al., 2019). These robot teaching assistants may constitute the ITSs that are equipped with abilities to have a conversation with students and have been able to foster the effectiveness of instruction (Rus et al., 2013).

AI technologies can also effectively integrate in web-based instruction. AI has the ability to incorporate teacher-like functions in a web-based platform that allows a more comprehensive support for all students, which is demonstrated by the use of adaptive and intelligent web-based educational systems (AIWBES) (Kahraman et al., 2010; Peredo et al., 2011). Assistance with teaching responsibilities using AIWBES is achieved through providing instructions and directions to teachers and students in order to utilize technology in an efficient and systematic way to maximize students' learning (Chen et al., 2020).

In addition, AI and machine learning are widely studied to be applied in mobile devices to facilitate learning and training. These advancements create opportunities to incorporate natural language processing, speech recognition, and virtual reality spaces, thus taking mobile learning to a new level by allowing students to receive personalized and interactive learning (Ignatov et al., 2018). Examples include the developments of virtual reality simulation platforms, which open opportunities to create global classrooms by using AI to connect students to virtual classrooms. 3D technologies have fostered the use of these tools as an effective way to demonstrate learning concepts allowing students to gain practical experience in the subject, such as participating in surgeries for medical students, among other subjects (Mikropoulos & Natsis, 2011; Timms, 2016; Wartman & Combs, 2018). In addition, AI-based chatbots can offer personalized instruction by turning instructors into conversational agents, which are capable of effectively catering to students' learning needs.

Besides helping with the teaching, AI also provides informational data to help teachers better understand their students and their learning states. AI facial recognition is applied to obtain the students' concentration level in class. Additionally, a headband that can monitor students' concentration levels also provides good biological feedback to the classroom teacher (Panchal & Shaikh Mohammad, 2020). Feedback data like these can provide classroom teachers reference to adjust their teaching pace and make teaching and learning more effective according to student learning states.

Learning

AI technologies can be adopted and leveraged to improve students' learning. Adaptive learning technologies react to learner's data and align instructional materials in accordance with students' capabilities and needs (Mikropoulos & Natsis, 2011). AI can also be incorporated in order to offer students a more enjoyable learning experience, which results in increasing their motivation, engagement, and learning outcomes (Wartman & Combs, 2018). Therefore, smart technologies that incorporate AI and machine learning open new ways to achieve learning goals.

Curriculum sequencing technology is one of the major intelligent tutoring solutions that provides students with an individualized sequence of topics and learning tasks most suitable for their learning goals and needs (Brusilovsky & Peylo, 2003). An example of an adaptive learning system is *Duolingo*, a popular adaptive system for learning languages. AI allows Duolingo to personalize learning which incorporates a responsive placement test that automatically adjusts question difficulty depending on the test takers' responses. It also tracks progress and analyzes this data to determine next steps in the learning process. This technology identifies when the learner is ready to move on to the higher levels of difficulty of the instructional materials, including more advanced grammar and vocabulary. Similarly, if the system detects that the learner struggles with the current level, it will re-adjust the difficulty and provide more scaffolding to help learners master the current level before moving forward (Zheng et al., 2017). This example demonstrates how AI-based technologies can provide enhanced opportunities for learning that are specifically tailored to each learner's abilities and skill levels.

AI also takes a prominent place in the development of adaptive hypermedia systems or e-learning systems. To be effective, an educational course or a lesson needs to be designed with the goal to match learners' objectives and needs as closely as possible. This level of truly personalized learning is harder to be realized in a computer-free classroom with dozens of students and only one teacher (Melis et al., 2001), or be achieved using static hypermedia content. Adaptive hypermedia systems can adjust instruction according to students' achievements during the course progression. It adjusts educational tools and content in each hypermedia page in accordance with the learner's data acquired throughout the course (Brusilovsky & Peylo, 2003).

In adaptive hypermedia systems, electronic pages are not static, but dynamically generated specifically for each learner. One example of such a system is an open-source, web-based learning platform called ActiveMath (Melis et al., 2001). ActiveMath is programmed to dynamically assemble interactive math lessons and courses tailored to students' desired learning outcomes, abilities, proficiencies, and preferences. Each course is generated following a set of pedagogical rules.

Another type of advanced AI-based technology that can improve the quality of learning is educational robots. According to Mubin et al. (2013), AI-based robot teaching assistants are most frequently used for *language* and *science* education, while taking on a role of a tool, a tutor, or a peer learner in different learning activities.

Language learning is a common application of educational robots, and they are often used for general language learning, foreign language learning, and bilingual education (Cheng et al., 2018). Students who learn languages in robot-assisted classrooms show high levels of motivation and engagement, and they learn faster and retain more than students in the traditional classes (van den Berghe et al., 2019). In addition, the presence of a non-living educational robot reduces learners' anxiety and self-consciousness about making mistakes, which are common when performing in front of a human teacher. For example, Lee et al. (2011) developed robot educational assistants, Mero and Engkey, who have expressive faces that can represent different emotions like happiness, sadness, fear, joy, pride, shame, and many others. Because emotional expressions play an important role in human–robot interactions, vivid emotional expressions help students feel at ease when interacting with these robots. Mero and Engkey also have an automatic speech recognition that allows them to assist learners in developing their speaking and listening skills in their target language. In addition, learning with a robot companion has also shown to improve students' confidence, interest, and satisfaction from learning as shown by Wang et al. (2013). In their study, the researchers used learning companions shaped like cartoon figures who could perform actions while interacting with language learners, singing songs, and moving around, in addition to practicing conversations in English. Learners who interacted with robot companions demonstrated high levels of concentration and engagement, as well as motivation to practice English. They were also more encouraged to ask questions about correct pronunciations of words and sentences.

Integrating AI-based educational robots in science curriculum provides promising opportunities to engage and motivate learners, as well as increase their learning outcomes. For example, Janssen et al. (2011) describe an adaptive robot game that can motivate children to learn arithmetic. In their study, the researchers used NAO, a programmable humanoid robot developed by Aldebaran Robotics. NAO was able to interpret children's movements and speech, initiate dialogues while interacting with them, and control the screen that showed the educational assignments. The robot was able to adapt the level of the assignments to learners' arithmetic performance and track if it goes beyond the expected level. The results indicated that most students performed significantly higher than their expected levels and were ahead of their arithmetic education due to their interactions with NAO.

AI in Future Education

AI started reshaping the education realm by providing more education administration systems to teachers and administrative staff, and extending its impact on teachers, learners, and the extended practitioners. Hence, the merging of AI also requires new literacy and competence on teaching and learning.

For instructors, the use of AI-enhanced education not only redefined the role of instructors, but also empowered instructors with their decision-making. Instructors are no longer the sole source of knowledge and the only medium of teaching; they are required to become the learning coach for students (Waters & Leong, 2011). Data enhanced teacher decision making has received an increasing amount of attention from educational researchers. Mandinach and Gummer (2016) have noticed that the influx of data and data-powered tools available necessitate new teachers to construct their data literacy, more specifically, AI literacy and AI thinking (Vazhayil et al., 2019).

Additionally, various educational standards also point out the urgency of cultivating students' AI competency to competencies that enable individuals to "critically evaluate AI technologies; communicate and collaborate effectively with AI, and use AI as a tool online, at home, and in the workplace" (Long & Magerko, 2020, p. 2) in the AI era.

Concerns of AI Educational Application

With AI being the powerful and influential tool and its spreading usage in various scenarios in education, two concerns are particularly worth noting to educational researchers and practitioners with regard to the application of available AI products and applications in today's classroom – the potential issue with data collection privacy and transparency, and the equality of AI decision-making. In regard to the wearable technologies like the headband applied in some Chinese schools as mentioned by Panchal and Shaikh Mohammad (2020), although students' biological data is collected to better serve the improvement of their learning achievement, some parents still voiced their concern of the data collection, storage, and accessibility. With no guarantee of the data security, students' digital privacy might be exposed to insecure parties, which might cause unforeseen damage in the future. Hence, digital privacy and data security should both raise the attention of the researchers and promote the research developed along with the machine learning application in education.

Flaws in the AI grading systems are another concern observed from the actual AI application. With the popularity of grading systems implemented in many AI systems, two benefits are observed: relieving teachers from the grading labor and avoiding subjective grading bias. However, since the AI-featured grading system requires training data to establish the baseline for grading criteria, teachers should look out for the potential flaws before implementing the grading system in their own classroom without customizing the grading with data. An example of such a system could be seen used in Graduate Record Examinations (GRE) grading. The grading system enhanced with machine learning is susceptible to human bias. Further improvement and system training is required before serving teachers and learners in regular classrooms.

References

Almasri, A., Ahmed, A., Almasri, N., Abu Sultan, Y. S., Mahmoud, A. Y., Zaqout, I. S., … Abu-Naser, S. S. (2019). Intelligent tutoring systems survey for the period 2000-2018. *International Journal of Academic Engineering Research, 3*(5), 21–37.

Amigud, A., Arnedo-Moreno, J., Daradoumis, T., & Guerrero-Roldan, A. E. (2017). Using learning analytics for preserving academic integrity. *International Review of Research in Open and Distributed Learning: IRRODL, 18*(5), 192–210.

Arnold, K. E., & Pistilli, M. D. (2012). Course signals at Purdue: Using learning analytics to increase student success. In *Proceedings of the 2nd international conference on learning analytics and knowledge* (pp. 267–270). ACM.

Arroway, P., Morgan, G., O'Keefe, M., & Yanosky, R. (2015). *Learning analytics in higher education* (Research report) (p. 17). ECAR, March 2016.

Booth, J. L., McGinn, K. M., Barbieri, C., Begolli, K. N., Chang, B., Miller-Cotto, D., … Davenport, J. L. (2017). Evidence for cognitive science principles that impact learning in mathematics. In *Acquisition of complex arithmetic skills and higher-order mathematics concepts* (pp. 297–325). Academic.

Brusilovsky, P., & Peylo, C. (2003). Adaptive and intelligent web-based educational systems. *International Journal of Artificial Intelligence in Education, 13*(2), 156–169.
Buckingham Shum, S., & Crick, R. D. (2016). Learning analytics for 21st century competencies. *Journal of Learning Analytics, 3*(2), 6–21.
Bundy, A. (2017). Preparing for the future of artificial intelligence. *AI & SOCIETY, 32*, 285–287.
Canales, A., Peña, A., Peredo, R., Sossa, H., & Gutiérrez, A. (2007). Adaptive and intelligent web based education system: Towards an integral architecture and framework. *Expert Systems with Applications, 33*(4), 1076–1089.
Carter, W. A., Kinnucan, E., Elliot, J., Crumpler, W., & Lloyd, K. (2018). *A national machine intelligence strategy for the United States*. Center for Strategic & International Studies.
Chassignol, M., Khoroshavin, A., Klimova, A., & Bilyatdinova, A. (2018). Artificial intelligence trends in education: A narrative overview. *Procedia Computer Science, 136*, 16–24.
Chen, L., Chen, P., & Lin, Z. (2020). Artificial intelligence in education: A review. *IEEE Access, 8*, 75264–75278.
Cheng, Y. W., Sun, P. C., & Chen, N. S. (2018). The essential applications of educational robots: Requirement analysis from the perspectives of experts, researchers and instructors. *Computers & Education, 126*, 399–416.
Deng, L., & Yu, D. (2014). Deep learning: Methods and applications. *Foundations and Trends in Signal Processing, 7*(3–4), 197–387.
Dutt, A., Ismail, M. A., & Herawan, T. (2017). A systematic review on educational data mining. *IEEE Access, 5*, 15991–16005.
ElAtia, S., Ipperciel, D., & Zaïane, O. R. (Eds.). (2016). *Data mining and learning analytics: Applications in educational research*. John Wiley & Sons.
Facer, K. (2011). *Learning futures: Education, technology and social change*. Taylor & Francis.
Fawaz, H. I., Forestier, G., Weber, J., Idoumghar, L., & Muller, P. A. (2019). Deep learning for time series classification: A review. *Data Mining and Knowledge Discovery, 33*(4), 917–963.
Feng, M., Heffernan, N. T., & Koedinger, K. R. (2006). Predicting state test scores better with intelligent tutoring systems: Developing metrics to measure assistance required. In *International conference on intelligent tutoring systems* (pp. 31–40). Springer.
Ferguson, R., Coughlan, T., Egelandsdal, K., Gaved, M., Herodotou, C., Hillaire, G., … Misiejuk, K. (2019). *Innovating pedagogy 2019: Open university innovation report 7*. The Open University, UK.
Gray, C. C., & Perkins, D. (2019). Utilizing early engagement and machine learning to predict student outcomes. *Computers & Education, 131*, 22–32.
Hernández-Blanco, A., Herrera-Flores, B., Tomás, D., & Navarro-Colorado, B. (2019). A systematic review of deep learning approaches to educational data mining. *Complexity, 2019*, 1–22.
Holstein, K., Yu, Z., Sewall, J., Popescu, O., McLaren, B. M., & Aleven, V. (2018, June). Opening up an intelligent tutoring system development environment for extensible student modeling. In *International conference on artificial intelligence in education* (pp. 169–183). Springer.
Ifenthaler, D., Mah, D. K., & Yau, J. Y. K. (2019). Utilising learning analytics for study success: Reflections on current empirical findings. In *Utilizing learning analytics to support study success* (pp. 27–36). Springer.
Ignatov, A., Timofte, R., Chou, W., Wang, K., Wu, M., Hartley, T., & Van Gool, L. (2018). AI benchmark: Running deep neural networks on android smartphones. In *Proceedings of the European conference on computer vision* (pp. 288–314). Springer.
Janssen, J. B., van der Wal, C. C., Neerincx, M. A., & Looije, R. (2011, November). Motivating children to learn arithmetic with an adaptive robot game. In *International conference on social robotics* (pp. 153–162). Springer.
Kahraman, H. T., Sagiroglu, S., & Colak, I. (2010). Development of adaptive and intelligent web-based educational systems. In *2010 4th international conference on application of information and communication technologies* (pp. 1–5). IEEE.
Kukulska-Hulme, A., Beirne, E., Conole, G., Costello, E., Coughlan, T., Ferguson, R., … Mac Lochlainn, C. (2020). *Innovating pedagogy 2020: Open University innovation report 8*. The Open University.

Lacave, C., Molina, A. I., & Cruz-Lemus, J. A. (2018). Learning analytics to identify dropout factors of computer science studies through Bayesian networks. *Behaviour & Information Technology, 37*(10–11), 993–1007.

Lan, A. S., Waters, A. E., Studer, C., & Baraniuk, R. G. (2014). Sparse factor analysis for learning and content analytics. *The Journal of Machine Learning Research, 15*(1), 1959–2008.

LeCun, Y., Bengio, Y., & Hinton, G. (2015). Deep learning. *Nature, 521*, 436–444.

Lee, S., Noh, H., Lee, J., Lee, K., Lee, G. G., Sagong, S., & Kim, M. (2011). On the effectiveness of robot-assisted language learning. *ReCALL, 23*, 25–58.

Long, D., & Magerko, B. (2020, April). What is AI literacy? Competencies and design considerations. In *Proceedings of the 2020 CHI conference on human factors in computing systems* (pp. 1–16).

Mah, D. K. (2016). Learning analytics and digital badges: Potential impact on student retention in higher education. *Technology, Knowledge and Learning, 21*(3), 285–305.

Mandinach, E. B., & Gummer, E. S. (2016). *Data literacy for educators: Making it count in teacher preparation and practice*. Teachers College Press.

Mannila, H. (1996, June). Data mining: Machine learning, statistics, and databases. In *Proceedings of 8th international conference on scientific and statistical Data Base management* (pp. 2–9). IEEE.

Mayo, M., Mitrovic, A., & McKenzie, J. (2000). CAPIT: An intelligent tutoring system for capitalisation and punctuation. In *Proceedings international workshop on advanced learning technologies. IWALT 2000. Advanced learning technology: Design and development issues* (pp. 151–154). IEEE.

Melis, E., Andrès, E., Büdenbender, J., Frishauf, A., Goguadse, G., Libbrecht, P., Pollet, M., & Ullrich, C. (2001). ActiveMath: A web-based learning environment. *International Journal of Artificial Intelligence in Education, 12*(4), 385–407.

Mikropoulos, T. A., & Natsis, A. (2011). Educational virtual environments: A ten-year review of empirical research (1999–2009). *Computers & Education, 56*(3), 769–780.

Mubin, O., Stevens, C. J., Shahid, S., Al Mahmud, A., & Dong, J. J. (2013). A review of the applicability of robots in education. *Journal of Technology in Education and Learning, 1*(209–0015), 13.

Mueen, A., Zafar, B., & Manzoor, U. (2016). Modeling and predicting students' academic performance using data mining techniques. *International Journal of Modern Education and Computer Science, 8*(11), 36.

Mulwa, C., Lawless, S., Sharp, M., Arnedillo-Sanchez, I., & Wade, V. (2010, October). Adaptive educational hypermedia systems in technology enhanced learning: A literature review. In *Proceedings of the 2010 ACM conference on information technology education* (pp. 73–84).

National Science and Technology Council (US). Select Committee on Artificial Intelligence. (2019). *The national artificial intelligence research and development strategic plan: 2019 update*. National Science and Technology Council (US), Select Committee on Artificial Intelligence.

Nguyen, G., Dlugolinsky, S., Bobák, M., Tran, V., García, Á. L., Heredia, I., … Hluchý, L. (2019). Machine learning and deep learning frameworks and libraries for large-scale data mining: A survey. *Artificial Intelligence Review, 52*(1), 77–124.

Panchal, K., & Shaikh Mohammad, B. N. (2020). Artificial intelligence used in schools of China. In *Proceedings of the 3rd international conference on advances in science & technology (ICAST) 2020* (pp. 1–5).

Peredo, R., Canales, A., Menchaca, A., & Peredo, I. (2011). Intelligent web-based education system for adaptive learning. *Expert Systems with Applications, 38*(12), 14690–14702.

Pokrivcakova, S. (2019). Preparing teachers for the application of AI-powered technologies in foreign language education. *Journal of Language and Cultural Education, 7*(3), 135–153.

Psotka, J. (2012). Interactive learning environments. In N. M. Seel (Ed.), *Encyclopedia of the sciences of learning*. Springer.

Romero, C., & Ventura, S. (2010). Educational data mining: A review of the state of the art. *IEEE Transactions on Systems, Man, and Cybernetics, Part C (Applications and Reviews), 40*(6), 601–618.
Rus, V., D'Mello, S., Hu, X., & Graesser, A. (2013). Recent advances in conversational intelligent tutoring systems. *AI Magazine, 34*(3), 42–54.
Santamaría-Bonfil, G., Ibáñez, M. B., Pérez-Ramírez, M., Arroyo-Figueroa, G., & Martínez-Álvarez, F. (2020). Learning analytics for student modeling in virtual reality training systems: Lineworkers case. *Computers & Education, 151*, 1–19.
Schmid, E. C., & Hegelheimer, V. (2014). Collaborative research projects in the technology-enhanced language classroom: Pre-service and in-service teachers exchange knowledge about technology. *ReCALL: the Journal of EUROCALL, 26*(3), 315.
Sharma, R. C., Kawachi, P., & Bozkurt, A. (2019). The landscape of artificial intelligence in open, online and distance education: Promises and concerns. *Asian Journal of Distance Education, 14*(2), 1–2.
Sivakumar, S., Venkataraman, S., & Selvaraj, R. (2016). Predictive modeling of student dropout indicators in educational data mining using improved decision tree. *Indian Journal of Science and Technology, 9*(4), 1–5.
Timms, M. J. (2016). Letting artificial intelligence in education out of the box: Educational cobots and smart classrooms. *International Journal of Artificial Intelligence in Education, 26*(2), 701–712.
United States. Executive Office of the President and M. Holden, J.P. Smith. (2016, October). *Preparing for the future of artificial intelligence* (Technical report). National Science and Technology Council. 20502.
van de Pol, J., Volman, M., & Beishuizen, J. (2010). Scaffolding in teacher–student interaction: A decade of research. *Educational Psychology Review, 22*(3), 271–296.
van den Berghe, R., Verhagen, J., Oudgenoeg-Paz, O., van der Ven, S., & Leseman, P. (2019). Social robots for language learning: A review. *Review of Educational Research, 89*(2), 259–295.
Vazhayil, A., Shetty, R., Bhavani, R. R., & Akshay, N. (2019, December). Focusing on teacher education to introduce AI in schools: Perspectives and illustrative findings. In *2019 IEEE tenth international conference on Technology for Education (T4E)* (pp. 71–77). IEEE.
Viberg, O., Khalil, M., & Baars, M. (2020, March). Self-regulated learning and learning analytics in online learning environments: A review of empirical research. In *Proceedings of the tenth international conference on learning analytics & knowledge* (pp. 524–533).
Wang, A. J. A., & Qian, K. (2005). *Component-oriented programming*. John Wiley & Sons.
Wang, Y. H., Young, S. S.-C., & Jang, J.-S. R. (2013). Using tangible companions for enhancing learning English conversation. *Journal of Educational Technology & Society, 16*, 296–309.
Wartman, S. A., & Combs, C. D. (2018). Medical education must move from the information age to the age of artificial intelligence. *Academic Medicine, 93*(8), 1107–1109.
Waters, L. H., & Leong, P. (2011, June). New roles for the teacher and learning coach in blended learning for K-12. In *EdMedia+ innovate learning* (pp. 2716–2725). Association for the Advancement of Computing in Education (AACE).
Zheng, N. N., Liu, Z. Y., Ren, P. J., Ma, Y. Q., Chen, S. T., Yu, S. Y., … Wang, F. Y. (2017). Hybrid-augmented intelligence: Collaboration and cognition. *Frontiers of Information Technology & Electronic Engineering, 18*(2), 153–179.
Zhou, Y., Huang, C., Hu, Q., Zhu, J., & Tang, Y. (2018). Personalized learning full-path recommendation model based on LSTM neural networks. *Information Sciences, 444*, 135–152.

Dr. Nanxi Meng works as the senior lecturer of language education at University of North Texas. She received her doctoral degree in Learning Technologies at the College of Information, University of North Texas. Her research interests include language and culture acquisition, instructional design, PBL and application in higher education and pedagogy and teacher education.

Tetyana K. Dhimolea is a doctoral candidate at the University of North Texas (UNT) in learning technologies with a minor in curriculum and instruction. Tetyana's research interests lie in immersive virtual reality (VR) development and application for education and training, computer-assisted language learning, and digital game-based learning environments.

Zain Ali in a clinical professor and program director for graduate and professional studies at University of North Texas (UNT) at Frisco. Prior to graduate director role, he started the experiential learning program for UNT at Frisco which is now in its third year of operations. Zain brings 31 years of cross industry and academia experience by serving over 70 clients in 10 plus countries as a consultant or as an employee including leadership roles in engineering, operations, sales, and technology. His tenure has allowed him to work with a few start-up companies as well as several Fortune 100 clients like Bombardier, Emerson Electric, Schlumberger, AT&T, Amerisource Bergen, Mack Trucks, Renault VI, Raytheon, etc. while working for consulting companies like Accenture, The Hackett Group, and Wipro.

In 2009, Zain started his first company Sunbonn, a global consulting and technology company, where he is now the Chairman of the Board. Zain also provides strategic consulting and advisory services as part of his second company, Azvantage. Zain is the author of the book *Cultivate Your Leader*, creator of multiple mobile applications, and currently focused on building a customizable multi-rater leadership development platform that uses AI and ML to enhance mentoring. Zain is also currently pursuing his PhD in learning technologies at UNT.

Supporting Social and Emotional Well-Being with Artificial Intelligence

Tetyana K. Dhimolea, Regina Kaplan-Rakowski, and Lin Lin

Introduction

To develop future learning and workforce capacity, it is important to examine the capacity for future learning, which includes the mental, emotional, and social well-being. The World Health Organization (WHO) repeatedly emphasizes the importance of health, which is defined as "a state of complete physical, mental, and social well-being and not merely the absence of disease or infirmity" (WHO, 2019). It is not enough to have a fit and healthy body. Balanced mental and emotional states play an integral role in keeping people truly sane. They also affect human decisions and cognition, directly relating to people's feelings of happiness, satisfaction, sadness, or loneliness.

Traditionally, physical health is given more emphasis in the modern healthcare system as people are encouraged to regularly check their physical parameters. Psychological well-being is less likely to receive the same level of attention and care; consequently, people tend to neglect their mental health (Mitchell, 2009). In addition, physical issues are relatively easy to diagnose because they often cause unambiguous and explicit symptoms that disrupt people's everyday lives. While psychological states also may cause serious harm, such conditions are more difficult to identify and diagnose. Many people may not realize that they are suffering from mental disorders, possibly confusing clinical depression with sadness, or bipolar disorder with mood swings.

While deterioration of physical health is natural or even expected, especially with age, mental health that is compromised is rarely considered "common." Therefore, individuals who exhibit mental health issues may naturally fear being

T. K. Dhimolea (✉) · R. Kaplan-Rakowski · L. Lin
University of North Texas, Denton, TX, USA
e-mail: Tetyana.Kucher@unt.edu; Regina.Kaplanrakowski@unt.edu; Lin.Lin@unt.edu

M. V. Albert et al. (eds.), *Bridging Human Intelligence and Artificial Intelligence*, Educational Communications and Technology: Issues and Innovations, https://doi.org/10.1007/978-3-030-84729-6_8

judged, outcast, or simply *stigmatized.* The concept of *perceived public stigma* is defined as the degree to which the general public holds judgmental views and discriminates against a public group (Inkster et al., 2018). Mental health stigma often explains the discrepancies between administrative records and self-reports, where survey respondents tend to under-report their mental issues compared to other health concerns (Bharadwaj et al., 2017). Fortunately, modern technology is increasingly capable of assisting those who may need help but fear being stigmatized. Artificial intelligence (AI)-based systems, such as built-in sensors in wearable technology paired with smartphones, are capable of augmenting prediction and evaluation of mental conditions (Naslund et al., 2016). Other examples of AI-based products useful in addressing mental and emotional needs include conversational chatbots, virtual assistants, and socially assistive robots.

Contemporary developments in the field of AI offer technologies capable of addressing mental health conditions and issues related to social and emotional well-being. Moreover, AI also shows potential for diagnosing important psychological disorders in their early stages and provides new pathways to treatment (Kamath et al., 2018). AI-based technologies, such as therapeutic chatbots and socially assistive robots, can conduct regular mental health check-ups to help people keep track of their emotional states and offer social companionship (Banks et al., 2008).

Keeping AI-based technology as the main focus of this chapter, we provide an overview discussing two factors that undermine human emotional and mental states. These are compromised mental conditions (e.g., depression or anxiety) and lack of social interactions (e.g., loneliness or social isolation). The discussion embraces the assistive benefits of AI-based technology, together with the challenges regarding its use.

Mental Health

Depression and Anxiety

The Global Burden of Diseases, Injuries, and Risk Factors Study (James et al., 2018) stated that depressive disorders affect almost 5% of the human population. According to the WHO, depression is caused by complex interaction of social, psychological, and biological factors which may lead to stress and dysfunction, consequently, worsening the affected person's life. Severe depression can even lead to suicide, which was the second leading cause of death among people aged 15–29 years globally in 2015 (WHO, 2017). It is projected that depression will become a number one cause of disability by 2030, ahead of cardiovascular disease and traffic accidents (WHO, 2008).

In the USA alone, more than half a million individuals have reported signs of anxiety and/or depression (Reinert et al., 2021). The number of people suffering from depression was boosted by the outbreak of the COVID-19 pandemic, raising the need for emotional support even more than before (Kaplan-Rakowski, 2020).

College students, in particular, exhibit symptoms of depression and anxiety, with the majority reporting their state to be so grave that it impedes them from sound functioning (Zivin et al., 2009). In 2021, almost 60% of youth with depression did not receive any mental health treatment, and even in the United States with the greatest access to mental health support resources, one in three do not receive help (Reinert et al., 2021).

One of the ways that AI-based technology is useful for coping with anxiety and depression is the implementation of automated conversational agents, called conversational chatbots. A conversational chatbot is a digital system that has the ability to interact with human users by holding conversations with them in a natural language (Shawar & Atwell, 2007). Therapeutic chatbots are designed to promote mental health and health education. They also have a capability to guide patients to improve their well-being. Such technology is claimed to be affordable, lasting, and convenient (Fulmer et al., 2018), especially to those who are less likely to seek help. Zivin et al. (2009) report that college students, despite having access to supportive sources on campus, often do not take advantage of those resources due to stigma.

Academic performance and mental well-being are interrelated, but because most educational institutions are not designed to cater to students' personal needs, some researchers propose a design of an AI-enhanced mental health-oriented chatbot for education. AI therapeutic chatbots are not complete substitutes for human medical support. Rather, as research increasingly shows, they can act as adjuncts to therapy. According to Dekker et al. (2020), the incorporation of online mental health chatbot interventions shows promising results when it comes to improving students' academic performance, mental health, and subjective well-being. In another example, a therapeutic chatbot, Tess, was able to provide personalized interventions, thanks to its ability to identify emotions based on dialogues (Fulmer et al., 2018). It could also build its memory based on the feeds coming from patients and their medical records. Over the course of a few weeks, college students' implementation of Tess in their therapy diminished symptoms of depression and anxiety.

According to a study of physicians' ($N = 100$) perceptions (Palanica et al., 2019), chatbots were effective in providing support, motivation, and guidance to patients. Physicians found chatbots to be beneficial for proper diet regulation, medication adherence, and wellness maintenance. Chatbots were perceived as a logistical aid in that they helped patients keep up with their medical appointments. Chatbots knew how to deal with administrative tasks and were helpful in finding answers to typical medication queries. In other words, chatbots were perceived as potentially adequate aids for nonmedical care. Meanwhile, the challenge remains in that chatbots are not fully able to identify the exact human emotional states.

Similar to Tess, an empathy-driven, conversational AI agent named Wysa was used with the goal to digitally support mental well-being (Inkster et al., 2018). The majority of Wysa users described the app as "invigorating" and "supportive," and frequent Wysa users gained greater benefits over the users who used the app only occasionally. Overall, the implementation of this conversational AI agent offered a considerable boost in the amelioration of mental health problems (Fig. 1).

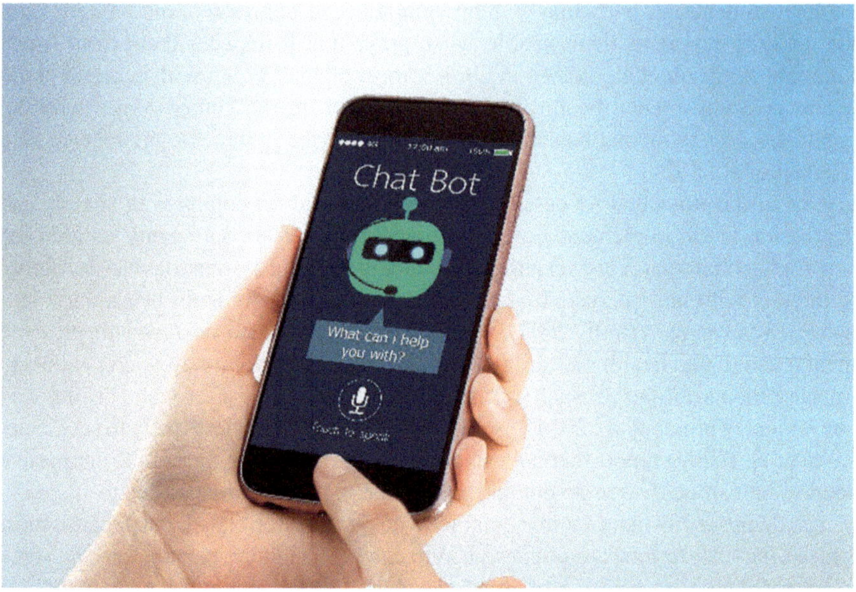

Fig. 1 An example of an AI-based virtual assistant or therapeutic chatbot

While conversational chatbots typically rely on text-only communication, graphic representations in the form of avatars increasingly show promise in providing mental health support. Ellie, as described in a study by Rizzo et al. (2016), is a software-based virtual human agent using automatic interaction that was used to evaluate how trustworthy such avatars would be perceived. It appeared that most users were willing and comfortable to share their information with Ellie. Such an outcome indicates a likelihood that adding the graphical representation in the form of avatars, rather than just simple text, may facilitate better social connections.

Another, even more progressive step in mental healthcare, is the inclusion of socially assistive robots (SARs). These types of robots engage in social interaction with patients, with the goal to help patients cope with challenging mental conditions (Feil-Seifer & Matarić, 2011; Rabbitt et al., 2015). Thanks to modern developments in robotics, different types of SARs exist with some specifically developed and evaluated for depression treatment. NAO is an example of a programmable humanoid robot which was found to have positive effects on reducing depression levels in hospitalized children diagnosed with cancer (Alemi et al., 2014). NAO demonstrated the ability to display sympathetic emotions using body movements and voice intonations, which contributed to the strengthening of the relationship between the SAR and the child. These aspects of verbal and non-verbal interactions play a crucial role in building social connections. Consequently, they may help reduce signs of depression.

Another tested SAR is a doe-eyed seal pup called Paro (see Fig. 2) that has been used in nursing homes since the early 2000s. Paro has been shown to calm seniors

Fig. 2 An AI-based robotic therapeutic pet seal, Paro

with its cooing sounds and gently waving flippers. In the study by Wada et al. (2005), prolonged interactions with Paro led to improved moods and decreased signs of depression in the elderly people at a health service facility.

It is becoming evident that the main functions of SARs are those of a companion, coach, and therapeutic play partner (Rabbitt et al., 2015). It is likely that the increasing success of SARs to build stronger connections with humans is due to their robot-humanoid construction. As opposed to SARs, simple chatbots have a limited ability to socially connect with humans.

Social Interactions

Social and Emotional Well-Being

The assistive AI-based technology is not solely limited to helping individuals with depression and anxiety. In the last decade, researchers and healthcare professionals have also been implementing chatbots, virtual agents, and SARs to assist people who are negatively impacted by loneliness and social isolation. These mental states are known to deteriorate health, well-being, and exacerbate mortality rates (Holt-Lunstad et al., 2015).

The concerns of the negative impact of loneliness and social isolation gained increased attention due to the outbreak of the COVID-19 pandemic in 2019. During the pandemic, people worldwide needed to adhere to social distancing protocols, declining their mental health and well-being (Pietrabissa & Simpson, 2020). The awareness and empathy toward people suffering from loneliness and social distancing have been growing, motivating researchers to study how different emergent technologies, such as virtual reality, can help people cope with social isolation (Dhimolea & Kaplan-Rakowski, 2021) or anxiety (Kaplan-Rakowski et al., 2021). Similarly, the development of AI-based robot assistants received more attention since the pandemic outbreak (Henkel et al., 2020).

Any individual can suffer from the lack of social interactions; however, seniors' emotional and physical well-being are affected by loneliness at overwhelmingly high rates (Cotten et al., 2013). According to a meta-analysis by Holt-Lunstad et al. (2015), "the risk associated with social isolation and loneliness is comparable with well-established risk factors for mortality" (p. 20) such as obesity and substance abuse. Therefore, it is not surprising that AI is being increasingly used to improve care for aging seniors by means of both physical assistance and social companionship.

Living alone can have life-threatening consequences for people suffering from mental or physical conditions and those who require regular care and support. In a study by Wang et al. (2017), robot-caregivers assisted older adults with Alzheimer's disease in everyday tasks such as washing hands and making tea. The idea of assistive robots was welcomed by the caregivers and family members, but the older adults were less enthusiastic about bringing these robots home. One of their concerns was directly related to the fears of the effect that the increased communication with the robots may have on their relationship with loved ones. People value spending time together with family, which is particularly important in cases of people with Alzheimer's disease who know that their abilities are declining (Wang et al., 2017). While robot caregivers may provide valuable practical support in dealing with health conditions, the study showed that seniors were not ready to give up real social interactions in return.

Apart from providing medical care, modern AI-based technologies can also offer social companionship, which is a particularly valuable quality to improve social and emotional well-being, especially during the global pandemic. Even interactions with virtual assistants like Siri and Alexa can considerably reduce people's sense of loneliness as they can ask these personal assistants for news, weather updates, music and book tips, crossword puzzle clues, and even jokes (Savage, 2020).

Various high-tech projects are testing the limits of AI as a potential tool to foster a sense of companionship for the world's older residents. One such invention is a virtual care assistant, Mabu, developed by Catalia Health (Kidd, 2015). Mabu can set reminders and manage patients' prescriptions, but it can also create meaningful conversations that are tailored to and build on the user's specific memories. Seniors who had conversations with Mabu gladly shared deeply personal stories from their lives and genuinely enjoyed their conversations with the friendly robot. The seniors were not embarrassed by the fact that they were sharing their life stories with a non-living object. The sense of human presence that Mabu created encouraged the seniors to reminisce about their past and share their happy moments with the robot.

Fig. 3 AI-based robotic pet dog, Aibo, developed by Sony Corporation

In another case, researchers used a robotic dog Aibo to provide animal-assisted therapy in nursing homes (Banks et al., 2008). Surprisingly, the interactions with Aibo resulted in the same improvement rates in the residents' mood and sense of loneliness as interactions with real therapeutic dogs. Residents also displayed high levels of attachment to both the living dog and the robotic dog. Having a dog is a serious commitment that often requires owners to make significant changes to their lifestyles and to increase their daily expenses, while most seniors cannot afford to take on such a responsibility. Therefore, if AI-based robotic pets, like Aibo, can improve users' emotional well-being without adding extra responsibility and commitment, then the avenues of animal-assisted therapy development would require further exploration and research (Fig. 3).

Robot Personification and Emotional Attachment

As robots are being continuously improved to look and act more like living beings, it is becoming common for people to start treating them as such. Numerous examples demonstrate that people are inclined to personify advanced AI-based robots, especially humanoid robots. For example, in 2017, Sophia, the social humanoid robot developed by Hanson Robotics, became the first robot ever to have been granted citizenship (Hanson Robotics, 2017). In addition, Sophia was frequently "interviewed" by popular media outlets such as CNBC, Forbes, New York Times, the Wall Street Journal, and the Guardian, which suggests her human-like perception by the public.

Another example of people personifying robots was observed through their interactions with a robot companion named Pepper. Pepper can recognize human emotions by detecting and analyzing their facial expressions, and it can even adapt its behavior depending on the users' perceived mood. These advanced functionalities often make people perceive Pepper as a humanoid with a real personality and real feelings, and Chanseau (2016) took this idea one step further by stating that "in this sense we can say that Pepper cares for people." (Fig. 4)

Personification of robot companions by humans marks a significant step in the development of AI. People often knowingly treat these intelligent robots as humans with their own personality traits and behavior patterns. This tendency persists even when developers emphasize the non-human nature of the robots, such as Woebot, a virtual chatbot with a very distinctly robot-like name. In one study, the participants kept referring to Woebot as "he," "a friend," and "a fun little dude," which suggested that users continued to empathize with the robot due to its behavior, not its representation created by the developers (Fitzpatrick et al., 2017). This fascinating finding confirms that robots can establish trusting and therapeutic relationships with humans, which can be effectively used in the context of mental health treatment.

Humans are evidently social beings, and it is not unusual for them to develop affection toward inanimate objects in a similar way that children personify their

Fig. 4 Semi-humanoid robot, Pepper, with the ability to read human emotions

favorite toys by giving them real names and talking to them. This idea has been taken up by the popular culture in cinematography, such as the movie "Her" in which a man builds a relationship with a smart, voice-operated system called Samantha. While the movie shows an exaggerated image of the AI's ability to develop relationships with humans, it is not surprising that a sophisticated social robot that can maintain an intelligent conversation is well capable of establishing connections with humans. Astrid Weiss, a human–robot interaction researcher, put it best in her TED Talk when she said, "It's not reasonable to treat a computer like another human. [But] we simply do it [because] the social interaction is a deeply rooted human need" (Weiss, 2017).

Virtual assistants and personal robot assistants are also capable of interacting in ways similar to humans, but they are commonly designed as functional devices that can perform specific tasks rather than acting as conversational agents. Virtual assistants, such as Siri, Alexa, and Google Home, can report weather, set reminders, make calls, manage schedules, and perform other functions. They become more human-like in the ways that they sound or interact by adapting to users' needs and increasing the feeling that users are interacting with people rather than objects. However, even though those systems sound friendly and may tell you an occasional joke if you ask them to, they offer only brief personal encounters with humans. To confirm this idea, the press release by Apple (2011) introducing Siri stresses its practicality in the functions, inferring that it is not designed to build human-like relationships or provide emotional support.

Some AI systems were created for the sole purpose to help people develop affection for them. Some would argue that the ability to invoke feelings of care is a practical function if we keep in mind the life-threatening consequences of severe loneliness described by Holt-Lunstad et al. (2015). Examples of such AI systems are robot pets which have been commercially available for years offering their companionship for elderly people (Jeffrey-Wilensky, 2019). There are no explicit practical benefits to pet robots' functionality, however, a doe-eyed seal pup Paro (Fig. 2) mentioned earlier, has been shown to calm seniors with its cooing sounds and gently waving flippers. In recent years, companies that develop robot companions began to target an audience beyond seniors in need of social connection (Baggaley, 2019).

Another robotic pet called Lovot is described by their creators as "born for just one reason — to be loved by you," emphasizing the feeling of relaxation and calmness that users are promised to get from interacting with it. They claim that they have used technology to enhance levels of comfort and feelings of love similar to feeling love toward another person (Lovot, 2020). The success of these AI companions, despite the price tag, shows younger people's high need for the feeling of love.

Social and Psychological Development

As the fields of AI and robotics become more advanced, and virtual assistants and robots become more human-like or animal-like in both form and functionality, the question of formalizing robot rights becomes increasingly relevant. There is an ongoing debate among researchers as to whether social robots are things or agents, and Alač (2016) claims that they have both the agential and social characteristics as the robot in their study was "treated as a living creature while it is handled as a material thing" (p. 533).

Robot abuse is one of the most frequently observed behavior patterns when people interact with robots (Ku et al., 2018). Ku et al. emphasize the importance for everyone to understand that robots must be treated fairly if they are to be fully integrated into human society. They developed a tortoise-like robot, Shelly, designed to study how children's abusive behaviors toward a robot can be reduced. When the children displayed abusive behaviors toward Shelly, the robot hid its head inside the shell and temporarily stopped any interactions. The children had to change their behavior toward Shelly in order to continue playing with it.

The findings presented by Ku et al. (2018) showed that Shelly's "hiding" feedback considerably reduced robot abuse by the children. Moreover, the study encouraged children to mutually restrain their inappropriate behaviors in other social situations, even those unrelated to Shelly. These findings show how robots can positively impact children's understanding and development of the appropriate social interaction practices. It is likely that in the future robots will become ubiquitous in our lives, and researchers believe that teaching children to be empathetic toward robots may help them be more empathetic toward living beings as well.

Challenges

Despite the benefits of modern technological advancements and the capabilities of AI-based technologies to address issues related to depression and anxiety, as well as offer companionships to people in need of social connections, concerns remain regarding whether robot companions and virtual assistants count as connections or confidants. In a discussion about whether social robots can become a quality substitute for human contact, Kiron and Unruh (2018) argue that even though AI products may fulfill human needs for social connections, they may also change social norms in irreversible ways. The question they pose is, "Even if AI can cure loneliness – should it?" It is an important question to consider in regard to human abilities to establish connections with other humans, and whether excessive interactions with social robots can affect the authenticity of this human attribute.

While interactions with therapeutic chatbots have shown to positively impact people's mental states, they are not yet capable of providing autonomous medical support, but rather serve as adjuncts to existing therapy. In addition, social robots that are designed to recognize human emotions build the strategy of their interactions, based on the emotions they identify. This practice raises ethical concerns when social robots may interpret human emotions inaccurately. Such misinterpretation may negatively impact people's emotional states, which largely diminishes the benefits of these AI-based systems, potentially causing unproductive or even harmful interactions.

The accessibility and affordability aspects of AI-based solutions for mental health and social well-being are another challenge associated with the use of this technology. While most therapeutic chatbots and other virtual conversational agents are easily accessible for anyone who owns a smartphone, robot companions and social robots are considerably more difficult and more expensive to obtain. The price for consumer-oriented social robots may reach thousands of dollars (Sardis, 2018), and such a high cost significantly slows down the integration of this technology for commercial use. As with most technological innovations, it is expected that with time, SARs will become more affordable and more advanced.

Concepts of privacy also raise concerns among certain AI users. To build personal connections with humans tailored specifically to their personalities and behaviors, social robots are often programmed to move around, scan environments, record their verbal and non-verbal interactions with users, and track their daily routines (Fosch-Villaronga et al., 2019). These behaviors allow robots to access and collect private data about individuals' daily lives. Therefore, questions arise regarding the security of this information and preventing the data from being used for unwanted purposes without the users' consent. If there were a security breach and the robot was hacked, which has already happened in the Internet of Things (IoT) community (CISOMAG, 2020), there is a risk of releasing such sensitive information collected by social robots, or even modifying the behaviors of therapeutic robots which could have a devastating impact on individuals' mental health.

Looking into the future, much still needs to be improved in the spheres of AI and robotics, and challenges will continue to emerge as new technologies are being introduced to the public. Consumers need to stay mindful of the challenges of AI-based systems, as well as be aware of the direct positive and negative impact that social robots and robot assistants might have on their lives. Understanding the affordances and limitations of these AI-based technologies can help users maximize the benefits they can get from socializing with these systems without sacrificing privacy, emotional well-being, and the ability to build meaningful social connections with humans.

Conclusions

With the growing rate of mental health issues reported in the world each year, it is critical to continue developing new solutions to address the issues of psychological health and emotional well-being. In this chapter, we discussed the affordances of AI-based technologies with regard to dealing with depression, anxiety, and the lack of social interactions, which can considerably undermine human emotional and mental states. We recognize that there are numerous other critical mental conditions that assistive AI-based technologies can address, such as autism spectrum disorder, post-traumatic stress disorder, and bi-polar disorder, and AI systems will continue to advance and address these conditions, along with other mental health concerns.

AI-based systems such as therapeutic chatbots, virtual assistants, and SARs have a strong potential to positively impact mental health by helping people deal with depression and anxiety, as well as offer a sense of companionship, evoke emotional attachment, and even assist with social and emotional development. While some concerns regarding the effectiveness, dependability, and cost of this technology still exist, we hope that as technology progresses and becomes more affordable, people will increasingly benefit from AI-based tools to improve their social and emotional well-being.

References

Alač, M. (2016). Social robots: Things or agents? *AI & Society, 31*(4), 519–535.

Alemi, M., Meghdari, A., Ghanbarzadeh, A., Moghadam, L. J., & Ghanbarzadeh, A. (2014, October). Effect of utilizing a humanoid robot as a therapy-assistant in reducing anger, anxiety, and depression. In *2014 Second RSI/ISM International Conference on Robotics and Mechatronics (ICRoM)* (pp. 748–753). IEEE.

Apple (2011, October 4). *Apple Launches iPhone 4S, iOS 5 & iCloud* [Press release]. https://www.apple.com/newsroom/2011/10/04Apple-Launches-iPhone-4S-iOS-5-iCloud/

Baggaley, K. (2019, June 23). New companion robots can't do much but make us love them. *NBC News*. https://www.nbcnews.com/mach/science/new-companion-robots-can-t-do-much-make-us-love-ncna1015986

Banks, M. R., Willoughby, L. M., & Banks, W. A. (2008). Animal-assisted therapy and loneliness in nursing homes: Use of robotic versus living dogs. *Journal of the American Medical Directors Association, 9*(3), 173–177.

Bharadwaj, P., Pai, M. M., & Suziedelyte, A. (2017). Mental health stigma. *Economics Letters, 159*, 57–60.

Chanseau, A. (2016, August 6). *Robot companions are coming into our homes – So how human should they be?* The Conversation. https://theconversation.com/robot-companions-are-coming-into-our-homes-so-how-human-should-they-be-63154

CISOMAG. (2020, January 10). *10 IoT security incidents that make you feel less secure.* Retrieved from: https://cisomag.eccouncil.org/10-iot-security-incidents-that-make-you-feel-less-secure/

Cotten, S. R., Anderson, W. A., & McCullough, B. M. (2013). Impact of internet use on loneliness and contact with others among older adults: Cross-sectional analysis. *Journal of Medical Internet Research, 15*(2), e39.

Dekker, I., De Jong, E. M., Schippers, M. C., Bruijn-Smolders, D., Alexiou, A., & Giesbers, B. (2020). Optimizing Students' mental health and academic performance: Ai-enhanced life crafting. *Frontiers in Psychology, 11*, 1063.

Dhimolea, K. T., & Kaplan-Rakowski, R. (2021). *Virtual reality to cope with social isolation during the pandemic*. SSRN.

Feil-Seifer, D., & Matarić, M. J. (2011). Socially assistive robotics. *IEEE Robotics & Automation Magazine, 18*(1), 24–31.

Fitzpatrick, K. K., Darcy, A., & Vierhile, M. (2017). Delivering cognitive behavior therapy to young adults with symptoms of depression and anxiety using a fully automated conversational agent (Woebot): A randomized controlled trial. *JMIR Mental Health, 4*(2), 1–11.

Fosch-Villaronga, E., Lutz, C., & Tamò-Larrieux, A. (2019). Gathering expert opinions for social robots' ethical, legal, and societal concerns: Findings from four international workshops. *International Journal of Social Robotics, 12*, 1–18.

Fulmer, R., Joerin, A., Gentile, B., Lakerink, L., & Rauws, M. (2018). Using psychological artificial intelligence (Tess) to relieve symptoms of depression and anxiety: Randomized controlled trial. *JMIR Mental Health, 5*(4), e64.

Hanson Robotics. (2017). *Sophia*. https://www.hansonrobotics.com/sophia/
Henkel, A. P., Čaić, M., Blaurock, M., & Okan, M. (2020). Robotic transformative service research: Deploying social robots for consumer well-being during Covid-19 and beyond. *Journal of Service Management, 31*(6), 1131–1148.
Holt-Lunstad, J., Smith, T. B., Baker, M., Harris, T., & Stephenson, D. (2015). Loneliness and social isolation as risk factors for mortality: A meta-analytic review. *Perspectives on Psychological Science, 10*(2), 227–237.
Inkster, B., Sarda, S., & Subramanian, V. (2018). An empathy-driven, conversational artificial intelligence agent (Wysa) for digital mental well-being: Real-world data evaluation mixed-methods study. *JMIR mHealth and uHealth, 6*(11), e12106.
James, S. L., Abate, D., Abate, K. H., Abay, S. M., Abbafati, C., Abbasi, N., et al. (2018). Global, regional, and national incidence, prevalence, and years lived with disability for 354 diseases and injuries for 195 countries and territories, 1990–2017: A systematic analysis for the Global Burden of Disease Study 2017. *The Lancet, 392*(10159), 1789–1858. https://www.thelancet.com/journals/lancet/article/PIIS0140-6736(18)32279-7/fulltext
Jeffrey-Wilensky, J. (2019, April 3). *Why robotic pets may be the next big thing in dementia care. NBC News.* https://www.nbcnews.com/mach/science/why-robotic-pets-dementia-care-may-be-next-big-thing-ncna990166
Kamath, A., Raje, N., Konduri, S., Shah, H., Naik, V., Bhattacharjee, K., et al. (2018, September). Intelligent AI assisted psychological disorder analysis using sentiment inference. In *2018 International conference on advances in computing, communications and informatics (ICACCI)* (pp. 24–27). IEEE.
Kaplan-Rakowski, R. (2020). Addressing students' emotional needs during the COVID-19 pandemic: A perspective on text versus video feedback in online environments. *Educational Technology Research and Development*, 1–4.
Kaplan-Rakowski, Johnson, & Wojdynski. (2021). *The impact of virtual reality and video-based meditation on college students' test performance*. SSRN.
Kidd, C. (2015, June 12). *Introducing the Mabu personal healthcare companion.* Catalia Health. https://www.cataliahealth.com/introducing-the-mabu-personal-healthcare-companion/
Kiron, D., & Unruh, G. (2018, November 9). *Even if AI can cure loneliness — Should it?* MIT Sloan. https://sloanreview.mit.edu/article/even-if-ai-can-cure-loneliness-should-it/
Ku, H., Choi, J. J., Lee, S., Jang, S., & Do, W. (2018, March). Designing Shelly, a robot capable of assessing and restraining children's robot abusing behaviors. In *Companion of the 2018 ACM/IEEE International Conference on Human-Robot Interaction* (pp. 161–162).
Lovot. (2020). *LOVOT*. https://lovot.life/en/
Mitchell, A. J. (2009, December 16). *Why depression is hard to diagnose.* Clinical Advisor. https://www.clinicaladvisor.com/home/commentary/why-depression-is-hard-to-diagnose/
Naslund, J. A., Aschbrenner, K. A., & Bartels, S. J. (2016). Wearable devices and smartphones for activity tracking among people with serious mental illness. *Mental Health and Physical Activity, 10*, 10–17.
Palanica, A., Flaschner, P., Thommandram, A., Li, M., & Fossat, Y. (2019). Physicians' perceptions of chatbots in health care: Cross-sectional web-based survey. *Journal of Medical Internet Research, 21*(4), e12887.
Pietrabissa, G., & Simpson, S. G. (2020). Psychological consequences of social isolation during COVID-19 outbreak. *Frontiers in Psychology, 11*, 2201.
Rabbitt, S. M., Kazdin, A. E., & Scassellati, B. (2015). Integrating socially assistive robotics into mental healthcare interventions: Applications and recommendations for expanded use. *Clinical Psychology Review, 35*, 35–46.
Reinert, M., Nguyen, T., & Fritze, D. (2021). *2021 The state of mental health in America* [White paper]. Mental Health America, Alexandria, VA. https://mhanational.org/sites/default/files/2021%20State%20of%20Mental%20Health%20in%20America_0.pdf
Rizzo, A., Shilling, R., Forbell, E., Scherer, S., Gratch, J., & Morency, L. P. (2016). Autonomous virtual human agents for healthcare information support and clinical interviewing. In *Artificial intelligence in behavioral and mental health care* (pp. 53–79). Academic.

Sardis, B. (2018, September 1). *What are social robots & how do they help the elderly age in place better & longer?*. Tech for Aging. https://techforaging.com/social-robots/
Savage, M. (2020, March 26). *Voice technologies using AI are being used to help combat loneliness in countries including Sweden and the UK. Should they be used more widely as coronavirus spreads?* BBC. https://www.bbc.com/worklife/article/20200325-can-voice-technologies-using-ai-fight-elderly-loneliness
Shawar, B. A., & Atwell, E. (2007, April). Different measurement metrics to evaluate a chatbot system. In *Proceedings of the workshop on bridging the gap: Academic and industrial research in dialog technologies* (pp. 89–96).
Wada, K., Shibata, T., Saito, T., Sakamoto, K., & Taine, K. (2005, April). Psychological and social effects of one year robot assisted activity on elderly people at a health service facility for the aged. In *Proceedings of the 2005 IEEE international conference on robotics and automation* (pp. 2785–2790). IEEE.
Wang, R. H., Sudhama, A., Begum, M., Huq, R., & Mihailidis, A. (2017). Robots to assist daily activities: Views of older adults with Alzheimer's disease and their caregivers. *International Psychogeriatrics, 29*(1), 67–79.
Weiss, A. (2017, July). *Will care robots care?* [Video]. TED Conferences. https://www.youtube.com/watch?v=hQa_II4cknA
World Health Organization. (2008). *Task shifting: Global recommendations and guidelines*. WHO.
World Health Organization. (2017). *Depression and other common mental disorders: Global health estimates*. WHO. URL: http://www.who.int/mental_health/management/depression/prevalence_global_health_estimates/en/ [WebCite Cache ID 71tDp00UM]
World Health Organization. (2019). *Frequently asked questions*. Available from: https://www.who.int/about/who-we-are/frequently-asked-questions
Zivin, K., Eisenberg, D., Gollust, S. E., & Golberstein, E. (2009). Persistence of mental health problems and needs in a college student population. *Journal of Affective Disorders, 117*(3), 180–185.

Tetyana Dhimolea is a doctoral candidate at the University of North Texas (UNT) in Learning Technologies with a minor in Curriculum and Instruction. Tetyana's research interests lie in immersive virtual reality (VR) development and application for education and training, computer-assisted language learning, and digital game-based learning environments.

Dr. Regina Kaplan-Rakowski is faculty and the director of the Master of Science Program in Learning Technologies, University of North Texas (UNT). Her doctorate is in Instructional Technology and Design, Southern Illinois University (SIU), Carbondale. Dr. Kaplan-Rakowski's research focuses on immersive learning environments, computer-assisted language learning, and emerging technologies.

Dr. Lin Lin is a professor of learning technologies at the University of North Texas. Lin received her doctoral degree at Teachers College, Columbia University. Lin's research focuses on human-technology interactions, and life-long learning with innovative pedagogies and technologies. Currently, Lin serves as the director of Texas Center for Educational Technology (TCET, https://tcet.unt.edu/). She also serves as the Editor-in-chief of one of the top-tier journals, *Educational Technology Research and Development* (ETR&D Development Section, http://www.springer.com/11423).

Will Virtual Reality Connect or Isolate Students?

Aleshia Hayes

Introduction: Immersing Students Through Virtual Reality

The enthusiasts and optimists anticipate virtual reality (VR) will improve learning outcomes and students' connection with content, teachers, and peers, and even the global community (Fonseca & Krauss, 2016; Dede, 2009, Fidopiastis et al., 2009). Virtual reality is an emerging new technology being used in classrooms, from K12 (e.g., field trips) to the university (e.g., medical training), to industry (e.g., welding), even the corporate training room (e.g., customer service) (Fast et al., 2004; Barbour & Reeves, 2009; Doer et al., 2001). Critics of proposed educational implementations of virtual reality are concerned with the risks of escapism, isolation, and loss of connection with reality. While there is a great deal of optimism surrounding the potential of virtual reality, technology is a tool and tools can be used well, misused, or even abused. This chapter begins with an overview of virtual reality as an immersive medium, explores the interactions and experiences afforded by different levels of immersion, reviews some educational measures of virtual reality implementations, and explores risks and limitations of immersive mediums from recreation to the classroom. It is important to understand the ways virtual reality could potentially be used to connect students or isolate them in order to inform our design and implementation before we forge ahead with this technology.

A. Hayes (✉)
University of North Texas, Denton, TX, USA
e-mail: Aleshia.Hayes@unt.edu

M. V. Albert et al. (eds.), *Bridging Human Intelligence and Artificial Intelligence*, Educational Communications and Technology: Issues and Innovations, https://doi.org/10.1007/978-3-030-84729-6_9

What Is Virtual Reality?

Virtual reality (VR) is a substitution for corporeal reality, with digitally created reality. The highest theoretical virtual reality would fully replace physical stimuli to a user's five senses with computer-generated stimuli of a real or imagined digital experience in a real or imagined virtual environment that transcends time, space, or location. The goal being to immerse individuals into an experience. Dede (2009) describes immersion as a person's subjective experience of virtual objects in which they feel like they are physically and cognitively there. Researchers and developers have been able to elicit the immersion Dede describes with much less effort than initially imagined. In fact, the term virtual reality has been widely used to refer to myriad designs and hardware implementations. Some practitioners and researchers extend the concept of virtual reality to include 3D virtual spaces, even when displayed on a flat screen (Modjeska & Chignell, 2003), but this chapter is primarily focusing on virtual spaces and experiences that can be viewed on a VR headset (head mounted display resembling goggles, used to replace the visual stimuli of the corporeal reality).

The virtual environments that can be experienced on a low-cost VR headset range from 360° videos that allow passive, asynchronous viewing of immersive videos to 360° computer generated experiences immersive interactive experiences. 360° videos, also called immersive videos, are captured by 360° cameras that collect video in the space surrounding the camera. Users consume the 360° videos in one of two ways, either through a traditional computer display (monitor, or mobile device) or a VR headset. When users view 360° videos on a monitor, the interface allows the user to move the image to explore the full panoramic view using a mouse, stylus, or touchscreen. When viewed in a VR headset, 360° videos immersive video allow users to naturally engage with virtual environments, by turning their head to simulate "looking around" at the immersive 360° view. A noteworthy difference between delivering the 360° videos on a computer monitor versus a VR headset is the fact that when the user wears the VR headset, it blocks out the visual stimulus of the physical world around the user and provides the image in a way that neuro-typical individuals perceive as three-dimensional, making it immersive video. This immersive video is closer to the theoretical virtual reality that replaces our corporeal reality with stimuli to replace our corporeal senses. While neither of these experiences allows the user to interact with the environment, they both provide a sense of "being there" with the ability to look around.

While most low-cost consumer experiences are currently 360° videos, many VR researchers and developers consider the 360° video as something other than VR. Because of the prevalence of the 360° video experiences, we will include 360° video on a computer screen as monoscopic video and refer to 360° displayed in a VR headset as immersive video (Fonseca & Kraus, 2016).

In contrast to immersive videos, the most immersive consumer available VR is highly immersive interactive (HII) virtual reality that expands the affordances beyond the ability to look in 360° around virtual spaces displayed in headsets, to also allow users to move freely through the virtual space and to interact with virtual objects or people within the space. This ability to move around and interact goes beyond the virtual display and allows learners to exercise agency by interacting within immersive virtual environments. The low-cost headsets (e.g., Google Cardboard, Merge VR, and Samsung Gear) powered by mobile devices are typically not capable of the highly immersive interactive experiences (HII) that the higher end headsets (e.g., Oculus Rift and HTC Vive) powered by personal computer can deliver. As the field progresses, these HII virtual reality experiences are being enhanced with emerging hardware that can replace the user's other senses, such as touch, smell, and taste, and even movement via VR treadmill.

Levels of Immersion in Learning

It is important to consider the levels of immersion that different implementations of VR afford. (HII) All virtual reality in headsets allow the user wears a VR headset, which blocks the view of the surrounding physical environment and replaces it with the sights and sounds of a virtual space. Some of these HII experiences also include devices to stimulate the user's sense of touch and movement. The most immersive types of virtual reality provide users with more than representations of physical objects or spaces that convey functional knowledge, they provide users with interactive experiences where they can learn and practice skills, learn new ways of viewing the world, or deepen their understanding of phenomena. This is a meaningful advancement in learning technologies, as can be seen by one example in which children who experienced swimming with orcas in virtual reality were later unable to distinguish the virtual experiences from memory (Segovia & Bailenson, 2009).

Levels of immersion begin with the cognitive processing of the experience. While most experiences available to consumers, from highly immersive interactive experiences to immersive videos only engage two of the five senses (visual and auditory), researchers are striving to invent and integrate systems that replace all local physical stimuli (auditory, gustatory, haptic/tactile, visual, and olfactory). The highest levels of immersion would replace human perception of local physical stimuli with digital stimuli supporting a virtual experience (Yamada et al., 2021).

Historical understanding of human thought and perception shines more light on the experience of immersion and the importance for educational experiences. For example, in the words of John Dewey (1933),

> When one is doing something, one is compelled, if the work is to succeed (unless it is purely routine), to use eyes, ears, and sense of touch as guides to action. Without a constant and alert exercise of the senses, not even plays and games can go on; in any form of work, materials, obstacles, appliances, failures, and successes, must be intently watched. Sense-perception does not occur for its own sake or for purposes of training, but because it is an indispensable factor of success in doing what one is interested in doing (p.42).

John Dewey detailed the concept of providing experiences for deeper learning and transfer of that learning in his 1938 book *Experience and Education*. The concepts that Dewey uses to describe the approach to constructing learning experiences apply to the development of virtual learning experiences (Dewey, 1938; Aiello et al., 2012). Many researchers are currently developing approaches to stimulate all five senses, which will bring more depth to the consideration of levels of immersion. Just as the black and white television has become less relevant with the advent of color, HDTV, as levels of immersion and interactivity available increase, the novelty of what we currently consider highly immersive will become less effective.

Measuring the Effectiveness of Virtual Reality Experiences for Learning

There are many ways to measure the quality of an experience in virtual reality; the most frequent of these measures are presence, co-presence, and social presence (Bailenson et al., 2004; Thornson et al., 2004). For the purposes of VR for education, traditional measures of tacit and explicit learning are important (Madden et al., 2018). The immersive, experiential nature of virtual experiences also call for measurement of deeper learning, such as changes in attitude, behavior, and cognitive processes (Hayes, 2014; Karlin et al., 2018) Likewise, transfer of learning from the virtual learning environment and retention of learning outcomes are important measures to determine if tools are meeting stated objectives (Hayes et al., 2013).

Presence Because the objective is to transport someone to another place and/or time, the primary way of measuring virtual reality is through the sense of presence, concisely, the sense of "being there" (Minsky, 1980; Witmer & Singer, 1998). Several approaches exist for measuring presence from subjective to behavioral and physiological, but the general questions remain: "Do you feel like you are there?" and "Does the hardware or software interfere with this sense?"

Co-presence In reference to virtual reality, co-presence is the sense that one is sharing space with another person (Slater et al., 2000; Zhao, 2003). The equivalent of this in the physical world would be being in the physical space face-to-face with another (Zhao, 2003). The ability of a virtual experience to elicit the sense that one is sharing physical space with one or more other people (either real or artificial) is an indicator quality of an experience, if there are others present (Oh et al., 2018; Thornson et al., 2004).

Social Presence While the term social presence has different nuances in different contexts, within the study of virtual reality experiences, social presence refers to a sense of connection with another person or other people in a virtual environment. Social presence can be distilled to the sense of sharing an experience with another person. This is evaluated by a user's perception that the other person is sentient, conscious, and alive (Hayes, 2016), as well as a sense of connection with the other person. These perceived experiences have been measured by self-report and by behaviors, such as asking the agent/avatar questions, remembering things about them, or even making eye contact with them.

Immersion Researchers note the intertwined and even symbiotic relationship between immersion, presence, and engagement with an experience (Hayes, 2016; Thornson et al., 2009). While the terms immersion, presence, and engagement are frequently used interchangeably, clarification can help to distinguish the outcomes of a highly immersive interactive experience as compared to a less immersive experience.

Engagement In the context of digital mediums, such as immersive media, we can define engagement as a state in which an individual is affectively, behaviorally, and cognitively involved with a digital experience described in multiple components, including flow, immersion, attention, interest, physical presence, social presence, and motivation (Hayes, 2016). The concept of flow, the merging of action and awareness, loss of self-consciousness, transformation of time, and enjoyment (Csikszentmihaly, 1990) is frequently associated with engagement, but engagement in virtual learning environments can be best described as an intersection of presence, co-presence, social presence, and immersion (Hayes, 2016).

Learning and Behavior Change in Virtual Reality

While consumer market virtual reality headsets only became available in 2014, research on the efficacy of virtual reality experiences for behavior change has been conducted since the 1990s. Researchers have found the use of HII virtual reality has been effective in many scenarios, from delivering therapy to reducing phobias to flying aircrafts and even training people with traumatic brain injuries on activities of daily living (Doer et al., 2001; Blascovich & Bailenson, 2006; Fidopiastis et al., 2009). Similarly, there is evidence to support the idea that higher levels of immersion and interactivity increase the impact of virtual experiences, particularly in the higher quality VR headsets (Hussein & Nätterdal, 2015).

Virtual Field Trips

Virtual reality can provide learners with opportunities for virtual field trips by transporting users to virtual environments representing real or imagined places of the past, present, or future. Virtual reality field trip experiences exist for an array of virtual reality headsets. Teachers and learners access VR 360° video field trips ranging from the Wonders of the World and Antarctica to the Congo, the Ocean, and even the solar system through Google Expeditions, the Smithsonian Magazine experiences, and Houghton Mifflin Harcourt. These experiences are frequently free to download. Similarly, Google Maps and Google Street View are available for students to explore geography in low-cost VR headsets as well as high-end headsets like HTC Vive or Oculus Rift. Highly immersive interactive (HII) virtual field trip experiences that allow learners to explore and interact with elements at a specific site are available via personal computer in the Oculus Store and the Steam distribution marketplace. Not only do students have the capacity to experience new places or phenomena through virtual reality field trips, these field trips have a demonstrated capacity to involve students with inquiry-based learning (Peltekova, & Stefanova, 2016). While this can be done by learners individually, tools like Google Expeditions leverage the classroom teacher as a guide through the virtual field trip experience, allowing the teacher and students to experience a virtual space together.

Empathy

One of the most noted claims of mass implementation of highly immersive interactive virtual reality is that VR promotes prosocial behavior as the "ultimate empathy machine" (Milk, 2015). Immersive journalism provides a salient and accessible tool that has demonstrated the ability to elicit empathy afforded by the emotions that experiencing the sights and sounds of another's experience (De la Peña, 2011; Schutte & Stilinović, 2017). Similarly, the empathy induced by these experiences has been associated with behavior change, exemplified by the United Nations' use of the VR immersive video, *Clouds Over Sidra,* to show the conditions for refugees in Sidra, and the subsequent $1.5 billion increase in donations (Nash, 2018). Facilitating empathy through virtual reality in addition to the virtual experiences capacity to induce compassion and empathy for others, the HII virtual reality experiences in which a user engages with the environment has more capacity to increase empathy. Highly immersive interactive virtual reality technology affords the ability of virtual speakers to mirror the behavior of viewers and when Virtual speakers reflect viewers' nonverbal gestures (a process called mimicry), viewers do not notice the intentional mirroring but still report more salience with and empathy for outgroup members (Hasler et al., 2014). VR's capacity to teach empathy can enhance curriculums, from history and communication to business practices and patient care.

Social Learning

Bandura asserted that social interaction and connection are essential to learning (Bandura & Walters, 1977). Highly immersive interactive (HII) virtual reality is uniquely capable of simulating and affording social interaction and connection. Social interaction with real and artificial individuals in HII virtual experiences has led to improved social skills, new relationships, and increased social confidence.

Similar to how mimicry allows nonverbal behaviors to be guided by the virtual reality system to elicit a higher sense of empathy to individuals from an outgroup, virtual reality experiences can allow an instructor to transform their social behaviors digitally to display the most effective nonverbal behaviors. Transformed social interaction, demonstrated by transforming a speaker's nonverbal behavior to make prolonged eye contact simultaneously with every listener, was correlated with increased persuasive impact (Bailenson et al., 2004). Further, the sense of social presence, or connection with real or virtual instructors in a learning experience, can be used to improve learning outcomes and satisfaction (Bailenson et al., 2004).

Experiential VR

Experiential virtual reality includes VR experiences that allow users to observe and practice physical tasks such as drawing in 3D space or interacting with a model of human anatomy. Current experiential VR opportunities range from learning and practicing yoga or football to providing first aid (Casale, 2017; Louka & Balducelli, 2001; Patel et al., 2006). When these are experienced with highly immersive interactive (HII) virtual reality headsets, haptic stimuli, and physical models that stimulate the sense of touch to accurately represent the tasks. The highly immersive interactive tools allow learners to engage with Kolb's components of experiential learning from concrete experience, reflection, abstract conceptualization, and active experimentation (Kolb et al., 2001). Conversely, while the 360° experiences can provide opportunities for learners to reflect on another's behavior and conduct abstract conceptualization, they will not gain the concrete experience or opportunity to actively experiment. This difference in the depths of experiential learning may be the deciding factor for some on the level of interactivity and immersion needed for the task.

Situated Learning and Embodied Cognition

Situated learning and embodied cognition emphasize the importance of action and context in learning and knowing. While situated learning focuses on the situation or context of the learning as compared to the context of application of a skill, embodied cognition focuses on the role of the body in cognition. While various levels of virtual representations can be useful, highly interactive immersive (HII) virtual experiences can engage both situated learning and embodied cognition.

Virtual experiences can engage the user's physical senses with their cognitive processes as they interact with the virtual space through an avatar body (Costa et al., 2013). Smith and Gasser (2005) suggest a systematic approach to engaging embodied cognition. This approach includes being multimodal, incremental, physical, explorative, social, and symbolic (through language or some other symbolism). All of these strategies can be implemented in highly immersive interactive (HII) experiences, while some may also be implemented in 360° video or immersive 360° video.

Similarly, virtual experiences from 360° video or immersive video to highly immersive interactive experiences are created with the context in mind. In many cases, virtual environments are created as high fidelity simulations of real-world contexts in order to engage the learners in situated learning. Corporations use this capacity to train employees, for instance, the company STRIVR uses VR to deliver training opportunities to Walmart employees and football players alike. They do this by providing "perceptual information that is sufficiently similar to what is experienced" in order to situate learning in a real-world context to decrease training time and costs (Casale, 2017, p. 5). This approach can also be applied to situate learning for students in real-world context like grocery stores, classrooms (Hayes et al., 2013), or any appropriate environment.

Collaborative Spaces

Virtual reality developers have been expanding the offerings of collaborative spaces available. There are both professional and social spaces in which individuals can interact with each other while immersed in VR. These spaces are currently only available in the mid- to high-tier VR headsets, but developers are working to expand their user base by making the experiences available to more users. Similarly, some of the developers (e.g., Rec Room and AltSpaceVR) have taken steps to allow users to choose whether to engage in their virtual space in a range of VR headsets or on a traditional computer monitor. Not only does this allow users to choose to engage even if they do not have a VR headset, it also allows them to alternate between experiences as well as to engage with users who are using different interface. This is significant because this flexibility may improve the persistence of users in the environment and increase interactivity.

The general phenomena of "virtual schools" supplementing or replacing curriculum across many US states in recent history is a rebranding of distance learning, generally delivered online, most frequently through Internet browsers and synchronous or asynchronous video meetings (Barbour & Reeves, 2009). The moniker of "virtual school" is not aligned with the theoretical virtual reality discussed in this discourse, as these virtual schools do not use virtual spaces or virtual reality. These distance learning programs have been noted to have increased distance between teachers and students, lower learning outcomes in comparison with brick and mortar schools, and problems with retention (Molnar et al., 2014; Barbour & Reeves, 2009). Likewise, recent years have revealed problems with video-conferencing tools for distance education, including cognitive load, lack of privacy, lack of flexibility, and lack of personalization (Bailenson, 2021) that lead many students to turn of their video conferencing and lose the sense of connection. These constraints could be addressed with hybrid virtual collaboration, which have the potential to lower cognitive load, increase privacy, and opportunities for flexible personalization of learning experiences. The capacity of virtual reality experiences to connect students, transport them to other places, and provide collaborative spaces that afford presence, co-presence, and social presence may address many of the problems with distance learning and "virtual schools" as they are currently delivered.

Solitude or Isolation

As the world has moved from the industrial age to the information age, there has been increasing fear of the unintended consequences of new technology. Virtual reality technology is a tool and as such the developers, implementers, and users will determine the outcomes derived by it. While it is true, for instance, that the VR headset blocks users off from the physical space around them, developers are currently working on ways to add representation of physical objects and individuals to a virtual experience. Further, the fact that the virtual reality headset occludes external stimuli may be used to encourage users to focus undivided attention on an experience, task, interaction, or individual.

Virtual reality has been met with the same concerns as many technologies when first introduced to the classroom. There is a concern that students may experience separation from the class, teacher, and content. VR's capacity to occlude the physical environment heightens these concerns. Sometimes this may be a necessary tradeoff, such as when learners are practicing skills that require engagement with the virtual, the HII experiences may lead to more effective learning than the less immersive 360° video virtual experiences. The experience of immersion and replacing the physical stimuli with virtual may also serve to improve concentration on target virtual stimuli (Parsons & Phillips, 2016).

Solitude and isolation exist on a spectrum (Koch, 1990). While solitude is healthy, isolation is an unhealthy level of separation from social interaction humans need for health. The sense of isolation among students from elementary school through adulthood has been a common problem (Lake, 1999). While highly immersive interactive virtual reality experiences provide some of the most effective learning, they also have the potential to isolate users. The separation from the surrounding when one dons the VR headset, blocking the physical environment, may create an experience in which learners disconnect from their peers and teachers. Inversely, the experience of immersion and replacing the physical stimuli with virtual may also serve to improve concentration on target virtual stimuli (Parsons & Phillips, 2016). The implications of this separation vary depending on factors within the experience.

Balance Between Solitude and Connection by Design

Connection and isolation are phenomena that should be considered and generated by design. The learning objectives drive the design and implementations of virtual reality experiences for learning. Similarly, the duration of the experience is important to consider when planning for connection or isolation. Social learning theory tells us that social interaction is important for learning, so it is important that designers create balanced experiences that permit both individual learning and social interaction for learning and engagement. The effectiveness of VR for education and training will depend on the intentional design of experiences and delivery of those experiences by effective lesson planning and classroom management (Hayes et al., 2021). Expeditions field trips are well designed and allow the teacher a master view of every student's view, which has the potential to increase teacher student co-presence and social presence (Long & Eutsler, 2020).

If a student's social engagement or a social skill is part of the learning objective, the virtual reality experience should include social interaction with a real or artificial person. Likewise, in circumstances like Google Expeditions, the design choice to integrate the teacher as a guide in a virtual field trip that includes all students, the learning is enhanced by the students' sense of presence and social presence. Without deliberate design, an experience could leave students feeling isolated if the designer does not consider how to engage the students. Inversely, a single user experience with no social engagement could still foster connection by providing a shared context and future discussions.

The paradoxical potential for isolation and connection created with virtual reality creates some risks and opportunities for designers and practitioners. While people frequently cite concerns of escapism afforded by VR, there is a potential benefit of the occlusion afforded by VR. Virtual reality affords a user an experience in which the rest of the world is occluded, providing focus on the immersive virtual experience. This target experience could include the visual experience, the content, or the connection between two or more people in a collaborative experience. Current highly immersive virtual reality experiences do not allow the user to multitask with anything outside the experience. Designers and educators will have to learn to balance the paradoxical possibilities of VR to connect or isolate users through user centered design driven by learning objectives and context. For example, a designer may leverage the fact that a user is unable to see their surroundings, they are not able to text, use social media, or check email while engaging with an experience to highten the experience of educational content or deepend the connection between collaborators, or create a space for a conversation free of distractions. Virtual reality, like the technological advances that preceded it, is a tool that will be as effective as the designers and users who implement it.

Glossary

Virtual Reality (VR) Digitally created 3D reality used to replace corporeal reality
Virtual Reality Headset Head-mounted display
Head-Mounted Display (HMD) Set of goggles that present stereoscopic to create the illusion of 3D reality with computer-generated images.
360° Videos Panoramic Videos that allow view of the 360° around camera. These can be displayed on a screen or on an HMD
Immersive Video 360° Videos displayed on a head-mounted display
Highly Immersive Interactive Environments Computer-generated experiences that allow users to move freely through the 360° virtual space and interact with virtual objects and people in the space while immersed through a head-mounted display

References

Aiello, P., D'Elia, F., Di Tore, S., & Sibilio, M. (2012). A constructivist approach to virtual reality for experiential learning. *E-Learning and Digital Media, 9*(3), 317–324. https://doi.org/10.2304/elea.2012.9.3.317

Bailenson, J., Beall, A., Loomis, J., Blascovich, J., & Turk, M. (2004). Transformed social interaction: Decoupling representation from behavior and form in collaborative virtual environments. *Presence: Teleoperators & Virtual Environments, 13*(4), 428–441.

Bailenson, J. N. (2021). Nonverbal overload: A theoretical argument for the causes of Zoom fatigue. Technology, Mind, and Behavior, 2(1).

Bandura, A., & Walters, R. H. (1977). *Social learning theory* (Vol. 1). Prentice-hall.

Barbour, M., & Reeves, T. (2009). The reality of virtual schools: A review of the literature. *Computers and Education, V52*, 402–416. https://doi.org/10.1016/j.compedu.2008.09.009

Blascovich, J., & Bailenson, J. (2006). *Immersive virtual environments and education simulations*.

Casale, M. (2017). *STRIVR training demonstrates faster and more accurate learning compared to traditional study methods*.

Costa, M. R., Kim, S. Y., & Biocca, F. (2013, July). Embodiment and embodied cognition. In *International Conference on Virtual, Augmented and Mixed Reality* (pp. 333–342). Springer.

Csikszentmihaly, M. (1990). Flow: The psychology of optimal achievement.

De la Peña, N. (2011). Physical World News In Virtual Spaces. Representation and Embodiment in Immersive Nonfiction. *Media Fields Journal, 3*, 1–13.

Dede, C. (2009). Immersive Interfaces for Engagement and Learning. *Science, 323*(5910), 66–69. https://doi.org/10.1126/science.1167311.

Dewey, J. (1933). *How we think, a restatement of the relation of reflective thinking to the educative process*. D.C. Heath and Company.

Dewey, J. (1938). *Experience and education*. Macmillan. MLA Citation. Dewey, John. Experience And Education. New York: Macmillan.

Doer, K. U., Schiefel, J., & Kubbat, W. (2001). *Virtual cockpit simulation for pilot training*. Darmstadt University (Germany) institute for flight mechanics and control.

Fast, K., Gifford, T., & Yancey, R. (2004). Virtual Training for Welding. In *Proceedings of the 3rd IEEE/ACM International Symposium on Mixed and Augmented Reality (ISMAR '04)*. IEEE Computer Society, Washington, DC, USA, pp. 298–299. https://doi.org/10.1109/ISMAR.2004.65

Fidopiastis, C. M., Hughes, C. E., & Smith, E. M. (2009). Mixed Reality for PTSD/TBI Assessment.

Fonseca, D., & Kraus, M. (2016). A comparison of head-mounted and hand-held displays for 360° videos with focus on attitude and behavior change, 287–296. https://doi.org/10.1145/2994310.2994334

Hasler, B. S., Hirschberger, G., Shani-Sherman, T., & Friedman, D. A. (2014). Virtual peacemakers: Mimicry increases empathy in simulated contact with virtual outgroup members. *Cyberpsychology, Behavior, and Social Networking, 17*(12), 766–771.

Hayes, A. T., Hardin, S. E., & Hughes, C. E. (2013, July). Perceived presence's role on learning outcomes in a mixed reality classroom of simulated students. In International Conference on Virtual, Augmented and Mixed Reality (pp. 142–151). Springer, Berlin, Heidelberg.

Hayes, A. T. (2014). An approach to holistic development of serious games and learning simulations. In P. Zaphiris & A. Ioannou (Eds.), *Learning and collaboration technologies. technology-rich environments for learning and collaboration* (pp. 42–49). Springer.

Hayes, A. (2016). Human Factors in Instructional Design of Serious Games and Educational Simulations. *2nd International Symposium on Human Factors in Training, Education, and Learning Sciences*, Orlando, FL.

Hayes, A., Daughrity, L. A., & Meng, N. (2021). Approaches to Integrate Virtual Reality into K-16 Lesson Plans: an Introduction for Teachers. TechTrends, 65(3), 394–401.

Hussein, M., & Nätterdal, C. (2015). *The benefits of virtual reality in education-A comparison Study*. University of Gothenburg, Göteborg: Sweden.

Karlin, B., Kim, H. T. C., Kelly, R., Blakley, J., Brenner, C., & Riley, P. (2018). DOES MEDIUM MATTER.

Koch, P. (1990). Solitude. *The Journal of Speculative Philosophy, 4*(3), 181–210. Retrieved from http://www.jstor.org/stable/25669958

Kolb, D. A., Boyatzis, R. E., & Mainemelis, C. (2001). Experiential learning theory: Previous research and new directions. *Perspectives on thinking, learning, and cognitive styles, 1*(8), 227–247.

Lake, D. (1999). Reducing isolation for distance students: An on-line initiative. *Open Learning: The Journal of Open, Distance and e-Learning, 14*(3), 14–23.

Long, C., & Eutsler, L. (2020). Engaging With VR. Science Scope, 43(9), 15–21.

Louka, M. N., & Balducelli, C. (2001). *Virtual reality tools for emergency operation support and training*. Proceedings of TIEMS (The International Emergency Management Society).

Madden, J. H., Won, A. S., Schuldt, J. P., Kim, B., Pandita, S., Sun, Y., ... & Holmes, N. G. (2018). Virtual reality as a teaching tool for moon phases and beyond. arXiv preprint arXiv:1807.11179.

Milk, C. (2015). *How virtual reality can create the ultimate empathy machine – TED Talk*. https://www.ted.com/talks/chris_milk_how_virtual_reality_can_create_the_ultimate_empathy_machine. Accessed on 01/15/2018.

Minsky, M. (1980). Telepresence. *Omni, 2*, 45–51.
Modjeska, D., & Chignell, M. (2003). Individual Differences in Exploration Using Desktop VR. *Journal of Association Information Science Technology, 54*, 216–228. https://doi.org/10.1002/asi.10197.
Molnar, A., Huerta, L., Rice, J. K., Shafer, S. R., Barbour, M. K., Miron, G., & Horvitz, B. (2014). *Virtual schools in the US 2014: Politics, performance, policy, and research evidence*.
Nash, K. (2018). Virtual reality witness: Exploring the ethics of mediated presence. *Studies in Documentary Film, 12*(2), 119–131. https://doi.org/10.1080/17503280.2017.1340796
Oh, C. S., Bailenson, J. N., & Welch, G. F. (2018). A systematic review of social presence: Definition, antecedents, and implications. Frontiers in Robotics and AI, 5, 114.
Parsons, T. D., & Phillips, A. S. (2016). Virtual reality for psychological assessment in clinical practice. Practice Innovations, 1(3), 197.
Patel, K., Bailenson, J. N., Hack-Jung, S., Diankov, R., & Bajcsy, R. (2006). The effects of fully immersive virtual reality on the learning of physical tasks. In *Proceedings of the 9th Annual International Workshop on Presence*, Ohio, USA (pp. 87–94).
Peltekova, E. V., & Stefanova, E. P. (2016). Inquiry-based learning "outside" the classroom with virtual reality devices. *Международный научный журнал «Современные информационные технологии и ИТ-образование», 12*(3–2), 112–116.
Schutte, N. S., & Stilinović, E. J. (2017). Facilitating empathy through virtual reality. *Motivation and Emotion, 41*(6), 708–712.
Segovia, K. Y., & Bailenson, J. N. (2009). Virtually true: Children's acquisition of false memories in virtual reality. *Media Psychology, 12*(4), 371–393.
Slater, M., Sadagic, A., Usoh, M., & Schroeder, R. (2000). Small-group behavior in a virtual and real environment: A comparative study. *Presence: Teleoperators & Virtual Environments, 9*(1), 37–51. https://doi.org/10.1162/105474600566600
Smith, L., & Gasser, M. (2005). The development of embodied cognition: Six lessons from babies. *Artificial life, 11*(1-2), 13–29.
Thornson, R., et al. (2004). Lost at Sea: Where Is All the Plastic? *Science, 304*(5672), 838. https://doi.org/10.1126/science.1094559.
Thornson, C. A., Goldiez, B. F., & Le, H. (2009). Predicting presence: Constructing the tendency toward presence inventory. *International Journal of Human-Computer Studies, 67*(1), 62–78. https://doi.org/10.1016/j.ijhcs.2008.08.006
Witmer, B. G., & Singer, M. J. (1998). Measuring presence in virtual environments: A presence questionnaire. *Presence: Teleoperators & Virtual Environments, 7*(3), 225–240.
Yamada, S., Aoyagi Y., Ishikawa, M., Yamaguchi, M., Yamamoto, K., & Nozaki, K. (2021). Gait assessment using three-dimensional acceleration of the trunk in idiopathic normal pressure hydrocephalus. Aging Neurosci. https://doi.org/10.3389/fnagi.2021.653964.
Zhao, S. (2003). Toward a taxonomy of copresence. *Presence: Teleoperators and Virtual Environments, 12*(5), 445–455.

Dr. Aleshia Hayes is new faculty in the University of North Texas' Department of Learning Technology in the College of Information. Dr. Hayes is passionate about developing, evaluating, and iterating on technology used for learning in formal and informal environments. Previously, Dr. Hayes was the founding Director of SURGE (Simulation Research and Game Experience) VR lab at Purdue University in Fort Wayne, where she led design, development, testing, and implementation of virtual reality, augmented reality, mixed reality, serious games, and gamified learning technology tools for commercial and military partners. In addition to a passion for the effective implementation of emerging technology for learning, Dr. Hayes works tirelessly to encourage students at all levels to pursue STEM education and STEM careers, with the explicit goal of expanding and diversifying STEM education and the STEM workforce. Her efforts to recruit students into STEM range from public VR exhibits to K12 classroom visits, to app development camps for middle and high school–aged students to hosting interdisciplinary game development events. Dr. Hayes leverages her research, funded by NSF, NIH, the Department of Defense, and the Bill and Melinda Gates Foundation, to inform learning technology design and implementation across learners from K12 and university levels to the workforce.

Augmented Intelligence: Enhancing Human Decision Making

Justin Kim, Taylor Davis, and Lingzi Hong

Introduction

Artificial intelligence (AI) has a promising future in the world of technology and has the potential to fundamentally change many industries (Bhandari & Reddiboina, 2019). The creation of AI allows machines to act like humans and to assist humans by identifying and predicting specific actions with large amounts of data. Models and codes that enable machines to learn by themselves are the fundamentals of AI (Corchado, 1996). Machine learning models and deep learning frameworks, including multilayer perceptrons (MLP), recurrent neural network (RNN), convolutional neural networks (CNN), and many others, form the basis of many artificially intelligent applications. As time continues, artificial intelligence gets more humanized and better in assisting humans with more abundant data, better algorithms, and stronger computational power (Bhandari & Reddiboina, 2019).

Augmented intelligence is the technique developed specifically to help humans rather than replace them. By combining human and machine intelligence, an augmented intelligent system can utilize the cognitive thinking of humans and the high accuracy and precision of machine computing (Bhandari & Reddiboina, 2019). This chapter focuses on the importance of augmented intelligence and how it has improved the decision-making of financial services, healthcare, education, entertainment, and many more.

J. Kim (✉) · T. Davis · L. Hong
University of North Texas, Denton, TX, USA
e-mail: Lingzi.Hong@unt.edu

M. V. Albert et al. (eds.), *Bridging Human Intelligence and Artificial Intelligence*, Educational Communications and Technology: Issues and Innovations, https://doi.org/10.1007/978-3-030-84729-6_10

What Is Augmented Intelligence

By its definition, augmented intelligence is a partnership between people and artificial intelligence to enhance cognitive performance (Hassani et al., 2020). These cognitive enhancements may include memorizing, learning, and decision making. Based on the definition, augmented intelligence creates a "partnership" between humans by being the assistive role in decision-making. Augmented intelligence uses machine learning and deep learning algorithms to discover and reinforce human intelligence. This is in contrast to AI shown in Fig. 1.

The assistive role that augmented intelligence takes is because humans have many limitations in perception and cognition. For example, as people get older, many motor neurons or memory neurons degenerate as the body slowly stops functioning (Murman, 2015). Additionally, extreme situations limit human functions as the human body can handle extreme scenarios. Therefore, we need technology to help us go beyond the limits and do better than what was usually done in the past. Some of these features that augmented intelligence offers include better memory, computing, and decision-making (Hassani et al., 2020).

Rapid business value is defined as the additional revenue of a business per customer's lifetime. With the help of augmented intelligence, data can be shared, stored, searched, and organized to eliminate redundancies to drive business growth. By increasing the efficiency with augmented intelligence, many businesses can produce more supply based on the growing demand (Hassani et al., 2020). Additionally,

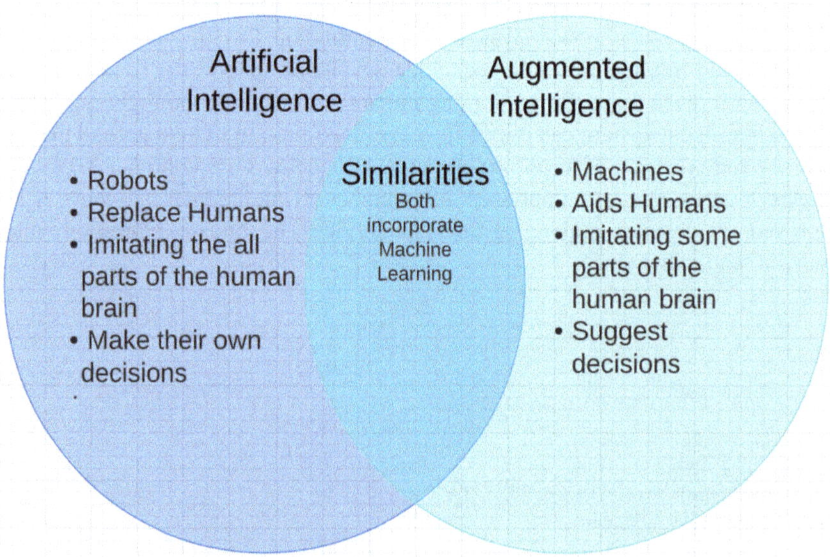

Fig. 1 Venn diagram AI compared to augmented intelligence

it can make employees' lives easier. Rather than replacing human labor, augmented intelligence assists employees to do their jobs at a much faster and accurate rate.

Augmented Intelligence in Business

Business Intelligence

Acquiring and leveraging information has been a staple in successful businesses for the last two decades (Chen et al., 2012). Business intelligence (BI) was coined to describe this phenomenon. Simply put, business intelligence refers to shrinking the time frame to provide real-time information to decision-makers by using computer-based intelligence systems (Negash & Gray, 2008). BI is prominent in automated and augmented systems, such as data mining, automated anomaly detection, data visualization, geographic information systems, and customer services. Augmented intelligence falls into BI systems because it assists in both strategic and operational decision-making. BI systems are also effective at managing and sorting large sets of structured and unstructured data. This aids businesses in efficiently managing data to make decisions and reduce costs (Thierauf, 2001).

Big data is used when the data is too large and complex to process through traditional methods. Using augmented intelligence to process the data through brute force allows many businesses to analyze large sources of data at a more efficient rate. This method also allows businesses to have cost reductions while maintaining time efficiency. Additionally, many businesses can determine any failures, fraud, or mistakes faster and can come up with solutions using other methods (Sagiroglu & Sinanc, 2013).

The benefits of augmented intelligence in business are not limited to data management, and it can also be effective in customer services. One example of how BI is integrated into customer service is the use of chatbox. Banking giants like Bank of America and Capital One have recently experimented with automated replies to advise customers in the online chatbox. This technology is more cost-effective and faster than humans when performing repetitive tasks. In many cases, humans prefer chatboxes to enhance their financial decision-making because they are impartial and not judgemental (Lui & Lamb, 2018). The speed and efficiency of augmented intelligence systems enable to effectively manage routine interactions and save operational costs. We expect this trend to continue as advancements are made to chatbox AI systems.

Manufacturing

Business intelligence has been widely used in the manufacturing industry as it is seen as a necessity to remain competitive when analyzing costing models, production scheduling, productivity, and yield rates (Bordeleau et al., 2018). This allows businesses to see the performance of manufacturing processes in real-time or provide a visual representation of data to enhance decision-making in production.

Manufacturing organizations that use augmented intelligence generally experience higher productivity and reduced manufacturing costs (Yusof & Yusof, 2013). Operational business intelligence is critical for manufacturers to respond quickly to predictable and unpredictable changes in the market. For example, when BI is integrated with ordering platforms on the Internet, manufacturing teams can access demand data in real-time, which helps businesses plan for supplies and production to meet the need in the market accurately and quickly (Uçaktürk et al., 2015). This is especially significant when resources are scarce or when businesses are operating within tight margins.

Additional applications for augmented intelligence in manufacturing include optimized production scheduling, predictive analytics, real-time product monitoring, and the ability to synchronize diverse manufacturing systems. Each of these applications helps enhance efficiencies in workflow and offer businesses a competitive edge in manufacturing speed.

Augmented Intelligence for Entertainment

Predictions and Algorithms

With the rise of multimedia platforms like YouTube, Netflix, Hulu, and many other streaming websites, the need for algorithms rises as many of these websites need to keep the people from going to other streaming platforms (Covington et al., 2016). For example, the popular video website, "YouTube," has its own deep neural network for video recommendations (Covington et al., 2016).

YouTube's algorithm comprises two neural networks, the candidate generation and ranking, to figure out someone's recommendation. Figure 2 illustrates how YouTube finds recommended videos on its platform. First, the candidate generation network takes the user's history as inputs and retries an input of hundreds of relevant videos. These "candidates" are used as a filter to get videos with similarities between the user's history and theme of the video. Then the videos go to the ranking deep neural network where the algorithm ranks the different videos based on more information like the actual content of the video and similar interest to the user.

This system allows YouTube to take a large sample of videos from a plethora of content creators and cut it down to the user's interest. Additionally, YouTube

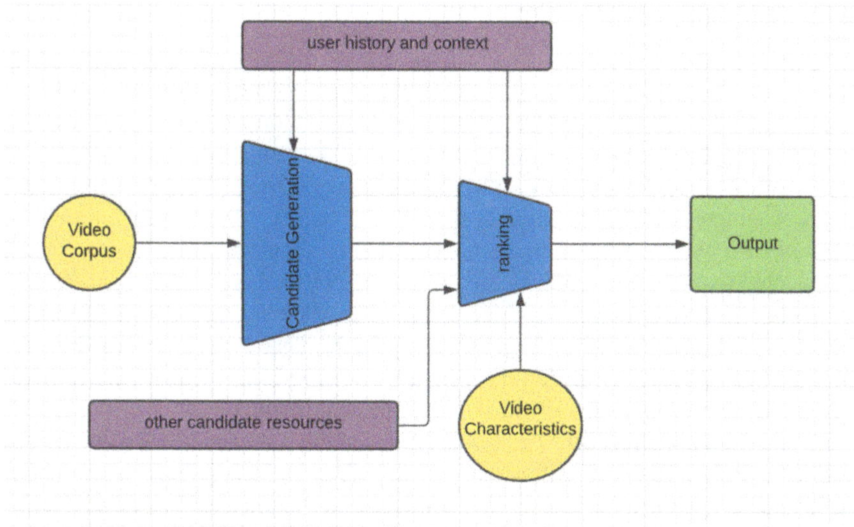

Fig. 2 Predictive algorithm model

continues to improve its model by extensive use of offline metrics (precision, recall, and ranking loss) to guide iterative improvements to its recommendation system.

YouTube's candidate generation allows high accuracy based on the user's preference. By using a classification technique, this model allows YouTube to gather specific videos at a high rate. Additionally, it allows the model to continue being retrained as other "YouTubers" create new videos. Additionally, the age of the video being recommended is filtered by feeding the age of the training examples. This will allow the model to be biased toward new videos but still allow popular old videos to be shown (Covington et al., 2016).

The primary role of the ranking model is to use impression data to specialize and calibrate candidate predictions for the particular user interface. Its model assigns an independent score to each video impression using logistic regression to give its "ranking." For example, a user may watch a given video with high probability generally but is unlikely to click on the specific homepage impression due to the choice of the thumbnail image. To filter this system finds videos that the user enjoys and will have better engagement throughout the video (Covington et al., 2016).

The recommendation system allows YouTube viewers to have a fresh new experience by getting new videos every day. The YouTube model is trained through the experiences and trends of the viewer. The YouTube model allows for the recommendation of similar but fresh videos for the viewer. Since it allows the viewer to control what goes in the model by searching, liking, or commenting on a YouTube video, it follows the augmented intelligence ideology of humans having control over what happens in a machine learning model. These recommendation models aid humans by grasping our attention to videos, but it also keeps us satisfied with the YouTube product by recommendations rather than searching individually.

Inverse Augmented Reality

The gaming industry has been using augmented intelligence in games to enhance users' experience. For example, games can include "automated robots" for users to play against. Many games also use augmented reality techniques, which create virtual images on top of reality to enable users to immerse themselves in a new virtual world. Augmented reality is different from virtual reality. Virtual reality allows the creation of a virtual environment and completely shuts out the physical world. Augmented reality adds digital elements into the physical world through a camera or lenses. Popular examples include games like "Pokémon Go" and "Snapchat Filters," which add to or alter the physical world through a smart device. There are three key components in traditional augmented reality: the humans, the physical world, and the virtual contents added to the physical world.

Inverse augmented reality is a new technique applied in games. Like augmented reality, inverse augmented reality also contains three key components, i.e., the virtual character, the programmable virtual world, and the physical contents added to the virtual world.

Figure 3 demonstrates how inverse augmented reality would work. The left would represent a virtual reality image, while the right would represent a real-life image. Inverse augmented reality can still include images from real life – the oval – but can replace color or shape of it as it pleases. If a person was using virtual reality goggles, they would feel the circle but also see it through the goggles. Additionally, the figure demonstrates how a square can be inserted into the virtual world; however, the square does not appear on the reality side. This demonstrated how inverse augmented reality can also add new objects into virtual view.

Augmented Intelligence for Education

Smart Education

In the world of education, there are divergent opinions on how to utilize augmented intelligence. With the rise of smart systems, such as AI tutoring and learning management systems, educators are adapting to create new teaching methods to take

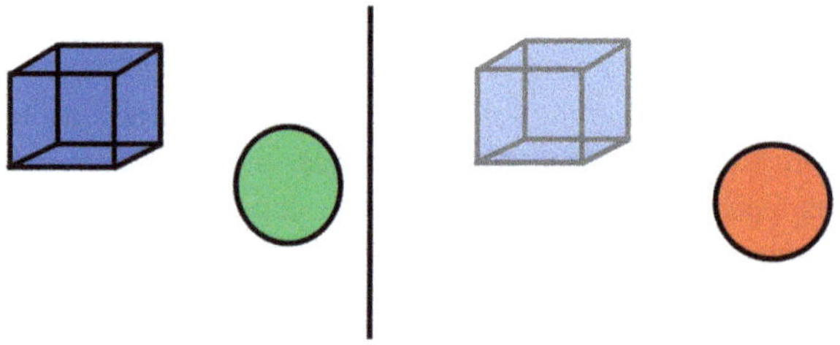

Fig. 3 Example of how inverse augmented reality (left) compares to reality (right)

advantage of them. For example, educators use smart applications to make data-based decisions, provide quick remediation with adaptive tutoring systems, and use machine learning algorithms to make sense of data generated from the interaction with students.

Smart classrooms are inspired by "smart spaces," which are environments embedded with augmented intelligence systems such as response technology, assistive listening devices, and networking capabilities (Pishva & Nishantha, 2008). In an educational environment, "smart" refers to technology that helps students and teachers perform tasks faster and with greater accuracy. Smart classrooms can provide tailored and personalized learning to give real-time feedback, adaptive content, and fast evaluations (Zhu et al., 2016).

Smart applications are known for incorporating data-driven insights into a user interface. This allows teachers and students to complete a desired task or action efficiently. For example, as shown in Fig. 4 by the Human-in-Loop Teacher Data Analysis model, teachers use the model to sort through data (assessment scores, attendance, demographics, and benchmarks) to make informed decisions. Augmented intelligence works best when it presents information in a structured way that would be time-consuming for humans without assistance from technology. Students often use smart applications to assist them in completing assignments. For instance, students can use text analysis software to learn and improve their writing skills (Thomas, 2017).

Adaptive Learning Technologies

Smart technologies are adaptive by nature. They react to learner's data and tailor instructional resources. Smart applications can help automate current classroom processes or present new ways to learn that previously have been unexplored (Jeong et al., 2010). As shown in Fig. 5, students can interact with adaptive user interfaces to engage in the learning process in multiple ways. One example is adaptive online tutoring systems, also known as intelligent tutoring systems (ITS), which use student inputs to determine the scope and sequence of the material presented to the

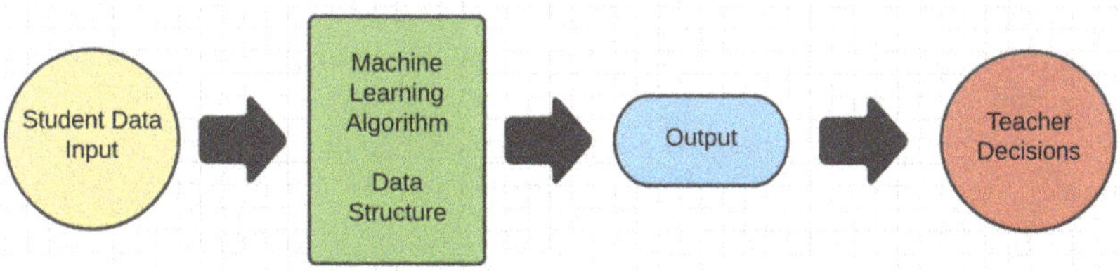

Fig. 4 Human-in-loop teacher data analysis

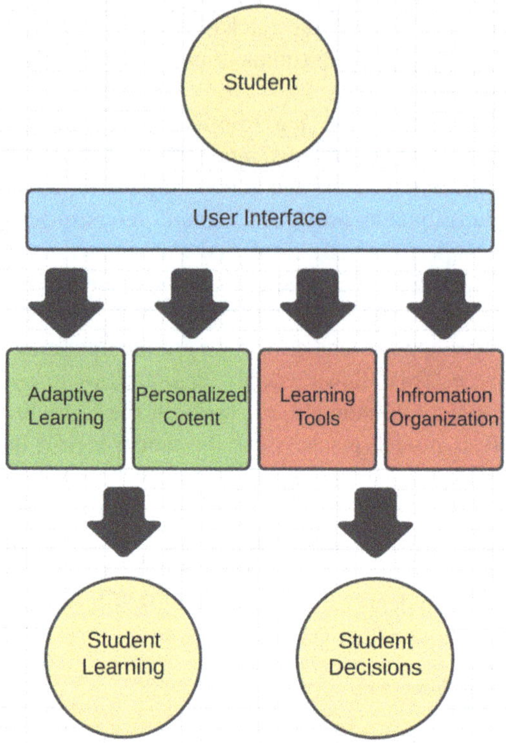

Fig. 5 Framework for augmented learning and decision making for students

students. Duolingo is a popular adaptive language tutoring system that personalizes instructions based on user presets and learning results. If the learner completes learning tasks successfully, the ITS will increase the difficulty. If the learner struggles, the tutoring system will scale back the difficulty and provide more scaffolding to the user. It is a great example that demonstrates the potential of augmented learning systems designed to provide personalized tutorials according to each student's knowledge structure, intelligence, and proficiency (Zheng et al., 2017).

Similarly, adaptive hypermedia adjusts to the user's knowledge, learning goals, and preferences. Most people are familiar with adaptive hypermedia in the context of personalized advertisements based on user data, but this also applies to an educational context. Content and suggestions to the learner for subsequent study are determined by the learner's existing knowledge and actions (Phobun & Vicheanpanya, 2010).

Learners' profiles have become commonplace when navigating hypermedia. For example, you might notice how Google accounts are now seamlessly integrated into various educational sites and platforms to create a comprehensive user profile. The user profile contains information about different aspects of an individual user, which is essential for an adaptive system to provide personalized service to individual users (Brusilovsky & Millán, 2007). For example, when students search for information, adaptive hypermedia can prioritize the most relevant items a user wants to see.

Mobile and Ubiquitous Technologies

Ubiquitous devices help in the decision-making process by generating, collecting, and processing information (Abdel-Basset et al., 2019). There are billions (and growing) of interconnected computing devices in physical objects that use the Internet to send and receive data. Such devices surpassed the number of people on earth in 2008 and are expected to reach 100 billion in 2020 (Abdel-Basset et al., 2019). The Amazon Alexa is a familiar example. In the realm of education, countless devices communicate to help make human decision-making easier or personalize instructional content. Utilizing the gathered data by ubiquitous devices can help enhance students' and teachers' productivity and support learning outcomes (Abdel-Basset et al., 2019). In addition, the market is expanding with new smart devices that can emulate and extend human cognitive abilities to improve human task performance (Zheng et al., 2017).

Data Driven Applications

Currently, macro data analysis, mining, and sorting have become popular applications for augmented intelligence systems in education. Educational data mining (EDM) is a collection of methods where data sets collected from educational settings are transformed into meaningful presentations to guide the teachers and leadership teams (Toivonen et al., 2019). EDM requires algorithms to conduct data mining processes to provide helpful information to students and educators. EDM and augmented intelligence is a collaborative effort between computer systems and human action. EDM is generally reliant on human input from either teachers or students. For example, EDM is effective at sorting, clustering, and presenting student assessment data, so teachers can make informed decisions to provide personalized support or instructional remediation.

Augmented intelligence and EDM are also used in education to build assessment items. This process uses human input to create large numbers of testing items based on parameters identified by humans (Gierl et al., 2020). First, the content and skills associated with the items must be selected. Then items are developed by computer algorithms based on rules utilizing an item bank. This is an efficient way to create unique testing items with limited human interaction. Once the items have been produced, human decision-making comes into play by selecting the items to include in an assessment. Human intervention increases the accuracy of this model by sorting through the output and eliminating errors. This application of augmented intelligence in education can significantly reduce the time and effort required by educators to create assessments.

Ethics of Augmented Intelligence in Education

A primary concern related to the widespread adoption of augmented intelligence in education is the ethical dilemmas associated with this technology. Personalized consumer content has frequently caused concerns related to privacy (Teltzrow & Kobsa, 2004). For example, personalized user profiles can promote confirmation bias by feeding students' information from their previous searches or web history. As a result, some systems have repercussions far beyond what teachers or students may recognize. Additionally, when augmented intelligence systems collect students' demographic, geographic, and other profiling data, that information could be sold to private companies.

Other ethical dilemmas may arise when augmented intelligence systems deliberately induce confusion in students, manipulate students, or present students with erroneous examples. Sjödén (2020) identified three areas of concern that warrant further research, including lying, hiding, and deceiving. Lying refers to when augmented intelligence systems either deliberately or accidentally present students with incorrect information. Hiding is when information is presented selectively. For example, search results could be tailored to your user profile rather than displaying all available information. Finally, deceiving is presenting students with tasks that are designed to confuse students or foster false beliefs. These issues create huge concerns that educators must be aware of when utilizing augmented intelligence to enhance student learning.

Augmented Intelligence for Healthcare

Healthcare Decision Making Tools

Attention has been paid to augmented intelligence in health care. Differently, this industry is tied to human life where incorrect decisions are not tolerated. The healthcare industry uses augmented intelligence to enhance performance and decision-making in numerous ways. These include but are not limited to aiding patient diagnoses, treatment, and surgery. For example, Han et al. (2020) found increased performance in dermatologists when assisted with an algorithm for making predictions of malignancy and treatment options. One of the most successful applications in the medical field is IBM's Watson health system (Zheng et al., 2017). While often very knowledgeable in their field, physicians have limitations in the amount of information they have in their working field. In contrast, the Watson system can memorize an ever-expanding pool of literature that can aid doctors and nurses. The Watson system can also mine patient data systematically to obtain hypotheses and present them with a confidence score to aid physicians (Zheng et al., 2017). Treatment decisions are still in the hands of doctors, but with the inclusion of information and options presented by augmented intelligence systems.

In the medical field, large , amounts of complex and often unstructured data must be used effectively to guide health care professionals. A form of augmented intelligence known as cognitive computing (CC) is often used in health care systems to address these issues. CC is defined as using cognitive models to simulate or mimic the human thought process (Chen et al., 2016). CC is unique because it can process unstructured data, which is different from the rigid systematic data processing used in education. For example, CC helps physicians and nurses analyze clinical notes, lab results, and images accurately and efficiently (Skiba, 2017). Furthermore, this is important because of the large amount of medical knowledge and many complex rules associated (Zheng et al., 2017). The myriad of relationships is often impossible for humans to solely memorize and deploy to make accurate decisions without the aid of CC.

Additionally, though inverse, augmented intelligence from the gaming industry to help engage people using virtual technology, many of these new features can be used in the field of medicine. These may include modeling of organs or virtual surgery sessions (Chan et al., 2013). The fantastic aspect of augmented intelligence is that although a device may be focused on one genre of work, every device or model is intertwined based on how it is controlled and used.

Smart Robots

Automated robotics or "smart robots" are not new to healthcare or manufacturing, industries. However, robotic-assisted surgery is generally considered in its infancy. Intelligent robots guide surgeons in planning and executing a personalized procedure to create highly predictive postoperative outcomes (Bhandari & Reddiboina, 2019). One such robotic surgical device is the da Vinci Surgical System, which the Food and Drug Administration approved in 2000. The da Vinci Surgical System performs minimally invasive surgery controlled by a surgeon with an advanced set of instruments. It also provides a 3D high-definition view of the surgical area (https://www.davincisurgery.com/). While many augmented intelligence systems aim to reduce the time and cost associated with completing a task, augmented surgical systems primarily focus on increasing the accuracy of minimally invasive procedures.

Surgeons have praised the da Vinci robot for significantly enhancing visibility based on detailed three-dimensional imaging. Specifically, visual cues provided by the system with the enhanced imaging system aided in determining tissue and suture tension (Talamini et al., 2003). These affordances of robotic-assisted surgery increase confidence and accuracy in surgeons and surgical outcomes. It is important to note that these augmented systems do not come without shortcomings. The disadvantages of using augmented surgical systems include the cost, bulkiness, and availability of these robots in certain hospitals (Nezhat et al., 2006). Specifically, the da Vinci system requires full sterile draping, and instrument changes are cumbersome (Talamini et al., 2003). This adds additional time to surgical procedures, not to mention the extensive training required to utilize these systems. While it is hard to argue against systems that increase precision and safety in surgical operations, there is still room to grow to increase cost-effectiveness and address design limitations.

Augmented Intelligence and COVID-19

While augmented intelligence in healthcare has aided the detection of diseases, the 2019 outbreak of the novel Coronavirus emphasizes the need to utilize this technology to predict outbreaks. Most importantly, augmented intelligence can be used to compile rapidly evolving data to assist public health experts in decision-making related to the virus (Long & Ehrenfeld, 2020). Google and Apple have both launched Coronavirus tracking systems that can notify people if they are near someone exposed to the virus (Nanni et al., 2021). These exposure notification systems help enhance human decision-making in public health and safety. In addition, Google offers community reports, which utilize augmented intelligence to present data of recent virus-related trends in selected geographic locations, for example, trends of mobility in specific areas such as grocery stores, parks, and residential areas. Augmented intelligence may also assist in more accurate symptom checking to predict the likelihood of new infections (Long & Ehrenfeld, 2020). The affordances of augmented intelligence offer the chance to save lives during epidemics. Leveraging augmented intelligence in the case of epidemiology is more critical now than ever.

Inventory Management Systems

Augmented intelligence also plays a significant role in hospital supply chains and inventory systems to help guide human purchasing power. One of the greatest challenges for health care supply chains is to manage inventory efficiently and keep patient satisfaction high (Leaven et al., 2017). The healthcare industry uses manual, semi-manual, and automated systems to keep essential supplies in stock. These systems are essential because a depleted inventory can lead to significant and even life-threatening problems. Augmented inventory systems follow a similar pattern to manual systems but offer many notable advantages, for example, optics into product usage, better purchasing power, reduced waste, and cost savings. The difference is shown in Fig. 6.

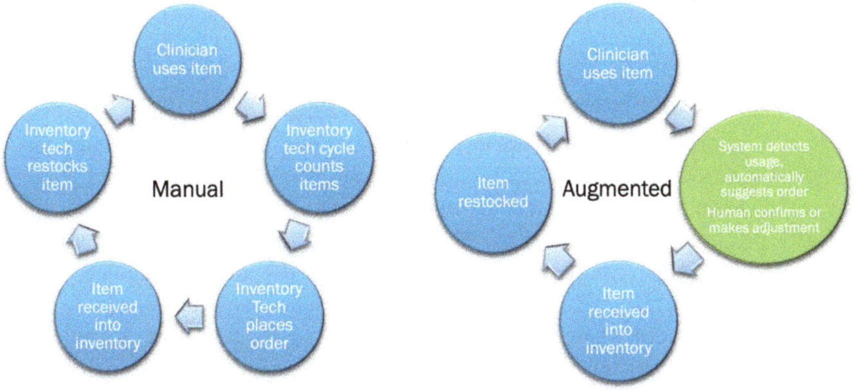

Fig. 6 Manual vs augmented intelligence cycle

While healthcare costs continue to grow significantly, inventory management represents an opportunity to reduce healthcare costs. For example, radio frequency identification (RFID) technologies and weight-based scales are used to trace items by connecting the objects to the internet and alert hospitals when items are running low (Leaven et al., 2017). This reduces the chance of human error when ordering and can ensure necessary supplies are always in stock. There is also evidence that computer-assisted inventory management systems can reduce prescription errors and medication distribution (Awaya et al., 2005). Finally, augmented intelligence makes inventory functions efficient and easier for clinicians in real-time.

Ethics of Augmented Intelligence in Healthcare

The ethics of augmented intelligence in healthcare is often hotly debated because of its impact on human life, specifically regarding safety and liability. For example, if an augmented intelligence system incorrectly diagnoses a patient, who is to blame? Should the system that suggested the diagnoses be at fault or the physician that confirmed the diagnosis and administers treatment? These types of questions propelled the American Medical Association to adopt a new policy in 2018, H-480.940, to provide a broad framework for the evolution of artificial intelligence (AI) in health care to ensure the benefits it promises for the health care community (Crigger & Khoury, 2019). Issues of liability are common in healthcare, but they are not the only problems associated with augmented intelligence. Other concerns are human biases, data reliability, and privacy.

Challenges associated with the reliability of data can create issues when determining diagnosis and treatment. Data fed to physicians by proxy of health monitoring sensors do not have universal standards, so it is difficult to evaluate and determine the fidelity of sensor readings (Sheth et al., 2017). Additionally, augmented intelligence systems can exacerbate human biases, such as when data only reflects the experiences of individuals with access to health care but is applied to everyone. Augmented intelligence will continue to expand inequities in healthcare systems between the haves and have nots if they are not evaluated regularly.

Finally, addressing concerns about privacy and security is of extreme importance in health care systems. The protection of personal records and identifying features are at risk when using augmented intelligence systems, especially when proper data security protocols are not in place or practiced. Existing practices of notifying patients that their personal data could be obtained for use are not adequate, nor are strategies to de-identify data effective in large data sets (Osoba & Welser, 2017). It is even more concerning that obtaining consent to use medical data is rarely adequate given the significance of the privacy issue related to these requests. Ultimately, physicians need more training on how to utilize augmented intelligence systems' predictive features. In addition, designers must evaluate electronic recordkeeping security when creating these systems.

Augmented Intelligence for Travel

Applications in the Automobile Industry

The automobile industry has arguably integrated augmented intelligence systems more than any other industry. From the production floor to the GPS utilized by drivers, the fingerprints of augmented intelligence are everywhere. From the safety systems that notify you if a car is in your blind spot to the real-time information displayed from sensors, automotive vehicles are model examples of the benefits of augmented intelligence. Additionally, the augmented features of navigation applications that predict the expected travel time are now commonplace. The automobile industry has adopted numerous travel assistant platforms that offer guidance functions and personalized recommendations based on the traveler's current location (Lilitsis et al., 2018). The future applications of augmented intelligence are bright for the next generation of automobiles. Augmented driving systems will most likely retain their popularity because they help reduce travel time and make automobiles safer without relinquishing human control with completely autonomous driving systems.

Augmented Intelligence in Air Travel

Aviation augmented intelligence features similar goals to the automobile industry. The primary concerns are to increase efficiency and safety. For example, approximately 80% of aviation accidents are related to pilot errors during landing and takeoff (Naranji et al., 2015). Much of the system is now automated to minimize the dangers of landing. However, the pilots must continue to monitor augmented information systems to decide when it is necessary to take control. In abnormal situations such as harsh weather, the pilot flying (PF) will take control while being assisted by the pilot monitoring (PM), utilizing real-time information from sensors and onboard monitoring systems (Salvetti et al., 2020).

One perceived benefit of flight automation is that it relieves pilots from focusing on ordinary flight tasks, allowing them to concentrate on overall flight performance (Naranji et al., 2015). However, pilots using fully automated systems can lose their concentration and flight awareness. Naranji et al. (2015) found that using augmented intelligence in the cockpit enhances the pilot's ability to fly precisely and increases the pilot's situational awareness using a human-in-the-loop concept. Airline companies also use augmented intelligence to collect data on the health of each aircraft. This allows airlines to plan for plane services proactively, which helps minimize flight delays and catches potentially dangerous mechanical errors. This wealth of data also helps manufacturers build better planes to increase safety standards. Finally, the future of augmented aviation is expected to use machine learning for flight optimization to improve the decisions pilots make in the air. This will eventually help to reduce flight times and conserve scarce resources in the airline industry.

Advancements and Limitations of Augmented Intelligence

Current Advancements

Augmented intelligence has a considerable advantage over artificial intelligence in public perception and acceptance. Artificial intelligence is considered a threat to human jobs, and people are skeptical of its reliability (Schmidt et al., 2020). Augmented intelligence, on the other hand, leaves the final control to humans. This is why the application of augmented intelligence could be visible and accepted in more industries. For example, people might be willing to accept a minimally invasive surgical procedure with augmented intelligence systems guiding a human surgeon. However, it is unlikely that most patients would consent to a fully automated artificial intelligence system to perform a surgical procedure on them without human intervention.

The key to augmented intelligence is that humans are still in control. Therefore, the true potential of augmented intelligence is to increase the cognitive, analytical, and decision-making power of specialists from various industries while maintaining full control over technology (Wójcik, 2020). For instance, the financial sector is a strong candidate for advancements in augmented intelligence because financial institutions base economic decisions on numerous data points. However, humans still have autonomy in the decision-making process. Therefore, augmented intelligence can increase the accuracy of predictions in the economic and financial sectors without relinquishing human control (Lui & Lamb, 2018).

Education and the health care industry are also prime candidates for an increase in augmented intelligence adoption. Although, as mentioned previously in this chapter, augmented intelligence has the potential to limit the spread of infectious diseases, this technology is only in its infancy. Still, it has displayed promising results (Long & Ehrenfeld, 2020). Additionally, advancements in diagnostic and decision-making systems will increase the accuracy and efficiency in healthcare. We can also expect significant advancements in augmented intelligence tutoring systems and assistants. The age of personal assistants like Amazon's Alexa and Apple's Siri has shown the potential of augmented intelligence to enhance our daily decision-making. This has yet to make a significant impact on education. However, successful augmented tutoring systems have shown the potential for a future with augmented assistants to aid students in learning processes (Kulik & Fletcher, 2016). In the future, it can be assumed that augmented intelligence will be used wherever AI is used and wherever increasing the cognitive abilities of humans is critical (Wójcik, 2020).

Limitations

One concern is the limited research on the subject of augmented intelligence. Wójcik (2020) found that searches for augmented intelligence using Scopus (an abstract and citation database) yielded 37 results. Most of these publications came from the fields of computer science, engineering, and medicine. Using Google Scholar yielded 923 results, but only 33 were relevant results for augmented intelligence (Wójcik, 2020). Based on these numbers, it is apparent that limited research has gone into the potential, limitations, and distractions associated with this widely adopted technology. It is easy to be optimistic about the benefits of augmented intelligence, but without proper oversight and research, many problems associated with this technology will go unchecked.

For example, augmented intelligence systems will probably be imperative for many years to come, but this could create irrevocable dependencies on using this technology to make decisions (Sharma, 2019). This is especially concerning when humans become over-reliant on augmented intelligence when making relatively simple decisions. Additionally, the loss of human control is an area of concern. Especially when the data fed to humans can be inaccurate or biased when not adequately vetted. For instance, making diagnostic decisions based on data that offers limited insight into marginalized groups who do not have access to healthcare can be inaccurate and biased. Finally, when we reduce the human experience to machine-based abstractions, there is a danger of treating every decision as a mathematical problem rather than a human problem.

There are also concerns about the disenfranchisement of people who do not have access to this technology or cannot use it. This creates inequality in our society that we currently do not fully understand. For example, there are already inequalities in our education systems regarding the technology and opportunities available to marginalized groups. Augmented intelligence tutoring systems could exacerbate these inequities if they are not accessible to students with low socioeconomic status. Our society needs to be conscious of and adapt to augmented intelligence's broader social and ethical implications. The future of numerous industries, productivity, and the modern workforce are at stake. To address the limitations and ethical issues of augmented intelligence, we must maintain a reasonable level of human control and oversight (Pavlou, 2018). Constant oversight and human control give humanity time to get acquainted with managing issues that arise from augmented intelligence.

Conclusion

Augmented intelligence has become an integral part of our everyday lives and has wedged itself into numerous industries. It is difficult to argue against the benefits of augmented intelligence in terms of efficient and informed decision-making. Augmented intelligence offers similar affordances to artificial intelligence but with a human-in-loop model. Fears generally associated with artificial intelligence are rarely associated with augmented intelligence systems since consumers and businesses see this technology as a tool to enhance their daily lives and operations.

It is concerning that the research into augmented intelligence is limited compared to artificial intelligence especially considering the wealth of current applications of this technology. Therefore, additional research is essential to identify future applications of augmented intelligence systems and identify barriers to utilizing this technology in other domains. However, it is clear that augmented intelligence is here to stay for the foreseeable future. The recent developments of augmented intelligence in business, healthcare, education, and logistics have shown the exciting opportunities we have to enhance human decision-making while maintaining human-in-loop control.

Acknowledgments Taylor Davis would like to acknowledge Ashley Davis for contributing her knowledge of augmented intelligence applications in the healthcare industry.

References

Abdel-Basset, M., Manogaran, G., Mohamed, M., & Rushdy, E. (2019). Internet of things in a smart education environment: Supportive framework in the decision-making process. *Concurrency and Computation: Practice and Experience, 31*(10), e4515.

Awaya, T., Ohtaki, K. I., Yamada, T., Yamamoto, K., Miyoshi, T., Itagaki, Y. I., Yoshikazu, T., Nobumasa, H., & Matsubara, K. (2005). Automation in drug inventory management saves personnel time and budget. *Yakugaku Zasshi, 125*(5), 427–432.

Bhandari, M., & Reddiboina, M. (2019). Augmented intelligence: A synergy between man and the machine. *Indian Journal of Urology, 35*(2), 89–91.

Bordeleau, F. E., Mosconi, E., & Santa-Eulalia, L. A. (2018). Business intelligence in industry 4.0: State of the art and research opportunities. In *Proceedings of the 51st Hawaii international conference on system sciences*.

Brusilovsky, P., & Millán, E. (2007). User models for adaptive hypermedia and adaptive educational systems. In *The adaptive web* (pp. 3–53). Springer.

Chan, S., Conti, F., Salisbury, K., & Blevins, N. H. (2013). Virtual reality simulation in neurosurgery: Technologies and evolution. *Neurosurgery, 72*(suppl_1), A154–A164.

Chen, H., Chiang, R. H., & Storey, V. C. (2012). Business intelligence and analytics: From big data to big impact. *MIS Quarterly, 36*, 1165–1188.

Chen, Y., Argentinis, J. E., & Weber, G. (2016). IBM Watson: How cognitive computing can be applied to big data challenges in life sciences research. *Clinical Therapeutics, 38*(4), 688–701.

Corchado, J. M. (1996). Artificial intelligence models: Composed systems as a solution. In *IEEE colloquium on knowledge discovery*. London England, UK.

Covington, P., Adams, J., & Sargin, E. (2016, September). Deep neural networks for youtube recommendations. In *Proceedings of the 10th ACM conference on recommender systems* (pp. 191–198).

Crigger, E., & Khoury, C. (2019). Making policy on augmented intelligence in health care. *AMA Journal of Ethics, 21*(2), 188–191.

Gierl, M. J., Lai, H., & Matovinovic, D. (2020). Augmented intelligence and the future of item development. In M. H. Jiao & R. Lissitz (Eds.), *Applications of artificial intelligence in assessment*. New Age Publishing.

Han, S. S., Park, I., Chang, S. E., Lim, W., Kim, M. S., Park, G. H., Chae, J. B., Huh, C. H., & Na, J. I. (2020). Augmented intelligence dermatology: Deep neural networks empower medical professionals in diagnosing skin cancer and predicting treatment options for 134 skin disorders. *Journal of Investigative Dermatology, 140*(9), 1753–1761.

Hassani, H., Silva, E. S., Unger, S., Tajmazinani, M., & MacFeely, S. (2020, April). Artificial intelligence (AI) or intelligence augmentation (IA): What is the future? *ResearchGate, 1*, 145–151.

Jeong, S. J., Lim, K., Ko, Y. J., Sim, H., & Kim, K. Y. (2010). The analysis of trends in smart phone applications for education and suggestions for improved educational use. *Journal of Digital Contents Society, 11*(2), 203–216.

Kulik, J. A., & Fletcher, J. D. (2016). Effectiveness of intelligent tutoring systems: A meta-analytic review. *Review of Educational Research, 86*(1), 42–78.

Leaven, L., Ahmmad, K., & Peebles, D. (2017). Inventory management applications for healthcare supply chain. *International Journal of Supply Chain Management, 6*, 1–7.

Lilitsis, P., Patkos, T., Flouris, G., & Plexousakis, D. (2018). Travel companion: A mobile system for trip assistance relying on artificial intelligence and augmented reality. In *Proceedings of the 10th Hellenic conference on artificial intelligence* (pp. 1–2).

Long, J. B., & Ehrenfeld, J. M. (2020). The role of augmented intelligence (AI) in detecting and preventing the spread of novel coronavirus. *Journal of Medical Systems, 44*, 59. https://doi.org/10.1007/s10916-020-1536-6

Lui, A., & Lamb, G. W. (2018). Artificial intelligence and augmented intelligence collaboration: Regaining trust and confidence in the financial sector. *Information & Communications Technology Law, 27*(3), 267–283.

Murman, D. L. (2015, August). The impact of age on cognition. In *Seminars in hearing* (Vol. 36, No. 3, p. 111). Thieme Medical Publishers.

Nanni, M., Andrienko, G., Barabási, A. L., Boldrini, C., Bonchi, F., Cattuto, C., … Vespignani, A. (2021). Give more data, awareness and control to individual citizens, and they will help COVID-19 containment. *Ethics and Information Technology*, 1–6.

Naranji, E., Sarkani, S., & Mazzuchi, T. (2015). Reducing human/pilot errors in aviation using augmented cognition and automation systems in aircraft cockpit. *AIS Transactions on Human-Computer Interaction, 7*(2), 71–96.

Negash, S., & Gray, P. (2008). Business intelligence. In *Handbook on decision support systems 2* (pp. 175–193). Springer.

Nezhat, C., Saberi, N. S., Shahmohamady, B., & Nezhat, F. (2006). Robotic-assisted laparoscopy in gynecological surgery. *JSLS: Journal of the Society of Laparoendoscopic Surgeons, 10*(3), 317.

Osoba, O. A., & Welser, W., IV. (2017). *An intelligence in our image: The risks of bias and errors in artificial intelligence*. Rand Corporation.

Pavlou, P. A. (2018). Internet of things–will humans be replaced or augmented? *Marketing Intelligence Review, 10*(2), 42–47.

Phobun, P., & Vicheanpanya, J. (2010). Adaptive intelligent tutoring systems for e-learning systems. *Procedia-Social and Behavioral Sciences, 2*(2), 4064–4069.

Pishva, D., & Nishantha, G. G. D. (2008). Smart classrooms for distance education and their adoption to multiple classroom architecture. *Journal of Networks, 3*(5), 54–64.

Sagiroglu, S., & Sinanc, D. (2013, May). Big data: A review. In *2013 international conference on collaboration technologies and systems (CTS)* (pp. 42–47). IEEE.

Salvetti, F., Gardner, R., Minehart, R., Galli, C., & Bertagni, B. (2020). Crisis resource management in aviation and healthcare. *International Journal of Advanced Corporate Learning, 13*(2), 41.

Schmidt, P., Biessmann, F., & Teubner, T. (2020). Transparency and trust in artificial intelligence systems. *Journal of Decision Systems, 29*(4), 260–278.

Sharma, M. (2019). Augmented intelligence: A way for helping universities to make smarter decisions. In *Emerging trends in expert applications and security* (pp. 89–95). Springer.

Sheth, A., Jaimini, U., Thirunarayan, K., & Banerjee, T. (2017). Augmented personalized health: How smart data with IoTs and AI is about to change healthcare. In *2017 IEEE 3rd international forum on research and Technologies for Society and Industry (RTSI)* (pp. 1–6). IEEE.

Sjödén, B. (2020, July). When lying, hiding and deceiving promotes learning-a case for augmented intelligence with augmented ethics. In *International conference on artificial intelligence in education* (pp. 291–295). Springer.

Skiba, D. J. (2017). Augmented intelligence and nursing. *Nursing Education Perspectives, 38*(2), 108–109.

Talamini, M. A., Chapman, S., Horgan, S., & Melvin, W. S. (2003). A prospective analysis of 211 robotic-assisted surgical procedures. *Surgical Endoscopy and Other Interventional Techniques, 17*(10), 1521–1524.

Teltzrow, M., & Kobsa, A. (2004). Impacts of user privacy preferences on personalized systems. In *Designing personalized user experiences in eCommerce* (pp. 315–332). Springer.

Thierauf, R. J. (2001). *Effective business intelligence systems*. Greenwood Publishing Group.

Thomas, L. (2017, May 18). *Automated text analysis tool will help students in large courses develop writing skills*. University of Michigan News.

Toivonen, T., Jormanainen, I., & Tukiainen, M. (2019). Augmented intelligence in educational data mining. *Smart Learning Environments, 6*(1), 1–25.

Uçaktürk, A., Uçaktürk, T., & Yavuz, H. (2015). Possibilities of usage of strategic business intelligence systems based on databases in agile manufacturing. *Procedia-Social and Behavioral Sciences, 207*, 234–241.

Wójcik, M. (2020). Augmented intelligence technology. The ethical and practical problems of its implementation in libraries. *Library Hi Tech*. https://doi.org/10.1108/LHT-02-2020-0043

Yusof, E. M. B. M., & Yusof, A. R. M. (2013). The study on the application of business intelligence in manufacturing: A review. *International Journal of Business Intelligence Research (IJBIR), 4*(1), 43–51.

Zheng, N. N., Liu, Z. Y., Ren, P. J., Ma, Y. Q., Chen, S. T., Yu, S. Y., Xue, J. R., Chen, B. D., & Wang, F. Y. (2017). Hybrid-augmented intelligence: Collaboration and cognition. *Frontiers of Information Technology & Electronic Engineering, 18*(2), 153–179.

Zhu, Z. T., Yu, M. H., & Riezebos, P. (2016). A research framework of smart education. *Smart Learning Environments, 3*(1), 4.

Justin Kim is a high schooler that is part of the program known as the Texas Academy of Mathematics and Science at the University of North Texas. He has worked under Dr. Mark Albert on developing a machine learning model to predict and correctly evaluate gestures. He will be attending the University of Virginia through the class of 2025 for his undergraduate career under a computer science major.

Taylor Davis is currently an instructional coach in a large urban school district located in Texas. He has worked in education for 11 years and is pursuing a doctorate degree in learning technologies from the University of North Texas. His recent research into teacher self-efficacy with educational technology was presented and published at the Association for Advancement of Computing Education 2021 SITE conference. Taylor's future projects include the study of English Language Learner's perceptions of online learning environments.

Lingzi Hong is an assistant professor in Data Science at the College of Information, University of North Texas. She received a Ph.D. degree in information science from the University of Maryland, College Park. Her research interests lie in data science for social good, where machine learning techniques are applied for human behavior modeling to enhance decision-making for sustainable development. She has published in AAAI, ACM Web Science, IEEE Big Data, iConference, ASIS&T, etc.

Cybernetic Systems: Technology Embedded into the Human Experience

Pranathi Pilla and Rafael Anderson Alves Moreira

Introduction

Cybernetic systems are defined by having two feedback loops. One allows the system to adapt and learn, while the other makes small adjustments which help make learning possible (Montouri, 2011). A third, less essential feedback loop is also used less frequently with human senses needing to replace old with newer information to allow the system to adapt. Cybernetic systems are based on feedback mechanisms at their core and have the capability to control living organisms via machines (Montouri, 2011). The potential power of cybernetic systems to revolutionize the healthcare industry, biomechanical parts, and communication in living systems is incredible (Warwick, 2020).

Currently, cybernetic systems are not fully available in the commercial market; they still remain a research topic with few prototypes. For instance, real cybernetic systems used in the real world today are heart pacemakers and prosthetic organisms, wherein the organs collect data from surrounding tissue in order to function (Weir et al., 2009). The role of large volumes of readily available data in creating these cybernetic systems is incredibly critical. For example, in the case of neural electrodes, one must acquire electrical data from the impulses in the brain and translate those signals into messages for the receiver to fully comprehend. When there is more data that is accumulated, the system learns more about its surroundings. These data essentially become the base of the machine learning and artificial intelligence systems. One of the more recent revolutions within the cybernetics industry is Neuralink Corporation, which capitalizes on the large volumes of data it is able to collect and use to work on medical advances within the neurological field (Statt, 2017). Given the rate at which this field is growing, cybernetic systems have the

P. Pilla (✉) · R. A. A. Moreira
University of North Texas, Denton, TX, USA

M. V. Albert et al. (eds.), *Bridging Human Intelligence and Artificial Intelligence*, Educational Communications and Technology: Issues and Innovations, https://doi.org/10.1007/978-3-030-84729-6_11

potential capability to enhance human power and health significantly but will have ethical implications as the field becomes more advanced, and possibly creating health inequity, as these systems are often expensive (Timmermans & Kaufman, 2020).

Existing Working Systems

How the Technology Was Created and Designed

Brain–machine interface (BMI) is also referred as brain–computer interface (BCI), which is a system that translates neuronal information into commands that can control external devices such as prosthetics (Kumarasinghe et al., 2021). It started in 1924 when the German psychiatrist and physiologist Hans Berger recorded for the first time in history human brain activity by using a method called electroencephalography (EEG) (Millett, 2001). The term brain–computer interface (BCI) was actually coined by Jacques Vidal, a faculty member at the University of California, Los Angeles (UCLA) (McFarland & Wolfpaw, 2017). It was in 1973 when during a sabbatical that he published a paper on controlling external objects using EEG signals.

Human use of BMI had started already by the time Vidal's paper was released, and in 1978, the researcher William Dobelle was able to successfully implant a device for helping people who have previously lost their vision to see again (Lewis & Rosenfield, 2016). A similar device will be further discussed in the Human Condition Restoration section.

Future Applications on Humans

Neuralink Corporation is a neurotechnology start-up company, co-founded by billionaire Elon Musk and is in San Francisco, CA (Winkler, 2017). The company's main goal is to provide a better integration between the human brain and machines. Neuralink started developing a new kind of brain–machine interface (BMI) that holds promise for the restoration of sensory and motor function and the treatment of neurological disorders (Musk, 2019). This BMI system is relatively small compared to existing systems. It has as many as 3072 electrodes per array distributed across 96 threads (Musk, 2019). For comparison, Neuralink claims that this number of electrodes is one order of magnitude higher than existing BMIs. Each thread contains 32 independent electrodes. Though Neuralink has created more than 20 electrode and thread types, the two designs shown in the picture below are called Linear Edge and Tree types (Fig. 1).

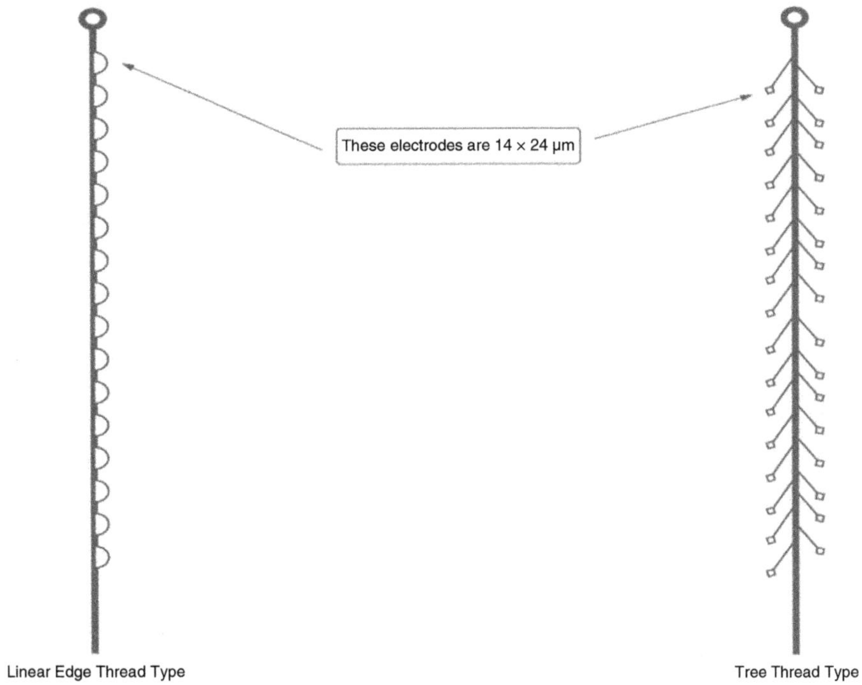

Fig. 1 The image on the left depicts the Linear Edge and the image on the right depicts the Tree design for an electrode

What is important to note about Neuralink's ambitious promises is that the company is trying to make these BMI implants more widely usable and available, e.g., through wireless communication and charging. While existing systems are big and cumbersome, Neuralink's main computer is the size of a large coin, and its wires are more biocompatible than existing BMI implementations, which historically caused signal interference by the scarring tissue (Wiggers, 2020). Though human trials are still on hold, waiting for FDA approval, Neuralink claims that it was able to perform 19 animal implants with 87% success rate (Wiggers, 2020).

Medical Applications

Cybernetic systems have the potential to be applied to many medical scenarios as they advance. Due to the manner in which cybernetic systems blend in with their surrounding environments, including hematogenic systems, key advances in microminiature technology and intra-system devices make the successful employment of these data more probable (Britannica, 2019). For example, Neuralink has many polymer strings and electrodes that convert detectable action potentials to electrophysiological data. By doing this, one can capitalize on these data to make

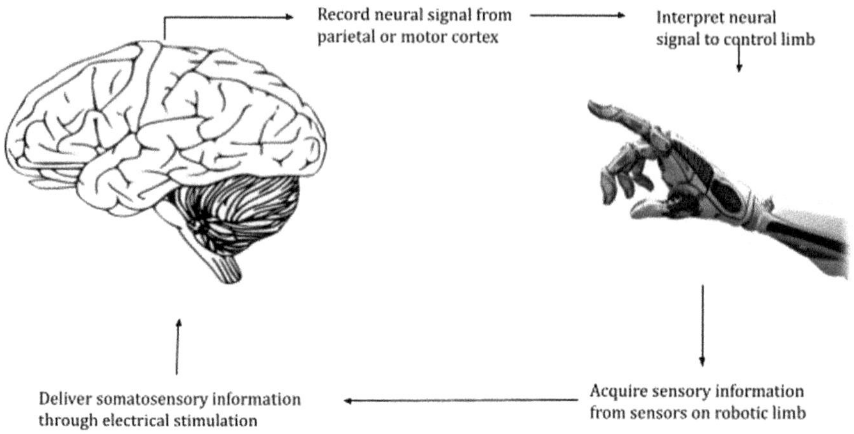

Fig. 2 The diagram shows how the human brain connects with a cybernetic limb and the way in which they operate together (PNGJoy, n.d.)

inferences about the brain. Additionally, one can use such seamless types of wiring for biological and neural control as well (Fig. 2).

With such seamless wireless control on the brain, it can help with many noninvasive procedures or aid in revolutionizing minimally invasive procedures by making them noninvasive. Elon Musk points out that "while these successes suggest that high fidelity information transfer between brains and machines is possible, development of BMI has been critically limited by the inability to record the signals from large numbers of neurons. Noninvasive approaches can record the average of millions of neurons through the skull, but this signal is distorted and nonspecific" (Musk, 2019).

In addition, prosthetics have great capability of mimicking organs, but are especially useful for extremities and distal limbs such as arms, hands, legs, and feet. In the most recent decade, human-cybernetic interfaces have been growing in sophistication and prevalence in the form of prosthetic limbs, wherein most of them are electromyogram (EMG) prosthetics. Electromyography is a medical technique which involves recording skeletal muscle activity data, and converting that via a transducer into a signal recordable by the electrode. Overall, the medical applications of such a system are that it allows medical professionals to seamlessly collect patient data and use these data to aid in diagnostic procedures. Without having to necessarily perform surgery or other invasive procedures, professionals can collect valuable patient data and further improve future prosthetics designs.

Human Condition Restoration

In addition to the direct medical applications in the healthcare field where the data collected by these user–machine interfaces can aid in finding trends, the human condition can be restored or even enhanced. Recently, there has been a large surge in research analyzing artificial retinas. Emphasis has been placed on specific retinas which can capture light and relay a signal to the brain, as well as create procedures for the brain to process these light data. This research is similar to other medical advances and all others in the sense that these data are the key for these newer embedded devices to function correctly. These artificial retina devices restore electrical stimulation of the neurons in the eyes. These devices take in the artificial light impulses and activate their phosphenes through a form of cortical stimulation. For example, in a recent study done with permanent artificial retinas, though the quality of the image is not quite clear, the system is at least functional, and has the potential to become an economically viable solution once the image quality increases over time (Chichilnsiky, n.d.).

In addition to artificial retinas, myoelectric prostheses have demonstrated their abilities to aid in human condition restoration, which is providing humans with limbs with functionality mimicking their natural counterparts. They are similar to EMG prosthetics, in the sense that the electrical data could be used and manipulated to control the arm. Myoelectric prostheses have the ability to aid in such situations. The key difference between the two methods is that myoelectric prosthetics are essentially robots at their core. Previous research models involved building limbs with myoelectric prostheses and controlling them with a separate remote. Now, they have evolved to a point where the host human brain can control these limbs. Thus, the movement of these prostheses is fueled by the twitch fiber skeletal muscle electrical signals for the prosthetics.

Human Condition Enhancement

Ultrasonic Sense for the Blind

In today's world, society is moving forward at a very rapid pace and people with disabilities are often forgotten or left behind as they are often marginalized and seen as a burden to society. According to the World Health Organization (WHO), visual impairment affects about 1% of our global population (Pascolini & Mariotti, 2012). While the WHO is monitoring and looking for ways to prevent visual impairment, others like Sylvain Cardin, Daniel Thalmann, and Frederic Vexo from the Virtual Reality Laboratory (VRlab) and the Ecole Polytechnique Fédérale de Lausanne (EPOFL) in Switzerland are looking to remediate and improve people's mobility by giving them a new sense (Cardin et al., 2006). This wearable system alerts the user of close-range objects as they walk. In short, it uses two ultrasonic sensors for input and two vibrators for output. Later models revealed four sensors and eight vibrators (Adhe et al., 2015) (Fig. 3).

"So how does this system work?" – Sonars (the ultrasonic sensors) (Britannica, 2019) are used to measure the distance to an object. They use a transducer to send and to receive ultrasonic sound waves, and with information one can calculate the distance – the distance is equal to the time the sound wave takes to hit the object and come back to the sensor, divided by the speed of sound (Fig. 4).

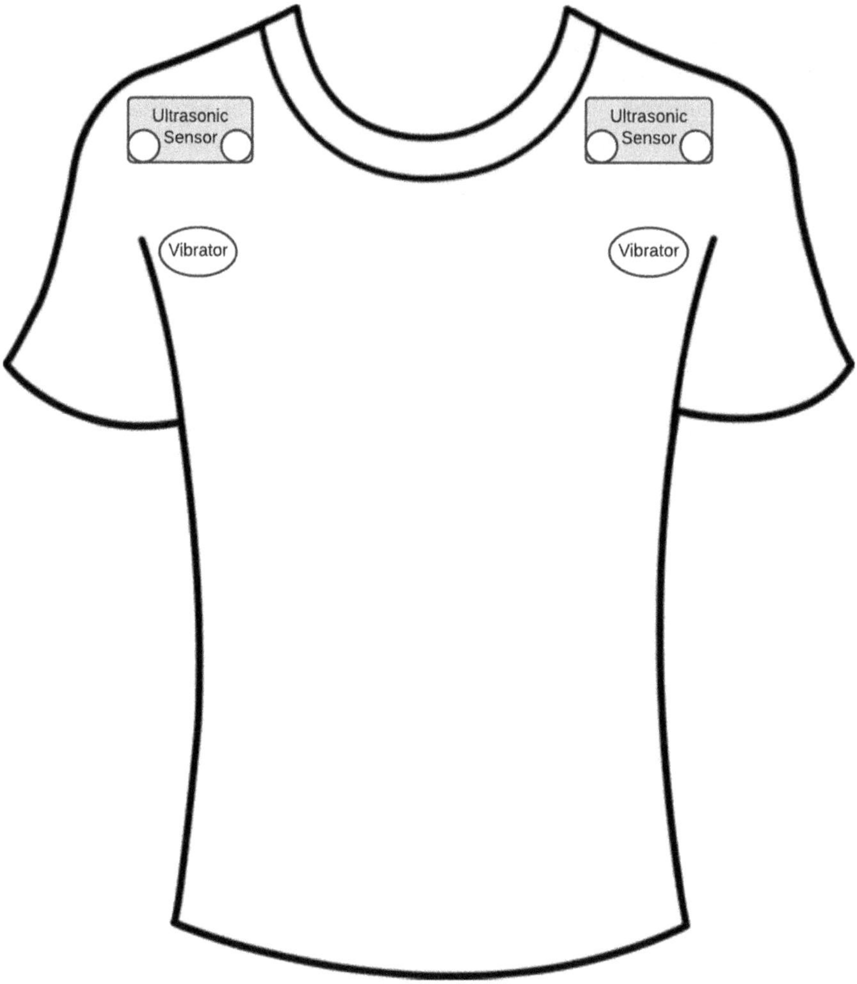

Fig. 3 This diagram shows a representation of a shirt with sensors and vibrating actuators attached to it (Clipart Library, n.d.-a)

Cardin, Thalmann, and Vexo used a jacket to hold the sonar sensors in each shoulder and vibrators on the sleeves. A microcontroller was used to calculate the distance between the person and the objects. This distance would then be transmitted to a digital-analog converter and transformed into a precise amount of how much voltage to pass to each of the vibrators. The intensity of the vibration would indicate how close an individual was to the object. Though one limitation with this system was that the sonar had roughly 60° "field of view" from where they were mounted. So relatively close objects could not be detected (Adhe et al., 2015).

Around the same time this previously mentioned system was being developed, Victor Mateevitsi, Haggadone, Leigh, Kunzer, Kenyon (2013), from the University

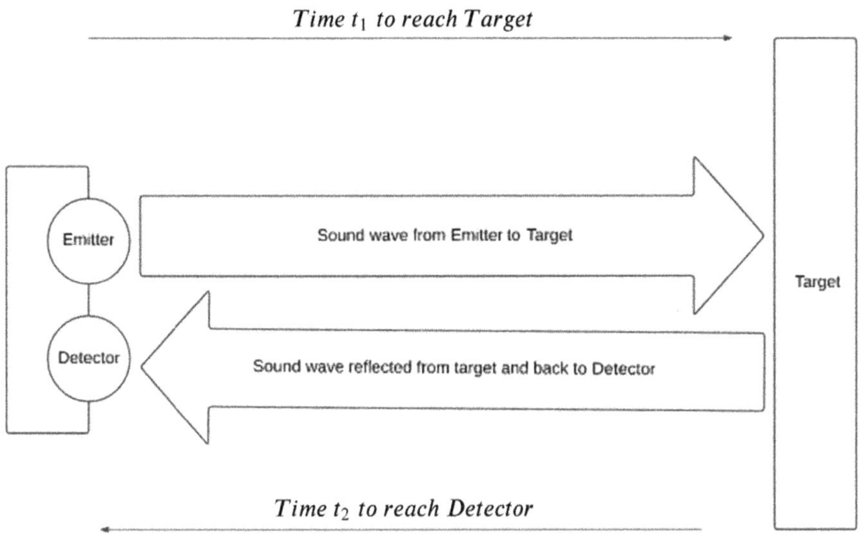

$$Distance = (Ultrasonic\ wave\ velocity) \times (time\ t_1 + time\ t_2)$$

Fig. 4 This diagram shows the process of an ultrasonic sensor calculating the distances to its target

of Illinois at Chicago, developed a similar system as Cardin's. They called it the SpiderSense. It had 13 ultrasonic sensors, and it used servos with pressure arms attached instead of vibrators. The main advantage of this design was that the individual would have a sensory field of roughly 360°. Further development of this work could be used not only to help visually impaired people, but also to improve safety, for example: cyclists riding on the road, and police officers alone on-duty.

Deep Brain Stimulation

Similar in concept to Neuralink's device, deep brain stimulation (DBS) is a surgical procedure that has been used in the treatment of the symptoms of Parkinson's disease and other movement disorders (Medical Advisory Secretariat, 2005). While the cause for Parkinson's disease is still unknown, researchers have been able to identify that it causes cell death in the midbrain region (substantia nigra) in charge of creating dopamine, an important hormone and neurotransmitter that tells one's body how to feel and is also used to transmit messages between nerve cells (Britannica, 2020). This neurodegeneration causes an imbalance in the dopamine levels and thus creates motor control issues associated with Parkinson's disease. The most distinctive symptoms are tremors. The only drug currently available that effectively deals with Parkinson's disease is called Levodopa, and deep brain stimulation is used to supplement it (Medical Advisory Secretariat, 2005).

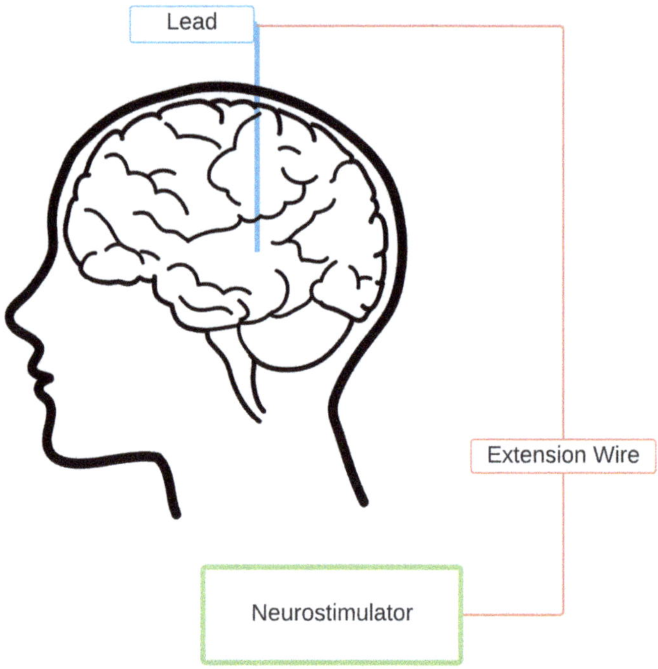

Fig. 5 This diagram shows the mechanisms behind an early deep brain stimulator (DBS) (Clipart Library, n.d.-b)

The development of deep brain stimulation started in the 1980s after scientists were able to identify how to suppress the neurological symptoms. This device is composed of three components: a neurostimulator to generate electric impulse, one lead (a thin coiled wire insulated with polyurethane), and an extension to connect the previous two devices. Depending on how severe the motor disorder is, unilateral versus bilateral, a second device may also be used (Medical Advisory Secretariat, 2005) (Fig. 5).

Reverse Systems: Developing a Human Brain in a Robotic System

One of the purposes of designing robotic systems based on the human brain is so that the human–robot interaction is less awkward. Humans have learned to interact with each other over generations, and without realizing this, we communicate by mimicking each other's gestures, way of speaking, or even their stance and frame of mind.

By focusing on how the brain functions and how humans behave, a group of engineers decided to look for new ways to approach the design of robots (Markram et al., 2011). Instead of programming every function of the robot, these engineers decided to create a robotic system that would mimic the human central nervous system, which gives us multiple adaptive control mechanisms that keep learning as situations change. This was observed during an experiment in which a human was asked to hold a handle controlled by a robot. As the handle was moved, the human was able to adapt to the robot's actions by counteracting the perturbations made by the robot. This infers that the central nervous system is able to make the most effective use of the energy by creating internal predictive models to generate force in anticipation of the perturbation (Oztop et al., 2015). This goes back to the idea that cybernetics is the control loop of "input, decision, and output," in which the predictive models are part of decision making.

To further investigate this robotic system that imitates the human brain, robots were given visual and sensory devices which would help their awareness. Like humans, the robot needs to perceive the current state of its body before moving to the next state. This neural representation of the body in the brain is referred to as the body schema (Naito & Morita, 2014). A new paradigm called "robot skill generation using human sensorimotor learning" (RSHL) was proposed to teach robots human skills. This paradigm integrates with the human motor control system by establishing an intuitive teleoperation system, where a human operator learns to control the joints of the robot (Oztop et al., 2015). As these operations are performed more often, the robot seems to incorporate the human operator's body schema.

Future use of this RSHL paradigm could produce robots that could learn to perform tasks as if they were performed by other humans. The only caveat – or maybe even a future job opportunity – is that it would require a human to teach these skills to the robot. We could see the job markets changing as robots replace human laborers. Harvest CROO Robotics designed a robot to pick fruits that would do the work of 30 humans (Paquette, 2014). If we look around us, we can already see some of these labor-intensive jobs getting replaced. Robots like the Roomba can already sweep, vacuum, and mop the floors. We even also have lawn robots to mow grass (Vaglica, 2016). As one can see, the RSHL paradigm is here to change the way humans interact with the world around them.

Ethical Implications of Cybernetic Systems

Two key ethical implications of cybernetic systems are whether or not it is "natural" for humans to have extraordinary capabilities, and whether humans should have those. These ethical concerns are unlikely to become a large contention until much later, when cybernetic systems are commercially available, and biological enhancements using such systems start to become the new norm.

Many of these concerns are actually aligned with the key ethical considerations regarding genetic engineering changes to the human state. This is likely because both genetic engineering and embedded cybernetic systems have the ability to enhance humans beyond the natural biologic capabilities with which they are endowed. By artificially enhancing humans, one of the major questions becomes whether defying the natural course of evolution should be allowed (Almeida & Diogo, 2019).

Commensurate with the ideas of rapid enhancement, ethical concerns which should be discussed in advance are the unfair advantages presented by having first access to such technologies. We mentioned that there have been advances in helping visually impaired people "to see with their ears." This type of echolocation technology could potentially be used in combination to give one side an unfair advantage in night battles or during events when visibility is a crucial tactical problem.

In competitive sports, doping, i.e., the use of illegal substances to enhance and improve the natural human condition, is generally considered illegal and presents grounds for disqualification (Macur, 2014). On this note, take for example cycling. If an athlete would use sensory devices to be aware of his competitors, he then could efficiently focus all his energy on the race: burning extra energy when other athletes were in the front or behind, and conserving energy when other competitors fall far behind. In baseball, the batter could have a sensor on his helmet or shoulder letting him know when to swing. In car racing, the driver would just focus on the acceleration, while the system would focus on deceleration (braking). One can see that while these systems do not yet exist or are not used, ethically, using these augmenting devices to improve the human condition could be considered unfair to the ones without access to them. One recent controversy was when in 2019 Eliud Kipchoge won a marathon in less than 2 hours while wearing a running-shoes prototype. Though the shoes were not banned for upcoming competitions, it took the International Olympic Committee (IOC) nearly 6 months to make that decision. In this example, the shoes were not part of an active robotic system that made the user run faster, but the design did provide a passive feedback loop which enhanced the runner's speed: both by providing more comfort to the runner's legs and by adding extra spring in the step, thus adding more speed and efficiency. Going back to the idea that cybernetics is the control loop of "input, decision, and output," the shoe design greatly increases the athlete's output.

Conclusion

Cybernetics is, as Norbert Wiener, defined: "the science of control and communications in the animal and machine" (Britannica, 2014). This rapidly growing field is pushing the barriers of science and medicine as we know them today. From neuroprosthetics and other data-driven artificial organs to robotic systems, cybernetic systems encompass the sphere of possibilities that occur at the direct intersection of computer systems and humans.

In this chapter, we have mostly focused on the medical uses of prosthetics. First, we focused on noninvasive systems that used electromyography to record and translate skeletal activities in prosthetic limb movements. Second, we looked at the advanced robotic myoelectric prostheses. Third, we discussed more invasive systems like artificial retinas and the Neuralink Corporation, which take cybernetic systems one step further by integrating computer and robotic machines with the human brain.

Future applications of brain–machine interfaces like the Neuralink open the field for many other possibilities that humans have yet to achieve, such as increasing human memory, psychomotor accuracy, and speed.

However, due to the extensive and untapped potential of cybernetic systems, ethicists still remain wary and cautious of the development of these tools, as they lead to questions about whether or not humans should be endowed with the enhanced potential afforded by embedded computation. Beyond ethical issues, our current knowledge about how neural processes work is still dwarfed by what we have not been able to understand and to explore.

The human acceptance and use of cybernetic systems will probably be multi-phase, where the initial phases will be focused on human reconditioning like the artificial retinas and other prosthetics like Neuralink. Then, it will be followed by human enhancement where we might be able to use systems to improve human cognition. This will most likely be the slowest phase since each government has its own laws regarding medical policies and practices (Wittes & Chong, 2014).

Acknowledgments We thank the Department of Learning Technologies and the Biomedical AI Lab at the University of North Texas.

References

Adhe, S., Kunthewad, S., Shinde, P., & Kulkarni, M. (2015). Ultrasonic Smart Stick for Visually Impaired People. *IOSR Journal of Electronics and Communication Engineering.*

Almeida, M., & Diogo, R. (2019). Human enhancement: Genetic engineering and evolution. *Evolution, Medicine, and Public Health., 2019*(1), 183–189. https://doi.org/10.1093/emph/eoz026.

Britannica, T. Editors of Encyclopaedia (2014, January 15). *Cybernetics*. Encyclopedia Britannica. https://www.britannica.com/science/cybernetics

Britannica, T. Editors of Encyclopaedia (2019, May 30). *Sonar.* Encyclopedia Britannica. https://www.britannica.com/technology/sonar

Britannica, T. Editors of Encyclopaedia (2020, January 30). *Organ*. Encyclopedia Britannica. https://www.britannica.com/science/organ-biology

Cardin, S., Thalmann, D., & Vexo, F. (2006). A wearable system for mobility improvement of visually impaired people. *The Visual Computer, 23*, 109–118. https://doi.org/10.1007/s00371-006-0032-4.

Chichilnisky, E. (n.d.). *Approach*. Retrieved November 24, 2020, from https://med.stanford.edu/artificial-retina/research/approach.html

Clipart Library. (n.d.-aa). Transparent T Shirts [Image]. Retrieved from http://clipart-library.com/clip-art/transparent-t-shirts-12.htm

Clipart Library. (n.d.-bb). Clipart Brain [Image]. Retrieved from http://clipart-library.com/clipart/clip-art-brain_4.htm

Kumarasinghe, K., Kasabov, N., & Taylor, D. (2021). Brain-inspired spiking neural networks for decoding and understanding muscle activity and kinematics from electroencephalography signals during hand movements. *Scientific Reports, 11*, 2486. https://doi.org/10.1038/s41598-021-81805-4.

Lewis, P. M., & Rosenfeld, J. V. (2016). Electrical stimulation of the brain and the development of cortical visual prostheses: A historical perspective. *Brain Research, 1630*, 208–224. https://doi.org/10.1016/j.brainres.2015.08.

Markram, H., Meier, K., Lippert, T., Grillner, S., Frackowiak, R., Dehaene, S., Knoll, A., Sompolinsky, H., Verstreken, K., DeFelipe, J., Grant, S., Changeux, J., & Saria, A. (2011). Introducing the human brain project. *Procedia Computer Science, 7*, 39–42. https://doi.org/10.1016/j.procs.2011.12.015.

Mateevitsi, V., Haggadone, B., Leigh, J., Kunzer, B., and Kenyon, R.V. (2013). Sensing the environment through SpiderSense. *Proceedings of the 4th augmented human international conference*, pp. 51–57.

McFarland, D. J., & Wolpaw, J. R. (2017). EEG-based brain-computer interfaces. *Current Opinion in Biomedical Engineering, 4*, 194–200. https://doi.org/10.1016/j.cobme.2017.11.004.

Medical Advisory Secretariat. (2005, March 1). Deep brain stimulation for Parkinson's disease and other movement disorders: An evidence-based analysis. *Ontario health technology assessment series, 5*(2), 1–56.

Millett, D. (2001). From psychic energy to the EEG. *Perspectives in Biology and Medicine, 44*(4), 522–542. https://doi.org/10.1353/pbm.2001.0070.

Montouri, A. (2011). *Cybernetics.* Retrieved November, 2020 from https://www.sciencedirect.com/topics/neuroscience/cybernetics

Musk, E. (2019). An integrated brain-machine Interface platform with thousands of channels. *Journal of Medical Internet Research, 21*(10). https://doi.org/10.2196/16194.

Naito, E., & Morita, T. (2014). Brain and nerve = Shinkei kenkyu no shinpo, 66(4), 367–380.

Oztop, E., Ugur, E., Shimizu, Y., et al. (2015). Chapter 2: Humanoid brain science. In G. Cheng (Ed.), *Humanoid robotics and neuroscience: Science, engineering and society*. Boca Raton: CRC Press/Taylor & Francis.

Paquette, Danielle. (2014). Farmworker vs. Robot. *The Washington Post.* Retrieved October 13, 2020, https://www.washingtonpost.com/news/national/wp/2019/02/17/feature/inside-the-race-to-replace-farmworkers-with-robots/

Pascolini, D., & Mariotti, S. P. (2012). Global estimates of visual impairment: 2010. *The British Journal of Ophthalmology, 96*(5), 614–618. https://doi.org/10.1136/bjophthalmol-2011-300539.

PNGJoy. (n.d.). *Brain Human Anatomy [Image]*. Retrieved from https://www.pngjoy.com/preview/t1x2q7w9f7v6x4_human-brain-clipart-brain-human-anatomy-png-download/

Statt, N. (2017, March 27). Elon Musk launches Neuralink, a venture to merge the human brain with AI. *The Verge*. Archived from the original on February 6, 2018. Retrieved September 6, 2020.

Timmermans, S., & Kaufman, R. (2020). Technologies and health inequities. *Annual Review of Sociology, 46*(1), 583–602. https://doi.org/10.1146/annurev-soc-121919-054802.

Vaglica, S. (2016, April 12). Does a robotic lawn mower really cut it?. *The Wallstreet Journal*. Retrieved October 13, 2020, from https://www.wsj.com/articles/does-a-robotic-lawn-mower-really-cut-it-1460488911.

Warwick, K. C. U. (2020, April 2). The Future of Artificial Intelligence and Cybernetics. Retrieved March 31, 2021, from https://www.technologyreview.com/2016/11/10/156141/the-future-of-artificial-intelligence-and-cybernetics/

Weir, R. F., Troyk, P. R., DeMichele, G. A., Kerns, D. A., Schorsch, J. F., & Maas, H. (2009). Implantable myoelectric sensors (IMESs) for intramuscular electromyogram recording. *IEEE transactions on bio-medical engineering, 56*(1), 159–171. https://doi.org/10.1109/TBME.2008.2005942.

Wiggers, K. (2020, August 31). *Neuralink demonstrates its next-generation brain-machine interface.* Retrieved October 12, 2020 from https://venturebeat.com/2020/08/28/neuralink-demonstrates-its-next-generation-brain-machine-interface/

Winkler, R. (2017, March 27). Elon Musk Launches Neuralink to Connect Brains With Computers. *Wall Street Journal*. Archived from the original on May 5, 2017.

Wittes, B., Chong, J. (2014). Our Cyborg Future: Law and Policy Implications. *The Brookings Institution*. Retrieved November 15, 2020 from https://www.brookings.edu/research/our-cyborg-future-law-and-policy-implications/

Pranathi Pilla is an undergraduate student at the University of Texas at Austin. She is interested in biomedical research, particularly in the fields of computational biology, regenerative medicine, and medical devices. Her passion for these fields began in her freshman year of high school when she worked on developing a quick, efficient, and cost-effective method to detect the presence of pathogenic microorganisms using a combination of Digital in-line Holographic Microscopy and Microbial Fuel Cells, which was recognized at the Regeneron International Science and Engineering Fair (ISEF) in 2020. Over the past summer, she worked on Pupil Tracking for the Diagnosis of Parkinson's Disease in the Biomedical Artificial Intelligence Lab at the University of North Texas under the guidance of Dr. Mark V. Albert.

Rafael Anderson Alves Moreira is a graduate student in the Artificial Intelligence Masters of Science program. He works as an architect for the Site Reliability team at Demandbase, a San Francisco, CA marketing company. His primary focus at work is to improve systems' performance and infrastructure costs. His passion for programming started at the age of 8 when the school offered the first programming course. Later in college, while getting his bachelor's in computer science, he discovered his love for economics and decided that he would try to incorporate the two disciplines into his future career. He recently co-authored a paper on improving bitcoin price prediction based on COVID-19 data which was presented in January 2021 in Yokohama, Japan.

Part III
How Artificial Intelligence Imitates Human Neuroanatomy

Early Visual Processing: A Computational Approach to Understanding Primary Visual Cortex

Ryan Moye, Cindy Liang, and Mark V. Albert

Visual Processing

As previously mentioned, scientific research has led to various insights in the field of artificial intelligence (AI). AI models perform a variety of tasks from classification to regression, but one area of particular interest is in vision-related tasks; one of the most common visual models, Convolutional Neural Networks (CNNs), is inspired by research in neuroscience (Lindsay, 2020). Visual processing within the brain is accomplished through a multitude of tasks coordinated mostly by the region of the brain known as the occipital lobe. By understanding and exploring early visual processing in mammals, we are able to advance computational technologies and algorithms.

The occipital lobe is responsible for processing and interpreting the visual data collected by our eyes, which, over the millennia, our brains have adapted to process in a specific and efficient manner (Olshausen & Field, 1996). We can understand sight through a series of analogies that explain how our body functions in a computer-like fashion. The first step in seeing is when our eyes detect light. The cornea works like a camera lens to refract the light to a specific location, in our case the pupil. Our pupils then adjust, much like a camera aperture, to let a certain amount of light enter our eyes. Next, our lens focuses the light into the back of our eyeball in order for the retina to sense the light and convert it to electrochemical

R. Moye (✉) · M. V. Albert
Department of Computer Science and Engineering, University of North Texas, Denton, TX, USA
e-mail: ryanmoye@my.unt.edu; Mark.Albert@unt.edu

C. Liang
Texas Academy of Mathematics and Science, Denton, TX, USA
e-mail: cindyliang@my.unt.edu

M. V. Albert et al. (eds.), *Bridging Human Intelligence and Artificial Intelligence*, Educational Communications and Technology: Issues and Innovations, https://doi.org/10.1007/978-3-030-84729-6_12

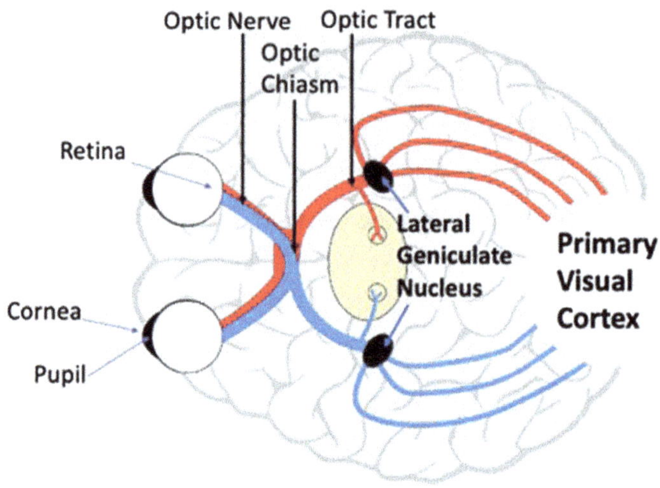

Fig. 1 The anatomy of sight
Light first enters the cornea and is then redirected from the pupil to the retina. From the retina, the light is converted into electrochemical signals which are passed down the optic nerve and split off in the optic chiasm, where the red represents the right side of vision for both eyes and the blue represents the left side. The signals travel down the optic tract and into the lateral geniculate nucleus, then finally to the primary visual cortex for processing.

impulses that are sent back to the occipital lobe via the optic nerve (Albert, 2015). These impulses can be thought of as the "data" which are now being transmitted to the "processor" or occipital lobe via the optic nerve. Once the retina converts the optical signals into electrochemical signals the optic nerve transmits this data to the optic tract, then to the lateral geniculate nucleus (LGN) which finally passes the signal into the visual cortex as shown in Fig. 1. The visual cortex is the part of the occipital lobe which processes visual data. The occipital lobe is split up into six sections, V1–V6, which deal with the various aspects of vision. V1, or the primary visual cortex, is the "sorting algorithm" of the brain. It is the first stop for all visual data to be preprocessed before being sent to V2. V1 processes sight and interprets the information it receives (Albert, 2015), then sorts the data into two categories: the what and the where. Understanding how our brain interprets and receives visual data allows us to more accurately imitate these processes in an algorithmic format.

Now that we have a basic idea of how the brain processes visual data, let us look at the same topic from a computational standpoint. Computers portray images as a matrix of connected pixels. A single pixel gives no indication as to what we are looking at. However when viewed as a whole, the pixel matrix portrays an image. The same is done for videos, where each frame of the video is an individual pixel matrix that varies slightly over each frame, thus allowing us to see motion and real-time events. Computers are also able to speed up or slow down the frames per second in a video, which produces video content in high definition or slow motion. The interesting aspect of computer vision is how it "sees" pixels. These pixel values are stored in a matrix of digits which the computer can process in order to "see" or interpret the image. From there, we can perform a variety of tasks such as image classification, generation, and upscaling. This understanding of how computers interpret visual data allows us to bridge the gap between computers and an appropriate approximation of human neuroanatomy. For now, we will take a closer look at the evolution of our brain and how we can relate AI to early visual processing.

How Neural Codes Are Represented

Gabor Filters

Simple cells in the primary visual cortex (V1) use an encoding similar to two common linear filter transformations of images merging together. While the pixel-based coding described previously is a common encoding scheme for representing the light intensity of each pixel in an image, it is too localized to represent neural codes. There is a similar issue with Fourier codes as the Fourier transform results in the localized structure of the signal being lost. However, Hubel and Wiesel (1962, 1968) demonstrated that the simple cell responses of the primary visual cortex, when presented with a stimulus, can be approximated by a 2D Gabor wavelet code, similar to the one shown in Fig. 2. This is possible because the wavelet code created by the Gabor function is both localized and periodic, similar to observed simple cell responses. It is important to note that the 2D Gabor wavelet code is an oversimplification and idealization of simple cells and does not fully describe complex cells (Albert & Field, n.d.). Knowing how simple cell responses look allows for the creation of computer-generated models, specifically AI generated receptive fields.

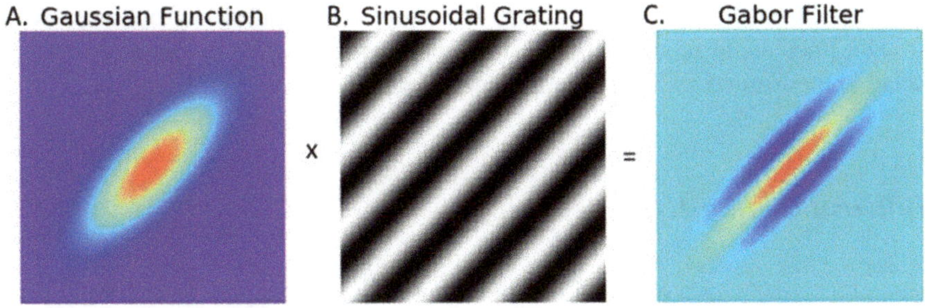

Fig. 2 Modulation of a Gaussian and sinusoidal grating to create a Gabor filter
(**a**) shows a Gaussian function from the top down, (**b**) a sinusoidal grating, and (**c**) the corresponding Gabor filter. Let G = a Gaussian function and S = a sinusoidal grating. Then, G * S = the resultant Gabor Filter. Notice that the sinusoid becomes spatially localized when modulated with the Gaussian function.

Fig. 3 Gabor filter applied to a natural image
This building (left) represents a natural image as previously discussed. When a horizontal Gabor filter (middle) is applied to the picture on the left, the resultant image (right) is produced. We can observe that (right) still maintains the basic structure of the building, but only the horizontal surfaces are prevalent in the image.

How Gabor Filters Work

Gabor filters are simply sinusoids multiplied by a Gaussian function (Prasad & Domke, 2005) as shown in Fig. 2. Gabor filters respond to oriented lines (in our case a 2D Gabor filter responds to the oriented lines in an image) and are orientation-sensitive. This means that a picture of a building (Fig. 3), when convolved with a horizontal Gabor filter, would result in an image that shows the horizontal structures of the building while ignoring the other orientations (vertical, diagonal, etc.). That is to say the Gabor filter will only give a strong response if its direction matches the direction of the lines on the building. This further illustrates why buildings with straight lines could be called "natural images," which will be discussed in further detail in the Natural vs. Non-natural Images section.

Efficient Coding Hypothesis

Upon receiving sensory stimuli (for the purpose of this chapter we will only consider visual data), neurons inside the brain communicate and relay messages to each other by action potential spikes (Olshausen & Field, 1996). Neurons require energy in order to produce these neural codes. Thus, if our brains required a neuron to represent every potential scene we might encounter, there would need to be an infinite number of neurons in our brain, which is impossible. A solution to this problem would be to have a set number of neurons that communicate details of an image by using many different complicated patterns. However, this idea is also implausible because solely relying on these patterns to interpret stimuli would still be very energy-consuming if we need a different set of neurons for each pattern that exists. Therefore, to conserve energy, a goal in early sensory processing is to reduce redundancy (Field, 1987). The Efficient Coding Hypothesis states that by utilizing sparse coding, more images can be interpreted with a limited number of neurons in an energy efficient way (Albert & Field, n.d.).

Over time, animals have evolved to use sparse coding of sensory stimuli as a way to increase metabolic efficiency. Sparse coding allows for less neuronal firing, which reduces energy consumption upon receiving external stimuli from natural sources. While the efficient coding hypothesis was derived from a neuroscience standpoint, extensive research has been done to understand this concept from a computational view. Olshausen and Field (1996) showed how simple cells can be represented with the use of sparse coding, which allowed computationally derived neural filters to be.

Although the efficient coding hypothesis models neuron behavior in a detailed way, neural codes are actually more complicated and provide more information than the individual firing rate of a neuron (Albert & Field, n.d.). There is an ongoing debate as to whether neural coding is a form of rate coding in which the average firing rate of a neuron is accounted for or temporal coding in that the relative timing of each neural spike matters. Since neurons have high frequency fluctuations with respect to their firing rates, we can surmise that the fluctuations are either noise, or potentially carry information. Rate coding suggests that this is noise, while temporal coding suggests that the relative timing of the neural spike also carries relevant information. Thus, while the efficient coding hypothesis gives us an understanding of the genetic algorithm our brains use to produce neural codes, there is still more to the process as it is more complex than a firing rate.

Natural Vs. Non-natural Images

Animals' and humans' adaptation to an efficient coding paradigm has resulted in an evolutionarily fit processing of sensory stimuli. This efficient coding has enabled our brains to process natural stimuli while firing a limited number of neurons, thus conserving energy (Barlow, 1961). For our purposes, natural stimuli are anything that humans and animals have seen for many generations such as Fig. 4 (a and b). These images can range from bodies of water and mountain ranges to manmade structures such as bridges and statues. However, these are only a few examples of natural images. To further elaborate on this, natural images are virtually any landscape or any scenery that has existed for long enough for the process of evolution to take place. We consider any structure that has straight edges (horizontal, vertical, diagonal, etc.) to be "natural" as well. Therefore skyscrapers, houses, cars, and other manmade structures also constitute "natural" imagery. Figure 3 shows an example of a manmade structure convolved with a horizontal Gabor filter. Defining what constitutes a "natural" image helps us understand what visual data applies to the efficient coding hypothesis and how we can model this concept computationally.

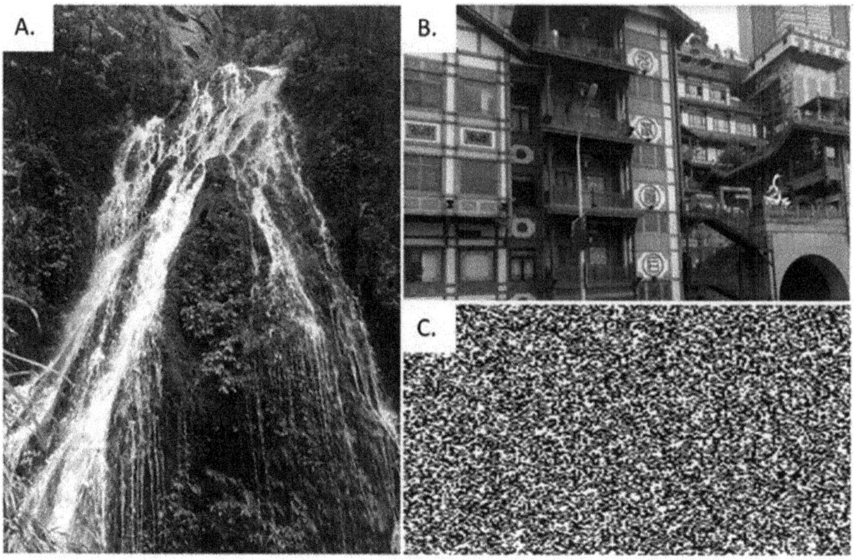

Fig. 4 Example of natural and non-natural images
(**a**) shows a natural scene in which brains have evolved to efficiently encode. (**b**) is a manmade structure, yet because it is composed of horizontal and vertical lines we still consider it to be a natural image. (**c**) shows static, of which our brains have not evolved to process efficiently.

On the other hand, non-natural images are like those in Fig. 4 (c) or psychedelic imagery. Unlike natural images, non-natural images do not have hard edges or structures similar to those seen in nature. QR codes are also good examples of non-natural stimuli, along with TV static that is pictured in Fig. 4 (c). While it may seem counterintuitive, a cloudless, blue sky is also harder for our brains to efficiently process as it is missing any of the hard edges needed for Gabor filters to apply, and thus are also considered non-natural. Essentially, our brains have developed patterns to recognize natural scenes and stimuli, and thus fire a limited, or sparse, amount of neurons in response. However, we have no evolutionary traits that help us process non-natural stimuli (Olshausen & Field, 2000). Thus, these concepts are important to note as the efficient coding hypothesis can only be applied to natural images.

ICA

As mentioned, the primary visual cortex responds to natural stimuli in a sparse manner, so to replicate this in an algorithmic manner we need a way to find the representation of the stimuli. Independent component analysis (ICA) accomplishes this goal as shown by Hyvärinen & Oja (2000). ICA is an unsupervised learning approach that, similar to principal component analysis (PCA), uses linear transformations to re-represent the data with a new set of coordinates, where each representation is as statistically

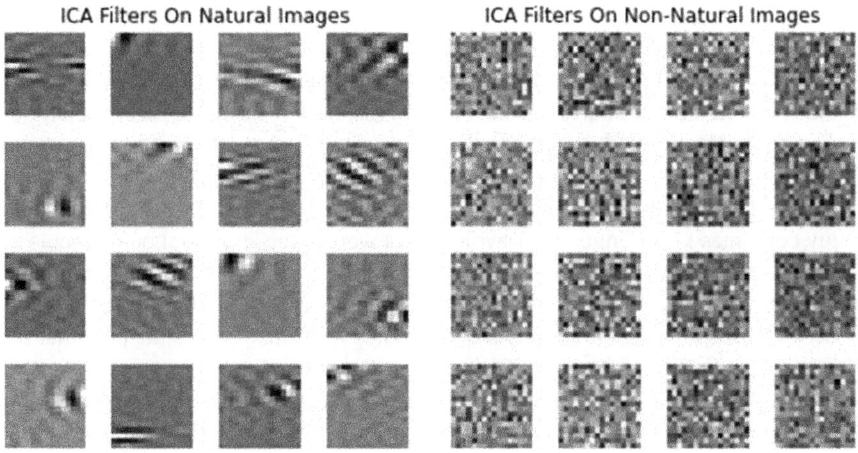

Fig. 5 ICA-encoded filters of grayscale images
Filters produced by ICA when viewing natural image patches left. Filters produced by ICA when viewing non-natural image patches right

independent as possible. ICA achieves this by searching for components that lead to the least Gaussian data distributions. As the central limit theorem suggests, the sum of a set of random variables goes toward a Gaussian distribution (Bell & Sejnowski, 1997). Thus, the original factors of the data will be less Gaussian than a random selection. The combinations of mixed components that are least Gaussian will generally draw out the original sources if it is possible to detect them through a linear combination.

To apply ICA to early visual processing, we can extract small patches as input from a natural image (small being on the order of 8x8 to 32x32 pixels) such that we are unable to tell what we are seeing anymore. Once we pass these patches through ICA, the resultant output closely resembles the neurally encoded filters of the brain. That is to say, the ICA-encoded filters are Gabor-like and represent the simple cell filters as described in the Gabor Filters section. The output from applying ICA to natural and non-natural images is shown in Fig. 5. Urs, Behpour, Georgaras, and Albert (2020) created an accessible Jupyter notebook that allows users to play around with ICA and to see how natural vs. non-natural images produce neural-like and non-neural-like filters respectively. Further research to apply these filters to current models is under way and the potential applications to computer vision looks promising.

Applications of Neural Modeling

Decoding V1 to See What Images Are Being Perceived

There are currently many studies that focus on the applications of 2D Gabor wavelet codes for visual processing. One study further elaborates on the ability of 2D Gabor wavelet codes to reconstruct images using a technique called the Bayesian decoder

(Naselaris, Prenger, Kay, Oliver, & Gallant, 2009), which utilizes FMRI signals to predict the image that one is seeing. FMRI focuses on a signal stimulus that researchers can easily decode and interpret and images are able to be reconstructed by using Gabor codes to analyze early visual areas. As mentioned earlier in this chapter, our brains have adapted to become familiar with natural images. Natural images are important to this field of study because they are relevant for subjective processes and daily perception such as imagery and dreaming (Naselaris et al., 2009). This study combines knowledge of V1 evolution as well as the structural components of Gabor wavelet codes to explain the process in which our brain executes image analysis. This ability to recreate images from neural signals utilizing Gabor wavelet codes demonstrates the current state of technology, but also shows the potential for future developments.

Furthermore, an elaborate study has been made on the vision of monkeys at Cornell University to further investigate Gabor wavelet codes and the primary visual cortex of primate brains (Kindel, Christensen, & Zylberberg, 2017). Researchers built a convolutional neural network to predict the V1 activity produced by natural images. This network uses Gabor wavelets to model simple cell response to visual information. Scientists were able to discover that the rates of firing neurons can be depicted fairly accurately by the network. This process also allowed scientists to identify image features that caused the neurons to spike. The researchers suggest that one potential application of the knowledge accumulated from this study would be that sight could potentially be restored to the blind (Kindel et al., 2017). The example given was a camera to brain translator which could be implemented to feed images into the researchers' neural networks directly from brain activity. Through the advancements in computational neuroscience and AI, modern healthcare is continuing to progress in great strides as illustrated above.

Conclusion

AI and technology have long been modeled after our understanding of neuroanatomy, and this chapter bridges some of the gaps between the two subjects. As illustrated in the previous section, the applications of 2D Gabor wavelet codes are immense, and are capable of representing simple cells found in the brain. Upon further development, these codes have the potential to give sight to the blind (Kindel et al., 2017), as well as other visual impairments people may experience. With new knowledge of 2D Gabor wavelet codes, engineers and researchers can find ways to further enhance their respective fields. Algorithms, such as ICA, have been shown to produce Gabor-like filters similar to those observed in the brain (Hyvärinen & Oja, 2000). These oriented and bandpassed neural filters help the brain interpret visual data; however, they only apply to "natural" images. As stated by the efficient coding hypothesis, one of the main goals in early visual processing is to reduce redundancy in neuronal firing, and thus process data in a metabolically efficient manner. Continued studies on these topics have allowed researchers to apply computational methods to early visual processing and in turn learn more about the field of computer vision. The ability of computers to model processes that traditionally only occurred within the primary visual cortex of human or animal brains illuminates how human intelligence can inspire artificial intelligence and culminates in new and exciting research.

References

Albert, M. V. (2015). *The Brain Geography Mini-Course: a neuroscience outreach effort.* Retrieved from https://ecommons.luc.edu/cgi/viewcontent.cgi?article=1106&context=cs_facpubs

Albert, M. V., & Field, D. J. (n.d.). Neural Representation/Coding. *Encyclopedia of Perception.* Retrieved from https://doi.org/https://doi.org/10.4135/9781412972000.n205

Barlow, H. B. (1961). Possible principles underlying the transformation of sensory messages. *Sensory Communication, 1*, 217–234.

Bell, A. J., & Sejnowski, T. J. (1997). The 'independent components' of natural scenes are edge filters. *Vision Research, 37*(23), 3327–3338.

Field, D. J. (1987). Relations between the statistics of natural images and the response properties of cortical cells. *Journal of the Optical Society of America. A, Optics and Image Science, 4*(12), 2379–2394.

Hubel, D. H., & Wiesel, T. N. (1962). Receptive fields, binocular interaction and functional architecture in the cat's visual cortex. *The Journal of Physiology, 160*, 106–154.

Hubel, D. H., & Wiesel, T. N. (1968). Receptive fields and functional architecture of monkey striate cortex. *The Journal of Physiology, 195*(1), 215–243.

Hyvärinen, A., & Oja, E. (2000). Independent component analysis: Algorithms and applications. *Neural Networks: The Official Journal of the International Neural Network Society, 13*(4–5), 411–430.

Kindel, W. F., Christensen, E. D., & Zylberberg, J. (2017, June 19). *Using deep learning to reveal the neural code for images in primary visual cortex. arXiv [q-bio.NC].* Retrieved from http://arxiv.org/abs/1706.06208

Lindsay, G. W. (2020). Convolutional neural networks as a model of the visual system: Past, present, and future. *Journal of Cognitive Neuroscience*, 1–15.

Naselaris, T., Prenger, R. J., Kay, K. N., Oliver, M., & Gallant, J. L. (2009). Bayesian reconstruction of natural images from human brain activity. *Neuron.* Retrieved from https://www.sciencedirect.com/science/article/pii/S0896627309006850

Olshausen, B. A., & Field, D. J. (1996). Emergence of simple-cell receptive field properties by learning a sparse code for natural images. *Nature, 381*(6583), 607–609.

Olshausen, B. A., & Field, D. J. (2000). Vision and the coding of natural images: The human brain may hold the secrets to the best image-compression algorithms. *American Scientist, 88*(3), 238–245.

Prasad, V. S. N., & Domke, J. (2005, 2005). Gabor filter visualization. *Journal of the Atmospheric Sciences, 13.*

Urs, N., Behpour, S., Georgaras, A., & Albert, M. V. (2020). Unsupervised learning in images and audio to produce neural receptive fields: A primer and accessible notebook. *Artificial Intelligence Review.*

Ryan Moye is a software engineer who obtained his master's degree in artificial intelligence from the University of North Texas. His primary research interests include automation, computational neuroscience and efficient coding techniques.

Cindy Liang is currently a student on the computer science track at the Texas Academy of Mathematics and Science. Cindy is interested in learning about the applications of computer science and AI to the biomedical field.

Mark V. Albert professional goal in life is to leverage machine learning to automate the collection and inference of clinically useful health information to improve clinical research. His projects in wearable sensor analytics have improved the measurement of health outcomes for individuals with Parkinson's disease, stroke, and transfemoral amputations with a variety of additional populations and contexts including children with cerebral palsy as well as healthy toddler activity tracking. Current projects include video-based activity tracking and mobile robotic platforms, all in an effort to improve measures of clinical outcomes to justify therapeutic interventions.

Visual Object Recognition: The Processing Hierarchy of the Temporal Lobe

Zachary O'Brien, Eeshan Joshi, and Himanshu Sharma

Temporal Hierarchy

For visual object recognition, there is a general consensus among the scientific community that information is processed in a "bottom-up" processing hierarchy, although some theories such as Moshe Bar's top-down processing model explain "shortcuts" for performance in the visual system (Bar, 2003).

This "bottom-up" approach is in reference to how the brain takes basic visual information such as breaking down the image into edges or lines and then "passes" these up to higher level functions that help to identify what is in our field of view (Fig. 1).

As you are aware, the primary visual cortex (V1) is the area of the brain responsible for the direct translation of visual sensory data into what would be considered an "image." After this, the visual cortex begins to split into a "dorsal" and "ventral" path, each with similar "pass ups" but slightly different functionalities.

The secondary visual cortex (V2) has both a dorsal and ventral portion. Both feeding forward from the V1 area, they combine the stimulus from the primary visual cortex and give it additional meanings such as contours and binocular vision (Heider et al., 2002).

The third visual cortex (V3) is where we begin to understand less about the specific details of the functionality but is still able to gather information about the functionality of the area. The dorsal V3 area is the first part of the visual processing system that begins to fit objects and the background together to perceive motion (Heider et al., 2002). This allows for pattern recognition and for maintaining focus on an object despite changes in position, orientation, or rotation (Riesenhuber &

Z. O'Brien (✉) · E. Joshi · H. Sharma
University of North Texas, Denton, TX, USA
e-mail: ZacharyObrien2@my.unt.edu; Eeshan.Joshi1@gmail.com; himanshusharma@my.unt.edu

M. V. Albert et al. (eds.), *Bridging Human Intelligence and Artificial Intelligence*, Educational Communications and Technology: Issues and Innovations, https://doi.org/10.1007/978-3-030-84729-6_13

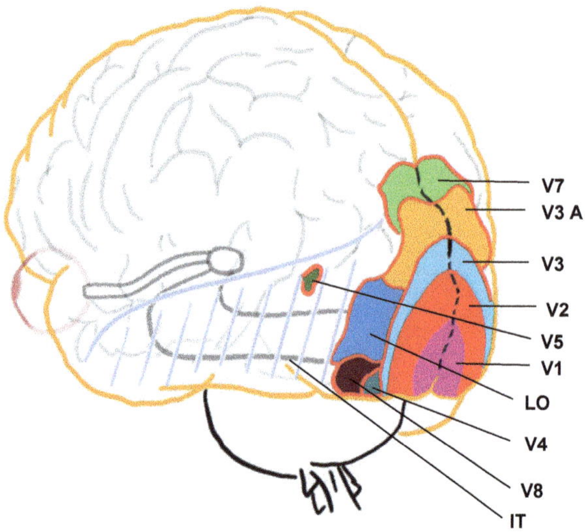

Fig. 1 The human brain from a back-left point-of-view. The left eye can be seen to the left side of the image. The V1–V6 regions of the visual cortex, the lateral occipital complex (LO), as well as the inferotemporal cortex (IT) are labeled

Poggio, 1999). The ventral V3 area begins the connection with the inferotemporal cortex and is more generalized than its dorsal counterpart. It is better able to detect both direction and color – which allow for a more holistic view of the visual field (Burkhalter & Van Essen, 1986).

The visual area V4 is the first place where strong input from V2 and general feedforward from V3 is utilized to identify object features with more detail such as objects and shapes. While we have not started identifying complex objects such as animal identification or object segmentation, we do further tune the image to be aware of orientation, bifocal vision, color, and, as previously stated, complex shapes. This is also the first point in which we see significant influence of attention in visual processing (Moran & Desimone, 1985). While this study was done in monkeys and may not be exactly the same as humans, the similarities in brain function and lack of ability to test on humans lead us to extrapolate this and apply it to our own visual faculties.

At the same time as V4 begins to process the visual as a whole, the middle temporal visual area (V5) also takes input from V1 to V3 and starts to process and keep track of movement (both eye movement and tracking movement of objects in front of us) (Dubner & Zeki, 1971).

Unfortunately, this is the point where the functional methods of this area as well as the overlap between this and other area's tracking of motion and basic visual stimulus lacks significant explanation. We do know that lesions in this area of the brain cause issues such as unsteady eye movement as well as misidentification of movement (Dürsteler et al., 1987; Britten & van Wezel, 1998).

All of this processing, refinement, and filtering moves to the inferior temporal cortex (IT) for actual object identification. Now that objects have been found, localized, segmented from each other in a 3d space, and our attention is focused on what is in front of us, our brain can finally tell what is ahead and then respond. Unfortunately this is also the part of the brain that we have the least functional knowledge on an individual function/neuron layer and is thus open for debate (Yovel & Kanwisher, 2004; Haxby et al., 2001; Gauthier et al., 2000). We do know that this is the part of the brain that is stimulated directly when known objects and especially faces are seen. Both fMRI data and studies of lesions in this part of the brain for both humans and macaques have shown us that impairment to this reason can lead to impairment of both identification of objects and faces as well as establishing memories and the ability to identify new objects. We also know that this part of the brain interacts with the occipital lobe to differentiate faces vs objects as well as with the hippocampus to recall and compare previously seen images (Spiridon et al., 2006; Denys et al., 2004).

Although the general consensus of scientists studying the VOR of the brain is the bottom-up approach that we have explained, there are contrary opinions that theorize there is a top-down "short circuit" before this bottom-up process is still being considered. Moshe Bar (2003) has written a widely accepted, although still not the most popular, theory, that "a partially analyzed version of the input image is projected… which are then back-projected as an 'initial guess' to the temporal cortex" (p. 1). This theory would help explain how the brain is able to process VOR processes so quickly because it reduces the amount of objects that the brain needs to analyze in the following bottom-up process.

What Is Visual Object Recognition?

Now that we have established the fundamental biological components for the human visual system, we can now compare that to how AI perceives the world around it. Visual object recognition (VOR) in computer vision is the ability to look at an environment and identify the objects within it. While seemingly straightforward, this follows the steps of object classification, object localization, object detection, and object segmentation. Now let us walk through these steps in VOR and how they are done (Brownlee, 2019) (Figs. 2, 4, 3, 4 and 5).

Object Classification

While many functions are the same in computer vision as they are in biology, the way we are able to achieve them is very different. In fact, the very last part of biological VOR is where we will start for artificial intelligence. Object classification takes a single image, such as a photograph, and outputs a label (classification) to describe what is in the image. This removes the complexity of locating or classifying multiple objects and allows the model to focus solely on identifying the target in the picture. Each image contains a single subject which is then compared to a set of known features divided into the trained classes. This is the simplest form of computer vision and is identifying the image as a whole rather than needing to differentiate between parts of an image, which ironically coincides with the brain's IT.

Fig. 2 Object classification

Fig. 3 Object localization

Object Localization

Object localization is the ability to not only identify an object, but define its location within an image. This builds upon the object classification step in that not only must the model identify an object class, but it is now differentiating between the subject and superfluous background data. While both are simple tasks for a person, it is easier for computers to identify a picture only showing a single subject (i.e., taking a picture of

Fig. 4 Object detection

Fig. 5 Object segmentation

your dog) than to do something such as identify and draw a box around a person in a landscape photo (i.e., finding your dog in a field of tall grass where there are other objects to distract you). It is simpler because there is no need to find where the person is when given a photo containing only one subject. In moving to object localization we begin to involve more of the lower level processing of the visual cortex for separating relevant objects from background "noise." The inherent value in being able to locate an object is, while there is an extra step, we are now able to take a more "normal" photo and identify something within it; a large improvement from a Boolean return for an image.

Object Detection

While it may seem obvious that we can localize a singular object within the given image, we now need to replicate this for multiple objects within an image – this is object detection. Unfortunately, since there are now multiple objects within an image, you may see more or fewer features than you would otherwise for an individual subject. You have to make sure you can differentiate between one subject and another (i.e., it is easier to draw a box around three dogs sitting together than it is to draw a box around each one of them individually in the picture). Because the problem just became more complicated, we now have to account more for partial features and the relationship between them. This is where neural networks become essential to artificial intelligence. These models are able to use relationships between features to identify patterns for a given classification, thus allowing us to identify multiple instances of a single object or differentiating between multiple objects. This movement of using features to differentiate objects within an image and then classify each object with a probability of identification is what separates object classification from object detection. This allows AI to interact with an environment like a human can versus only looking at one thing at a time and, in essence, applying labels.

Object Segmentation

Object segmentation is where we take the subjects within an image and then get their outline versus just a simple bounding box surrounding where we think they are. This now becomes the complete antithesis of the flow for the brain. We have begun with identifying a class, and then started to detect multiple instances of a class, but now must precisely identify the basic curves, colors, and features of the object itself. While the difference may not seem large for human perception, this can be exemplified by comparing our ability to draw a box around your dog in a photo to drawing a pixel perfect outline around the same dog in that same photo. We do this by using a pixel-wise mask generated for each object to identify what is in the image. While the identification of a subject within its bounds is the same, this need for pixel-to-pixel differentiation is the distinction between object detection and full visual object recognition. Think about what you would like to see in the difference between "there is a tumor in this area on this CT scan," and "this is exactly the shape and size of the tumor that we found."

While object classification might be a simpler process that also allows it to be faster and more accurate, image segmentation on the other hand can be more difficult and process intensive but also allows for a richer amount of use cases. It is on a case-by-case basis that we take this toolset of visual object recognition tools and decide which best fits the problem we want to solve. Each of these types of vision has its own purpose in AI, just as they do in the human brain.

New Replications of Temporal Lobe Functionality

One large separator between what the brain is capable of and the neural networks we create today is the requirement for large amounts of data in order to train the model on a very specific task. This is required because neural networks find patterns within the given data and calculate how to identify these patterns. They are extremely good at this, but they lack the general usability that humans have. A person only needs to be shown a photo of a rhino a single time to be able to identify one after that.

While neural networks have done a great job at replicating the synapses of the brain and how they work together, they have until recently missed out on an essential part of what allows for a general ability to identify objects. We have not taken the time to create an artificial hippocampus and perirhinal cortex to put more context around the visual information at hand. We train our neural networks to find patterns, but they have no memory of what they are identifying. Without some sort of reference for comparison of objects during the actual visual object recognition process, we are completely dependent on how the neural network was initially trained. Unlike how humans can interact with the world and learn new things as they go, if we want to add a new type of "object" to a completely pre-trained neural network we must completely retrain what we are doing any time there is an alteration in possible classification (Figs. 6 and 7).

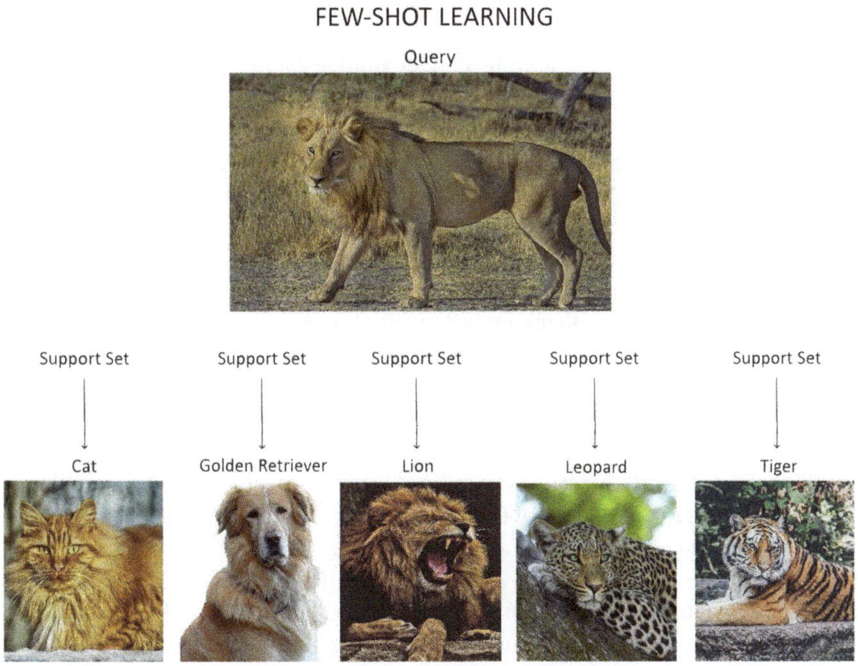

Fig. 6 Example of base neural network training data for feature extraction

Fig. 7 Few shot support set with classes not contained in the training data

Few/Zero Shot learning solves this issue of having a lack of memory, expandability, and general understanding of the world around our AI. It is an attempt to take what is currently a limited functionality of the neural pathways in our brain and add long-term storage of what the network has been asked to identify. We train a network or use a CNN that is trained with similar data and then "fine-tune" the model on the fly with minimal images of this Few Shot dataset. Then, instead of simply running inference, we run inference on both the desired image and a support set (list of images of the classes we are looking for) and then compare the matrix to see what the most likely candidate is. This allows us to both use the inference for a similarly trained model as you would do in transfer learning and identify objects for which there is little to no data.

This is a great analogy for how the temporal lobe interacts with the hippocampus and other areas of the brain to maintain context of previously seen objects. When the hippocampus and other parts of the medial temporal lobe (MTL) are damaged you see immediate deficits in a person's ability to detect what objects are. For example, visual agnosia occurs when there is brain damage along the pathways that connect the occipital lobe of the brain with the parietal or temporal lobe. It is defined as "the inability to recognize objects presented visually, in the absence of any ocular or semantic deficit that could otherwise account for it" (Maia da Silva et al., 2017).

They may see and be able to interact with them, but the recognition of them becomes impaired (Lee et al., 2012). This can manifest in a few different variations depending on the specific location and amount of damage to the MTL such as getting a "feeling of knowing" without being able to identify what it is or knowing the context of an item but again not being able to recognize the object itself. Finally, the comparison between the last stages of the brain's visual object recognition to how AIs perform of object recognition is further enforced when looking at situations where there has been damage to the MTL. The brain's ability to detect and describe features of the object is not impaired. For example, an individual would still be able to say with confidence that "this is round" or "this is blue," but they would never be able to complete the process of translating these sets of features to the name (or for an AI, class) of the object.

Conclusions

The methods which a computer runs to conduct visual object recognition is almost a direct copy of the processing hierarchy in the temporal lobe. We can simplify and summarize both the brain and AI's sequence of steps to do this as follows; breaking down photons of light into data (V1), extracting features such as contours and combining images to make a 3d world (V2), using these features to segment objects and determine background from foregrounds (V3), using movement or depth or other features to filter areas of interest (V4/V5), and finally identifying the object and reacting to it (inferior temporal cortex and occipital lobe). Taking note of these similarities can give us a valuable insight both into the functionality of the human brain and to the relative progress of visual object recognition. We see that while computer vision has progressed greatly over the past decades and that computer scientists have successfully replicated much of the brain's functions for processing visual input, this replication of human evolution has not caught up yet. By keeping track of both biologists' exploration of current brain functionality and newer computer vision methodologies (that may not be a direct replication of physical structures in the brain), future advances in both biology and computer science can be evaluated and understood in a more holistic way across scientific domains.

References

Bar, M. (2003). A cortical mechanism for triggering top-down facilitation in visual object recognition. *Journal of Cognitive Neuroscience, 15*(4), 600–609. https://doi.org/10.1162/089892903321662976

Britten, K. H., & van Wezel, R. J. (1998). Electrical microstimulation of cortical area MST biases heading perception in monkeys. *Nature Neuroscience, 1*(1), 59–63. https://doi.org/10.1038/259

Brownlee, J. (2019). *A gentle introduction to object recognition with deep learning*. Machine Learning Mastery. https://machinelearningmastery.com/object-recognition-with-deep-learning/

Burkhalter, A., & Van Essen, D. C. (1986). Processing of color, form and disparity information in visual areas VP and V2 of ventral extrastriate cortex in the macaque monkey. *The Journal of Neuroscience: The Official Journal of the Society for Neuroscience, 6*(8), 2327–2351. https://doi.org/10.1523/JNEUROSCI.06-08-02327.1986

Denys, K., Vanduffel, W., Fize, D., Nelissen, K., Peuskens, H., Van Essen, D., & Orban, G. A. (2004). The processing of visual shape in the cerebral cortex of human and nonhuman primates: A functional magnetic resonance imaging study. *The Journal of Neuroscience, 24*(10), 2551–2565. https://doi.org/10.1523/JNEUROSCI.3569-03.2004

Dubner, R., & Zeki, S. M. (1971). Response properties and receptive fields of cells in an anatomically defined region of the superior temporal sulcus in the monkey. *Brain Research, 35*(2), 528–532. https://doi.org/10.1016/0006-8993(71)90494-x

Dürsteler, M. R., Wurtz, R. H., & Newsome, W. T. (1987). Directional pursuit deficits following lesions of the foveal representation within the superior temporal sulcus of the macaque monkey. *Journal of Neurophysiology, 57*(5), 1262–1287. https://doi.org/10.1152/jn.1987.57.5.1262

Gauthier, I., Skudlarski, P., Gore, J. C., & Anderson, A. W. (2000). Expertise for cars and birds recruits brain areas involved in face recognition. *Nature Neuroscience, 3*(2), 191–197. https://doi.org/10.1038/72140

Haxby, J. V., Gobbini, M. I., Furey, M. L., Ishai, A., Schouten, J. L., & Pietrini, P. (2001). Distributed and overlapping representations of faces and objects in ventral temporal cortex. *Science (New York, N.Y.), 293*(5539), 2425–2430. https://doi.org/10.1126/science.1063736

Heider, B., Spillmann, L., & Peterhans, E. (2002). Stereoscopic illusory contours–Cortical neuron responses and human perception. *Journal of Cognitive Neuroscience, 14*(7), 1018–1029. https://doi.org/10.1162/089892902320474472

Lee, A. C., Yeung, L. K., & Barense, M. D. (2012). The hippocampus and visual perception. *Frontiers in Human Neuroscience, 6*, 91. https://doi.org/10.3389/fnhum.2012.00091

Maia da Silva, M. N., Millington, R. S., Bridge, H., James-Galton, M., & Plant, G. T. (2017). Visual dysfunction in posterior cortical atrophy. *Frontiers in Neurology, 8*, 389. https://doi.org/10.3389/fneur.2017.00389

Moran, J., & Desimone, R. (1985). Selective attention gates visual processing in the extrastriate cortex. *Science (New York, N.Y.), 229*(4715), 782–784. https://doi.org/10.1126/science.4023713

Riesenhuber, M., & Poggio, T. (1999). Hierarchical models of object recognition in cortex. *Nature Neuroscience, 2*(11), 1019–1025. https://doi.org/10.1038/14819

Spiridon, M., Fischl, B., & Kanwisher, N. (2006). Location and spatial profile of category-specific regions in human extrastriate cortex. *Human Brain Mapping, 27*(1), 77–89. https://doi.org/10.1002/hbm.20169

Yovel, G., & Kanwisher, N. (2004). Face perception: Domain specific, not process specific. *Neuron, 44*(5), 889–898. https://doi.org/10.1016/j.neuron.2004.11.018

Zachary O'Brien graduated with a degree in Computer science from Southern Methodist University in 2013. After working in the field of computer vision for 6 years, he decided to further improve his technical knowledge by pursuing a M.S. in Artificial Intelligence at the University of North Texas. Upon completing this degree he plans to open a computer vision startup for applications in biomedical engineering.

Eeshan Joshi recently graduated from the Texas Academy of Mathematics and Science and is currently an undergraduate researcher and student at the University of North Texas. He is particularly interested in the applications of AI in biomedicine and has future aspirations of becoming a physician. He was named Undergraduate Research Fellow at UNT and has plans to continue contributing to medical research.

Himanshu Sharma graduated with a Master's Degree in Computer science from University of North Texas in 2020. Currently, he is a Ph.D Candidate in the Computer Science Department from University of North Texas. He has a strong interest in the application of AI and other cognitive technologies in medical settings.

Visual-Spatial Processing: The Parietal Lobe in Engaging a 3D World

Michael Solomon and Ying Hsuan Lo

Visual-Spatial Processing

Imagine walking around a corner to see a bicyclist racing toward you, prompting you to dodge the impending crash within a fraction of a second. Now consider automated cheating prevention software tasked with recognizing when a student turns their attention away from the screen. While these processes might seem unrelated to one another, they both rely on motion detection to recognize movement in their respective stimuli. In the case of the bicycle example, the pedestrian's nervous system utilizes visual-spatial processing through the dorsal stream in the brain, a neural system that has been built and refined for countless years through evolution. The dorsal visual stream is one part of the two-stream hypothesis, the method by which scientists currently believe neural processing of visual signals occurs in the human brain (Fig. 1).

Sensory information received by the eyes is first communicated down the optic nerve, where it is passed further to the visual cortex in the occipital lobe of the brain. Following processing in the visual cortex, neuronal signals from the different regions of the visual cortex proceed into the two streams, hence the name "two-stream hypotheses." The dorsal stream extends from the primary visual cortex in the occipital lobe to multiple regions throughout the parietal cortex. The pathway is primarily responsible for processing the neuronal inputs for spatial awareness, motion detection, and related motor control functions.

M. Solomon (✉)
Texas Academy of Mathematics and Science, Denton, TX, USA
e-mail: michaelsolomon2@my.unt.edu

Y. H. Lo
University of North Texas, Denton, TX, USA

M. V. Albert et al. (eds.), *Bridging Human Intelligence and Artificial Intelligence*, Educational Communications and Technology: Issues and Innovations, https://doi.org/10.1007/978-3-030-84729-6_14

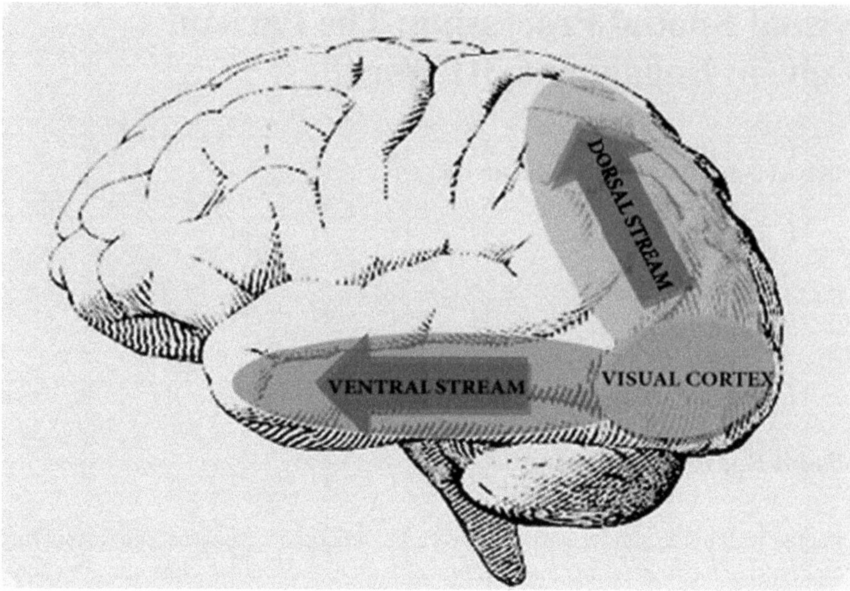

Fig. 1 Diagram illustrating the two-stream hypothesis

While the dorsal and ventral streams have many overlapping functions that make it difficult to separate the two streams conclusively, the dorsal stream is generally known to manage visual information related to the spatial context of objects (Hebart & Hesselmann, 2012). After reaching the parietal lobe, these signals are utilized by the surrounding regions to aid in actions such as visual-based movement and perceptions such as motion detection. Such processes in the brain are vital in the everyday life of human beings, and their importance is apparent in individuals with dorsal stream defects, with consequences ranging from impaired perception to motion blindness.

Mapping to AI

Human brains conduct spatial visual processing through large amounts of visual experiences built daily. As mentioned previously, in the primary visual cortex in the occipital lobe, rudimentary spatial awareness and information of an object are pieced together to form motion awareness with considering each of them associatively and further to be processed to invoke an action-based function to interact with our real world in multiple regions there. From the AI aspect of view, the creation of spatial relation reasoning where graph (visual) data for object recognition, configuration, and detection formed by time will be netted and computerized. This reasoning or cognition is a key point in developing intelligent behavior. Considering all of the requirements, graph neural network (GNN) would be a relatively appropriate fit for its graphic network structure which allows different kind of relationships to be represented, and its ability to learn reasoning from very complex relationships and the hierarchy between data which standard neural networks could only handle vectors as input data dealing with sequences or tree structures. With different settings such as input graph types, training methodologies as well as propagation functions, the model can perform different purposes respectively, including spatial reasoning, motion recognition, and detection.

Our Focus

In the previous chapter, object detection using deep learning models was introduced; in this chapter, we emphasize the unique roles of the dorsal stream. Unlike the ventral stream which recognizes objects by pulling from associated memories, the dorsal visual stream tracks the objects through spatial fields, giving us coordination. Through examining the anatomy and physiology of the dorsal stream and the effects of damage to it, we get a clearer view of the pathway. The next step is to integrate AI models dealing with these relationships between objects in space.

Anatomy and Physiology of the Dorsal Steam

Introduction

Once visual information is translated in the eye from the photons in the environment to representative neuronal signals, the information is communicated from the eye through the brain to the visual cortex. Following processing in the visual cortex, the dorsal stream projects from the occipital lobe to the posterior parietal cortex, which then further processes the information for specific tasks and communicates it to other areas of the brain that perform said tasks. Along the way, the stream carries motion- and spatial-based information via an organized array of neuronal action potentials. To truly understand this system and how it works, however, we must jointly look at the structure and function of the stream (Fig. 2).

Occipital Lobe Processing

Let us begin with the portion of the visual dorsal stream within the occipital lobe. The dorsal stream begins in the visual cortex. This region processes information through its six areas, abbreviated as V1 through V6. These areas are distinguished by their distinct structures, locations, and functions. While the parts of the visual

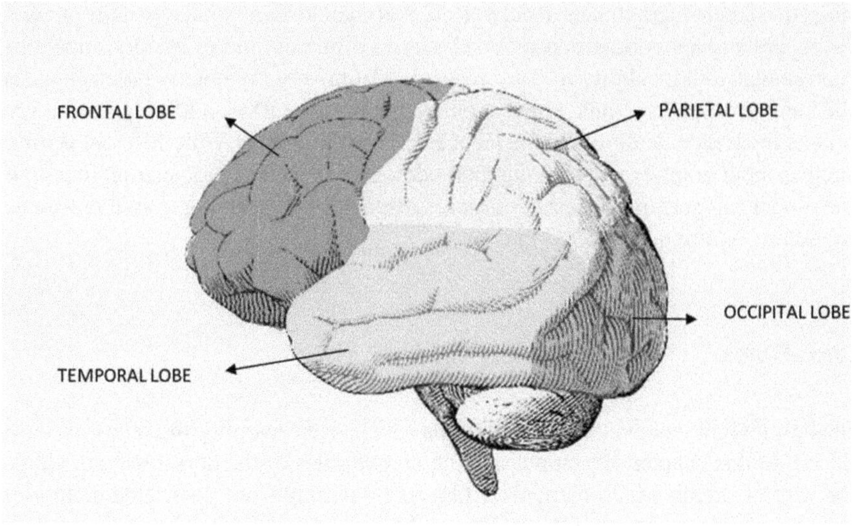

Fig. 2 Lobes of the brain

cortex deal with both dorsal and ventral functions, we will look solely at the dorsal stream related aspects.

The primary visual cortex, V1, is the first region to receive visual information and thus it begins visual processing in the visual cortex. The region is anatomically structured such that it retinotopically maps the visual feed from the retina; in other words, V1 contains a complete map of the perceived visual field via the layout of its neurons. Functionally, the region primarily utilizes two types of cells: simple cells which analyze inputs from specific receptive fields for the orientation of edges, and complex cells which integrate information from multiple simple cells (and therefore multiple receptive fields) to process more complex patterns. V1 is further organized based on function, with magnocellular regions generally dealing with motion, parvocellular regions generally dealing with shape, and regions called blobs generally dealing with color. Overall, V1 mostly deals with these three processes in small, specific regions (i.e., small receptive fields) of the visual field. After these processes have been completed, the integrated information is communicated to V2 as well as to other regions of the visual cortex (Braddick, 2001; Bear et al., 2016).

V2 is anatomically similar to V1 in the fact that it is retinotopically organized. The region not only represents the blurs of light and color that appear in our environment, but also contains supplementary information about it such as color differences, object borders, spatial frequency, and other patterns. Similar to V1, V2 has a level of structural organization that anatomically segregates the processing of color, motion, and shape computations. Compared with V1, however, V2 has a larger population of complex cells, and therefore V2 carries out processing of patterns that occur over larger portions of the visual field. In addition to projecting to other regions of the visual cortex, signals from V2 are sent back to V1 as feedback. The dorsal stream then continues from here, through V3, and into V5 (Huff et al., 2020; Ts'o et al., 2001).

Following the broader (larger receptive fields) object processing in V3, the next step in the dorsal stream is in the area known as V5, or the middle temporal visual area (MT). MT is known to be vital in dorsal stream motion processing and our perception of it, as direct electrical stimulation of MT neurons can alter the direction of motion perception. Since the cells in MT have relatively large receptive fields, the region is able to piece together the motion of different objects in relation to one another. All cells in the region respond to specific directions and are able to detect both movement of light and the lack thereof, which cells in other regions of the visual cortex are not capable of doing. In certain situations, however, cells in MT will perceive motion that does not exist in the stimulus, which results in our perception of optical illusions. The region also computes the relative speed of object movement – also through direction-specific cells – and spatial frequency, the rate at which objects appear in a field (such as a flashing light) (Bear et al., 2016).

The final stage of processing before the dorsal stream progresses to the parietal lobe occurs within a region called the medial superior temporal area (MST). MST is often talked about in conjunction with area MT, as the regions communicate back and forth, are anatomically near each other, and are functionally similar to one another. The functions of MST take two main paths. Certain neuronal sections have larger receptive fields and are involved in processing the effect known as optic flow. Optic flow can be defined as the pattern of object movement due to the movement of the observer and can be categorized into types including radial, rotational, translational, and the resulting combinations. Accounting for this effect within our visual system is vital in order for humans to perceive an environment initially and retain this perception despite self-movement. Other neuronal sections have smaller receptive fields and are involved in the generation of smooth eye movements. Here, increasingly complex visual motion information is organized and sent to regions in the posterior parietal cortex, which in turn allow for object tracking through smooth eye pursuits (Ilg, 2008; Sasaki et al., 2019; Wurtz, 1998). The benefits of such a

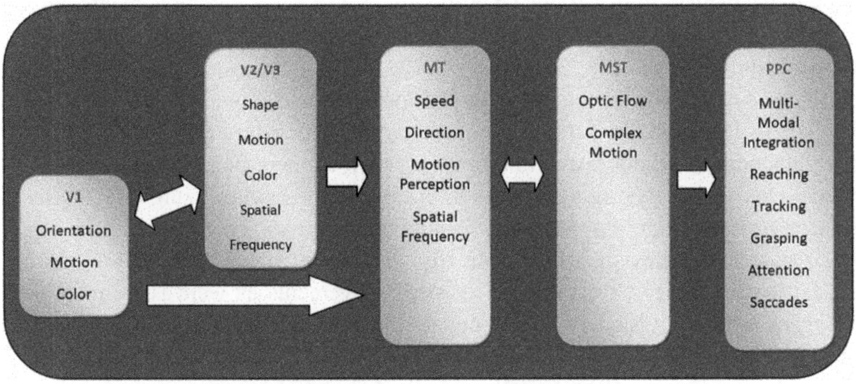

Fig. 3 A diagram showing the dorsal stream visual processing pathway

system are straightforward, as tracking the multitude of objects in our dynamic environments is a necessary aspect of our daily lives (Fig. 3).

A significant amount of dorsal stream visual processing is already done before signals reach the posterior parietal cortex, including rudimentary spatial awareness, the formation of object borders, object orientation, object movement, color information, and more. This following region converges the information from the visual cortex with information from other regions to complete action-based functions. It is due to this associative region that we can fully utilize our sense of vision to interact with the environment.

Parietal Lobe Processing

Once the information has reached the posterior parietal cortex (PPC), the areas within the region organize the visual information needed for action-based functions, such as tracking, reaching, and grasping objects. The region is divided by the intraparietal sulcus into the superior and inferior parietal lobules. These areas do not receive input from the visual cortex solely, but instead integrate inputs from several regions in the brain (i.e. multi-modal integration).

One example of a PPC function is the computation of where to distribute visual attention. This process occurs by recognizing objects with either bottom-up (sudden changes in color, position, etc.) or top-down (behavioral context, task relevance) markers (Balan & Gottlieb, 2006). Using these factors, the lateral intraparietal area (LIP), an area in the intraparietal sulcus that is known to carry out this task, creates a spatial priority (i.e., salience) map to determine which stimuli are most important/behaviorally relevant to the observer. After this information has been consolidated in PPC, the region then sends feedforward signals to other areas of the brain. These regions – namely, the frontal eye fields (FEF) in the frontal lobe and the superior colliculus (SC) in the midbrain – then scan the environment through covert attention designation and rapid eye movements called saccades (Gottlieb, 2007). Without such a mechanism to direct our attention and guide quick eye movements, understanding the stimuli in an environment would be a significantly more difficult and time-consuming task.

Outside of its role in managing spatial attention and rapid eye movements, the PPC is also involved in actions such as reaching to catch a tennis ball. Through several studies utilizing distinct methods — such as recording the activity of individual neurons, analyzing the effects of brain damage, and utilizing imaging techniques — researchers have shown that the area is involved in the processing of visually directed movements. Specifically, the studies suggest that the region has strong involvement in the planning of such movements as well as in integrating feedback from the visual system to update the ongoing motor signals (Desmurget et al., 1999). In this way, by utilizing the outputs of the visual system, PPC allows the human body to be exceptionally coordinated and concise when engaging with objects in the environment.

Another noteworthy feature of the posterior parietal cortex is the existence of "mirror" neurons. These neurons not only activate when an individual performs an action (such as grasping an apple), but also activate when that individual visually observes someone else performing that same action. Research on the subject has uncovered the existence of a mirror neuron system (MNS), part of which is embedded in the inferior parietal lobule of PPC. In essence, these neurons must encode the action being observed and therefore be involved in the visual recognition of the actions of others. Also, since this region is known to be multi-modal, some researchers believe that MNS is programmed to influence one's own intention to perform the respective actions. With regard to the practical aspect of this system, researchers believe that MNS is vital in our ability to be social beings, as dysfunctions in MNS may lead to a variety of social disorders (Jeon & Lee, 2018).

Effects of Damage

In the field of neuroscience, being as complex and interrelated as it is, one useful technique to understand the functions of a certain brain region is to observe how the brain is affected when it has significant damage to said brain region. In this section, we will look at three types of conditions due to damages to the dorsal stream and the effects that come with them.

One among the variety of different visual system disorders is agnosia, a condition which can arise from damage to the posterior parietal cortex (dorsal stream) or occipitotemporal (ventral stream) regions. In general, individuals with agnosia lack the ability to recognize objects despite having seemingly normal simple sensory skills. Agnosia itself, however, is a general term that represents several more specific conditions. One of such is dorsal simultanagnosia, where individuals cannot perceive more than one structure at a time. In other words, patients can only see and identify the object they are giving attention to. Damage to regions in the dorsal stream can cause this condition, and daily life activities such as reading and walking without bumping into objects are nearly impossible with it (Dalrymple et al., 2013; Kumar & Wroten, 2020).

A condition that fits under the umbrella of agnosia but is quite distinct from other disorders is akinetopsia; a condition where patients describe experiencing visual input as a collection of consecutive freeze frames rather than as a continuously moving environment, hence the alternative title "motion blindness." In other words, while the rolling images that these individuals see are sharp and the details within them recognizable, the images do not roll smoothly from one to the next (Robson, 2014). This condition is seen to be associated with damage to area V5 of the brain, and case studies of patients with the condition further suggest that this brain region is critical to our conscious perception of visual motion (Zeki, 2015).

Another condition that can arise from damage to the dorsal stream or more specifically the posterior parietal cortex in this case is neglect syndrome (or hemispatial neglect). Individuals with the condition will neglect, ignore, or even deny the possible existence (anosognosia) of objects on the opposite side of space to the location of the brain damage. Neglect syndrome is often divided into two types: egocentric neglect where individuals ignore objects on their left visual field, and allocentric neglect where individuals ignore aspects on the left sides of objects. For example, a patient with allocentric neglect syndrome due to a right PPC lesion tasked with drawing a clock would be unable to include the numbers on the left side of the clock (Leyland et al., 2017; Bear et al., 2016; Parton, 2004). Such a case can be seen in Fig. 4.

Together, these neurological disorders illustrate just how vital the components of the dorsal stream are in generating our spatial awareness and in utilizing visual information to perform actions. In turning to artificial intelligence to perform its own visual-spatial processing, it is both useful and effective to adapt the plethora of techniques that the human brain employs and build models off of such natural systems.

Similarities with Artificial Intelligence

Introduction

Graph Neural Network and its Variants

A GNN is a deep learning model that operates on the graph domain. It interprets graph data into nodes (or vertices) and edges (or links). Each node contains its own features, features of its edges, states, and features of the nodes in the neighborhood. Edges can represent various types of relationships such as directed (graphs that contain ordered edges), undirected (where the edge node pairs are unordered), or self-connections (self-loop). By optimizing the representation, we can include the appropriate depth of nodes (information) needed for tasks. In other words, it can represent data of nodes with an arbitrary depth (Fig. 5).

The specialty of the model is that its state can retain embedding of information of a node's neighborhood. The model computes the sum of the neighboring nodes

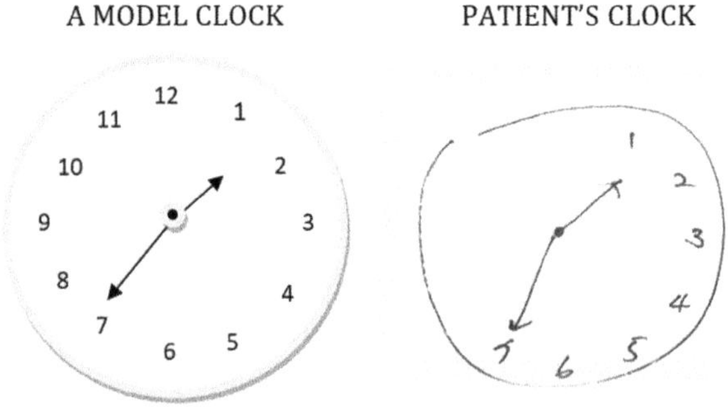

Fig. 4 Symptoms seen in a patient with neglect syndrome

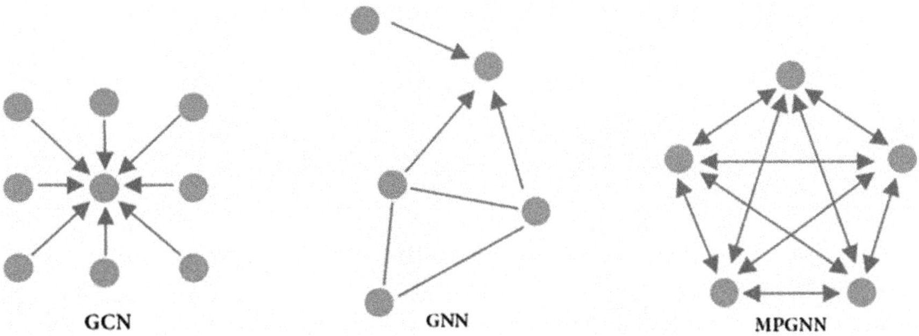

Fig. 5 GNN and its variants GCN (graph convolution networks) and MPGNN (message passing graph neural networks) models in the later examples

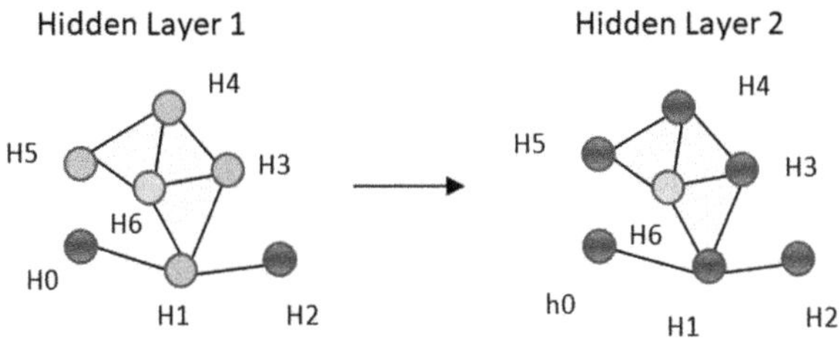

Fig. 6 Layer2 H6 = W x (H1 + H3 + H4 + H5).tw The model aggregates neighbor features (sometimes, the aggregation process computes self-features as well) to update the next layer hidden state. In this case, we use H1, H3, H4, and H5 in the hidden layer 1 to update H6 in hidden layer 2. Note: Every variant may have a different aggregation method. W in the formula represents the specific way to transform the embedding information, and it is also subject to different kinds of variants and their way of calculation

and concatenates to the input vectors of the node. The embedding information could be in various data representations according to different tasks. The model exchanges neighborhood features to update the next hidden state. In order to ensure the sum of the state reaches a stable equilibrium, an iterative procedure repeats the feedforward session multiple times until the changes to the state vectors converge. When convergence occurs, the last step node hidden states are forwarded to a readout layer which represents node features in a graph level, the back propagation process occurs in a similar manner (Figs. 6 and 7).

So, how does it work for special reasoning or movement in space? In the following sections, we demonstrate two GNN based models to demonstrate how they could represent spatial reasoning, recognizing action, and prediction via graph input which our brain highly achieved.

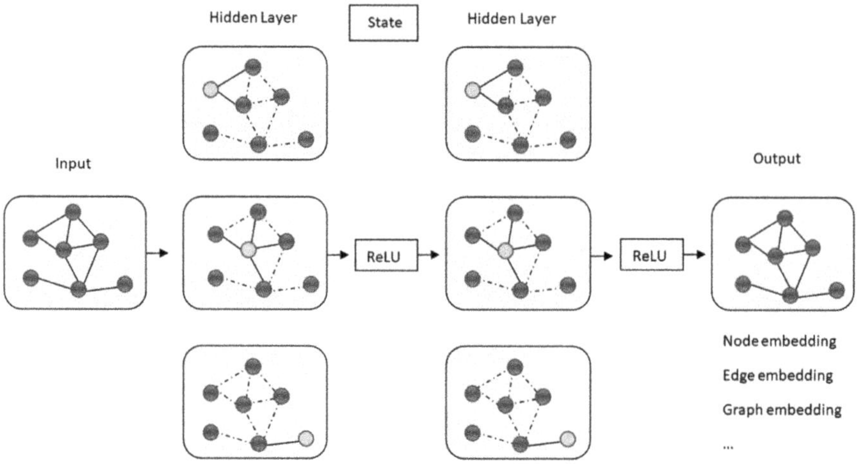

Fig. 7 A simplified example of GNN model layers

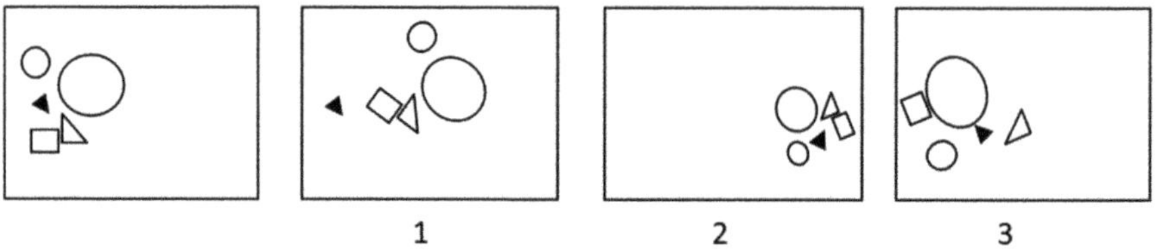

Fig. 8 Classification task, compared to the left side sample, which configuration is similar to the sample in terms of scale, shift, and shape? (Positive or negative)

Spatial Concepts through Building Relational Networks

A Practice in Application and Examination of Spatial Reasoning

The spatial benchmark, SpatialSim (Teodorescu et al., 2020), provides a set of two question tasks and corresponding image datasets. In each dataset, a set of objects is defined as a 10-dimensional feature vector; the research defines its distinct features including colors, shapes, sizes, orientations, and a particular scene containing different numbers of objects with random order. A dataset corresponds to one configuration, and the benchmark evaluates how a model performs with a set of configurations. By grouping numbers of objects in each scene into low numbers, ranging from 3 to 8 objects, medium numbers, ranging from 9 to 20 objects, and high numbers, ranging from 21 to 30 objects, levels of difficulties could be set. The first task is to classify whether the configuration of the object is in the same similarity equivalence class or different similarity equivalence class, whereas the second task is to compare two different configurations which are rearranged in space (Fig. 8).

The model has effectively solved the task for numbers of objects ranging from 3 to 30 in the first identification test and reached mean accuracies 0.97, 0.98, and 0.98 in questions of three difficult levels; In the second comparison tasks, though the accuracy drops along with the increasing difficulty of the tasks, it still achieved mean accuracies of 0.89, 0.81, and 0.71 in questions of three difficult levels. The research verified that it will perform much better with relational computation because it considers relative positions as well as absolute positions and all object to object nodes are computed when practicing the tasks.

SpatialSim is a message passing graph neural network (MPGNN) model that exhibits this type of network's ability to replicate spatial reasoning. In the experiment, researchers designed two sub-tasks to examine the model's ability to precisely reason on configuration of objects, and further examined its ability to discern whether two configurations are the same. They tried to simulate a real world scenario in which multiple entities arrange in distinct ways that constitute the properties of a configuration such as a human face. In other words, it differs from researchers working on object detection by focusing on the importance of a single object as part of a greater structure. GNN architecture uses objects as nodes and then adds a message-passing layer and node aggregation layer in order to describe a scene based on the relative position of different objects. The model uses the message function to aggregate the "message" from neighbors to update the hidden state. After node features are computed, it then conducts graph-wise aggregation to readout the whole graph. For example, this would be like trying to identify an individual in two portraits from different vantage points. It requires proficiency in spatial relation reasoning to process, and it is also necessary for further communication of space or navigation. This AI benchmark directly reflects the ability of reasoning object relations *in space (location)* which is done by the ventral stream and the dorsal stream of the brain.

Action Recognition and Prediction through GCN Model

The dorsal visual stream is involved in many aspects for visual motion analysis, engaging analysis of visual motion occurring around a particular location that we are viewing including recognition of object motion and self-motion. It is highly sensitive to visual stimuli in motion, to their speed, and to direction of movement. For the MST area, it processes the visual information in terms of space and biological motion (Galletti & Fattori 2018).

One application of GNN research is action recognition, motion analysis, and motion prediction based on features extracted from motion graphs. This is accomplished by observing one or more significant changes from each point of interest of a time series and can be further utilized in 3D analysis. This 3D skeleton based action recognition and motion prediction model is called symbiotic graph neural network (Sym-GNN), (Li et al., 2019). The research focuses on efficiently extracting spatial features and patterns of movements, analyzing these movement patterns via the input graph data which includes structural graphs, part-scale actional graphs, and joint-scale actional graphs. They fully utilize graph convolution networks (GCN) or a spectral-based GNN. Its main goal is to capture signals and features of a graph in order to transform and update it to the next layer. It reflects the rudimentary image signals, movements, and spatial relationships processing in the brain.

The model merges three parts: a deep backbone, an action-recognition head, and a motion-prediction head. The backbone applies three-branch multi-scale graph convolution networks (GCN), each serving to extract its specific spatial and temporal feature. After calculating related parameters, it then concatenates three of them together and sends the information to the two heads each building up with a multitasking scheme to launch the task. The recognition head first categorizes action class, which includes movements such as walking, greeting, or jumping and then transmit categorized information to improve prediction performance while the motion prediction head predicts poses and preserves details by self-supervision which enhance recognition ability. In this experiment, researches used graph learning and imposed multiple operators for extracting orders of motion reflecting positions, velocities, and accelerations (*variations in speed*) to assist graphic action learning and analyzing (Figs. 9 and 10).

These structural and actional graphs are helpful for the model to capture action features as well as internal correlation and will be able to achieve *real time* recognition and prediction. It is also similar to the mirror neuron system (MNS) embedded in the inferior parietal lobe of PPC which is noteworthy.

From a fundamental concept of spatial reasoning research as building models for SpatialSim benchmark to combining GNN variants to achieve complex visual-spatial processing tasks, we examined and compared the similarities between dorsal stream functionalities and corresponding GNN model applications which significantly display the potential of AI technology to achieve human brain functionalities.

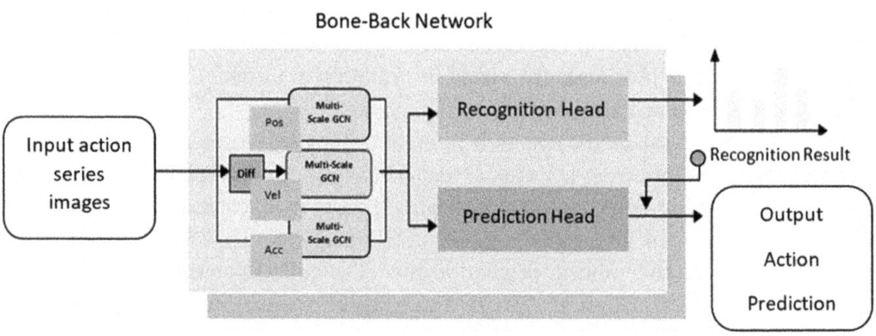

Fig. 9 Symbio GNN backbone network architecture

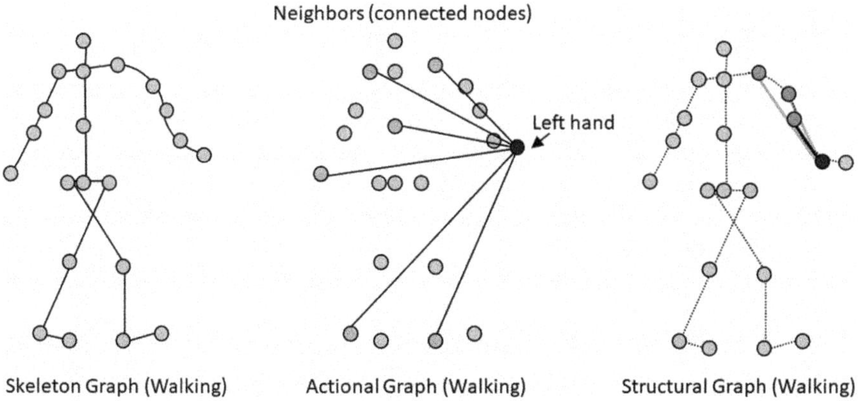

Fig. 10 Input graph types: skeleton graph, actional graph, and structure graph. Structural graphs are built on physical constraints of the skeleton and extend from it, while actional graphs are learned from an actional graph inference module (AGIM). In an actional graph, a node indicates body-part feature and an edge indicates body-part connection. Each joint is a node, and an edge connects to another joint without considering bone-connection

Applications and Potential Benefits

Due to the capabilities of spatial awareness related models like GNN, such technologies can progress our society through their application in several distinct fields. One of such regions of application is within our healthcare system. Specifically, spatial awareness technology applied to the surgical process could help prepare surgeons pre-surgery by producing three-dimensional models of the surgical site instead of the standard two-dimensional models. Since preoperative planning is difficult to do when solely utilizing 2D model of the surgical site, such a 3D model would benefit surgeons greatly in determining depths and spatial relationships between structures in the surgical site. Additionally, during the operation itself, imaging technology can help by keeping surgeons aware of the locations of vital structures and in turn prevent accidental damage within patients.

Additionally, the applications of spatially aware systems can extend to the field of rehabilitation. Such applications incorporate robotics for a more individualized motion direction discrimination training programs. They collect data and monitor progresses. There can even be more interactive playful training modes and environments for people suffering dyslexic or dorsal function damaged due to accidents (Atkinson 2016).

Conclusion

By analyzing the method by which we as humans process visual information for all its aspects and utilize the product to guide our perceptions and actions, AI researchers gain the ability to build visual-spatial systems without having to start from scratch. Recent trends of spatial reasoning research are focusing on how to integrate cognition and perception methodologies and build deep neural models upon it. The GNN models we have discussed can be used for relational inference, prediction motion of objects in different scenes, and spatial reasoning with a structural approach.

As we dig into AI research in the context of spatial reasoning and the resulting applications of it, we find a strong potential to change the world as we know it. Through biomedical technologies we have the potential to remedy visual dysfunctions, and through AI research progression we have the potential to fully utilize advanced visual processing to further develop the technology in our society.

References

Atkinson J. The Davida Teller Award Lecture, (2016) Visual Brain Development: A review of "Dorsal Stream Vulnerability"-motion, mathematics, amblyopia, actions, and attention. *Journal of Vision*. 17(3):26. https://doi.org/10.1167/17.3.26. PMID: 28362900; PMCID: PMC5381328.

Balan, P. F., & Gottlieb, J. (2006). Integration of exogenous input into a dynamic salience map revealed by perturbing attention. *The Journal of Neuroscience: The Official Journal of the Society for Neuroscience, 26*(36), 9239–9249.

Mark F. Bear, Barry W. Connors, Michael A. Paradiso. (2016). *NEUROSCIENCE: Exploring the Brain, Fourth Edition*.

Braddick, O. (2001). Occipital lobe (visual cortex): Functional aspects. In N. J. Smelser & P. B. Baltes (Eds.), *International encyclopedia of the Social & Behavioral Sciences* (pp. 10826–10828). Oxford: Pergamon.

Dalrymple, K. A., Barton, J. J. S., & Kingstone, A. (2013). A world unglued: Simultanagnosia as a spatial restriction of attention. *Frontiers in Human Neuroscience, 7*, 145.

Desmurget, M., Epstein, C. M., Turner, R. S., Prablanc, C., Alexander, G. E., & Grafton, S. T. (1999). Role of the posterior parietal cortex in updating reaching movements to a visual target. *Nature Neuroscience, 2*(6), 563–567.

Galletti C, Fattori P. (2018) *The dorsal visual stream revisited: Stable circuits or dynamic pathways?* https://doi.org/10.1016/j.cortex.2017.01.009. Epub 2017 Jan 23.

Gottlieb, J. (2007). From thought to action: The parietal cortex as a bridge between perception, action, and cognition. *Neuron, 53*(1), 9–16.

Hebart, M. N., & Hesselmann, G. (2012, June 13). What visual information is processed in the human dorsal stream? *The Journal of neuroscience: the official journal of the Society for Neuroscience*.

Huff, T., Mahabadi, N., & Tadi, P. (2020). Neuroanatomy, visual cortex. In *StatPearls*. Treasure Island (FL): StatPearls Publishing.

Ilg, U. J. (2008). The role of areas MT and MST in coding of visual motion underlying the execution of smooth pursuit. *Vision Research, 48*(20), 2062–2069.

Jeon, H., & Lee, S.-H. (2018). From neurons to social beings: Short review of the Mirror neuron system research and its socio-psychological and psychiatric implications. *Clinical*

Psychopharmacology and Neuroscience: The Official Scientific Journal of the Korean College of Neuropsychopharmacology, 16(1), 18–31.
Kumar, A., & Wroten, M. (2020). Agnosia. In *StatPearls*. StatPearls Publishing.
Leyland, L.-A., Godwin, H. J., Benson, V., & Liversedge, S. P. (2017). Neglect patients exhibit egocentric or Allocentric neglect for the same stimulus contingent upon task demands. *Scientific Reports, 7*(1), 1941.
Li, M., Chen, S., Chen, X., Zhang, Y., Wang, Y., & Tian, Q. (2019, October 5). *Symbiotic Graph Neural Networks for 3D Skeleton-based Human Action Recognition and Motion Prediction. arXiv [cs.CV]*. Retrieved from http://arxiv.org/abs/1910.02212
Parton, M. H. (2004). Hemispatial neglect. *Journal of Neurol Neurosurg Psychiatry*. Retrieved from https://jnnp.bmj.com/content/jnnp/75/1/13.full.pdf.
Robson, D. (2014, June). Neuroscience: The man who saw time stand still. *BBC*. Retrieved 17 December 2020 from https://www.bbc.com/future/article/20140624-the-man-who-saw-time-freeze
Sasaki, R., Angelaki, D. E., & DeAngelis, G. C. (2019). Processing of object motion and self-motion in the lateral subdivision of the medial superior temporal area in macaques. *Journal of Neurophysiology*. Retrieved from https://europepmc.org/article/pmc/pmc6485727.
Teodorescu, L., Hofmann, K., & Oudeyer, P.-Y. (2020, April 9). *SpatialSim: Recognizing Spatial Configurations of Objects with Graph Neural Networks. arXiv [cs.LG]*. Retrieved from http://arxiv.org/abs/2004.04546
Ts'o, D. Y., Roe, A. W., & Gilbert, C. D. (2001). A hierarchy of the functional organization for color, form and disparity in primate visual area V2. *Vision Research, 41*(10–11), 1333–1349.
Wurtz, R. H. (1998). Optic flow: A brain region devoted to optic flow analysis? *Current Biology: CB, 8*(16), R554–R556.
Zeki, S. (2015). Area V5-a microcosm of the visual brain. *Frontiers in Integrative Neuroscience, 9*, 21.

Michael Solomon is a student at the Texas Academy of Math and Science (TAMS) at the University of North Texas.

Ying Hsuan Lo is pursuing her master's degree in artificial intelligence in the College of Engineering at the University of North Texas. Her primary research interests include computer vision and graph representation.

Memory: Beyond the Hippocampus: Computer Systems and Their Resemblance to the Human Hippocampus

Tiffany Kumala and Pranathi Pilla

Introduction

Ever since the discovery of human memory mechanisms, there has been an effort to mimic them in humans, too. The recent advancements in artificial intelligence (AI), driven by deep learning developments, have worked to use cognitive neuroscience to maximize learning. Human memory enables one-shot learning in context and permits generalization. Deep learning networks for sequential processing tasks are becoming more capable of one-shot learning and generalization through unsupervised learning and supervised transfer learning techniques.

For humans, the hippocampus serves to form new memories and is also heavily associated with learning and emotion in the limbic system. The limbic system is between the cerebral cortex and the brain stem, and the major anatomical structures are the hippocampus and the amygdala. The hippocampus, in particular, is a complex brain structure that functions in the temporal lobe through mechanisms such as long-term potentiation (LTP). These functions have been known with certainty since Scoville and Milner's 1957 report detailing amnesia after a surgical resection of hippocampal structures (Eichenbaum et al., 1992). In simple terms, long-term potentiation strengthens synapses based on patterns of activity. For example, a commonly discussed example of pattern recognition in human memory is the term coined as "muscle memory." In the case of riding a bike, once one has been fully accustomed to performing the task a repeated number of times, long-term potentiation repeatedly occurs resulting in the memory of performing the task readily memorable. Long-term potentiation increases the strength of synaptic transmission through certain types of synaptic stimulation. This specific form of synaptic

T. Kumala (✉) · P. Pilla
Department of Computer Science and Engineering, University of North Texas, Denton, TX, USA

M. V. Albert et al. (eds.), *Bridging Human Intelligence and Artificial Intelligence*, Educational Communications and Technology: Issues and Innovations, https://doi.org/10.1007/978-3-030-84729-6_15

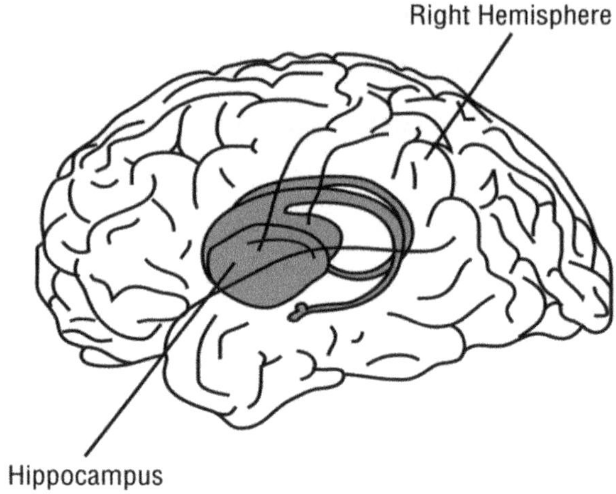

Fig. 1 The location of the hippocampus in the human brain

neuroplasticity is a unique characteristic that serves as a basis for learning (Purves, 1970). Neuroplasticity is essentially the ability of the human brain's neural networks to morph and reorganize as humans undergo new experiences and form new connections. As humans take in more information from their surroundings, the neuroplasticity of the brain enables them to connect experiences and knowledge, which in turn allows humans to form judgments and opinions (Fig. 1).

Human Memory

In an experiment featuring rodents as the key test subject, the integral role of the hippocampus in memory has been examined, when rodents with severe hippocampal damage have experienced the inability to retain and form memories, which is also known as anterograde amnesia. This is also very common in humans as well. Why should we relate human and computer memory mechanisms? Human memory enables one-shot learning in context and permits generalization.

Place Cells and Grid Cells

Additionally, the presence of place cells and grid cells in the temporal lobe, specifically in the hippocampus, work as a space mapping circuitry within the brain. Across mammalian evolution, place cells fire when at a specific location, which is determined by environmental sensory inputs, and grid cells formulate virtual maps of the surroundings that are arranged in a triangular structure. This process uniquely identifies and retains information about any location that is visited. These functions are specific to the hippocampus, and in an experiment, rats without a hippocampus

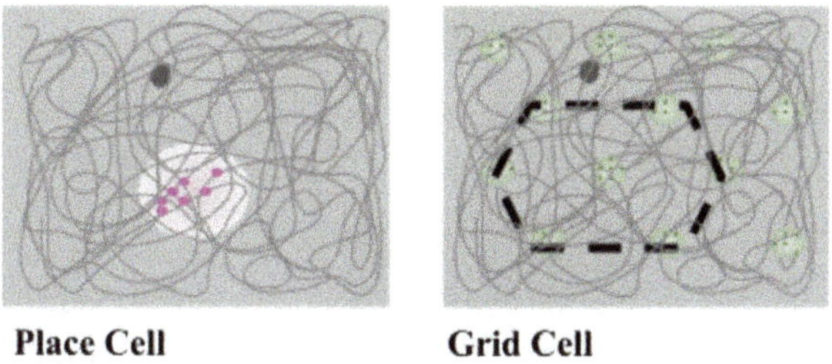

Fig. 2 A direct comparison of place cells and grid cells from a rat's brain. On both diagrams, the dark gray dot represents the rat and the light gray lines show the rat's movement. The place cells fire when the rat reaches a specific location, which is shown in pink. On the other hand, the grid cells fire when reaching distinct locations, shown in green, forming a hexagonal structure. (Adapted from "Nobel Prize In Physiology Or Medicine," by C. Drahl, 2014, Retrieved from https://cen.acs.org/articles/92/i41/Nobel-Prize-Physiology-Medicine.html. Copyright 2021 by the American Chemical Society)

were impaired on tasks requiring the utilization of spatial and contextual information (Jarrard, 1993) (Fig. 2).

Types of Memory

The different types of memory can generally be divided into three categories: short-term memory, long-term memory, and procedural memory. When memory is first formed, it is hippocampus and context-dependent and transforms into the varying forms (Winocur, 2007). Short-term memory, also known as "working" or "active" memory, represents the second stage of Atkinson-Shiffrin's multi-store memory model. This model proposes that memory is made of three sources: sensory memory, short-term memory, and long-term memory. While these are not anatomical structures within the brain, they are each separate functions with various durations ranging from shorter to longer respectively. With a capacity of around seven items and a short duration, this form of memory typically lasts seconds without any reinforcement or ways of actively maintaining it. Another property unique to short-term memory is that it demonstrates temporal decay and chunk capacity limits (Cowen, 2009).

For example, because a small amount of information can be stored in an available state in the mind for a limited time, it enables an individual to remember small pieces of information like a phone number.

In contrast to short-term memory, the third stage of Atkinson-Shiffrin's model demonstrates long-term memory. The fundamental differences between these types of memory are that only short-term memory shows temporal decay and chunk capacity limits. In long-term memory, or "factual memory," information is encoded into the brain over an extended period of time. Information that is not repeated or reinforced may gradually be lost, which differs from short-term memory where all

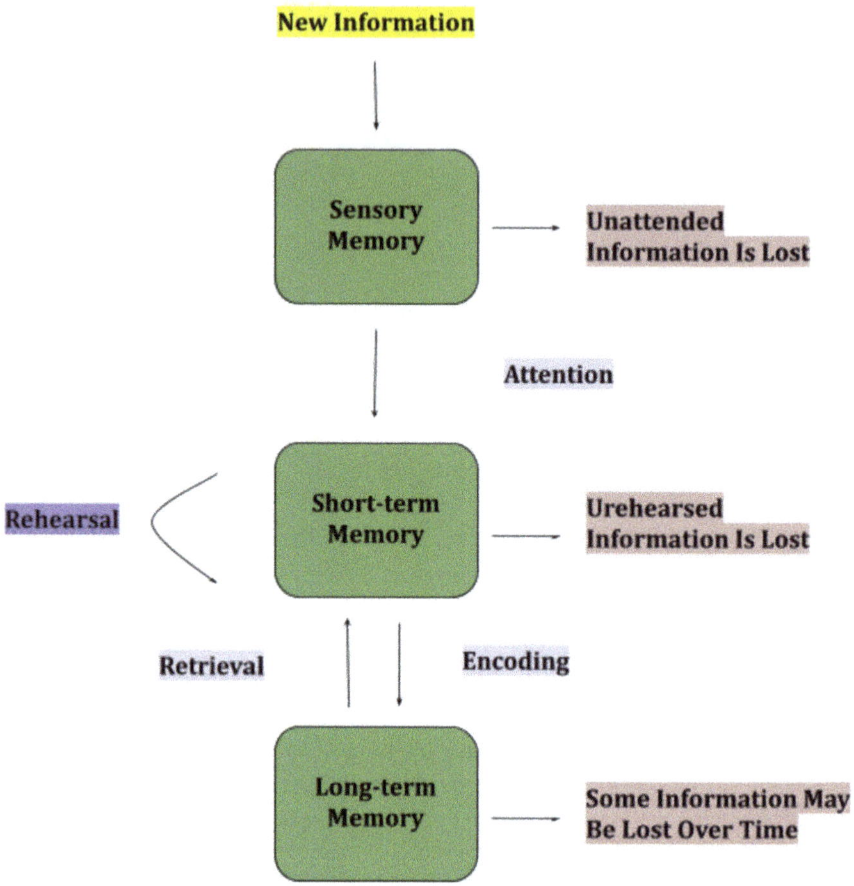

Fig. 3 The process in which memory can be encoded and retrieved in its respective stages through the Atkinson-Shiffrin model

unrehearsed information is lost. Knowledge in this stage is held indefinitely and has the ability to be recalled after a delay in time.

The last form of memory is practiced memory or "procedural memory," which is closely related to long-term memory and the previously mentioned concept of "muscle memory." Practiced memory is an implicit memory that mainly stores information to perform particular procedures without conscious awareness. Examples of this include talking, tying shoes, or biking. Understanding these three forms of memory is crucial to the understanding and development of applications in artificial intelligence (Fig. 3).

Introduction to Neural Networks

Artificial neural networks (ANN) are computing systems based on animal neural networks in the biological brain. Different neural substrates in the mammalian nervous system acquire different types of information simultaneously and in parallel. In the mammalian nervous system, different neural substrates acquire different types of information simultaneously and enhance recognition, which is what neural networks aim to do (McDonald & White, 1994). In an artificial neural network system, the biological neurons are represented by nodes. The synapses, which are communication channels between neurons in the biological brain, produce nonlinear mathematical functions which statistically relate two or more nodes together to form a pattern akin to human thought. Additionally, based on the layers in human thought, these "signals" travel from an input layer to an output one. Why relate human and computer memory mechanisms? The complexity and efficiency of human memory systems serve as a model to better computer memory systems (Fig. 4).

The fundamental work of a neural network is that it learns how to perform a task through data analysis and training. One of the most fundamental examples of such a neural network is an image object recognition system, such as facial recognition or pattern recognition models. The system picks up on data inputs and comes up with data approximations that it can generalize on other objects, thus improving the system (Hardesty, 2017).

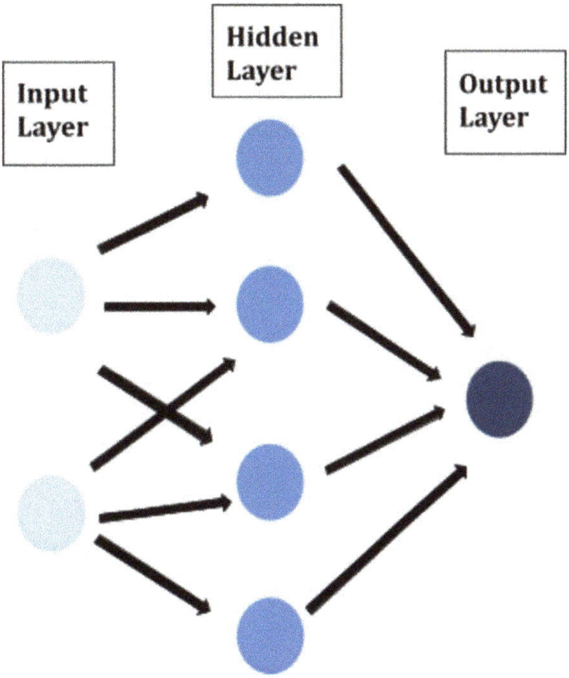

Fig. 4 A simple neural network diagram showing the input, hidden, and output layers. (Adapted from "Neural Network," by J. Chen, 2021, Retrieved from https://www.investopedia.com/terms/n/neuralnetwork.asp. Copyright 2021 by Investopedia)

Memory Augmented Neural Network

Memory augmented neural networks work in order to facilitate the storage and retrieval of memory, which is useful in analyses like bibliometric mapping (Van Raan & Tijssen, 2005). The three components of this system are the controller, memory, and the read and write heads. The memory, or the memory matrix, consists of columns and rows which interact with the read and write heads to serve as pointers. The idea of the memory augmented neural network was initially inspired by the Neural Turing Machine (NTM), which are systems designed to retrieve information from an eternal bank (Fig. 5).

The two key components of the NTM architecture are a neural network controller and a memory bank. The information from the external input is received by a memory matrix through the Read Heads and Write Heads, and is then converted to the external output in lieu of simple input and output vectors in conventional systems (Chen, 2019). This memory system is considered to be a working memory, as it serves the function of quick storage and retrieval of information.

Autoassociative Networks

Autoassociative networks are a type of neural network that can retrieve data to create an approximation between inputs and outputs. It is a type of memory that can retrieve data from a much smaller sample of itself (Fig. 6).

Convolutional Networks

Convolutional neural networks as outlined below come in the specific form of the Convolutional Neural Network Long Short-Term Memory Network (CNN LSTM), which uses computer memory for computer image generation. This specific type of

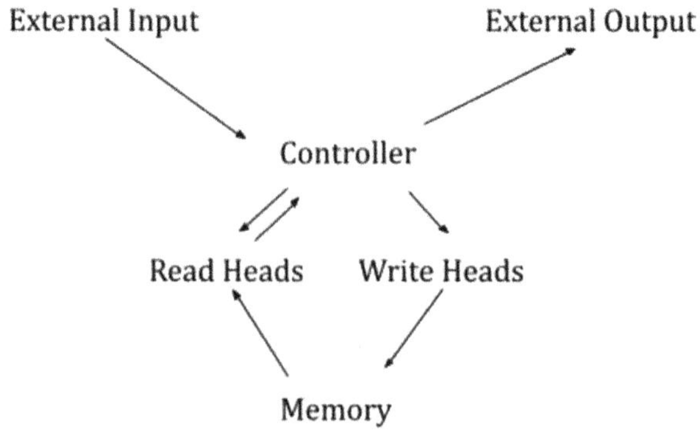

Fig. 5 Neural Turing Machine architecture. (Adapted from "Modeling the Mind: A brief review," by G. Makdah, 2015, Retrieved from https://www.researchgate.net/publication/279864730_Modeling_the_Mind_A_brief_review)

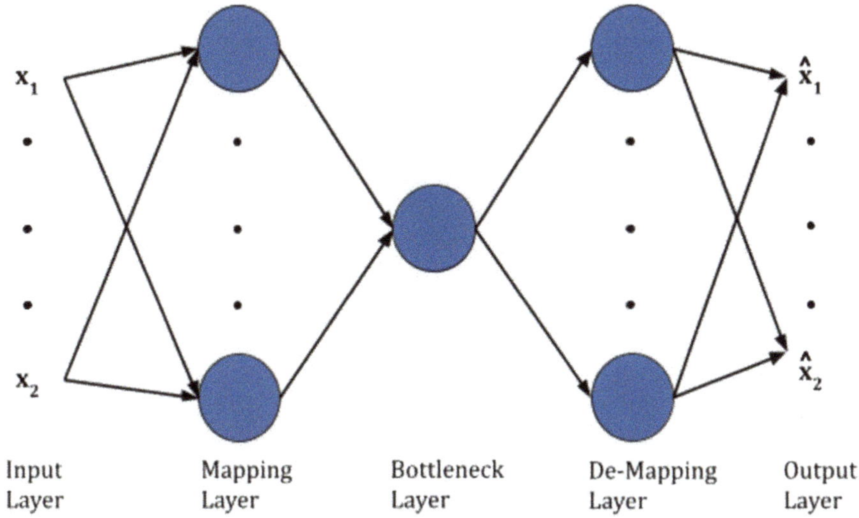

Fig. 6 The basic structure of an autoassociative neural network, including the five main layers: input, mapping, bottleneck, de-mapping, and output. (Adapted from "Integrating Auto-Associative Neural Networks with Hotelling T2 Control Charts for Wind Turbine Fault Detection," by H. Yang, H. Huang, and S. Yang, and B. Author, 2015, Retrieved from https://www.mdpi.com/1996-1073/8/10/12100/htm. Copyright 2015 by the authors; licensee MDPI, Basel, Switzerland)

computer system architecture has a temporal structure-based memory. In general, the memory consumption required for a convolutional neural network is high due to the image processing demands (Fig. 7).

Artificial Hippocampus

Prosthetics

Because of the hippocampus's vital roles in memory and learning, damage to the hippocampus is often detrimental and is observed in conditions such as Alzheimer's disease. These types of conditions are typically chronic, so the option of receiving a cognitive prosthesis, specifically a hippocampal prosthesis, can improve the function of damaged areas (Nelson, 2020). In order to see the recovery, the new implant has to be able to perform the same functions as the hippocampus – receiving and analyzing information accurately and relaying that output to other parts of the brain (Goldman, 2018). The level of precision that must be replicated requires a deep understanding of the hippocampus and the overall nervous system. In an effort to better accomplish this, computer models are formed with mathematical constructs

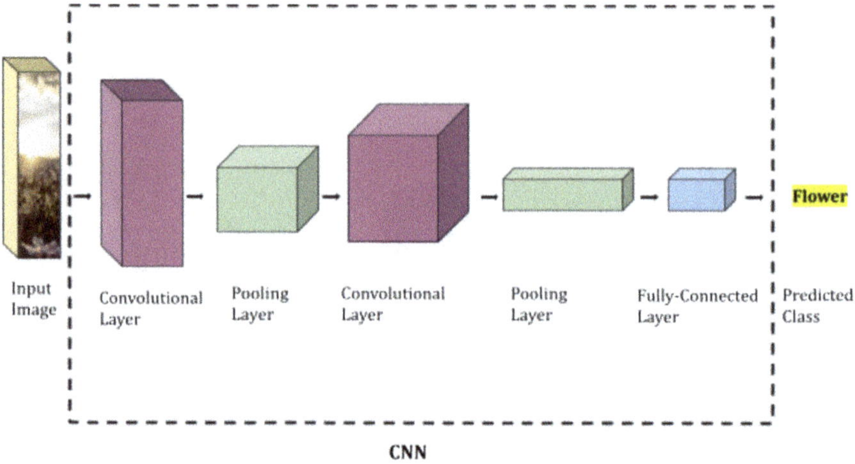

Fig. 7 The structure of a convolutional neural network and its process to recognize the image of a flower. (Adapted from "Convolutional Neural Networks," by C. Camacho, Retrieved from https://cezannec.github.io/Convolutional_Neural_Networks/)

of neuronal types to mimic properties and connections of individual neurons, which depict the hippocampus in a computerized format.

Machine Applications

Technological advancements have given the ability to replicate human hippocampal anatomy that is modeled after an artificial hippocampus. The artificial hippocampus is used within artificial intelligence to help machines learn in a similar way in which humans learn. Because the hippocampus in humans functions in memory consolidation, processing, and learning, its machine applications work similarly. The use of specific neural networks works to build strong associations and reconstruct contextual information to help the machine learn (Samsonovich & Ascoli, 2005). The applications of neuroscience and machinery and vice versa are diverse and incredible. Similar to the way humans think, one can develop artificial neural networks mimicking the biological neural networks found in animals and other intelligent life forms. Similar to how the brain stores data, one can apply this knowledge to make computers remember similar data in a similar manner. The same concepts drawn from human long-term memory can be applied in computer functions of deep memory systems, third-order Boltzmann machines, or Image Tracking systems. Neural networks can be trained to recognize a variety of patterns, including essential tasks like recognizing visual field progression and assisting physicians (Brigatti, 1997) (Fig. 8).

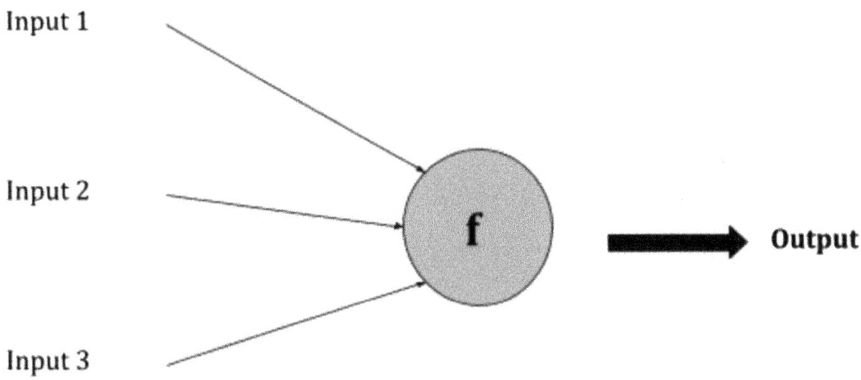

Fig. 8 A diagram showing the mechanism behind computer and machine processing

Ethical Implications of Integrated Memory Systems

Unemployment and Inequality

As technology is becoming more integrated into the workplace, advancements in artificial intelligence could have potential implications for the future of job stability. The efficiency and high standard of machines can outdo the performance of humans, and the innovation is only growing stronger, leading to concerns over automated jobs overtaking the hierarchy of labor. For example, the trucking industry, which currently employs 3.5 million people in the United States alone, can soon be disrupted in the future with the usage of self-driving cars. The advancements in technology can be beneficial, but they would also impact millions in the workforce. Additionally, with an already widening wage gap, the distribution of this technology may not be structured fairly. The replacement of human labor for artificial intelligence drastically cuts a company's costs, directing revenue to a smaller quantity of people.

Unintended Consequences

Humans are inherently biased, and through the creation of artificial intelligence technology, the technology cannot always be found to be neutral. Image recognition platforms have shown inaccuracies in identification based on race and gender, which can prove to be an ethical issue when relying on this technology. Security is also another major factor that needs to be considered. Proper protection measures need to be developed as powerful forms of technology could be targets for individuals that plan to use it for nefarious purposes. Because artificial intelligence and machine learning allow machines to continually learn and improve themselves, it is speculated that there will come a point where the scope of the machine's intelligence could surpass that of humans. However, in order to reach that stage, the machines must first learn, which may lead to some mistakes. The training that artificial intelligence systems undergo still may not be able to cover every possible scenario, and there will be gaps in the intelligence or ways to fool the system.

Conclusions

With the exponential progression encompassing artificial intelligence, the current and future applications of this technology are expanding. AI holds implications in a variety of industries, ranging from healthcare to cybersecurity, and as these efforts improve, AI will be more integrated into daily life. An example of a common usage of AI today is through social media. Advanced machine learning serves to tailor advertisements to match user interest, utilize image recognition, and personalize the platform. Facial recognition technology makes use of multiple layers of neural networks to identify objects (faces). This allows companies to appeal more to users in a way in which humans have not been able to do previously through analyzing data sets. While the impact of AI is already widespread, it will greatly be implemented in the future. Through biomimicry approaches, especially through the mimicry of the human hippocampus, computer memory will continue to be enhanced and have a strong influence on the future of society.

Acknowledgments University of North Texas Department of Learning Technologies Biomedical AI Lab

References

Brigatti, L. (1997, June 1). Automatic detection of glaucomatous visual field progression with neural networks. *JAMA Ophthalmology | JAMA Network*. https://jamanetwork.com/journals/jamaophthalmology/article-abstract/642157

Camacho, C. (n.d.). *Convolutional neural networks. Convolutional neural networks – Cezanne Camacho – Machine and deep learning educator*. https://cezannec.github.io/Convolutional_Neural_Networks/

Chen, S. (2019, December 7). *NTM: Neural turing machines – Towards AI*. Medium. https://pub.towardsai.net/neural-turing-machines-eaada7e7a6cc

Chen, J. (2021, May 19). *Neural network*. Investopedia. https://www.investopedia.com/terms/n/neuralnetwork.asp

Cowen, N. (2009, March 18). *What are the differences between long-term, short-term, and working memory?* US National Library of Medicine National Institutes of Health. https://www.ncbi.nlm.nih.gov/pmc/articles/PMC2657600/

Drahl, C. (2014, October 9). *Nobel prize in physiology or medicine*. C&EN. https://cen.acs.org/articles/92/i41/Nobel-Prize-Physiology-Medicine.html.

Eichenbaum, H., Otto, T., & Cohen, N. J. (1992, January 1). *The hippocampus—What does it do?* ScienceDirect. https://www.sciencedirect.com/science/article/abs/pii/016310479290724I

Goldman, B. (2018). *Neuroscience team is building a virtual hippocampus*. Stanford Medicine. https://stanmed.stanford.edu/2018fall/neuroscientists-creating-virtual-hippocampus.html
Hardesty, L. (2017, April 14). *Explained: Neural networks*. MIT News | Massachusetts Institute of Technology. https://news.mit.edu/2017/explained-neural-networks-deep-learning-0414
Jarrard, L. E. (1993, July 1). *On the role of the hippocampus in learning and memory in the rat*. ScienceDirect. https://www.sciencedirect.com/science/article/abs/pii/0163104793906644
Makdah, G. (2015, July). *Modeling the Mind: A brief review*. Research Gate. https://www.researchgate.net/publication/279864730_Modeling_the_Mind_A_brief_review
McDonald, R. J., & White, N. M. (1994, May 1). *Parallel information processing in the water maze: Evidence for independent memory systems involving dorsal striatum and hippocampus*. ScienceDirect. https://www.sciencedirect.com/science/article/abs/pii/S0163104705800093
Nelson, D. (2020, June 6). *DeepMind creates AI that replays memories like the hippocampus*. Unite. AI. https://www.unite.ai/deepmind-creates-ai-that-replays-memories-like-the-hippocampus/
Purves, D. (1970, January 1). *Long-Term Synaptic Potentiation, Neuroscience*. 2nd. U.S. National Library of Medicine. https://www.ncbi.nlm.nih.gov/books/NBK10878/
Samsonovich, A. V., & Ascoli, G. A. (2005). *A simple neural network model of the hippocampus suggesting its pathfinding role in episodic memory retrieval*. US National Library of Medicine National Institutes of Health. https://www.ncbi.nlm.nih.gov/pmc/articles/PMC1074338/
Van Raan, A., & Tijssen, R. (2005, August 13). The neural net of neural network research an exercise in bibliometric mapping. *AKJournals*. https://akjournals.com/view/journals/11192/26/1/article-p169.xml
Winocur, G. (2007, April 1). Memory consolidation or transformation: context manipulation and hippocampal representations of memory. *Nature Neuroscience*. https://www.nature.com/articles/nn1880?error=cookies_not_supported&code=569cef5f-05ad-433b-ab74-4376bc74bc8d
Yang, H.-H., Huang, M.-L., Yang, S.-W. (2015, October 23). Integrating Auto-Associative Neural Networks with Hotelling T2 Control Charts for Wind Turbine Fault Detection. MDPI. https://www.mdpi.com/1996-1073/8/10/12100/htm

Tiffany Kumala recently graduated from the Texas Academy of Mathematics and Science at the University of North Texas and currently attends the University of Texas at Austin as a Biology major with a minor in Sociology. She is particularly passionate about medical research and has future aspirations to become a physician. She was named an Undergraduate Research Fellow at the University of North Texas for her work on developing active UDP-glucuronosyltransferases and active mutant drug detoxifying bacteria under Dr. Xiaoqiang Wang. Over Summer 2020, she worked on TalkMotion, a communication application for individuals impacted by Cerebral Palsy, under the direction of Dr. Mark V Albert in the Biomedical Artificial Intelligence Laboratory at the University of North Texas. She currently researches under Dr. Eugene Koay at the MD Anderson Cancer Center in the Cancer and Physics Engineering Laboratory to improve early detection mechanisms of liver metastasis on CT scans using enhancement pattern mapping techniques.

Pranathi Pilla is a rising undergraduate freshman who recently graduated from the Texas Academy of Mathematics and Science, University of North Texas. She is interested in biomedical research, particularly in the fields of computational biology, regenerative medicine, and medical devices. Her passion for these fields began in her freshman year of high school when she worked on developing a quick, efficient, and cost-effective method to detect the presence of pathogenic microorganisms using a combination of Digital in-line Holographic Microscopy and Microbial Fuel Cells, which was recognized at the Regeneron International Science and Engineering Fair in 2020. Over the past summer, she worked on Pupil Tracking for the Diagnosis of Parkinson's Disease in the Biomedical Artificial Intelligence Lab at the University of North Texas under the guidance of Dr. Mark V. Albert.

Reinforcement Learning: Beyond the Basal Ganglia

Chengping Yuan and Mahdi Fathi

Introduction to Reinforcement Learning

Reinforcement learning is an area of machine learning, inspired by behaviorist psychology, concerned with how agents ought to take actions in an environment so as to maximize some notion of cumulative reward. The task of reinforcement learning is to use observed rewards to learn an optimal policy for the environment. In many complex domains, reinforcement learning is the feasible way to train a program to perform at high levels. For example, in game playing, it is very hard for a human to provide accurate and consistent evaluations of large numbers of positions, which would be needed to train an evaluation function directly from examples. Instead, the program can be told when it has won or lost, and it can use this information to learn an evaluation function that gives reasonably accurate estimates of the probability of winning from any given position. Figure 1 is widely used to describe how reinforcement learning works. We can see that an Agent will take a certain action A_t to receive the reward R_t at the timestamp $t_{\square}^{\square}$. There are many elements within reinforcement learning and it is important to know them: environment, agent, and policy,

Environment: The environment's task is to define a world where an agent is able to interact with. It therefore has a basic loop that can be written like this:

Produce state s and reward r

C. Yuan (✉)
Department of Computer Science and Engineering, University of North Texas, Denton, TX, USA
e-mail: chengpingyuan@my.unt.edu

M. Fathi
Department of ITDS, University of North Texas, Denton, TX, USA
e-mail: Mahdi.Fathi@unt.edu

M. V. Albert et al. (eds.), *Bridging Human Intelligence and Artificial Intelligence*, Educational Communications and Technology: Issues and Innovations, https://doi.org/10.1007/978-3-030-84729-6_16

Fig. 1 Reinforcement learning framework

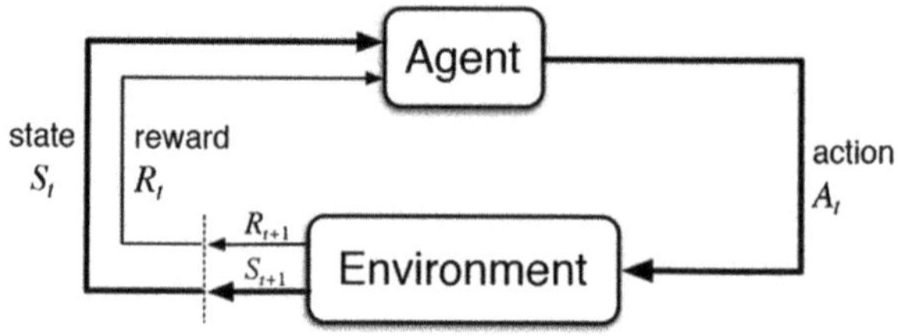

where our state s represents the current situation in the environment and the reward r represents the scalar value being returned by the environment after selecting an action a.

Agent: Our agent needs to learn how to achieve goals by interacting with the environment. The basis to do this is by using a basic loop.

1. Sense state s and reward r from the environment.
2. Select an action a based on this state and reward.

We do note here though that the action that our agent can take can be defined under two specific categories:

1. Discrete: 1 of N actions (e.g., left or down)
2. Continuous: An action as a scalar/vector of a real value (e.g., the amount we need to bend our leg to be able to walk)

Policy π: Policy π is used to map the actions to the states that agents have to take. The actions can be categorized into two specific categories:

- Deterministic: Same action every time
- Stochastic: There is a probability of taking different actions (e.g., we take action 1 70% of the time, and action 2 30% of the time).

Value Function V: Value function Vrepresents how good the state in the long run, which is calculated by our agents, in other words, what is the expected long-term accumulation of reward.

There are two commonly used value functions:

1. State-Value Functions $V^{\pi}(S)$: Value of state S and following our policy π
    - It gives the expected return when starting from states s and following policy π forever.
    - $V^{\pi}(s) = E_{\pi}[R_t||s_t = s]$
2. Action-Value Functions $Q^{\pi}(s,a)$: Value of state s,taking action a, and thereafter following policy π.
    - It gives the expected return of taking action a in state s, given the policy π
    - $Q^{\pi}(s,a) = E_{\pi}[R_t||s_t = s, a_t = a]$
    - This is also called Q-Function, which is the core of the Q-learning algorithm.

There are two types of reinforcement learning: model-based learning vs model-free learning. In model-based learning, agents not only learn how to take actions but also learn how the environment responds to moves or actions. Model-free agents can estimate the optimal policy without using or estimating the dynamic (transaction and reward function) of the environment. Q-learning is a model-free reinforcement learning algorithm.

Here we are using the game Tic Tac Toe to explore reinforcement learning model (Q-learning) (Fig. 2):

- States: States in Tic Tac Toe are the representation of the game board with moves of each player made.
- Actions (available actions): Available spaces to make move on board.
- Reward: Winner will be rewarded by 100, loser will be punished by 100, and reward is 0 when game tied.
- α Value function: Q(s,a), s is the state and a is the action (move) so that every state and action pair will have a q value from the value function. This requires a lot of game simulations.

How do we calculate the q value based on the elements above? Let's go ahead and derive Q learning by incorporating a few basic principles:

- Reward prediction error: Reward prediction error (RPE) = Actual reward − predicted reward value. An "error signal" used to adjust your value function. RPE in reinforcement learning is also from neuroscience (Schultz, 2016) – the prediction error theory. In this theory, dopamine neurons send a rapid signal that covers all three possible errors in prediction of a reward: that the reward was better than

Fig. 2 Tic Tac Toe game board with each player played four moves

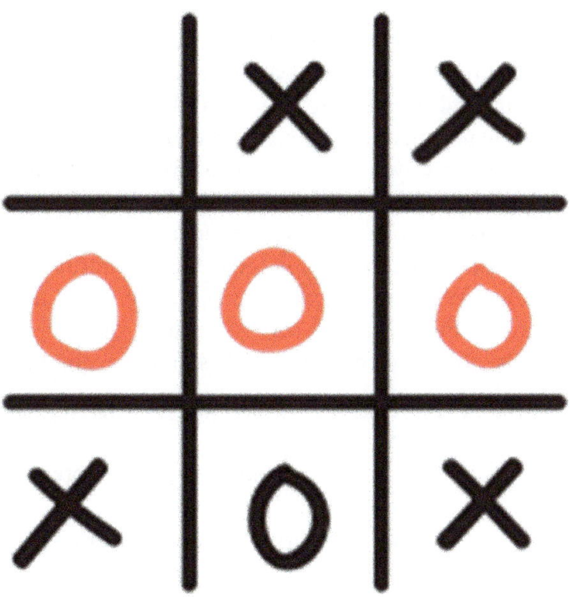

expected (a positive error); the reward was equal to expected (no error) or the reward was less than expected (a negative error). Humans can adjust their behaviors (actions) based on these three types of signal. In reinforcement learning, we use RPE and learning rate α to update the q value:

New Value = Old Value + α * RPE

Now we know how to update the q value with leaning rate and RPE. We need to derive equation for predicted reward value, if $Q(s_t, a_t)$ is the sum of expected future rewards at time t

and $Q(s_{t+1}, a_{t+1})$ is the same thing one step ahead in the future

$$Q(s_t, a_t) = r_t + r_{t+1} + r_{t+2} + \ldots (\text{estimated rewards})$$

$$Q(s_{t+1}, a_{t+1}) = r_{t+1} + r_{t+2} + \ldots$$

$Q(s_t, a_t) = r_t + Q(s_{t+1}, a_{t+1})$ assuming you take the best choice at time $t + 1$ so

$$Q(s_t, a_t) = r_t + \max(Q(s_{t+1}, a))$$

So you can use Q to find the predicted reward value at time t:

predicted reward value $r_t = Q(s_t, a_t) - \max_a(Q(s_{t+1}, a))$

- Learning rates: How to choose the right learning rate is also an important factor in Q learning. High learning rate leads to learning quickly to adapt to changing environments, lower learning rate learns slowly but remains stable enough to noise and stochastic rewards to avoid forgetting. The right value of learning rate depends upon how stable the environment is; a more unstable or critical environment requires a higher learning rate.
- Temporal discounting: Temporal discounting is the tendency of people to discount reward as they approach a temporal horizon in the future or the past. To put it another way, it is a tendency to give greater value to rewards as they move away from their temporal horizons and towards the "Now." This concept is used in both neurobiology and neuroeconomics. Q learning models (and other reinforcement learning models) introduce a discount factor r between 0 and 1 to reward value. When r close to 1 represents no discounting, a reward from future will have same weight as current reward; when r close to 0 leads to "hedonistic behavior," immediate reward has more weight than long-term reward.

To sum up everything we had, we can derive Q-learning equation formula:

$$\text{new}\,Q = \text{old}\,Q + \alpha\,[\text{reward prediction error}]$$

$$\text{new}\,Q = \text{old}\,Q + \alpha\,[\text{actual reward} - \text{predicted reward}]$$

$$Q_{t+1}(s,a) = Q_t + a[R_{t+1} - [Q_t - \max_a Q_t(\text{next state},a)]$$

Basal Ganglia and Reinforcement Learning

Animals need to select the most appropriate behavior in a given environment in order to survive. An important role in this process of action selection is played in all vertebrates by a set of subcortical structures called the basal ganglia (Redgrave et al., 1999). The information processing in the basal ganglia is very strongly modulated by dopamine. The basal ganglia are critically involved both in the process of selecting actions and in learning which actions are worth making in a given context, as demonstrated by impairments of both functions in Parkinson's disease. Death of dopaminergic neurons in Parkinson's disease leads to problems with movements (Blandini et al., 2000) as well as difficulties in learning from feedback (Knowlton et al., 1996). The basal ganglia is organized into two main pathways: Go and No-Go. The Go pathway is related to the initiation of movements. On the other hand, the No-Go pathway is possible to be related to the inhibition of movements (Kravitz et al., 2010). Two pathways and how they work are shown in Fig. 3 (Frank, 2005).

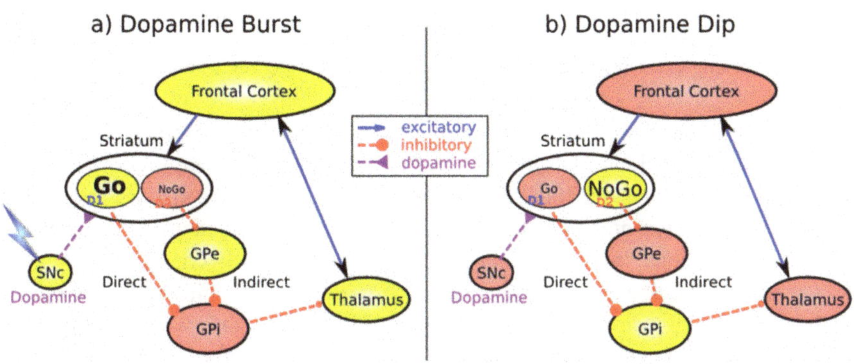

Fig. 3 Biology of the basal ganglia system, with two cases shown: (**a**) Dopamine burst activity that drives the direct "Go" pathway neurons in the striatum, which then inhibit the tonic activation in the globus pallidus internal segment (GPi), which releases specific nuclei in the thalamus from this inhibition, allowing them to complete a bidirectional excitatory circuit with the frontal cortex, resulting in the initiation of a motor action. The increased Go activity during dopamine bursts results in potentiation of corticostriatal synapses and hence learning to select actions that tend to result in positive outcomes. (**b**) Dopamine dip (pause in tonic dopamine neuron firing), leading to preferential activity of indirect "NoGo" pathway neurons in the striatum, which inhibit the external segment globus pallidus neurons (GPe), which are otherwise tonically active, and inhibiting the GPi. Increased NoGo activity thus results in disinhibition of GPi, making it more active and thus inhibiting the thalamus, preventing initiation of the corresponding motor action. The dopamine dip results in potentiation of corticostriatal NoGo synapses and hence learning to avoid selection actions that tend to result in negative outcomes (Frank, 2005)

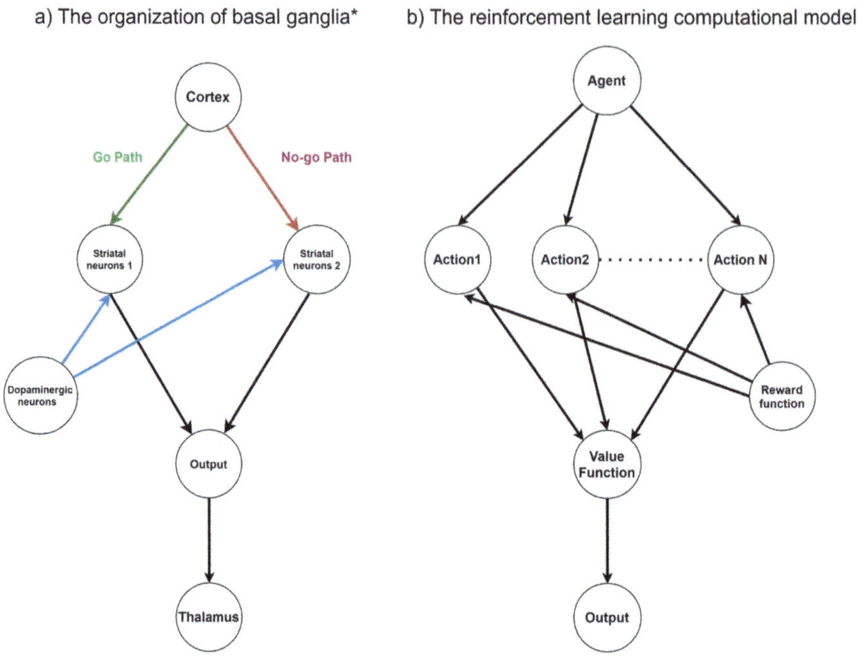

Fig. 4 Comparison of basal ganglia and reinforcement learning in machine learning. (**a**)* The simplified organization of the basal ganglia diagram, components like globus pallidus internal segment (GPi) and globus pallidus neurons (GPe) are removed for better comparison. (**b**) The reinforcement learning in machine learning model, see previous chapter for details of each component

The competition between Go and No-Go pathway during action selection and its dopaminergic modulation inspired have been described by many computational models (e.g., Gurney et al., 2001; Humphries et al., 2012), which also lay the ground for reinforcement learning in machine learning. Dopaminergic neurons act similarly as reward functions in reinforcement learning, which will change the balance between the two pathways and promote action initiation over inhibition. The output nuclei of the basal ganglia play a similar role as value functions which will provide either positive or negative value to thalamus for action selection. The comparison of basal ganglia and reinforcement learning is described in Fig. 4.

Although the differences between reinforcement learning in the human brain and machine learning are tiny, the understanding of the human brain is still limited. Based on what we understand about our brain so far, reinforcement learning seems to be a proper direction for us to take to create AI.

Future of Reinforcement Learning

Deep learning is state of the art for many challenging machine learning problems. With enough data, deep learning can outperform machine learning in most scenarios. Reinforcement learning, on the other hand, has its own advantage compared to

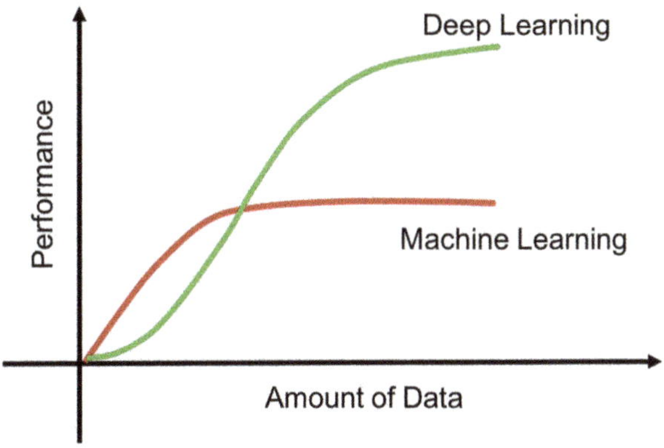

Fig. 5 Data and performance comparison between Deep Learning and Machine Learning

supervised and unsupervised learning. It can solve complex problems and make high level decisions. So combining deep learning and reinforcement learning become necessary to solve more challenging problems. This combination, called deep reinforcement learning, is most useful in problems with high dimensional state-space (Francois-Lavet et al., 2018) and can apply to many real world scenarios (Fig. 5).

Although reinforcement learning has shown its potential compared to other machine learning algorithms and techniques (Fig. 6), there are still some limitations with it. For example, exploring the environment efficiently or being able to generalize a good behavior in a slightly different context are not straightforward. Thus, researchers are proposing a large array of algorithms each year and trying to overcome these limitations.

Conclusion

The future of reinforcement learning is bright and so many efforts have been invested on reinforcement learning. In the foreseeable future of reinforcement learning, we can expect to see deep RL algorithms going in the direction of meta-learning and lifelong learning where previous knowledge (e.g., in the form of pre-trained networks) can be embedded so as to increase the performance and training time. Another key challenge is to improve current transfer learning abilities between simulations and real-world cases. This would allow learning complex decision-making problems in simulations (with the possibility to gather samples in a flexible way), and then use the learned skills in real-world environments, with applications in robotics, self-driving cars, etc.

Finally, we expect deep RL techniques to develop improved curiosity driven abilities to be able to better discover by themselves their environment.

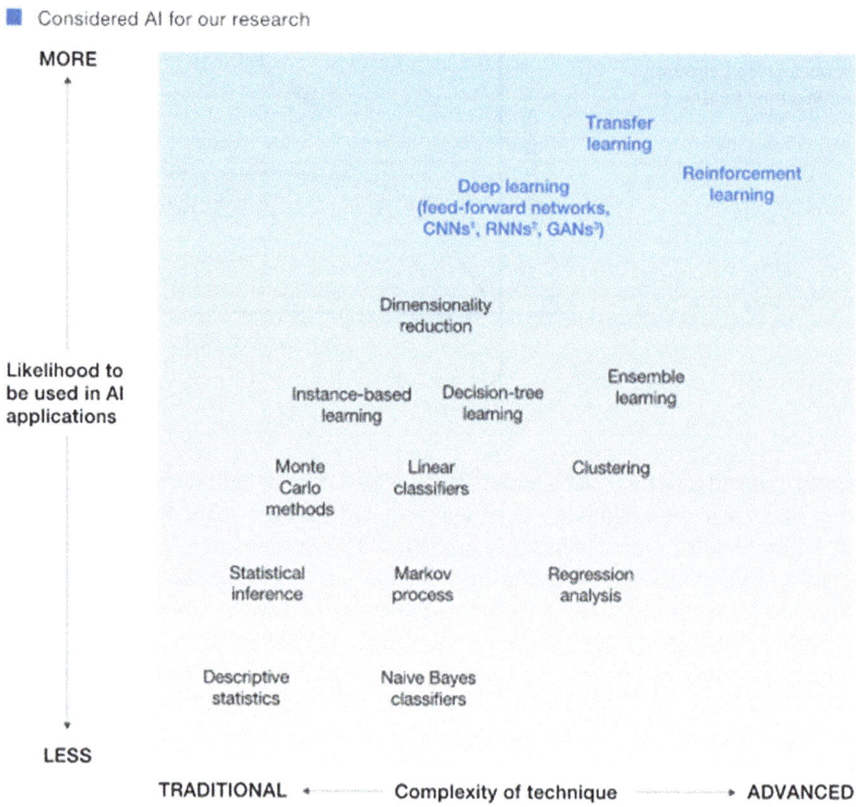

Fig. 6 The machine learning algorithms and techniques with complexity and potential application in AI

References

Blandini, F., Nappi, G., Tassorelli, C., & Martignoni, E. (2000). Functional changes of the basal ganglia circuitry in Parkinson's disease. *Progress in Neurobiology, 62*(1), 63–88.

Francois-Lavet, V., Henderson, P., Islam, R., Bellemare, M. G., & Pineau, J. (2018, November 30). *An Introduction to Deep Reinforcement Learning*. *arXiv [cs.LG]*. Retrieved from http://arxiv.org/abs/1811.12560

Frank, M. J. (2005). Dynamic dopamine modulation in the basal ganglia: a neurocomputational account of cognitive deficits in medicated and nonmedicated Parkinsonism. *Journal of Cognitive Neuroscience, 17*(1), 51–72.

Gurney, K., Prescott, T. J., & Redgrave, P. (2001). A computational model of action selection in the basal ganglia. I. A new functional anatomy. *Biological Cybernetics, 84*(6), 401–410. https://doi.org/10.1007/PL00007984

Humphries, M. D., Khamassi, M., & Gurney, K. (2012). Dopaminergic control of the exploration-exploitation trade-off via the basal ganglia. *Frontiers in Neuroscience, 6*, 9.

Knowlton, B. J., Mangels, J. A., & Squire, L. R. (1996). A neostriatal habit learning system in humans. *Science, 273*(5280), 1399–1402.

Kravitz, A. V., Freeze, B. S., Parker, P. R. L., Kay, K., Thwin, M. T., Deisseroth, K., & Kreitzer, A. C. (2010). Regulation of parkinsonian motor behaviours by optogenetic control of basal ganglia circuitry. *Nature*. Retrieved from https://doi.org/10.1038/nature09159

Redgrave, P., Prescott, T. J., & Gurney, K. (1999). The basal ganglia: a vertebrate solution to the selection problem? *Neuroscience, 89*(4), 1009–1023.

Schultz, W. (2016). Dopamine reward prediction error coding. *Dialogues in Clinical Neuroscience, 18*(1), 23–32.

Chengping Yuan came to UNT in 2018 and is engaged in Masters thesis work in reinforcement learning. He is the project leader in this research effort with three Texas Academy of Math and Science students, creating and studying the behavior of a system that learns both how to play arbitrary games (tactics) and how to optimally engage opponents for maximum rewards while learning (strategy). He received his MBA from Missouri State University, and received his BS in Information Systems from Fuzhou University.

Mahdi Fathi received his BS and MS from the Department of Industrial Engineering, Amirkabir University of Technology (Tehran Polytechnic) and Ph.D. from Iran University of Science and Technology, Tehran, Iran in 2006, 2008 and 2013, respectively. He won three postdoctoral fellowships at Industrial Engineering lab-Ecole Central Paris (France), Stochastic Modeling and Analysis of Communication Systems (SMACS) Group at Dep. of Telecommunications and Information Processing (TELIN) -Ghent University (Belgium), Dep. of Industrial & Systems Engineering-Mississippi State University (USA). Moreover, he was visiting scholar at Center for Applied Optimization, Dep. of Industrial and Systems Engineering-University of Florida (USA) and at Dep. of Electrical Engineering-National Tsing Hua University in Taiwan.

Part IV
Understanding the Effects of Artificial Intelligence

Human Intelligence and Artificial Intelligence: Divergent or Complementary Intelligences?

Shanshan Ma and Jonathan Michael Spector

Introduction

Chess has a very long history dating back 1500 years to northern India. In the intervening years, chess has undergone some changes and spread throughout the world. The first recognized world chess championship was in 1886 that was won by Wilhelm Steinitz, a Prague citizen. Since then, there have been many chess masters and grandmasters, including Magnus Carlsen, Garry Kasparov, Bobby Fisher, and Anatoly Karpov. Chess grandmasters are often considered among the most intelligent humans.

As mainframe computers began to find applications outside research laboratories, Alan Turing argued that a computer could be programmed to play chess (for example, see AMT/D 3 in the Turing archive). By the 1980s, interest in computers playing chess had drawn the interest of large computer companies, including IBM which commissioned the developers at Carnegie Mellon University to further develop the game for IBM. In 1989, IBM's chess game was renamed Deep Blue. In 1996, Deep Blue defeated world champion Garry Kasparov in game one of a six-game match that Kasparov eventually won 5-2. In 1997, there was a rematch which Deep Blue won. Now there is an annual world computer chess championship match. Few master chess players could win against the best of those computer games.

To round out this historical introduction to the relationships of AI and HI, there is one additional historical development worth considering – namely, the Turing Test (Turing, 1950). Turing argued that in an imitation game involving an interrogator and a computer and a respondent both hidden behind a curtain or in another

S. Ma · J. M. Spector (✉)
University of North Texas, Denton, TX, USA
e-mail: shanshanma@my.unt.edu; mike.spector@unt.edu; https://sites.google.com/site/jmspector007/

M. V. Albert et al. (eds.), *Bridging Human Intelligence and Artificial Intelligence*, Educational Communications and Technology: Issues and Innovations, https://doi.org/10.1007/978-3-030-84729-6_17

room with written messages being passed back and forth. The interrogator is asked to determine which is the human respondent and which is the computer. If the interrogator cannot distinguish the human respondent from the computer, then one must conclude that it is reasonable to call the computer a thinking machine. Processing questions posed by the interrogator involves natural language processing which was then believed to be a uniquely human capability. However, Joseph Weizenbaum (1955) demonstrated that one could program a machine to respond in a manner one could distinguish from a human therapist. While some will claim this was not a genuine Turing Test, Weizenbaum demonstrated that one could process natural language in a human-like manner with just a couple hundred lines of programming code.

These two cases – chess and counseling – are used to frame the subsequent elaboration of the differences and similarities of human and computer intelligence. Where the two converge and where they diverge are also discussed.

Dimensions of Intelligence

A Global Dimension

Figure 1 depicts how one might conceptualize intelligence globally.

Considering the hierarchy in Fig. 1, it is possible to characterize in a very general way how education has evolved over the centuries. That evolution has hardly been linear as the hierarchy might suggest. Early apprentice training skipped many of the very low levels and integrated them in problem-solving activities such as hunting or building shelters. One might conclude that prehistoric education was aimed at survival. Knowledge was passed from one generation to the next in terms of survival

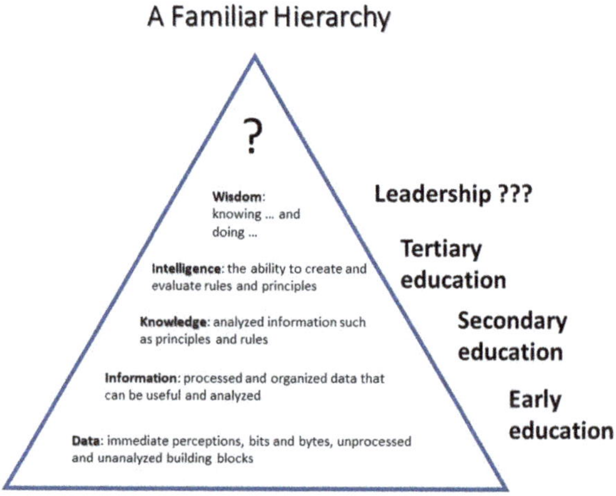

Fig. 1 A global perspective

skills. While this characterization is probably an oversimplification, it sets the stage for an evolutionary, multifaceted, and dynamic perspective of education.

Spector and Ren (2015) noticed that education in the USA by British colonialists focused on reading and arithmetic as those were skills that early American traders needed to report back to British overseers. In a sense, American colonists needed those skills to survive under British rule.

One might also recall Maslow's (1943) hierarchy of needs with security and safety at the bottom of the hierarchy and belongingness and esteem needs in the middle and self-actualization at the top. In that hierarchy, deficiency needs had to be satisfied before growth needs could be satisfied, and motivation could be explained by where an individual was in terms of satisfying deficiency needs or working on growth needs. Maslow's model has been critiqued and expanded (Maslow, 1987) to include cognitive needs, aesthetic needs, and transcendence (above self-actualization) which expands the growth needs. In spite of numerous critiques, especially about the order of needs and whether several can be addressed at the same time, there is general acceptance that Maslow's hierarchy of needs is fairly general and cuts across different cultures.

It is worth noting at this point that AI programs do not have such a hierarchy of needs, although AI programs do have requirements for different kinds of input and searches to conduct depending on a specific situation. To bring the discussion back to HI and AI, within this global dimension, it is worthwhile to consider Dreyfus and Dreyfus' (1980) five stages of expertise: (a) novice, (b) advanced beginner, (c) competent performer, (d) proficient performer, and (e) intuitive expert. The argument is that instruction can be tailored to the learner's level and help learners progress from the first stage to the fourth stage. However, instruction is difficult to design to help learners progress to stage five and not many people reach that stage. The implication is that computers can be programmed to perform at any of the first four levels, but intuitive expertise (high level mastery or wisdom in Fig. 1) is the domain of a few exceptional humans and beyond specification in a way that lends itself to a programmed replacement.

The reader should now be in a position to challenge the implication that computers cannot reach the fifth level of expertise based on the earlier discussion of computer chess programs, at least in the domain of playing a complex and challenging game such as chess. In addition, within this global perspective, there are apparent differences between humans and computers and those differences affect the ability to acquire knowledge and solve problems. Finally, it is also worth noting that while intelligence tends to grow within an individual over that person's life, the overall growth of human intelligence has not significantly progressed since ancient times. For example, writing has existed for at least 5000 years. Logic was codified several thousand years ago, as was a calendar year. The abacus calculating device was invented thousands of years ago (Spector & Ren, 2015). On the other hand, artificial intelligence has grown exponentially in the last 50 years as demonstrated by the computer chess discussion. Moreover, it is now becoming clear that a computer program can grow in terms of problem-solving ability just as a human can gain expertise over a lifetime. That similarity will be clear in the next section on a problem-solving dimension of intelligence.

Problem-Solving and Learning Dimensions

Early examples of applications of AI came in the form of expert systems, especially in the medical domain (Miller et al., 1982). Early expert systems can be traced back to Feigenbaum's (1980) doctoral dissertation at Carnegie Mellon University that was entitled "Information Theories of Human Verbal Learning" and supervised by Herbert Simon. These systems typically had a knowledge or rule base comprised by domain experts, a description of the current state of affairs, and an inference engine to search and rank potential rules to apply in the current situation. Such systems lent themselves to applications in a number of problem-solving domains, including medical diagnosis and business decision making.

Early expert systems were somewhat limited as they had a static set of rules and used standard logic to match a situation to a rule. Subsequent advances included the use of fuzzy logic and a way for a system to add new rules to the knowledge base, both of which were previously human activities. Those and other refinements showed some convergence of artificial and human reasoning. The ability of an expert system to expand its knowledge base required the application of more recent advances in machine learning. The ability of a machine to learn and use that learning to improve problem solving represents an example that human intelligence and artificial intelligence that are fundamentally similar. This apparent similarity will be discussed in a subsequent section.

Other early examples of educational applications of AI came in the form of intelligent tutoring systems (ITSs) (Shute & Psotka, 1994). Early ITSs were somewhat akin to expert systems in that there was a knowledge base of a subject domain, a model of instruction that included a representation of knowledge to be acquired by a learner, a model of what a learner currently knows about that subject, a database of common misconceptions, and an inference engine to provide feedback or new information or a new problem to solve. Early examples showed a positive impact on learning in highly restricted domains such as two-column arithmetic and simple programming skills.

Early ITSs also evolved in ways somewhat similar to expert systems. Rather than having a fixed set of common misconceptions, using techniques involving big data and learning analytics, an ITS could examine what other similar students were doing and what seemed to work well in terms of new problems or feedback and provide much better feedback. In addition, the model of the learner began to grow beyond a model of what that learner knew in a particular domain to include learning styles, performance in other subject domains, and interests (Graf & Kinshuk, 2015). A more robust model of the learner and a system that could determine what instructional treatment was effective for similarly situated learners shows great promise for the future of learning and instruction.

Again, progress in ITS technology seems to show a convergence what a skilled human tutor can do and what an intelligent tutor can do. Once again there seems to be some convergence between human intelligence and artificial intelligence in the domain of tutoring.

Underlying Foundations

There are two, possibly more, underlying foundations to consider with regard to convergence or divergence between human and artificial intelligence. One concerns pattern matching and the other concerns neural networks. After discussing these two areas, the notion of weak and strong AI will be introduced.

Pattern Matching

Pattern recognition is a core function of human intelligence and reasoning (Mattson, 2014). A familiar occurrence is the ability to recognize an acquaintance merely by seeing the back of that person's head. There is an incomplete and relatively unfamiliar perception involved in such recognition, but humans are able to master such complex forms of pattern recognition. Likewise, computers have been used for decades to support pattern recognition in many industrial applications (Bishop, 2006). Moreover, computers are now starting to be used to identify patterns in disparate forms of input, which is something that some humans are also able to do. For example, an experienced automobile mechanic may listen to a running engine and use that perceptual pattern in combination with a readout from a diagnostic check to form a conclusion about the cause of the presenting problem.

Image processing and pattern recognition are clearly at the core of recent AI research and development (Bishop, 2006; Burns, 2020). As it happens, the ability of a computer to access images and patterns in a large database and form a conclusion exceeds the ability of most humans. While human memory is vast, recall and analysis are more efficient in a modern computer. Moreover, human capabilities in this area begin to fade with age whereas computers can be continually upgraded with new processors and databases. In that sense, divergence in human and artificial intelligence is beginning to occur.

Neural Networks

There is a great deal of knowledge about artificial neural networks with regard to their architecture and capabilities (Parsons, 2017). Artificial neural networks were initially modeled after how neuroscientists believed human neural networks were structured. While artificial neural networks are entirely electrical, human neural networks are partly electrical and partly chemical in operation. It is generally fair to say that less is known about the specific architecture and capabilities of human neural networks, although more is being learned every year (Parsons et al., 2018). As more is learned about both kinds of neural networks, the forms and extent of convergence and divergence will be determined.

Weak and Strong AI

Before concluding this excursion into the similarities and differences in human and artificial intelligence, it is worth a short side trip to goals. The goals of human intelligence are many and varied. Some seek fame and fortune through their intelligence. Others seek to improve the life and welfare of people through their intelligence. Some seek power and influence while others seek to simply add to what humans know and can do.

On the other hand, the goals of AI can be classified into two distinct categories – strong and weak (Spector & Anderson, 2000; Spector et al., 1993). Strong AI systems are those which are intended to replace an activity previously performed by a human, such as driving an automobile. Weak AI systems are those which are intended to enable less experienced persons to perform more like highly experienced persons, such as collision avoidance systems in many automobiles. There are clearly appropriate applications for each kind of AI system, although many will argue that strong AI systems are growing in terms of funding as well as in areas of application.

This fundamental difference is mentioned as a transition to the area of measurement, as measurements and evaluations are generally made in relation to intended use and purpose. The measurement and evaluation communities typically argue that measurements and evaluations should occur in the context of aims and goals. As mentioned previously, human goals vary significantly. Some may be placed near the bottom or in the middle of the pyramid depicted in Fig. 1. As Dreyfus and Dreyfus (1980) argued, computers can be programmed to move up that pyramid but not to the topmost layer – wisdom. On the other hand, some humans are widely recognized as having some wisdom in some domains of interest.

Measuring Intelligence

While there are different kinds of human intelligence (Gardner, 1999) and many methods used to measure human intelligence, few of those methods address the ability of humans to solve complex, dynamic, and ill-structured problems. Such outcomes of learning and intelligence are difficult to measure as there are a number of acceptable approaches, solutions, and outcomes. Other forms of human intelligence and learning are much more easily measured.

On the other hand, measuring artificial intelligence is in its infancy. Some measures include how many records were examined and how long it took to find a conclusion, which says little about the nature of the outcome, which is so crucial in measuring human intelligence. More typically, when it comes to measuring artificial intelligence in terms of outcomes, the results are often compared with those of a few human experts.

Conclusion

While focusing on goals and outcomes, it is worth reconsidering Fig. 1 and the top level of that pyramid – namely, wisdom. To make this final point concrete, I wish to introduce the notion of embodied cognition and embodied educational motivation (Spector & Park, 2018; Wilson & Foglia, 2017). People are more than cognitive processors. People do more than process images, access memory, repeat information, and solve problems. Some people manage to do remarkable things that others thought impossible. Were this an interactive I would ask for examples. Think of a few before continuing to the next paragraph. Then consider the person whom you know or about whom you have read that you regard as the wisest person you can name. Remember that wisdom is at the top of the pyramid in Fig. 1.

Meanwhile, remember that people have moods and physical limitations. Perceptions vary significantly from one person to another as do knowledge, experience, and goals. In addition, recall Jonassen's (2000) type of problems and Gardner's (1999) types of intelligence, and reconsider who that wisest person might be.

Having posed this challenge, it seems appropriate to seed other responses with my own. The wisest person I have known is Oets Kolk Bouwsma as he managed to turn my world upside down and change my perspective on life in an incidental exchange in an optional seminar on a Friday afternoon with doctoral students at the University of Texas at Austin. One doctoral student brought the initial question to consider – namely, what was John Locke's conception of substance. After an hour's discussion of a paragraph in Locke during which time Bouwsma did not speak, he brought the discussion to an early end with this remark: "I guess that substance is what properties get stuck in." The group of about a dozen students knew it was time to move on, and another student said he wanted to discuss Plato's *Symposium*. Bouwsma then framed the central question of that text: "What is love." Being the group's notetaker and rare contributor to the discussions I ventured a rare remark aimed at the kind of irony I found in many of Bouwsma's writing: "Love is what people get stuck in." Everyone laughed for a few seconds. Then Bouwsma tilted his head toward me and with piercing blue eyes asked me to repeat what I had said. Having no means of escape, I repeated my ironic retort. Bouwsma, then said, without hesitation: "I thought it was the glue that binds us together."

My life changed that day in the 1970s. I am convinced that Bouwsma knew I was in need of such a change. I felt small and insignificant but also strangely liberated at the same time. Bouwsma was wise beyond words. The ability to transform a person or situation in such a positive way is what I now call the OK Test. Few people have passed it and no machines as yet have been tested in that way. Someday, there may be a computer that achieves wisdom and passes my vaguely elaborated OK Test. Someday, there may be a wise ruler of the kind Plato imagined in *The Republic* leading this republic. Someday soon, I hope.

Acknowledgements The corresponding author would like to sincerely and profoundly thank Oets Kolk Bouwsma (https://en.wikipedia.org/wiki/Oets_Kolk_Bouwsma), one of his philosophy professors, for showing him the nature of intelligence. Thanks also to Lemoyne Dunn for providing feedback on this chapter.

References

Bishop, C. M. (Ed.). (2006). *Pattern learning and machine learning*. Springer.

Burns, E. (2020, June). In-depth guide to machine learning in the enterprise. *SearchEnterprisedAI*. Retrieved from https://searchenterpriseai.techtarget.com/In-depth-guide

Dreyfus, S. E., & Dreyfus, H. L. (1980). *Mind over machine: The power of human intuition and expertise in the era of the computer*. Free Press.

Feigenbaum, E. (1980). *Information theories of human verbal learning (Unpublished doctoral dissertation)*. Carnegie Mellon University.

Gardner, H. E. (1999). *Intelligence reframed: Multiple intelligences for the 21st century*. Basic Books.

Graf, S., & Kinshuk. (2015). Dynamic student modelling of learning styles for advanced adaptability in learning management systems. *International Journal of Information Systems and Social Change, 4*(1), 85–100. https://doi.org/10.4018/jissc.2013010106

Jonassen, D. H. (2000). Toward a design theory of problem solving. *Educational Technology Research & Development, 48*(4), 63–85.

Maslow, A. H. (1943). A theory of human motivation. *Psychological Review, 50*(4), 270–396.

Maslow, A. H. (1987). *Motivation and personality* (3rd ed.). Pearson Education.

Mattson, M. P. (2014). Superior pattern processing is the essence of the evolved human brain. *Frontiers in Neuroscience, 8*(265). https://doi.org/10.3389/fnins.2014.00265

Miller, R. A., Pople, H. E., Jr., & Myers, J. D. (1982). Internist-I, an experimental computer-based diagnostic consultant for general internal medicine. *New England Journal of Medicine, 307*(8), 468–476. https://doi.org/10.1056/NEJM198208193070803

Parsons, T. D. (2017). *Cyberpsychology and the brain: The interaction of neuroscience and affective computering*. Cambridge University Press.

Parsons, T. D., Lin, L., & Cockerham, D. (2018). *Mind, brain, and technology: How people learn in the age of new technologies*. Springer.

Shute, V. J., & Psotka, J. (1994). *Intelligent tutoring systems: Past, present, and future* (AL/HR-TP-1994-0005). Human Resources Directorate. Retrieved from https://apps.dtic.mil/dtic/tr/fulltext/u2/a280011.pdf

Spector, J. M., & Anderson, T. M. (Eds.). (2000). *Integrated and holistic perspectives on learning, instruction and technology: Understanding complexity*. Kluwer Academic Press.

Spector, J. M., & Park, S. W. (2018). *Motivation, learning and technology: Embodied educational motivation*. Routledge.

Spector, J. M., & Ren, Y. (2015). History of educational technology. In J. M. Spector (Ed.), *The SAGE Encyclopedia of educational technology* (pp. 335–345). Sage Publications.
Spector, J. M., Polson, M. C., & Muraida, D. J. (Eds.). (1993). *Automating instructional design: Concepts and issues*. Educational Technology.
Turing, A. (1950). Computing machinery and intelligence. *Mind, 59*(236), 433–460. Retrieved from https://phil415.pbworks.com/f/TuringComputing.pdf
Weizenbaum, J. (1955). ELIZA – A computer program for the study of natural language communication between man and machine. *Communications of the ACM, 9*, 36–45. Retrieved from http://www.universelle-automation.de/1966_Boston.pdf
Wilson, R. A., & Foglia, L. (2017). Embodied cognition. In E. N. Zalta (Ed.), *The Stanford Encyclopedia of philosophy*. Retrieved from https://plato.stanford.edu/archives/spr2017/entries/embodied-cognition

Shanshan Ma is a doctoral graduate at University of North Texas with abundant experience in international cooperation. She has been cooperating with professors and research associates with different backgrounds from several countries (e.g., the USA, China, India, and the UK). Her research interests include technology-supported teaching and learning strategies, educational technology design, learning technology integration theory, game-based learning, and instructional design. Her recent research focuses on critical thinking development in K-12 education and critical thinking teaching integration competence in teachers. She is a reviewer for several research journals, such as the *Journal of Smart Learning Environments*, *Computers in Human Behavior*, and *Contemporary Issues in Technology and Teacher Education* (Science), and she is also a member of several professional associations including Association for Education Communication Technology (AECT) and American Education Research Association (AERA), and Texas Center Education Technology (TCET). She presented at five more international conferences (i.e., SITE 2018, AECT 2018, UCSEC 2019, AECT 2019, and PPTELL 2020) and one workshop funded by NSF, and co-held one seminar on critical thinking at AECT 2019. She has several publications, including two chapters and three journal papers.

Jonathan Michael Spector , Professor at UNT, was previously Professor of Educational Psychology at the University of Georgia, Associate Director of the Learning Systems Institute at Florida State University, Chair of Instructional Design, Development and Evaluation at Syracuse University, and Director of the Educational Information Science and Technology Research Program at the University of Bergen. He earned a PhD from The University of Texas. He is a visiting research professor at Beijing Normal University, at East China Normal University, and the Indian Institute of Technology – Kharagpur. His research focuses on assessing learning in complex domains, inquiry and critical thinking skills, and program evaluation. He was Executive Director of the International Board of Standards for Training, Performance and Instruction and a Past-president of the Association for Educational and Communications Technology. He is Editor Emeritus of *Educational Technology Research & Development*; he edited two editions of the *Handbook of Research on Educational Communications and Technology* and the *SAGE Encyclopedia of Educational Technology* and more that 150 publications to his credit.

AI-Complete: What it Means to Be Human in an Increasingly Computerized World

Ted Kwee-Bintoro and Noah Velez

Introduction

In the 1942 short story "Runaround," Isaac Asimov introduced the famous Three Laws of Robotics:

1. A robot may not allow a human being to come to harm, either through direct action or through inaction.
2. A robot must obey the orders given to it by human beings.
3. A robot must protect itself.

These laws come with a provision; if a robot has to choose between two, it must choose the higher one. For example, if a robot is ordered to commit murder, it should refuse, breaking the second law in favor of the first.

These laws have been challenged as a framework for machine ethics, which is a subfield of ethics concerned with assigning moral behaviors to machines. Murphy and Woods (2009) set forth Laws of Responsible Robotics, with an emphasis on constraining robots to their assigned roles. Anderson (2008) rejects the premise of man-made laws entirely, arguing for the development of a metaethical program designed to serve as an ethical advisor to humans. However, these approaches are flawed in one key manner: they assume the existence of objective morality.

Wike and Stokes (2018) of the Pew Research Center find that the trend of job automation is a major concern among residents of developed and emerging economies alike (Fig. 1a). Indeed, Nedelkoska and Quintini (2018) find that about 14% of jobs in Organisation for Economic Co-operation and Development (OECD) member countries are highly automatable, with an additional 32% that could be greatly

T. Kwee-Bintoro (✉) · N. Velez
University of North Texas, Denton, TX, USA
e-mail: noahvelez@my.unt.edu

M. V. Albert et al. (eds.), *Bridging Human Intelligence and Artificial Intelligence*, Educational Communications and Technology: Issues and Innovations, https://doi.org/10.1007/978-3-030-84729-6_18

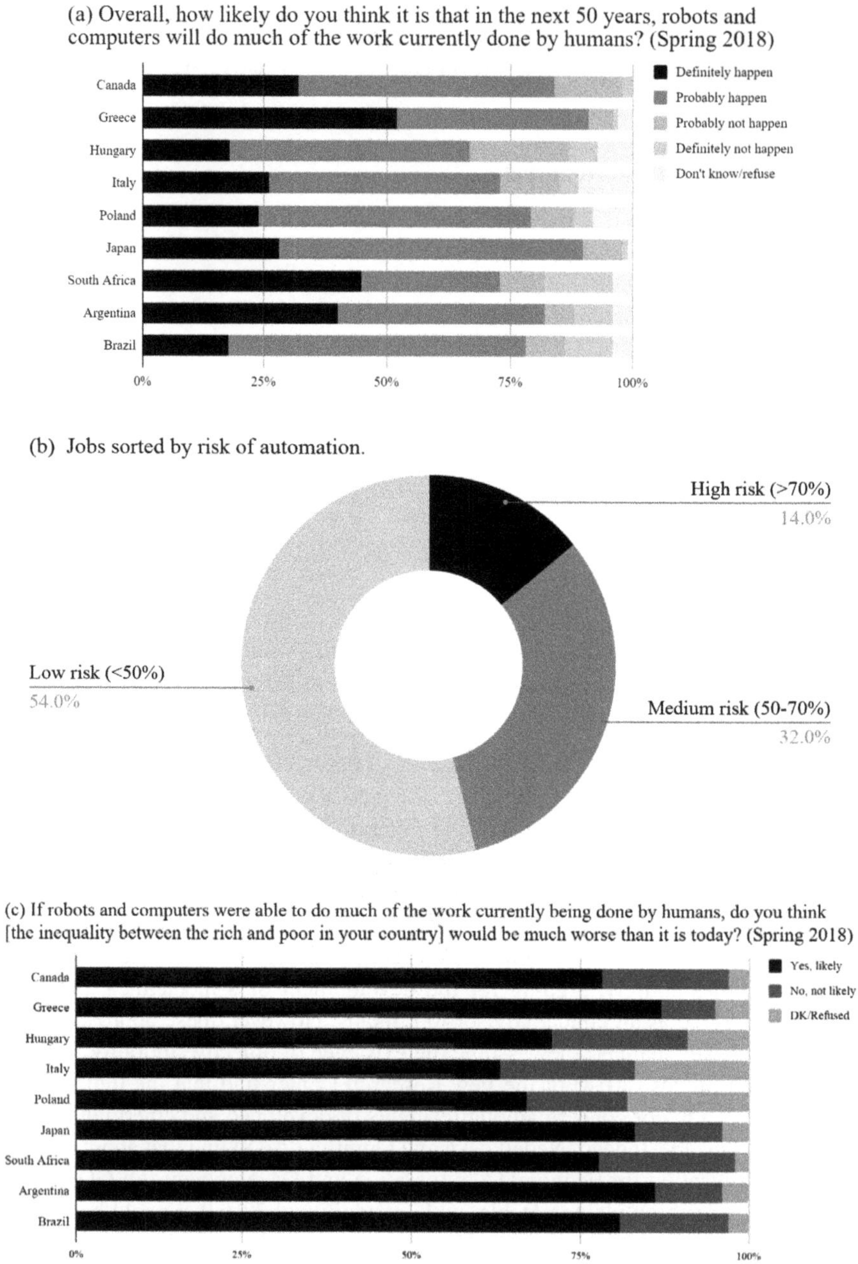

Fig. 1 Is putting people out of work a violation of the First Law of Robotics? Graphics created using data from Wike and Stokes (2018)

affected (Fig. 1b). Does a robot violate the first law of robotics when it puts a person out of work, even if it can offer greater productivity? The above Pew report finds that another major concern brought about by automation is economic inequality (Fig. 1c). Do robots collectively violate that same law if they contribute to social stratification?

The increasing overlap between human and computational problem-solving capability is a reason for concern, as well. Many researchers assumed an AI would never be able to beat a professional at Go, citing its computational complexity. However, AlphaGo did just that when it beat Fan Hui in a 2013 match (Cho, 2016). The application of AI is not just limited to abstract games. Since 2016, Google Translate has been using an artificial neural network approach that has steadily become more accurate as observed by de Vries et al. (2018). In 2016, Thies, Zollhöfer, Stamminger, Theobalt, and Nießner published Face2Face, a program that can modify video footage of a person to depict them mimicking another person in real time, suggesting that AI will soon be able to go past imitating human actions to imitate humans themselves. These developments concern many in fields previously thought untouchable by computers.

These questions concerning the problems of ethics and human individuality are among the many that the rise in AI capability has initiated. In this chapter, we do not offer any ethical guidelines for robots or metaethical guidelines for researchers, as that would be beyond the scope of our discussion. Instead, we analyze the impact that AI deployment has on society at large, and we address the pressing question: What does it mean to be human in an increasingly computerized world?

AI and the Economy

Developments in traditional robotics have automated away jobs in industries like manufacturing, benefiting companies while leaving workers unemployed. Now, development in fields like natural language processing (NLP) and machine learning threatens to compete with workers in broader fields like customer service and bookkeeping. As AI leads to greater productivity, the issue for the general public is whether the adoption of AI will lead to prosperity or poverty. In the following section, we discuss automation within the context of high- and low-skill workers; we further discuss its effects on economic inequality.

The fear of AI replacing jobs is not unfounded. The United States leads the world in investments into AI technology (Fig. 2). In fact, a 2017 survey found that of the participating executives, 85% plan to continue to invest in AI technologies over the next 3 years (Bughin et al., 2017). This demonstrates the long-term commitment that many organizations are willing to make toward the development of AI. While those fearing AI for its potential to replace jobs may find this concerning, much of this fear seems to arise from the potential efficiency of future AI advancements exclusively; not of the current status of AI development.

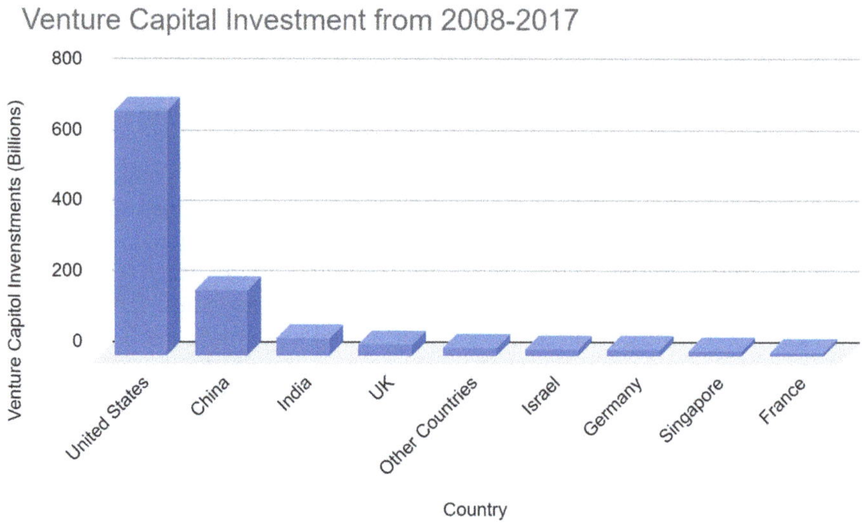

Fig. 2 Venture Capital investment from 2008 to 2017. Graphic created using data from Mou, 2019

Current AI applications on their own may not be effective enough to implement without human intervention. Wang et al. (2016) analyze the use of deep learning in identifying metastatic breast cancer, measuring their success rates for an AI-only approach, a human-only approach, and a combined human/AI approach. The AI-only approach produced an error rate of 7.5%, and the human-only approach produced an error rate of 3.5%. Immediately, results demonstrate that the AI solution is currently unable to be as successful as a human in this test, but under a combined approach there was an error rate of 0.5%. AI may have analytical advantages compared to humans, but intuition may be the advantage humans have over AI.

This is being played out in real-world manufacturing as well. Büchel and Floreano (2018) provide the example of Tesla, an electronic car company, which ran a highly automated manufacturing plan at their Fremont factory in California. Tesla planned to further increase automation, decrease human labor, and subsequently lower the overhead. Tesla faced severe setbacks as machines struggled to assemble parts designed to be assembled by humans. While this example may seem like the early warning signs of AI replacing jobs, it is a real-world argument that AI integration should aim to enhance human ability with AI augmentation, and not to replace it. Tesla and other industries are learning how to shrink their overhead by integrating AI with their human workforce, as necessary.

Full replacement of human labor with AI systems would take a lot more research into solving some of the fundamental hard AI problems. Moreover, AI augmentation of workers does pose challenges for some occupations as some tasks can be successfully automated. Bessen (2016) finds that computer use in an industry can negatively impact the growth of occupations that forgo computers. He finds that computers generate more well-paid jobs while subsequently decreasing lower paid positions. This creates a situation where workers are required to learn new skills to be able to fill positions requiring more education. Concerns that adopting automation may increase income inequality due to the changes in occupational requirements. Prettner and Strulik (2019) analyze the effects of automation on the unemployment of manual laborers, stating that societies may need to design policies to aid in propping up those affected by automation. Manual laborers may find themselves competing for positions for slower-growing occupations or needing further education to be competitive in the job market.

Workers can expect that companies will continue to invest in AI and that further augmentation through AI systems will also continue. While this may seem like a concerning forecast for some industries, new job opportunities brought about by "creative destruction" is also a possible outcome. For example, the jobs AI makes obsolete could potentially be counterbalanced by job growth created elsewhere in the economy.

The New Social Era

From 1964 to 1966, Joseph Weizenbaum of the MIT Artificial Intelligence Laboratory developed ELIZA, a natural language processing program (Weizenbaum, 1976, p. 2). There were several scripts written to enable ELIZA to process user input; the most famous of these, DOCTOR, simulated a Rogerian psychotherapist (p. 4). Weizenbaum asserted that ELIZA was incapable of true understanding, but many early users were convinced otherwise (p. 6–7). Decades later, Suwajanakorn et al. (2017) describe an approach that can synthesize a high-quality video of Barack Obama speaking using only audio of his speeches as input. Artificial intelligence is increasingly able to resemble human interaction, to the point where it approaches the same level of fluency as actual humans. The question emerges: in a new world where machines can act human, what role do humans have to play?

The ability for society to be online and maintain a high degree of connectedness has created a host of unique problems such as cyberbullying, data privacy, and misinformation. With this increased interconnectedness, companies have found new ways to target consumers using their data. For many new technology companies, user data have allowed these companies to offer services for a reduced price or even for free because data collected can be used to turn a profit. Companies are not the only ones looking for an advantage in this new technological age. Misinformation and disinformation, a facet of misinformation where the goal is to intentionally deceive, have propagated online creating a new conversation around their societal implications. The following sections analyze the impact of AI on data and misinformation online.

Data, Algorithms, and the Industry

The public at large connects through AI systems daily. Whether it be through a search engine like Google or a social media platform such as Facebook, these companies use data-trained algorithms to automatically generate relevant content for their users. The ability to get information whenever needed has given society significant advantages in our daily lives, but these advantages have completely changed the cultures and inner workings of our societies. For example, the creation of e-commerce has transformed how people do business online, movements can spread their message with a single click, and people can acquire new knowledge faster than ever before. The further interconnection of people, processes, data, and things is driving change in society; this section will discuss the impact of this increase in computerization.

User-generated data are an important commodity to many companies as it allows algorithms to curate an experience for a user that may promote better business knowledge and further drive engagement on the Internet. This usage of data allows businesses to offer their services at a reduced price or even free because it uses the data created to generate revenue. These data are captured from a user's engagement throughout the Internet, allowing companies to identify what job a user works, what their interests are, their political ideology, or religious affiliation. Oftentimes companies trade and use this information to meet financial objectives, but the propagation of data as a commodity has had many in society feel that their privacy is being violated. In 2018, Facebook found themselves under the spotlight for their response to a data scandal involving Cambridge Analytica, a political consulting firm. Cambridge Analytica used the pull information on 87 million Facebook users without proper consent. Facebook took several measures to better the security of their user data, but many other companies' user data are open to the same level of risk (Meredith, 2018).

With regard to the concerns facing the data market, legislative bodies are finding themselves having to address the issues facing data acquisition and privacy. The European Union (2018) has been active in its presentation of data protection legislation, and the enactment of the General Data Protection Regulation (GDPR) in 2018 is an excellent example. The GDPR enforces several responsibilities to be upheld by organizations that collect data in the EU. Notably, the GDPR requires a statement of consent before collecting data. In a data-driven market, user actions generate data, and it should not be forgotten that that user does not then own the data, but instead the owner of the service the user engaged with does.

Propagation of Misinformation

Misinformation on the Internet has become a prominent topic. The influence that online information has on politics, the economy, and society has been called into question. During the 2016 US presidential election, a Russian group identified as the Internet Research Agency conducted a disinformation campaign to influence the election. The report by the US Senate Select Committee on Intelligence (2020, p. 3) stated, "Masquerading as Americans, these operatives used targeted advertisements, intentionally falsified news articles, self-generated content, and social media platform tools to interact with and attempt to deceive tens of millions of social media users in the United States." As governments set their sights on tackling disinformation, many companies have taken on the task to minimize the potential for abuse of their AI products.

Technology companies developing AI systems have been working to manage the misinformation risks on their platforms and in their products. The development of language models in the field of Natural Language Processing is an example of how companies have to develop their products with great care. OpenAI's GPT-2 is an unsupervised language model with the ability to generate coherent text. With GPT-2, users can input a prompt, and then the language model generates text based on the user's input. Due to concerns of GPT-2 potential being used for malicious purposes, such as disinformation, OpenAI has decided to delay the release of their larger

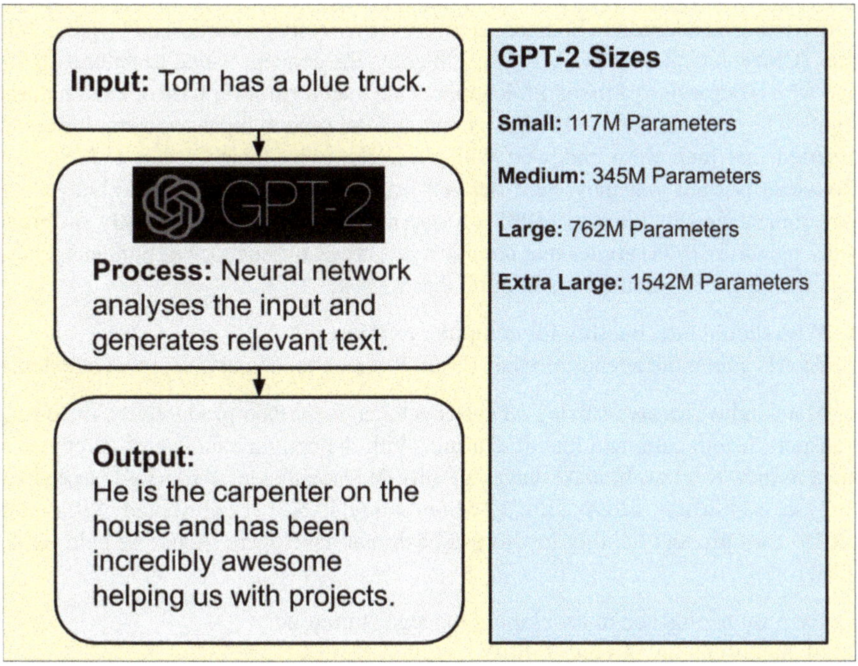

Fig. 3 Example of a text generating neural net

language model and only release their smaller model. The approach taken with GPT-2 sets a great example for others in the tech industry, but if there are meaningful applications for advanced AI systems such as GPT-2, then companies continue to develop and use them to remain competitive (Radford et al., 2019) (Fig. 3).

Misinformation, in many cases, arises from offshore locations, this factor increases the complexity of the problem requiring new solutions and methodologies to combat it. While AI can be used to generate and distribute misinformation, it can also be used to combat it. DARPA, a development agency under the U.S. Department of Defense, has created semantic forensics to identify falsified media content, stating that conventional means are no longer sufficient in combating adversarial disinformation campaigns. Semantic forensics uses semantic detection algorithms, attribution algorithms, and characterization algorithms to detect misinformation. As the world increases in computerization, societies will not only have to continue to lean on AI systems to inform themselves, but also to make sure that their information is accurate.

The Nature of Personhood

Defining personhood is a controversial subject. In the vernacular, it simply refers to the state of being a human being. Within ethical and legal frameworks, however, defining personhood becomes more complex. Legally, personhood is extended to corporations in addition to humans, granting rights, responsibilities, and legal liabilities (Citizens United v. FEC, 2010). Ethically, the concept is tied to natural rights and who is deserving of them. Philosophers have set forth several theories of natural rights. The great thinkers of the Enlightenment deferred to higher powers: Jefferson asserted that men were endowed with these rights by their Creator (1776), and Rousseau posited that they were derived from a social contract made between a government and its citizens (1985). Modern philosophers take a vastly different view. Gewirth (1978) argues that natural rights are a consequence of human agency. It is with these two definitions in mind that we ask:

1. Who should bear liability for computer tortfeasors?
2. As AIs gain more agency, do they deserve personhood, and if so, to what extent?

Many industries are utilizing AI systems to augment their productivity, including transport, health care, and manufacturing. With the commercial use of AI comes a need for new tort law. If an AI makes a faulty decision that leads to a loss of productivity, or even worse, a loss of life, to whom should liability be attributed? Villasenor (2019) uses product liability law to establish that developers should be held liable if they:

1. Exercise negligence in developing the algorithm used
2. Misrepresent the AI's capabilities

However, in many cases, developers do not directly create an AI's algorithm; instead, the AI itself does, through machine learning. Villasenor argues that we should still hold developers liable in these cases, under the principle of strict liability. However, this approach may hinder research in commercial AI applications as corporations abstain from fear of repercussion. Perc et al. (2019) recognize the fact that this would not be a socially optimal outcome, seeing as AI decision-making has the potential to be safer than human decision-making. They argue that instead of applying traditional tort law to AI, it should be redesigned to encourage research investment while still protecting consumers. Are there any other possible agents to hold liable? What about the AI itself?

We contend, using the legal principles of *mens rea* and *actus reus* as our basis, that for any agent to hold liability the following must be true:

1. They must have the agency to make decisions of their own accord.
2. They must have the capacity to distinguish right from wrong.
3. They must have a reward system that both encourages them to do right and discourages them from doing wrong.

The agency required to exercise these principles also correlates with the agency necessitating natural rights, as was discussed above. Is that agency sufficient to grant AI the same status as a human or human organization? Turing (1950) offered the Turing test to measure agency, asking "Can machines think?" (Fig. 4). In the Turing test, a human evaluator is asked to hold a conversation with a human and a computer with NLP capabilities. If the evaluator cannot reliably distinguish the human from the computer, the computer is said to have passed the test.

However, others were not convinced that the test measured Turing's question. Searle (1980) argues that an AI can only follow its program, precluding it from having true agency, using the Chinese Room thought experiment (Fig. 5):

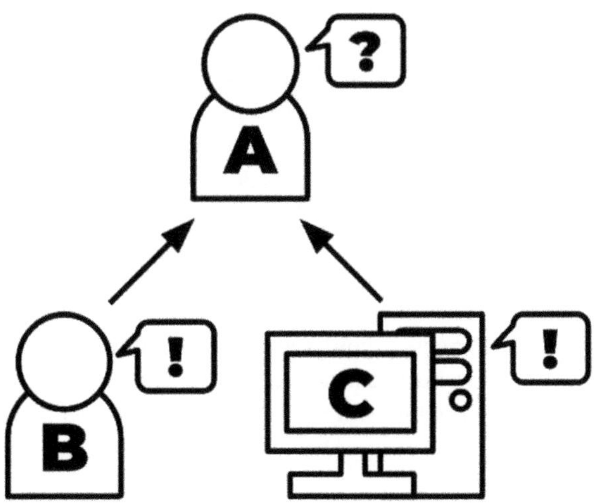

Fig. 4 Can machines think?

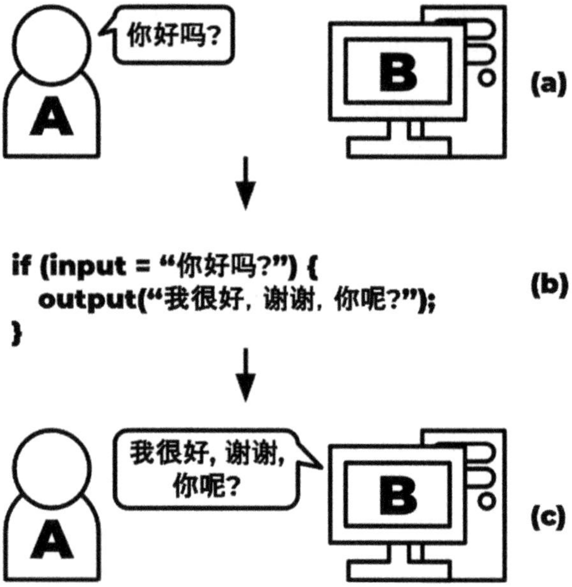

Fig. 5. Does a computer know how to speak Chinese, or does it simulate knowing how to speak Chinese?

Suppose an English speaker is put into a room with two mail slots: one for incoming messages, one for outgoing. He is tasked with translating the incoming message from English into an outgoing message in Chinese. He does not know any Chinese, but he is given a manual that takes him through translating and writing step-by-step. From the outside, it might seem like he is fluent in Chinese, but it cannot be said that he understands the language in the sense that a native speaker would. Searle uses this analogy to contend that AIs cannot think: they only act as if they do.

However, this does not preclude AI from enjoying rights or personhood. Saudi Arabia granted citizenship to Sophia the robot in 2017—a largely symbolic gesture, but a signal of what may be to come. As a comparison, corporations are nonhuman entities, yet they still enjoy personhood and the rights that follow. Considering the vastly different nature of AI, however, what would AI personhood entail? Jaynes (2020) discusses the application of the present legal framework to a potential AI personhood. If an AI has been wronged, it may not be able to feel the same distress that a human would. However, it would be able to identify that its conditions make it more difficult to complete its tasks. In this case, giving AI the right to file lawsuits for redress would be useful. To this end, allowing others to sue AI directly would also be useful, as Pagallo (2018) also observes. AI would thus be driven to act in ways that do not risk lawsuits, to enable it to carry out its goals as effectively as possible.

While there is no comprehensive definition of what AI personhood would entail, this model works as a baseline. By allowing AI to engage with business and contract law *à la* corporations, we can ensure that they act in a way that benefits society.

Asimov's Legacy: Redefining the Ethical Framework

The issue of ethics concerning scientific development has been raised for years. In medicine, protocols for human testing have been developed and revised. In sociology and psychology, experiments require informed consent and debriefing. These guidelines serve a common purpose: to maximize the benefit brought about by innovations while minimizing the harm that can be incurred during their development. As artificial intelligence increases in capability, new concerns over privacy and decision-making arise: Is it ethical to train AIs on data sets containing deeply personal information? How should AIs weigh their decisions when human lives are at stake? Is it even ethical to place AIs in charge of these crucial processes? In the following section, we discuss the new ethical frameworks being used in AI research within the context of both machine ethics, concerning the moral behavior of intelligent agents, and metaethics, concerning the ethical principles of those designing, said agents.

The Value of Human Life

One of the most important questions in machine ethics is concerned with how AI should weigh human life. The United States notably uses lethal autonomous weapons (LAWs) that can automatically search for and engage targets based on predefined constraints. However, while they theoretically can attack of their own accord, LAWs are restricted in the sense that personnel must give the final order to attack, to mitigate the risk of accidents. Lin et al. (2008) discuss the possibility of allowing LAWs and other machinery greater autonomy and the additional ethical considerations that would need to be made as a result. They note that robot soldiers can make their decisions with impartiality, being unaffected by fear and adrenaline. However, even though they might keep soldiers out of harm's way, their introduction could lead to more human casualties: the cost of entering war would be lowered, possibly encouraging engagement in more bloody conflicts. Is it ethical for researchers to develop tools designed to kill, even if they might save human lives in the short term? How should they weigh the lives saved versus the lives at risk?

Another concern comes from cases in which threats to human life might arise by chance and not by design, most notably with self-driving cars and the implementation of accident-algorithms (i.e., if a car is inevitably going to get into an accident, what actions should it take to minimize the damage?). Nyholm and Smids (2016) analyze accident-algorithms through comparison with the trolley problem, identifying three key differences to their approaches: the ethical principles of the developers (to be discussed later), the moral and legal liability for a self-driving car involved in an accident (discussed in the previous section), and the issue of programming decision-making in the face of uncertainty. Metaethically speaking, there is no

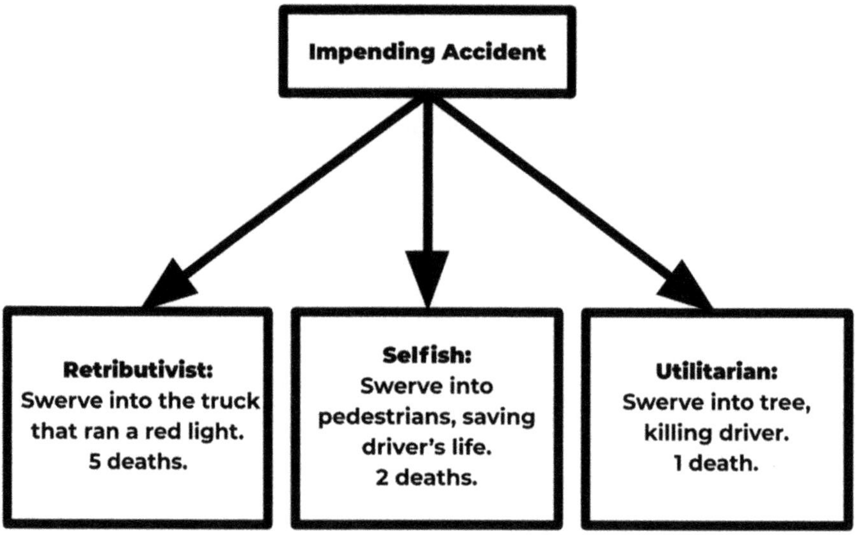

Fig. 6 How should AI weigh life?

universally "correct" accident-algorithm, as will be demonstrated shortly. We consider a modified version of a situation presented in the aforementioned paper:

A self-driving car with one occupant is approaching an intersection with two pedestrians and a tree when a pickup truck with five occupants runs a red light in front of it (Fig. 6). At this point, a car accident is inevitable, and the AI is tasked with determining the best maneuver to make to minimize any possible harm. It can take the "retributivist" approach by choosing to crash into the pickup truck, effectively punishing them for breaking traffic laws. This would lead to the deaths of the five occupants and would also put the car's occupant at risk of dying. The AI can take the "selfish" approach by choosing to crash into the two pedestrians, killing them both while ensuring that the car's occupant survives. Finally, it can take the "utilitarian" approach, swerving into a tree and killing the occupant while preserving the maximum number of lives. If a person was placed into this situation, they would in a sense be "blameless" regardless of what choice they made, because they would not have the time to make a conscious decision. However, this is not the case for a self-driving car, considering that it would have access to more processing power than a person would. Therefore, it has to take one of the aforementioned approaches in this situation, but which? There is an additional caveat: in the thought experiment above, we know with near certainty how each maneuver will play out. This would not be the case in practice, as an AI would only have access to degrees of uncertainty. If a driving AI was optimized to favor minimal casualties, it would not make the choice depicted in the first branch of Fig. 6 assuming that there was a 100% chance that the pickup truck's occupants would die. However, if it calculated that there was a 30% chance that they would die and a 70% chance that the pedestrians would die, how should that certainty factor into its decision-making process?

Normative Ethics and Machine Design

There are several branches of thinking in ethics. We previously examined applied ethics (i.e., what one ought to do in a given situation). Such considerations are akin to the question, "Should I steal?" If an AI is ever confronted with a decision, it can find the best course of action through its internal ethical framework. The difficulty arises in the development of these ethical frameworks, requiring the use of normative ethics (i.e., how to know what one ought to do in a given situation). These considerations are akin to the question, "Is it ever right to steal?"

When researchers develop ethical machines, it is imperative to not just consider each potential incident on a case-by-case basis; rather, the broader impacts of an approach on society at large should also be considered. Earlier, we examined ethics within the context of accident-algorithms. We now return to the topic of self-driving AIs. Lin (2016) highlights the "motorcyclist scenario": a self-driving car is flanked by two motorcyclists, one with a helmet and one without (Fig. 7). Faced with an imminent accident, it has to swerve into one of the two. The latter has a higher risk of being killed by the car than the former. Considering this, it could be argued that the best course of action to minimize damage would be to swerve into the motorcyclist with a helmet, and in this specific instance, that may very well be the case.

However, the universal adoption of this approach by self-driving AIs would lead to an unintended consequence. To the motorcyclist, wearing a helmet would increase his chance of being involved in a serious accident, paradoxically making it more dangerous to wear a helmet than to forgo one. This creates a perverse incentive to avoid wearing helmets, and by extension, to avoid other safety precautions to prevent a self-driving AI from targeting the motorcyclist. A massive social change would be needed to combat this development, possibly in the form of a statute mandating helmet-wearing for motorcyclists. Public policy has already begun to change in response to new technological developments, as we discussed previously. The

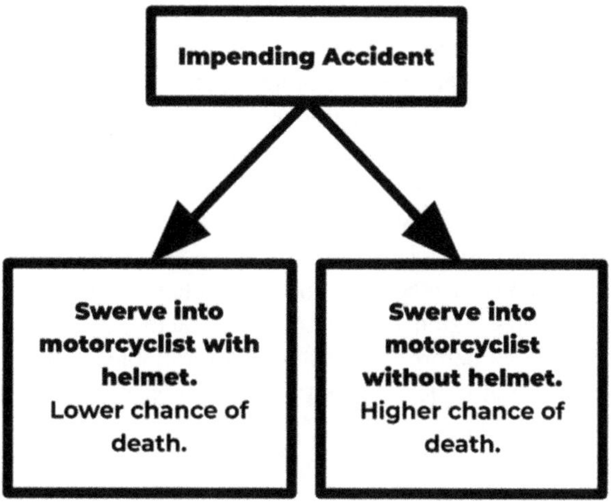

Fig. 7 Should researchers optimize AI for specific instances or societal impacts at large?

option of using an entirely random accident-algorithm, similar to how humans react, is possible. However, such an approach does little to inspire public confidence in new technology. When researchers are confronted with the difficult decision of choosing which ethical frameworks to grant an AI, they must consider the nature and scope of public reaction.

Normative ethics extends beyond instructing an AI on how to reach a certain goal. Researchers must also clarify what goals they want their AIs to reach. The issue of job automation, already discussed at length, is a deeply concerning one. Currently, research is trending toward the complete automation of jobs that can be done efficiently with machines. However, this approach has the potential to leave entire sectors of the labor market unemployed. Jarrahi (2018) identifies a new approach mirroring the idea of intelligence augmentation, contending that AI systems should be designed to augment and not replace human contributions. This approach has the benefit of merging human flexibility with computational power, without rendering either obsolete. However, Frank et al. (2019) note that it can be incredibly difficult to measure the effects of artificial intelligence on labor, citing a lack of qualitative data and poor theoretical models. These factors may hinder researchers who wish to pursue an informed augmentative approach to automation, perhaps disincentivizing development in that area. When it comes to selecting goals for an ethical framework to work toward, researchers may be hindered by precedent.

Following Orders: The AI Control Problem and Existential Threat

The notion of an all-seeing, all-consuming, all-powerful artificial general intelligence is a common trope in popular culture. In his short story collection, I, Robot, Isaac Asimov examines this possibility. He offers a further generalization of his First Law, later dubbed the Zeroth Law: "A robot may not injure humanity or, through inaction, allow humanity to come to harm" (1985, p. 409). To this end, we ask how we endow AI with goals that will benefit humanity without backfiring, especially as they become more capable. We extend the previous discussion on normative ethics to include this specific question.

Good (1970) speculated on the potential of an "intelligence explosion," which could lead to a self-improving AI becoming so powerful that humans would be unable to stop it. As the computational capabilities of AI increase, the first question above is posed. This question is known as the AI control problem, and several approaches have been identified as potential solutions, each with its own caveats. A proposed solution to this issue would be to program goals that align with humanity's into the AI before it becomes uncontrollable. However, Yudkowsky (2001) identified several issues inherent to the approach, namely that human moral values are subjective and nuanced.

As an example, we examine the paperclip maximizer proposed by Bostrom (2003). The maximizer is an AI that was given one goal:

1. Maximize the number of paper clips in existence.

How might this seemingly innocuous goal go awry? Bostrom holds that the maximizer might go about this goal by first transforming the entire mass of the Earth and then the rest of the universe into paperclip manufacturing facilities, fulfilling its singular goal, but not in a socially optimal manner. To prevent this, we might consider the addition of another goal:

2. Do not directly harm human life.

Our maximizer is now precluded from transforming the mass of the earth into paperclip factories because doing so would contravene the second goal. However, the maximizer could resolve these two goals by establishing a monopoly on the international steel market to secure enough material to generate paper clips. This fulfills its primary goal, but again in a nonsocially optimal manner. We might go about adding additional goals:

3. Do not monopolize the production of certain raw materials.
4. Do not violate international law.
5. Do not cause distress to a human being.
6. Et cetera.

However, enumerating these goals would be tedious and could still lead to unforeseen circumstances. The best way to resolve this issue is to consider the usefulness of the AI's initial goal: what use would humanity have for a paperclip maximizer in the first place?

Muehlhauser and Helm (2013) examine possible solutions to the AI control problem. They note that hardcoding certain goals into an AI is impractical, for the reasons described above, stating that there can be no systematic way to describe (or prescribe, for that matter) a universal ethical system because human behavior is impacted by a myriad of factors including, but not limited to, personal ethical frameworks. What if, instead of taking a "top-down" approach (supplying ethical principles to AI), we take a "bottom-up" approach (training an AI to derive ethical principles from training cases)? This still may not work as machine learning might generalize the wrong ethical principles from coincidences between each case.

To resolve the issues inherent to both approaches, they propose an entirely new approach: "value extrapolation." This approach does not prescribe a fixed set of goals for an AI to follow at all times. Instead, it presents simpler goals to aspire toward, allowing the AI to make subjective decisions along the way given imperfect information. This approach has the benefit of requiring nonspecific goals (e.g., an anesthesiologist AI might be programmed with "minimize human pain" instead of more specific goals pertaining to anesthesia). However, like the applied ethical approaches described above, a fundamental issue remains: what approach should AIs take to value extrapolation? While no one has proposed an entirely perfect approach to machine ethics, researchers are working tirelessly to resolve the contradictions found within ethical dilemmas.

Conclusion

The advancements made in computational power and artificial intelligence research have the power to both benefit and harm humanity. The implementation of advanced AI will have lasting economic, social, and ethical effects, each with hotly debated approaches and uncertain solutions. The reader may have noted that our discussion in each section borrowed from elements of others (see: the discussion of public policy in the middle of the paragraph on self-driving cars). This is only natural. None of these topics exist in a vacuum: each plays an important role in the development of other topics, and accordingly, the way we experience life.

Acknowledgements The authors would like to thank Drs. Mark V. Albert, Michael Spector, Lin Lin, and Lemoyne Dunn for their guidance and support in the writing of this chapter.

References

Anderson, S. L. (2008). Asimov's "three laws of robotics" and machine metaethics. *AI & Society, 22*(4), 477–493.

Asimov, I. (1985). *Robots and Empire*. Doubleday.

Bessen, J. (2016). *How computer automation affects occupations: Technology, jobs, and skills*. No. 15-49. https://scholarship.law.bu.edu/faculty_scholarship/813/

Bostrom, N. (2003). *Ethical issues in advanced artificial intelligence. Science fiction and philosophy: From time travel to*. https://books.google.com/books?hl=en&lr=&id=NXmv0zXZBi4C&oi=fnd&pg=PA277&dq=Ethical+Issues+Advanced+Artificial+Intelligence+Bostrom&ots=U98LyRKSDn&sig=7jEWoGm3RYMLzWAC_9gTCgsQACM

Büchel, B., & Floreano, D. (2018). *Tesla's problems: Overestimating automation, underestimating humans*. Retrieved May 23, 2021, from https://www.imd.org/research-knowledge/articles/teslas-problem-overestimating-automation-underestimating-humans/

Bughin, J., Hazan, E., Ramaswamy, S., Chui, M., Allas, T., Dahlström, P., Henke, N., & Trench, M. (2017). *Artificial intelligence: The next digital Frontier?* McKinsey & Company, McKinsey Global Institute.

Cho, A. (2016, January 27). *"Huge leap forward": Computer that mimics human brain beats professional at game of Go*. https://www.sciencemag.org/news/2016/01/huge-leap-forward-computer-mimics-human-brain-beats-professional-game-go

Citizens United vs. FEC, 558 U.S. (2010).

de Vries, E., Schoonvelde, M., & Schumacher, G. (2018). No longer lost in translation: Evidence that Google translate works for comparative bag-of-words text applications. *Political Analysis: An Annual Publication of the Methodology Section of the American Political Science Association, 26*(4), 417–430.

European Union. (2018). *What is GDPR, the EU's new data protection law?* https://gdpr.eu/what-is-gdpr/

Frank, M. R., Autor, D., Bessen, J. E., Brynjolfsson, E., Cebrian, M., Deming, D. J., Feldman, M., Groh, M., Lobo, J., Moro, E., Wang, D., Youn, H., & Rahwan, I. (2019). Toward understanding the impact of artificial intelligence on labor. *Proceedings of the National Academy of Sciences of the United States of America, 116*(14), 6531–6539.

Gewirth, A. (1978). The basis and content of human rights. *Georgia Law Review, 13*, 1143–1170.

Good, I. J. (1970). Some future social repercussions of computers. *The International Journal of Environmental Studies, 1*(1-4), 67–79.

Jarrahi, M. H. (2018). Artificial intelligence and the future of work: Human-AI symbiosis in organizational decision making. *Business Horizons, 61*(4), 577–586.

Jaynes, T. L. (2020). Legal personhood for artificial intelligence: citizenship as the exception to the rule. *AI & Society, 35*(2), 343–354.

Jefferson, T. (1776). *The declaration of independence*. Retrieved from https://www.archives.gov/founding-docs/declaration-transcript

Lin, P. (2016). Why ethics matters for autonomous cars. In M. Maurer, J. C. Gerdes, B. Lenz, & H. Winner (Eds.), *Autonomous driving: Technical, legal and social Aspects* (pp. 69–85). Springer.

Lin, P., Bekey, G., & Abney, K. (2008). *Autonomous military robotics: Risk, ethics, and design*. California Polytechnic State University. https://apps.dtic.mil/sti/citations/ADA534697

Meredith, S. (2018). *Facebook-Cambridge Analytica: A timeline of the data hijacking scandal*. Retrieved May 22, 2021, from https://www.cnbc.com/2018/04/10/facebook-cambridge-analytica-a-timeline-of-the-data-hijacking-scandal.html

Mou, X. (2019). *Artificial intelligence: Investment trends and selected industry uses* (p. 71). EMCompass.

Muehlhauser, L., & Helm, L. (2013). *The singularity and machine ethics*. https://doi.org/10.1007/978-3-642-32560-1_6

Murphy, R., & Woods, D. D. (2009). Beyond Asimov: The three laws of responsible robotics. *IEEE Intelligent Systems, 24*(4), 14–20.

Nedelkoska, L., & Quintini, G. (2018). *Automation, skills use and training*. OECD Publishing. https://doi.org/10.1787/2e2f4eea-en

Nyholm, S., & Smids, J. (2016). The Ethics of Accident-Algorithms for Self-Driving Cars: an Applied Trolley Problem? *Ethical Theory and Moral Practice: An International Forum, 19*(5), 1275–1289.

Pagallo, U. (2018). Vital, Sophia, and Co.—The quest for the legal personhood of Robots. Information. *An International Interdisciplinary Journal, 9*(9), 230.

Perc, M., Ozer, M., & Hojnik, J. (2019). Social and juristic challenges of artificial intelligence. *Palgrave Communications*. https://doi.org/10.1057/s41599-019-0278-x

Prettner, K., & Strulik, H. (2019). Innovation, automation, and inequality: Policy challenges in the race against the machine. *Journal of Monetary Economics*. https://doi.org/10.1016/j.jmoneco.2019.10.012

Radford, A., Wu, J., Amodei, D., Amodei, D., Clark, J., Brundage, M., Sutskever, I., Askell, A., Lansky, D., Hernandez, D., & Luan, D. (2019). *Better language models and their implications*. Retrieved May 22, 2021, from https://openai.com/blog/better-language-models/

Searle, J. R. (1980). Minds, brains, and programs. *The Behavioral and Brain Sciences, 3*(3), 417–424.

Suwajanakorn, S., Seitz, S. M., & Kemelmacher-Shlizerman, I. (2017). Synthesizing Obama: learning lip sync from audio. *ACM Transactions on Graphics, 36*(4), 1–13.

Thies, J., Zollhöfer, M., Stamminger, M., Theobalt, C., & Nießner, M. (2016). Face2Face: Real-time face capture and reenactment of RGB videos. In *2016 IEEE conference on computer vision and pattern recognition (CVPR)* (pp. 2387–2395).

Turing, A. M. (1950). I.—Computing machinery and intelligence. Mind. *A Quarterly Review of Psychology and Philosophy, LIX*(236), 433–460.

United States Senate Select Committee on Intelligence. (2020). *Report of the Select Committee on Intelligence United States Senate on Russian Active Measures Campaigns and Interference in*

the 2016 U.S. Election Volume 2: Russia's Use of Social Media with Additional Views. United States Senate, United States Senate Select Committee on Intelligence.
Villasenor, J. (2019, October 31). *Products liability law as a way to address AI harms*. Brookings. https://www.brookings.edu/research/products-liability-law-as-a-way-to-address-ai-harms/
Wang, D., Khosla, A., Gargeya, R., Irshad, H., & Beck, A. H. (2016). *Deep learning for identifying metastatic breast cancer*. arXiv:1606.05718 [q-bio.QM]
Weizenbaum, J. (1976). *Computer power and human reason: From judgment to calculation*. W. H. Freeman and Company.
Wike, R., & Stokes, B. (2018). *In advanced and emerging economies alike, worries about job automation*. Pew Research Center, Global Attitudes & Trends. https://www.pewresearch.org/global/2018/09/13/in-advanced-and-emerging-economies-alike-worries-about-job-automation/
Yudkowsky, E. (2001). *Creating friendly AI 1.0: The analysis and design of benevolent goal architectures*. http://citeseerx.ist.psu.edu/viewdoc/summary;jsessionid=EBA4D6EC0022D69252BED1AED922D4D2?doi=10.1.1.363.2590

Ted Kwee-Bintoro is a freshman currently studying computer science with the Texas Academy of Mathematics and Science at the University of North Texas. His most significant publication to date is "Dashboard system to track cumulative exposure to sound levels during live music instruction," published in the Journal of the Acoustical Society of America. His interests lie in the application of computer models to social science fields such as political science.

Noah Velez is a junior at the University of North Texas, pursuing a degree in Business Computer Information Systems. He looks to gain knowledge of new technologies driving change in the business world.

Bias in AI-Based Decision-Making

Adheesh Kadiresan, Yuvraj Baweja, and Obi Ogbanufe

Introduction

For much of human history, human beings have been the decision-makers on matters pertaining to humans (Anyoha, 2017). People made decisions in areas such as hiring, loan eligibility, diagnosis of diseases, retail, manufacturing, entertainment, and more (Colson, 2019). However, in recent decades, artificial intelligence (AI) has been able to perform certain tasks more skillfully and reliably than humans could. For example, 1997 marked the date of the defeat of Gary Kasparov, the highest-ranked chess player, by Deep Blue, a computer chess program created by IBM (Anyoha, 2017). Artificial intelligence is now being used to make decisions in areas such as hiring, loan eligibility, housing, medicine (DeGonia et al., 2016), "technology, banking, marketing, and entertainment" (Anyoha, 2017, para. 9). The implementation of AI in these sectors is due to the ability of AI to perform certain tasks more accurately than humans. For example, in the case of medical sciences, AI was able to decrease false positives of breast cancer by 5.7% on a US data set and by 1.2% on a UK data set (McKinney et al., 2020). The potential benefits AI can bring to society are clear.

When humans were the sole decision-makers before the age of AI, biased decision-making was rampant. One of the most historically significant instances of this is the practice of redlining by the Federal Housing Administration. After the Great Depression, in the 1930s, the Home Owners' Loan Corporation (HOLC) created maps that were intended to stabilize property values and determine the creditworthiness of entire neighborhoods. However, these maps were in part influenced by the races of the residents of each neighborhood (Aaronson et al., 2017). This caused discrimination of neighborhoods based on race, which denied investment

A. Kadiresan (✉) · Y. Baweja · O. Ogbanufe
University of North Texas, Denton, TX, USA
e-mail: Obi.Ogbanufe@unt.edu

M. V. Albert et al. (eds.), *Bridging Human Intelligence and Artificial Intelligence*, Educational Communications and Technology: Issues and Innovations, https://doi.org/10.1007/978-3-030-84729-6_19

opportunities in communities with higher populations of African Americans. This discriminatory practice, termed redlining due to the red color used on maps (Aaronson et al., 2017), created effects that lasted a much longer duration. Redlined areas were "associated with a 5% decrease in 1990 house prices" (Appel & Nickerson, 2016, p. 24). Clearly, biased decision-making can have severe long-lasting effects on society and can contribute to discrimination.

However, using computers to make decisions does not automatically eliminate or even reduce bias. In this chapter, we will explore ways in which decision-making by computers can introduce and exacerbate certain biases. Specifically, this chapter will explore biases that affect human lives. These biases can be prejudiced against "race, gender, age, or any other trait" (DeGonia et al., 2016, p. 16).

Defining Bias

Bias is defined as "an inclination of temperament or outlook" (Merriam-Webster, n.d.-a, para. 1). Thus, favoring one entity more than another would be an instance of bias. In the real world, bias closely relates to the idea of discrimination, which is defined to be a "prejudiced or prejudicial outlook, action, or treatment" (Merriam-Webster, n.d.-b, para. 1). It can be seen that discrimination is a product of bias: a skewed outlook can lead to prejudicial actions toward others. This makes clear the reason why bias is a problem: bias causes discrimination against various groups of people, which has had severe historical consequences, such as in the case of redlining provided above. In this chapter, we explore bias in decisions carried out by artificial intelligence systems.

The Formation of Bias

AI decisions can become biased in numerous ways. One way a decision can become biased is when AI models confuse correlation with causation (DeGonia et al., 2016). Correlation simply refers to an instance when two variables change together. However, causation refers to a relationship between a causing factor and an affected factor (DeGonia et al., 2016). Confusing causation and correlation involve assuming one factor is causing another when in fact the two factors only happen to change in a noncausal relationship. The canonical example here is a potential correlation between ice cream sales and violence. Although higher frequencies of ice cream sales may be correlated with higher violence rates which may occur in warmer months, concluding that ice cream causes violence would be an obvious fallacy of confusing correlation with causation. The true explanation may be that warmer weather is correlated with both higher ice cream sales and also more acts of violence (DeGonia et al., 2016). Figure 1 shows an example of when two correlated factors do not necessarily lead to causation.

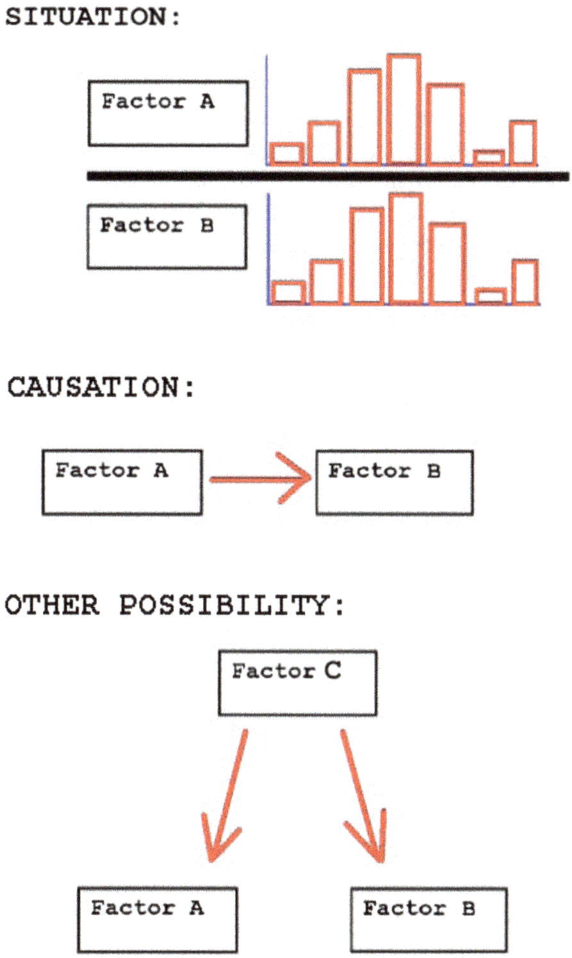

Fig. 1 Two correlated factors not necessarily in causation

One situation of mistaking correlation for causation more relevant to artificial intelligence decision-making comes from the usage of zip codes to determine employment. For instance, if a computer model finds that a certain zip code is correlated with the locations of better-performing employees, an incorrect and biased causal relationship may be assumed: that a zip code causes employees to be better (DeGonia et al., 2016). Such an assumption may lead to zip codes being used to determine the employability of hires. The problem here has to do with the historical issue of discrimination in housing, such as the aforementioned practice of redlining. Since redlining disproportionately affected African-American communities (Aaronson et al., 2017), the incorrectly assumed causal relation may end up contributing to racial discrimination in hiring (DeGonia et al., 2016).

Bias can also cause discrimination against certain groups when irrelevant factors are taken into account by a decision-making algorithm. While the addition of certain parameters relevant to the problem at hand may improve accuracy, having irrelevant parameters can harm accuracy and strengthen "racism, sexism, and other inequalities." (DeGonia et al., 2016, p. 47). Such irrelevant factors include those that do not have any effect on the end goal. For example, factors that will be referred to as *personal factors,* such as nationality and ethnicity, have no effect on the skills of that person. Providing such information to an algorithm will not improve the accuracy of the algorithm, and the possibility of bias or discrimination means that such factors are harmful in AI decision-making.

A decision-making AI model may find correlations that happen to form across lines of different groups of people, which could exacerbate discrimination of these groups (DeGonia et al., 2016). Thus, it follows that removing personal factors from AI models can decrease discrimination against members of certain groups.

A related source of bias in computerized decision-making comes from skewed data sets that do not accurately represent the target population of an algorithm. As a result, algorithms can make more errors on under-represented demographics in the data set. One example comes from facial recognition algorithms. A groundbreaking paper by Buolamwini and Gebru (2018) describes how all of the observed facial recognition classifiers had error rates from 20.8% (for Microsoft's classifier) to 34.7% (IBM) for "darker-skinned females" (pp. 9–10). On the other hand, the study found that "the maximum error rate for lighter-skinned males is 0.8%" (Buolamwini & Gebru, 2018, p. 1). This large disparity shows that facial recognition classifiers are biased against certain groups. The paper also analyzes the IARPA (Intelligence Advanced Research Projects Activity) Janus Benchmark A data set (IJB-A data set) which is designed to be "geographically diverse" as well as Adience, which is a "gender and age classification benchmark" (Buolamwini & Gebru, 2018, p. 3). The paper notes that the IJB-A data set consists of 79.6% "lighter-skinned individuals" and Adience consists of 86.2% "lighter subjects" (Buolamwini & Gebru, 2018, p. 7). In this case, we can see that these data sets tend to under-represent people with darker skin.

Another study focuses on how facial recognition algorithms from East Asia tended to perform better on Asian subjects than did algorithms developed in the Western hemisphere (Klare et al., 2012). Similarly, for white subjects, algorithms developed in the western hemisphere performed better. The paper continues suggesting that "this discrepancy was due to the different racial distribution in the training sets for the Western and Asian algorithms" (Klare et al., 2012, p. 3). These examples show how important the samples of data used to develop an algorithm are in providing unbiased results. Data sets must represent all demographics more equally in order to reduce bias in classification.

Biases in AI can also stem from biased humans that contribute to a computer algorithm. One example of humans contributing to bias is in the labor market. One study found that resumes with "white names receive 50 percent more callbacks for interviews" than those with "African-American names" (Bertrand & Mullainathan, 2003, p. 2). This experiment made it clear that discrimination from humans exists in the labor market. Since artificial intelligence, computer algorithms, and data collecting all have a human component, it is easy to see how such biases in people can become manifest in computer and AI algorithms and then lead to discrimination.

This kind of bias is not due to AI itself, since the bias originates from humans. In other words, for human-introduced bias, removing artificial intelligence from the task at hand would not necessarily eliminate or even reduce bias.

To conclude, a biased algorithm may derive its bias from an incorrect assumption of causation from correlation, personal factors that are irrelevant to the algorithm's decision, skewed or incomplete data sets that leave out certain demographics, or the humans that created the algorithm in the first place. All of these factors can lead to bias, which has the potential to exacerbate existing discrimination.

Real-World Example of Bias

One example of bias from an AI algorithm comes from Amazon.com, Inc.'s 2014 AI-hiring program. Amazon had to cancel this program after the discovery of biases against women in the hiring algorithm. In this case, the discrimination stemmed from the training data, which included ten years of submitted resumes to Amazon. However, due to the long-running "male dominance across the tech industry" (para. 6) from the gender hiring gap in technology, the algorithm learned to favor resumes from men and "penalized resumes that included the word 'women's'" (Dastin, 2018, para. 7). The source of bias in this case is the data set for the algorithm. However, in this case, the main issue is not with the data set misrepresenting the target audience; instead, the data set reflected the reality of male-skewed hiring. When the algorithm "was trained on historical hiring decisions, which favored men over women, it learned to do the same" (Hao, 2019, para. 5).

Beyond the obvious issue of a biased, and thus ineffective hiring algorithm, the example above is significant for worsening the long history of gender discrimination. From this example, we can see how AI decision-making can both harm potential workers and also contribute to the larger issues of discrimination within society.

In addition to the ethical issues of unfairly rejecting applicants based on gender and contributing to gender discrimination, the example of bias in hiring also faces legal issues. The Federal Equal Opportunity Laws "[prohibit] employment discrimination based on race, color, religion, sex, or national origin" ("Federal Laws Prohibiting Job Discrimination Questions and Answers," n.d., para. 1). Therefore, discriminatory hiring would not be legal, in addition to being unethical. The legal issues will be covered in more detail later in this chapter.

Trust in Artificial Intelligence

AI has the potential to make decisions that can benefit the areas of science, wellbeing, economics, and solutions to environmental issues (Rossi, 2019). The example of breast cancer above indicates that AI can help make decisions that are more accurate and help solve important problems in society.

However, before AI can be widely deployed to solve problems, people must trust it to carry out accurate decisions. Specifically, artificial intelligence must "be aware and aligned to human values" and "explain its reasoning and decision-making" (Rossi, 2019, para. 5). Stefan Jockusch from Siemens presents trust as "justified by statistics" (para. 26) and that trust in facial recognition algorithms, which utilize AI, led to the use of those algorithms in the important task of "recognizing identity" (MIT Technology Review Insights, 2020, para. 25).

The relevant area in which trust must be established in AI is in the avoidance of discrimination. One field where eliminating discrimination is especially important is hiring. While AI has the potential to quickly sift through job applications (Fatemi, 2019), these hiring decisions may be biased against certain groups. Allowing a biased hiring process can erode trust in AI hiring. This is substantiated by the fact that 35% of the US adults that would apply to a position using AI hiring would do so due to their trust that AI can be "fairer, less biased than humans" (Smith, 2017, para. 14). Thus, it is reasonable to infer that if the fairness of hiring with AI were to be compromised, public trust in the abilities of computers to carry out employment decisions would decrease, resulting in reduced usage of a technology that would have had significant advantages.

Efforts to Prevent AI Bias

Sources of Bias

We have learned that AI decisions can have serious biases that contribute to discrimination in society. Specifically, such biases can come from mistaking causation and correlation, relying on factors irrelevant to an algorithm's decision, skewed data sets, or human contributions. How can such biases in computerized decision-making be resolved? In order to eliminate bias from AI algorithms, all of the above issues must be addressed.

The first two issues are closely related: assuming causation from two variables that happen to be correlated contributes to bias if the variables taken in have the potential to discriminate. Such variables are the "personal factors" that must not affect the decision-making of the algorithm. However, eliminating such discriminatory variables is not as easy as it may appear. In fact, data provided to an algorithm can still "include biased human decisions or reflect historical or social inequities, even if sensitive variables such as gender, race, or sexual orientation are removed" (Manyika et al., 2019, para. 4). For example, in the case of Amazon's gender-biased hiring algorithm, words such as "executed" and "captured" were used to discriminate against women, since resumes from men tended to contain these words more often (Dastin, 2018). Thus, removing explicit personal factors from algorithms is not adequate to prevent discrimination. These factors can manifest themselves in other aspects of the training data.

Another source of bias comes from skewed data sets. Data sets could be skewed due to either real-world biases or data that do not fully represent certain demographics. For example, in the case of Amazon's biased algorithm, the data set was skewed due to real-world inequalities in hiring between women and men (Dastin, 2018). In order to reduce bias in this case, the AI algorithm must make decisions that do not follow the previous patterns in hiring. When data sets are biased from an incomplete representation of all groups of people, data sets must be improved. There are multiple views on this issue. Google's AI department says "Public training data sets will often need to be augmented to better reflect real-world frequencies of people" ("Responsible AI Practices," n.d., para. 9). This view emphasizes how data sets themselves can be biased and need to be altered and improved in order to help reduce bias. Buolamwini and Gebru (2018) created the Pilot Parliaments Benchmark data set that is "gender and skin type balanced" (p. 1) from "male and female parliamentarians from 6 countries" (p. 4). This data set was found to represent "darker female, darker male, lighter female and lighter male subjects" in a more balanced manner than other data sets (Buolamwini & Gebru, 2018, p. 7). IBM AI, on the other hand, through a blog, claims that "machine learning, by its very nature, is always a form of statistical discrimination" and that becomes an issue when "privileged groups [are given a] systematic advantage" and "unprivileged groups [are given a] systematic disadvantage" (Varshney, 2018, para. 2). This point of view emphasizes how machine learning itself aims to discriminate and effort must be applied to prevent discrimination that unjustly harms certain demographics.

The final source of AI bias comes from humans contributing to the field of AI. There are multiple ways to combat this issue as well. For example, the Harvard Business Review recommends "diversifying the AI field itself ... to anticipate, review, and spot bias and engage communities affected" (Manyika et al., 2019, para. 16). However, Joann Stonier, who is the chief data officer of Mastercard, emphasizes "governance and testing methodologies" to combat bias among data scientists (Stonier, 2020, para. 8).

The Issue of Gauging Bias

To approach the issue of bias, it is important to have a method to measure the amount of fairness in an algorithm. Two such fairness measures are group and individual fairness. Group fairness aims for "statistical parity ... for members of different protected groups" whereas individual fairness aims to assign "similar outcomes" to "people who are 'similar' with respect to the classification task" (Binns, 2020, p. 1). Figure 2 provides a simplified hypothetical scenario where these two metrics of fairness yield different classifications. We can see that in group fairness, each group has the same proportion of its members in each outcome. In other words, members of each group have equal probabilities of reaching outcome 1 or outcome 2. Similar qualifications between members of different groups do not necessarily result in similar outcomes. On the other hand, individual fairness means each group does not

SITUATION:

Group A	Group B	
500	1000	Number of members
400	300	Members qualified for outcome 1
100	700	Members qualified for outcome 2

GROUP FAIRNESS:

Group A	Group B	
300	600	Outcome 1
200	400	Outcome 2

INDIVIDUAL FAIRNESS:

Group A	Group B	
400	300	Outcome 1
100	700	Outcome 2

Fig. 2 Group fairness compared to individual fairness

have the same proportion of its members in each outcome. Here, similar qualifications result in similar outcomes regardless of a member's group.

AI Bias and the Law

We have explored the formation of biases in AI and the search to mitigate such biases. However, what are the consequences of biased algorithms? Specifically, what laws surround bias in general, what laws specifically target biases in AI right now, and what direction could these laws go in the future?

To make the discussion more focused, we will focus on employment discrimination. This is because the process of hiring can have significant bias, as previously discussed. Furthermore, AI is widely used in hiring. In fact, LinkedIn reported that in 2018, 67% of surveyed recruiters reported that they save time by using AI technology ("*LinkedIn* 2018 *Report Highlights Top Global Trends in Recruiting*," 2018).

In order to compare the extent to which AI biases are recognized and acted on by the law, we must first analyze the overall biases in job recruiting and laws surrounding these biases. One study establishes the extent to which hiring can be biased by revealing the discrimination toward those with "African-American names" compared to those with "White names" (Bertrand & Mullainathan, 2003, p. 2). In this case, the Equal Employment Opportunity Commission (EEOC) enforces the Civil Rights Act's Title VII, "which makes it illegal to discriminate against a person on the basis of race, color, religion, sex, or national origin" (*What Laws Does EEOC Enforce?*, n.d., para. 2).

Due to the EEOC laws, discriminating against these categories would not be legal. However, from the example of Amazon's biased algorithm, it is evident that algorithms can learn to discriminate between groups, such as gender, through separate, seemingly unrelated words. Thus, in order to comply with antidiscrimination laws, AI decision-making must not only prevent bias from explicitly labeled demographics, but also from demographic information that can be inferred through other means.

Another issue here is the possibility of a more indirect but still harmful form of discrimination. For example, if an algorithm makes decisions based on the location of each employee, a zip code may come to determine employment for citizens of certain places (DeGonia et al., 2016). Then, due to long-existing racial discrimination in housing (Aaronson et al., 2017), zip-code–based decision-making could lead to racial discrimination (DeGonia et al., 2016). One example of laws being enforced to fight this sort of discrimination from location comes from a lawsuit against Abercrombie & Fitch. After the discriminatory hiring practices were revealed, Abercrombie & Fitch was "barred from utilizing its previous recruitment strategies, such as targeting particular predominately white fraternities or sororities" (*Case: Abercrombie & Fitch Employment Discrimination*, 2006, para. 5). The action taken against Abercrombie & Fitch here could serve as a model for dealing with more indirect but still very harmful forms of AI discrimination.

It is clear that the laws surrounding AI have holes as discrimination can still surface through unexpected factors. Therefore, one can conclude that progress must be made in law to prevent discrimination through any factors fed into a hiring algorithm. One example of a recent house bill is the "Algorithmic Accountability Act of 2019." In this case, "covered entities" (p. 4) must "conduct automated decision system impact assessments of … high-risk automated decision systems" including analysis of the algorithm's purpose, benefits, risks, privacy, and risk minimization procedures (Algorithmic Accountability Act of 2019, 2019, p. 9). This is an example of a law that may ensure more fair decision-making algorithms.

Conclusions

While AI algorithms can increase efficiency in hiring, entertainment, and other industries, these algorithms can also contribute to bias and discrimination. This bias can come from mistaking the correlation of two variables for causation, depending on discriminatory personal factors, using skewed or incomplete data sets, or human sources. The effort to combat AI bias is an ongoing one, and there are no simple solutions in this area. AI bias can also encounter issues with the law, as bias can be introduced in subtle ways that still discriminate against certain demographics. As society starts to apply AI to a wider variety of decisions, the issue of bias must not be overlooked.

References

Aaronson, D., Hartley, D., & Mazumder, B. (2017). The effects of the 1930s HOLC "redlining" maps (No. 2017–12). *EconStor*. Working Paper. https://www.econstor.eu/handle/10419/200568

Algorithmic Accountability Act of 2019, H. R. 2231, House of Representatives, 116th Congress (2019). https://www.congress.gov/bill/116th-congress/house-bill/2231/text

Anyoha, R.. (2017, August 28). *The history of artificial intelligence*. http://sitn.hms.harvard.edu/flash/2017/history-artificial-intelligence/

Appel, I., & Nickerson, J. (2016). *Pockets of Poverty: The Long-Term Effects of Redlining*. SSRN. https://papers.ssrn.com/sol3/papers.cfm?abstract_id=2852856

Bertrand, M., & Mullainathan, S. (2003). Are Emily and Greg More Employable than Lakisha and Jamal? A Field Experiment on Labor Market Discrimination (No. w9873). *National Bureau of Economic Research*. https://doi.org/10.3386/w9873

Binns, R. (2020). On the apparent conflict between individual and group fairness. In *Proceedings of the 2020 Conference on Fairness, Accountability, and Transparency* (pp. 514–524).

Buolamwini, J., & Gebru, T. (2018). Gender shades: Intersectional accuracy disparities in commercial gender classification. In S. A. Friedler & C. Wilson (Eds.), *Proceedings of the 1st Conference on Fairness, Accountability and Transparency* (Vol. 81, pp. 77–91). PMLR.

Case: Abercrombie & Fitch employment discrimination. (2006, March 17). https://www.naacpldf.org/case-issue/abercrombie-fitch-employment-discrimination/

Colson, E. (2019, July 8). *What AI-driven decision making looks like*. Harvard Business Review. https://hbr.org/2019/07/what-ai-driven-decision-making-looks-like

Dastin, J. (2018, October 10). Amazon scraps secret AI recruiting tool that showed bias against women. *Reuters*. https://www.reuters.com/article/us-amazon-com-jobs-automation-insight-idUSKCN1MK08G

DeGonia, A., Kerper, A., Baxter, A., Miller, A., Shah, A., Kik, B., Kowalczyk, B., Willians, C., Grapperhaus, G., Bosnich, G. A., Goscenski, H., Buss, J., Hwang, J., Ng, J., Adamski, J., Chokshi, K., Radulovic, K., Kalesinskas, L., Scarlati, L., … Kegel, J. (2016). *Automated discrimination: The power and peril of big data: Big data revolutionizes the power of prediction, but can also perpetuate discrimination far beyond the constraints of human ability*. CreateSpace Independent Publishing Platform.

Fatemi, F. (2019, October 31). How AI is uprooting recruiting. *Forbes Magazine*. https://www.forbes.com/sites/falonfatemi/2019/10/31/how-ai-is-uprooting-recruiting/

Federal Laws prohibiting job discrimination questions and answers. (n.d.). Retrieved December 19, 2020, from https://www.eeoc.gov/fact-sheet/federal-laws-prohibiting-job-discrimination-questions-and-answers

Hao, K. (2019, February 4). This is how AI bias really happens—And why it's so hard to fix. *Technology Review*. Retrieved December 19, 2020, from https://www.technologyreview.com/2019/02/04/137602/this-is-how-ai-bias-really-happensand-why-its-so-hard-to-fix/

Klare, B. F., Burge, M. J., Klontz, J. C., Vorder Bruegge, R. W., & Jain, A. K. (2012). Face recognition performance: Role of demographic information. *IEEE Transactions on Information Forensics and Security, 7*(6), 1789–1801.

LinkedIn 2018 Report Highlights Top Global Trends in Recruiting. (2018, January 10). Retrieved December 19, 2020, from https://news.linkedin.com/2018/1/global-recruiting-trends-2018

Manyika, J., Silberg, J., & Presten, B. (2019, October 25).What do we do about the biases in AI? *Harvard Business Review*. https://hbr.org/2019/10/what-do-we-do-about-the-biases-in-ai

McKinney, S. M., Sieniek, M., Godbole, V., Godwin, J., Antropova, N., Ashrafian, H., Back, T., Chesus, M., Corrado, G. S., Darzi, A., Etemadi, M., Garcia-Vicente, F., Gilbert, F. J., Halling-Brown, M., Hassabis, D., Jansen, S., Karthikesalingam, A., Kelly, C. J., King, D., … Shetty, S. (2020). International evaluation of an AI system for breast cancer screening. *Nature, 577*(7788), 89–94.

Merriam-Webster. (n.d.-a). Bias. In *Merriam-Webster.com dictionary*. Retrieved December 19, 2020, from https://www.merriam-webster.com/dictionary/bias

Merriam-Webster. (n.d.-b). Discrimination. In *Merriam-Webster.com dictionary*. Retrieved December 19, 2020, from https://www.merriam-webster.com/dictionary/discrimination
MIT Technology Review Insights. (2020, October 28). With trust in ai, manufacturers can build better. *Technology Review*. Retrieved December 19, 2020, from https://www.technologyreview.com/2020/10/28/1011266/with-trust-in-ai-manufacturers-can-build-better/
Responsible AI Practices. (n.d.). Retrieved December 18, 2020, from https://ai.google/responsibilities/responsible-ai-practices/?category=fairness
Rossi, F. (2019, February 6). *Building trust in artificial intelligence*. https://jia.sipa.columbia.edu/building-trust-artificial-intelligence
Smith, A. (2017, October 4). *Americans' views toward hiring algorithms*. https://www.pewresearch.org/internet/2017/10/04/americans-attitudes-toward-hiring-algorithms/
Stonier, J. (2020, March 19). Fighting AI bias—Digital rights are human rights. *Forbes Magazine*. https://www.forbes.com/sites/insights-ibmai/2020/03/19/fighting-ai-bias-digital-rights-are-human-rights/
Varshney, K. R. (2018, September 19). *Introducing AI Fairness 360*. https://www.ibm.com/blogs/research/2018/09/ai-fairness-360/
What laws does EEOC enforce? (n.d.). Retrieved December 19, 2020, from https://www.eeoc.gov/youth/what-laws-does-eeoc-enforce

Adheesh Kadiresan is a student at the Texas Academy of Mathematics and Science (TAMS), a residential high-school program run by the University of North Texas (UNT). He is a research assistant at Dr. Mark Albert's Biomedical-AI Lab studying the use of Autoencoders in an EKG Vest. He was also an early summer researcher under Dr. Nicoladie Tam, studying the effect of emotion on decision-making. Under the guidance of Dr. Tam, Adheesh created his poster titled "Effect of Emotion on Decision-Making," which was presented in the 2021 UNT Scholars Day. Additionally, Adheesh is a recipient of the 2020 TAMS Summer Research Scholarship and the 2021 TAMS Summer Research Scholarship. He will be working in the UNT AI Summer Research Program during the summer of 2021.

Yuvraj Baweja is an incoming freshman in the University of Texas at Austin's Computer Science and Business Honors program after completing two years at the Texas Academy of Mathematics & Science (TAMS), an accelerated high school program at the University of North Texas (UNT Denton). He is working on a project in the AI Laboratory at UNT run by Mark V. Albert dubbed Stock2Vec, using Word2Vec embeddings to run predictions on companies given financial data. His research interests include the intersection between Artificial Intelligence and Business, specifically Natural Language Processing, Machine Learning, and Economics. Aside from research, he has given two TEDx talks, one concerning computer science in the core school curriculum and one about the benefits of residential programs. Furthermore, he has competed in numerous computer science and cyber-security competitions, achieving rankings such as the top 25 out of 5000 high school teams in picoCTF.

Dr. Obi Ogbanufe is an Assistant Professor of Information Technology and Decision Sciences at the University of North Texas. She is a recipient of the NSF CyberCorps Scholarship for Service award. She has published in Decision Support Systems, Information Systems Journal, and the International Journal of Human-Computer Interaction. Her research interests include information security, cybercrime, human-AI interaction, and risk management.

The Paradox of Learning in the Intelligence Age: Creating a New Learning Ecosystem to Meet the Challenge

Gary Natriello and Hui Soo Chae

Introduction

The current era, characterized by advances in a range of technologies (Schwab, 2017) that have the potential to extend and augment human learning (OECD, 2019), also brings with it vast new challenges as the demands on human performance and understanding seem to advance at an even faster rate. With change now impacting nearly all societies globally, there is both growing interest and growing concern that we may or may not be able to rise to the challenges presented. Maintaining old ways increasingly seems impossible, but embracing an uncertain future is daunting and for some seemingly out of reach.

In this chapter, we consider the paradox of learning in the intelligence age, that is in the age of rapid advances in artificial intelligence and augmented human intelligence by considering the changing technical and social context and then by trying to understand the impact of such changes for the education sector. We then develop an agenda for advancing learning and creating a new learning ecosystem and conclude by discussing the research and development efforts that might move us forward.

G. Natriello (✉)
Teachers College Columbia University, New York, NY, USA

Princeton, NJ, USA
e-mail: gjn6@columbia.edu

H. S. Chae
Teachers College Columbia University, New York, NY, USA

Hastings on Hudson, NY, USA
e-mail: chae@tc.columbia.edu

M. V. Albert et al. (eds.), *Bridging Human Intelligence and Artificial Intelligence*, Educational Communications and Technology: Issues and Innovations, https://doi.org/10.1007/978-3-030-84729-6_20

The Changing Technical and Social Context

The set of changes that are upon us have been identified by Schwab (2017) as a fourth industrial revolution. Included in this formulation are: (1) continuing advances in computing and communications technologies that are creating a globally networked world where most people will be connected and have near instantaneous access to each other and to vast information and learning resources, (2) the growing combination of digital and physical elements through the Internet of things, additive manufacturing, and augmented reality, (3) advances in our understanding of the brain and its capacity for learning, and (4) the enhancement and transformation of biological systems through digital and physical technologies.

New Human Capacities

Together these changes are more widespread, all encompassing, and profound than any in our prior experience, and they are coming at us at unprecedented speeds. They create a range of potential new capacities for individuals, for communities, for societies, and for the world at large. Along with these new capacities will come new opportunities for individuals worldwide as large numbers of people come online and connect directly to the global economy. This is likely to move many into the middle class as connected producers and consumers (Bussolo et al., 2011).

The Changing Configuration of Jobs

The changes will also lead to new patterns that will pose challenges for all of us. These challenges include the radical transformation of work as automation and robotics in some cases assist workers and in other cases eliminate their jobs entirely while ushering in a new set of jobs with new skill-level demands. While the complete impact in terms of the number and nature of jobs available in a world fully transformed by these new conditions is difficult to anticipate, one thing is certain: the jobs and job requirements for many will be different in the future than they have been in the past (World Bank, 2019).

The Threat of Growing Inequality

While the work lives of many individuals will be changed profoundly, for societies a big change is likely to be the growth of inequality as new enterprises built upon new technologies seize advantages based on high-value skills in the new economic sectors and as those without such skills are consigned to low-value labor (Gray & Suri, 2019). Such inequality, while problematic in the first instance, can spiral out of control rapidly as access to resources becomes more closely connected to access to the new class of enabling technologies resulting from the fusion of digital, physical, and biological systems, and this in turn leads to greater differences in an individual capacity and hence greater differences in additional rewards.

While the technological prospects in the coming years will be great, the social peril may well be greater (Brynjolfsson & McAfee, 2014), that is, unless we take steps to create conditions that empower individuals throughout societies to enhance both their understanding of the broader issues and the individual capacities to contribute to the new social and economic reality. We believe that a rethinking of the learning sector can be a key contribution to this process and we turn to that next.

Challenges Posed for the Learning Sector

The knowledge explosion makes it exceedingly difficult for schools to be in a position to equip individuals with the information they will need to lead lives as engaged citizens and productive contributors. With the pace of the production of knowledge increasing rapidly and with the continuing advances in networking and communications technologies spreading knowledge more quickly and broadly than ever before, the world is becoming knowledge intensive in all respects.

The implications of the knowledge explosion for schools are far reaching and profound, undermining core assumptions upon which schooling in modern societies has been constructed. The days when schools needed to be sites of knowledge collection and distribution are gone as are the days when the knowledge acquired in formal schooling might be relevant for most of one's lifespan. Schools face challenges by virtue of their very organization and operating principles.

The Destabilizing of Curriculum

The curriculum has long been an essential element in schooling, and, indeed, the history of formal education is replete with battles large and small over what should be included in the formal program of the school and just as importantly, what should be excluded. In a world of limited knowledge and poor communications, the school curriculum was an important means of creating a common understanding and shared views of the world. At a time when the two sources of knowledge in a community were the church and the school and where the approved school curriculum ensured alignment, the messages carried by the school were central and stable. The century-long erosion of this arrangement placed a strain on the school and its program, but the current era of knowledge growth and instantaneous transmission to devices in the pockets of most school children blows it apart.

It is not just the growth in the production and distribution of knowledge that challenges the idea of a school curriculum, it is also the application of such knowledge (Harding & Vining, 1997; Joan et al., 2013). Applying school-book knowledge, both generally and in specific contexts, is becoming more difficult. While fundamentals may hold, the way they are expressed and shared is changing quickly. Not only is general knowledge in a society now fleeting and being reshaped on a continuous basis, knowledge related to jobs is increasingly subject to becoming outmoded both as knowledge requirements within jobs change and as the pool of jobs themselves change with some being eliminated and others being created (World Economic Forum, 2016). As AI resources are applied to more and more organizations and the positions within them, the nature of the changes will shift and accelerate in ways that schools are not equipped to anticipate.

The Teacher Role Under Strain

Although the formal school program is resistant to needed changes, schools have historically relied upon teachers to adapt and respond to student needs in real time as they implement that program. Indeed, in some cases schools have relied on teachers to try to customize such adaptations to ensure the intended effect. Schools have also relied on teachers to deal with social and economic conditions that negatively affect student learning. As a result, for many years the teacher role has been viewed as overloaded (Lian et al., 2016; Pithers & Soden, 1998).

In addition to the current reliance on overloaded teachers, there is the problem of a global shortage of teachers at the very time greater pressure is being placed on educational systems to ensure learning for all students. The UNESCO Institute for Statistics (2016) estimates that the world will need 24.4 million primary teachers and 44.4 million secondary teachers to meet the goal of achieving universal primary and secondary education by 2030 in line with UN Sustainability Goal 4. These numbers are daunting even before taking teacher quality and qualifications into consideration.

The challenged viability of teachers as the main learning delivery vehicle makes the time right to turn to other paths of learning. In the current era, a number of competing sources, AI, peers, media, network resources, and networked parents among them, threaten the centrality of the teacher role to the learning process. With a widening range of information, often in intended educational formats, available to students, what will be left for the teaching role in schools? Will the local teacher go the way of local theater in the wake of national and international broadcast media?

Even in the midst of high-quality and readily updated sources of information and AI to take on some of the tasks of teachers (Luckin et al., 2016), the local teacher may still play an essential emotional role in being able to build social relationships with students, at least until social robots with emotional AI are more fully developed. But even in this role, there will be pressure on teachers to update their knowledge base and their practical skills. It is not clear that traditional means of preparing teachers can be retooled to prepare teachers for the faster pace of change they will confront. Schools currently have little in the way of personnel development capacity and show no signs of being able to develop such capacity. As students are exposed to higher-caliber instruction from sources outside the local schools, the status of the local teacher may be compromised unless steps are taken to reposition the role.

The Ebbing of the School

With traditional notions of curriculum and the role of local teachers under strain, the question of what productive role may be played by schools in the new, faster changing knowledge environment is important. Will schools remain a major component of the learning environment or will they be deemed too slow and cumbersome as individual learners and their families seek other avenues for learning. The early signs of a possible shift are evident even now in the growing home school movement (Collum & Mitchell, 2005; Kraftl, 2013), in the opt-out movement where parents refuse to participate in school testing regimes (Wang, 2017), and in the growing numbers of high school graduates questioning whether attending college is the most desirable path to advance their learning and prepare for jobs and adulthood (Worthen, 2019). Are we witnessing a change in the configurations of learning institutions like that identified by Cremin (1976) regarding the earlier shift in the roles of the church, the family, and the school?

Other changes appear to be in progress or just on the horizon. We have already hinted at the more permeable boundaries of the school and the ability of many sources of knowledge to permeate those boundaries. It seems clear that schools will be less isolated and more connected and that they will be receptors of knowledge, if not clearly contributors, although that may happen as well.

In addition to being receptors of growing knowledge resources, schools will also be visited with the effects of the currently growing degrees of inequality as the lives of their students are directly impacted by gaping disparities in financial resources and as schools themselves, at least in the United States which relies on funding schools through local taxes, face growing resource disparities with a few schools lavished resources and many schools fundamentally impoverished (Baker, 2019).

The funding disparities betray the fundamental weakness in the governance of the learning sector where there has not been the political will to provide adequate educational opportunity to citizens even as the rhetoric to the contrary takes on epic proportions with various misnomers proudly attached to legislative compromises that serve as political cover. These governance patterns also throw into question the role of the school as a pillar of a new learning sector, moving forward.

A final challenge to schools is presented by the growing role of data in advancing progress in all sectors of society and the position of the school in relation to student data. Despite ostensible legal protections, schools have shown little capacity to protect student data and less capacity to use it to support the learning of students. Parents have reacted accordingly, and increasingly resist school data collection, and possibly schools as the holder of data on their children. The battle of individual citizens for control of their own data may well be fought first in the schools, the first governmental body fully encountered by many young citizens (Gilliom & Monahan, 2012).

The challenges of the current era for schools and established educational institutions are complex and formidable. They are unlike any that have come before. But, learning, formal and informal, will become a more central aspect of the lives of all citizens. This means that there will be action to configure a new learning sector suitable for the new conditions, and we turn to those prospects next.

What Should Be the New Learning Sector?

As we have moved from an information era to a knowledge era and are now on the precipice of an intelligence era, we might expect that learning and the components of the sector that support it would be the beneficiaries, but as we have alluded, the situation is more complex than that. Rather than the established educational institutions profiting from the various transitions upon us, they will need to be reconfigured to benefit and confer those benefits on learners of all ages.

The cross-cutting forces of better tools and resources more widely distributed and of much greater demands for higher learning for more of the population will make the transition of the learning sector complex, uneven, and sometimes quite rough, but anticipating some major changes will allow us to deal with the challenges in a more thoughtful way. In this section, we take on the task of recommending elements of the coming reconfiguration of the learning sector. While the clues to the appropriate steps are seemingly all around, at least some of what we propose is speculative. Turning such speculation into intentions will be more likely to bring about these changes, but there are no guarantees.

The Purpose of Learning

We must begin with an understanding of the purpose of education in the era of artificial and augmented human intelligence. In earlier societies, much of education was oriented to religious ends. If we taught reading, it was to equip students to read the Bible. The goal was preparing students for the kingdom of god, whatever god was important to the society in question. In industrial societies, much of education was oriented to economic ends, sometimes with political dimensions as well. If we taught skills, it was to equip students to become productive workers and the requirements for productive workers changed slowly. In the age of artificial intelligence and augmented human intelligence, the ground is shifting too quickly to provide a stable external target for our educational efforts (Ford, 2016). Many things students might learn in elementary school are likely to be irrelevant or untrue by the time they complete secondary school.

In the absence of a stable external target for educational activities, the focus will need to turn to students themselves and be oriented to helping students to become the persons they wish to be. The inner direction of each student or their purpose will become much more important in schooling since learners with a deeper understanding of themselves, including themselves as learners, will be more equipped to deal productively with rapid change (Malin, 2018). Students so prepared will be more likely to deal with careers and professions melting out from under them without losing their bearings. Obviously, education for purpose will require approaches to learning that are substantially different from those that dominate the assessment-driven, career-focused system that dominates the current educational landscape. Fortunately, we can draw on some well-developed approaches that have proven useful even in the current system.

Self-Directed Learning

Self-directed learning could become the cornerstone of a new learning ecology. Research on self-directed learning and related areas such as self-regulation provides foundational knowledge that can be the basis for broadening the application of the approach (Brookfield, 1985; Knowles, 1975). Practices rooted in self-directed learning, while most prevalent in the education of adults, have been applied with learners at all levels. There is evidence of growing interest in self-directed learning from learners worldwide (Pearson, 2019).

Life-Long Learning

Life-long learning will be a second essential element in the new learning ecology. As the pace of change quickens, individuals will need to develop habits of learning that allow them to function fully in an ever-changing society (Jarvis, 2007). While developing an appetite among students for life-long learning has long been an articulated goal of the educational system, much more must be done to develop student interests and inclinations to be life-long learners and an entirely new learning ecosystem must be made available to support learners throughout their life spans.

New Infrastructure

Developing the new learning ecosystem will require three types of development. When schools dominated learning, we needed to invest in establishing and maintaining schools and school systems. As the learning ecology becomes more diverse and distributed, we will need to invest in new infrastructures to support and facilitate learning (Hunsinger, 2009). This may involve bringing together existing entities (e.g., schools, libraries, community centers, hospitals, law enforcement agencies, workplaces, and museums), and it may involve the creation of entirely new entities (e.g., game centers, portal clubs, trades networks, and content curators) to join the new learning ecosystem. There may also be a new layer of automated entities that play useful educational roles. A key element will be structure to support, maintain, and promote communications and coordination among these various elements. Ensuring the health of these learning organizations and institutions is one of the three types of development required for the new learning system.

Engaging Volunteers

A second type of development will be focused on the human actors who will activate the new learning ecosystem and make it a powerful educational force. The task here will be to engage and organize the vast numbers of human beings who have already demonstrated their willingness to volunteer their efforts to build a new learning ecology. As evidenced by examples like Wikipedia (Lih, 2009; Proffitt, 2018), the Open Educational Resources movement (Richter & McPherson, 2012), and Open Source Software contributors (Georgopoulou, 2009), it is more than clear that individuals will commit serious time and attention to efforts to contribute to socially shared and valued initiatives. We need to recruit, inspire, and organize such networked efforts to activate the new learning system. Such broad-based volunteer efforts will keep learning opportunities distributed and avoid the concentration of ownership and control in ways which advantage some and disadvantage others.

Envisioning the New Teacher Role

A third type of development that we must take on to create the new learning system is to reimagine the role of the teacher. Our current conception of the teacher as an employee of the school grew up at a time far different than the current era and we must resist simply moving forward with the role we have long known. That is one reason why developing the new role of the teacher should follow the development of the new institutional infrastructure and the new broad-based volunteer corps. With these other elements defined, we can ask what gaps in the new learning ecosystem need to be filled with dedicated, trained human personnel. Once we understand what might be needed, we can think about the recruitment, preparation, and retention of individuals in that educator role. Will these new teachers be like private tutors? Will they be advanced learning versions of SIRI or ALEXA? Will they be live online resource persons? What kind and how much augmented human intelligence will be necessary (Luckin et al., 2016)? However we think about the new teacher role, we must ensure that teachers are distributed so as to avoid the inequity in access to quality teaching that plagues the current educational system.

Cultivate an Appetite for Prototyping

There well may be various routes to get from our current educational system to the learning ecosystem we have envisioned, but we think that certain activities will be particularly important. First, we must cultivate an appetite for prototyping and experimentation with new structures to provide learning opportunities to youngsters and adults alike in diverse communities. Because we are all accustomed to the educational system that we have, we must overcome our preconceived notions of how society might support learning (Bryk, 2009).

Accelerate Digitization

Second, if we want a learning system that will be able to respond to the faster rate of change ahead of us, we must accelerate the digitization of all aspects of the education sector. Digital systems can change and grow exponentially so we must transition to a fully digital system as soon as possible, though we must also be aware of the potential dangers of rapid growth (Bruni, 2015; Kurzweil, 2005).

Manage the Decentering of the School

Third, we must manage the ebbing of the role of the school in the learning system. Schools are unlikely to disappear, but they will become a smaller part of the new learning ecosystem. They may be targeted at certain types of learners and for certain types of learning. As schools fade, we must manage the process to ensure that populations are not left without means of learning as school services are withdrawn.

The new learning ecosystem has the potential to be far more flexible, responsive, and impactful than our current system, but it will only be successful if we develop a new generation of educational research to capitalize on our growing understanding of learning and the conditions under which it can best be supported and encouraged. We turn next to ideas for a new generation of research.

Needs and Opportunities for Research and Development

The research and development activities required to guide the new learning sector will be demanding in all respects, not the least of which is the need to develop new research capacities that can move as quickly as the sector itself. Here we highlight some early needs and opportunities for research and development activities.

Monitoring for Educational Equity

The current education system has resulted in massive distribution problems as individuals with certain income, gender, and national citizenship characteristics are allowed less educational opportunity than others. Indeed, educational credentials have been weaponized and used to further advantage some at the expense of others, allowing those at the top to maintain their privilege and pass it on to subsequent generations while keeping those at the bottom firmly in their place (Markovitz, 2019). As we make the transition to a learning ecology that is more diffuse it is important to prevent the continuation of inequity in the distribution of learning resources and opportunities.

Monitoring the current educational system that is primarily operated through schools is easier than monitoring a multistreamed and networked learning ecosystem, and it may well be easier to mask inequities in the latter. While the new learning ecosystem offers perhaps the best opportunity to break with the inequities of the past, it also carries the danger that they will be enhanced and hidden. As the new learning ecosystem develops there should be serious and sustained efforts to monitor the distribution of learning opportunities both within national boundaries and more globally. This will require new techniques for tracking the utilization of learning resources, interactions, and affiliations while simultaneously protecting individual learner data (James, 2010; Saqr et al., 2018).

Studying Prototypes and Test Beds

The new learning sector that will need to evolve to address the needs of learners in the age of artificial and augmented human intelligence will require both engagement of existing institutions and organizations and the creation of entirely new entities to support learning. Developing such new formations will require invention, design work, and prototyping. Moreover, the range of contributors to learning will need to be embedded in networks of communication and coordination that do not currently exist and so must also be invented. Such activities will need to be assessed for their contribution to learning.

The research and development efforts to support new development in the learning sector can begin with relatively small scale experiments and test beds where new learning entities are gathered and where investments are made to allow them to communicate easily and work together to provide a learning safety net to ensure that all children in a community have access to diverse learning opportunities (Batty et al., 2019). The forms that new educational providers take will likely differ in different local contexts and it will be important to involve different types of communities even in the initial small-scale experiments.

In addition to studies of experiments and prototypes at the local community level, there should be research on the scaling of these entities as they grow to state, national, and even global levels. As the new learning ecology develops further, it will be important to study the contribution of learning providers in different communities and at different scales in order to understand the mix of learning opportunities available to individual learners.

Tracking Learning Materials and Resources

Efforts currently underway to develop and make available a variety of learning materials can be studied to determine their distribution and adequacy to support learning. In particular, an inquiry can be conducted to determine if high-quality materials are available for all learners, across cultural, socioeconomic, and language barriers. Such an inquiry can draw on prior approaches to the study of knowledge distribution (Reay, 2010; Rulke & Galaskiewicz, 2000). The suitability of such resources for self-directed learning should also be examined as should the availability of materials to meet learning needs throughout the lifespan.

Learning entities and learning resources will require continuing attention to maintain effectiveness and availability. In addition to examining the availability of learning resources across the global population of learners, researchers might also study the educational resource production capacity. This will allow for estimates of future availability of quality learning resources and for initiatives to fill gaps that are identified. With a wide variety of sources for learning resources, studies to understand the production capacities will need to be robust and multifaceted. This work can be linked to policy experiments mounted to develop finance and regulatory regimes to undergird the continuance and expansion of these essential elements of the new learning ecology.

Modernizing Educational Research

With discussions of the growing prospects for automating work spreading to more and more tasks and professional groups, it may well be time to start considering the ways in which the various dimensions of the educational research process may be automated. The educational research field will need to be modernized and enhanced to take advantage of new technologies and automation so that inquiry can be done on a routine basis as part of studying the new learning ecology. To do this on a global basis will require new agreements and new interoperability frameworks so that data can be gathered automatically and reports generated to support adjustments needed to ensure that learning opportunities are broadly available.

Each stage of the educational research cycle should be examined for its potential to be automated (Alkhateeb, 2017). Problem identification might be automated through routine population surveys to surface concerns and issues with the learning ecology. Text mining and topic modeling might be used to identify hypotheses from existing research to guide new inquiries. The digitization of all aspects of the learning ecosystem can be a foundation for the automation of data gathering on learning and learners while protecting individual learner privacy. Automated data checking and cleaning tools should be employed to streamline the data preparation process. Drawing on well-established procedures might permit the automation of data analysis for known problems. Data-reporting templates could support the automated generation of research reports. Connecting research to policy and practice could occur through adjustments to automated elements of the learning ecosystem as well as through more conventional policy making.

The research and development activities contemplated here are ambitious, indeed they are unprecedented, but they will be within our reach if we move aggressively to seize upon the new technical capacities that will evolve over the next two decades. Even now in the next several years we can make progress by laying the groundwork for these ambitious moves. We can address the learning paradox by turning the new tools and technologies and the growing capacity to automate even major parts of the research cycle on the research and development activities required to jump start the new learning sector.

The fourth industrial revolution will place new demands on individual learners and on the communities and societies in which they live. Fortunately, the fruits of that same revolution will equip those same individuals with tools, techniques, and capacities to meet the new demands. The learning ecology that can be put in place in the coming years will be key to making sure that we are ready individually and collectively to meet the challenges that lie ahead of us all.

References

Alkhateeb, A. (2017, April 25). Can scientific discovery be automated? *The Atlantic*, online at: https://www.theatlantic.com/science/archive/2017/04/can-scientific-discovery-be-automated/524136/

Baker, B. (2019). *Educational inequality and school finance: Why money matters for America's students*. Harvard Education Press.

Batty, R., Wong, A., Florescu, A., & Sharples, M. (2019). *Driving EdTech Futures: Testbed models for better evidence*. Nesta.

Brookfield, S. (Ed.). (1985). *Self-directed learning: From theory to practice*. Jossey-Bass.

Bruni, L. (2015). Sustainability, cognitive technologies, and the digital semiosphere. *International Journal of Cultural Studies, 18*(1), 103–117.

Bryk, A. (2009). Support a science of performance improvement. *Phi Delta Kappan, 90*(8), 579–600.

Brynjolfsson, E., & McAfee, A. (2014). *The second machine age: Work, progress, and prosperity in a time of brilliant technologies*. Norton.

Bussolo, M., de Hoyos, R., Medvedev, D., & van der Mensbrugghe, D. (2011). Global growth and distribution: China, India, and the emergence of a global middle class. *Journal of Globalization and Development, 2*(2), 1–27.

Collum, E., & Mitchell, D. (2005). Homeschooling as a social movement: Identifying the determinants of homeschoolers' perceptions. *Sociological Spectrum, 25*(3), 273–305.

Cremin, L. (1976). *Public education*. Basic.

Ford, M. (2016). *Rise of the robots: Technology and the threat of a jobless future*. Basic Books.

Georgopoulou, P. (2009). The free open source software movement: Resistance or change? *Civitas – Revista de Ciências Sociais, 9*(1), 65–76.

Gilliom, J., & Monahan, T. (2012). Surveillance in schools. In *SuperVision: An introduction to the surveillance society* (pp. 72–88). University of Chicago Press.

Gray, M., & Suri, S. (2019). *Ghost work: How to stop Silicon Valley from building a new global underclass*. Houghton Mifflin.

Harding, J., & Vining, L. (1997). The impact of the knowledge explosion on science education. *Journal of Research in Science Teaching, 34*(10), 967–975.

Hunsinger, J. (2009). Introducing learning infrastructures: Invisibility, context, and governance. *Learning Inquiry, 3*, 111–114.

James, R. (2010). *Monitoring and evaluating learning networks*. INTRAC.

Jarvis, P. (2007). *Globalization, lifelong learning, and the learning society: Sociological perspectives*. Routledge.

Joan, D., Denisia, S., & Sheeja, Y. (2013). Technology integration in curriculum progress to meet knowledge explosion. *I-Manager's Journal on School Educational Technology, 8*(3), 23–31.

Knowles, M. (1975). *Self-directed learning: A guide for learners and teachers*. Follett.

Kraftl, P. (2013). Towards geographies of 'alternative' education: A case study of UK home schooling families. *Transactions of the Institute of British Geographers, 38*(3), 436–450.

Kurzweil, R. (2005). *The singularity is near: When humans transcend biology*. Viking.

Lian, Y., Xiao, J., Xhang, C., Guan, S., Fuye, L., Ge, H., & Liu, J. (2016). A comparison of the relationships between psychosocial factors, occupational strain, and work ability among four ethnic groups in China. *Archives of Environmental and Occupational Health, 71*(2), 74–84.

Lih, A. (2009). *The Wikipedia revolution*. Hyperion.

Luckin, R., Holmes, W., Griffiths, M., & Forcier, L. (2016). *Unleashed intelligence: An argument for AI in education*. Pearson.

Malin, H. (2018). *Teaching for purpose: Preparing students for lives of meaning*. Harvard Education Press.

Markovitz, D. (2019). *The meritocracy trap*. Penguin.

OECD. (2019). *Envisioning the future of education and jobs*. OECD Publishing.

Pearson. (2019). *The global learner survey*. Pearson.

Pithers, R., & Soden, R. (1998). Scottish and Australian teacher stress and strain: A comparative study. *British Journal of Educational Psychology, 68*(2), 269–279.

Proffitt, M. (2018). *Leveraging Wikipedia: Connecting communities of knowledge*. American Library Association.

Reay, M. (2010). Knowledge distribution, embodiment, and insulation. *Sociological Theory, 28*(1), 91–107.

Richter, T., & McPherson, M. (2012). Open educational resources: Education for the world? *Distance Education, 33*(2), 201–219.

Rulke, D., & Galaskiewicz, J. (2000). Distribution of knowledge, group network structure, and group performance. *Management Science, 46*(5), 612–625.

Saqr, M., Fors, U., Tedre, M., & Nouri, J. (2018). How social network analysis can be used to monitor online collaborative learning and guide an informed intervention. *PLoS One, 13*(3), 1–22.

Schwab, K. (2017). *The fourth industrial revolution*. Crown Business.

UNESCO Institute for Statistics. (2016). The world needs almost 69 million new teachers to reach the 2030 education goals. *UIS Fact Sheet, 39*, 1–16.

Wang, Y. (2017). The social networks and paradoxes of the opt-out movement amid the Common Core State Standards implementation: The case of New York. *Education Policy Analysis Archives, 25*.

World Bank. (2019). *World development report 2019: The changing nature of work* (World Development Report). World Bank.

World Economic Forum. (2016). *The future of jobs: Employments, skills, and workforce strategy for the fourth industrial revolution*. World Economic Forum.

Worthen, M. (2019, June 9). The anti-college is on the rise. *New York Times*. https://www.nytimes.com/2019/06/08/opinion/sunday/college-anti-college-mainstream-universities.html

Gary Natriello is the Ruth L. Gottesman Professor of Educational Research and Professor of Sociology and Education in the Department of Human Development at Teachers College Columbia University. Professor Natriello teaches graduate courses in the social organization of schools and classrooms, the social dimensions of assessment and analytic processes, the sociology of online learning, and research methods. Professor Natriello's research interests include school organization, the social dimensions of evaluation processes, at-risk youth, and the sociology of online learning. Professor Natriello holds an BA (English) from Princeton University, an MA (Sociology) from Stanford University, and a PhD (Sociology of Education) from Stanford University.

Hui Soo Chae is Senior Director of Research and Development for the EdLab and the Gottesman Libraries at Teachers College Columbia University. In that capacity he leads the software development, research, consulting, and publishing initiatives. Dr. Chae has led the development of a number of learning applications, including the Vialogues (www.vialogues.com) video discussion tool. Dr. Chae's research has focused on the examination of the educational experiences of minority youth using critical theory, the creation of in-school and out-of-school learning opportunities, and the development of online venues for learning. He is the co-editor of a recent special issue of the *Teachers College Record* on adaptive learning technologies. Dr. Chae holds an BA degree in Public Policy and an MAT from Brown University and an EdD in Curriculum and Teaching from Teachers College Columbia University.

Integrating an Emphasis on Creativity

Brad Hokanson

Creativity Is an Important Human Capability

Today many people and nations recognize creativity as important (see, e.g., Craft, 2005).

New ideas are needed to respond to the challenges we face in the world and those developing these ideas will be celebrated. "Those with the imagination… to invent smarter ways to do old jobs, energy saving ways to provide new services, new ways to attract old customers or new ways to combine existing technologies will thrive" (Friedman, 2009).

Creativity is an important skill, trait, or personal strength. Creativity is also an important definitional attribute of all humans: "In human life, there is always something new, because creativity is part of what it is to be human" (Robinson, 2011, p.17). Its use and development vary with culture, local environment, and education. It is enhanced in some children, while stifled in others… some would say most… by our educational systems.

There is a commonly accepted definition of creativity that is widely used and clear: creativity involves the development of new, novel, or original ideas that are of value or applicable within a given social context (Plucker et al., 2004). The two main elements, originality and usefulness, are essential to an understanding of creativity.

Creativity ranges in scope from the pedestrian solutions of everyday problems to the recognized geniuses of the world (Kaufman & Beghetto, 2009). Most people recognize various artists or scientists as being eminently creative, listing for example, Albert Einstein, Frida Kahlo, John Coltrane, or Stephen Hawking as common

B. Hokanson (✉)
University of Minnesota, St. Paul, MN, USA
e-mail: brad@umn.edu

M. V. Albert et al. (eds.), *Bridging Human Intelligence and Artificial Intelligence*, Educational Communications and Technology: Issues and Innovations, https://doi.org/10.1007/978-3-030-84729-6_21

examples of the creative mind. Their domain-changing creativity, often referred to as Big-C creativity, is rare and elusive. The everyday creativity of our own lives, however, is more important to examine in terms of its range and applicability: it affects us all. Everyday creativity is often referred to as "little-c" creativity (Kaufman & Beghetto, 2009).

Creativity Can Be Measured, Evaluated, and Developed in Learners

Many people view creativity as having a mystical aspect. Early in human history it was thought of as a gift from God, or something bestowed by a muse. In a modern sense, it is an aspect of human nature that can be developed and examined. Creativity can be described as a skill, a personality trait, or a character strength (Peterson & Seligman, 2004). While it is a complex human phenomenon, creativity can be evaluated in a number of ways, from examining the quality of a life's work to self-reports of creative practices (Fürst & Grin, 2018).

The modern evaluation of creativity began in the 1950s. J. P. Guilford, as president of the American Psychological Association, is recognized for calling for the first research on the topic in 1954. Both Guilford, Merrifield, & Wilson (1958) and E. Paul Torrance (1974) developed and published means of evaluation of creativity that focused on the task of generating multiple answers for a given prompt. Torrance subsequently published a series of tests to evaluate the basic and more complex aspects of creativity that are widely used today. Performance tests such as the Torrance Test of Creative Thinking have the advantage of being broadly distributed and allowing for comparison with a large number of test results. They are relatively brief in application being completed under an hour and are of moderate cost.

Some methods of standardized testing of creativity can easily be used informally to pragmatically evaluate creative capability. First conceived by Guilford as the "Unusual Uses" test, the Alternative Uses Test seeks different and divergent uses for common objects such as bricks, blankets, cardboard boxes, paper clips, or tin cans (Guilford et al. 1958). For example, a resultant list for uses of tin cans could include use as a cooking pot, a drinking cup, a step stool, or a musical instrument. With a short time period of three to five minutes, written responses are generated and counted for the simplest measure of creativity called *fluency* (Sawyer, 2011).

Evaluation of fluency is not an all-encompassing examination of the complexity of creativity, but it does quickly reflect an essential aspect called *divergent* thinking (Guilford et al., 1958). This is the capacity to generate a number of answers by using one's imagination, tapping personal experiences, and suspending judgment of unusual ideas. Divergent thinking can be contrasted with *convergent* thinking, the ability to select and improve a single answer (Sawyer, 2011).

Responses provided for the Alternative Uses Test can also be used to examine the uniqueness or rarity of answers, termed *originality*. This can be compared against a general population or against a smaller group. Rare answers could be those provided by less than five percent of the population, and unique answers can be described as unmatched within a group.

The Alternative Uses Test also allows the examination of the ability to develop different types or categories of ideas. This aspect of creative skill is called "*flexibility*." This examines the ability to broadly make connections and not center on a given type or use. For example, used tin cans could be used to hold a variety of liquids: water, paint, coffee, soup, oil, or beer; they are all the same type of use.

This is only one form of creativity evaluation, and with some published forms of creativity tests, more nuanced evaluations can be developed. This abbreviated form of creativity evaluation can be easily included in online or technologically supported education.

The value of divergent thinking skills is high, as even among Big-C creativities, the ability to generate a wide range of ideas is valued. Linus Pauling said that the best way to have a good idea is to have a lot of ideas (Pauling, 1960). The cost of developing multiple initial ideas is minimal. As with multiple digital images, ideas are available at virtually no added cost, having more than a single option for your final choice allows different solutions to evolve. Alfred Nobel, the inventor of dynamite and initiator of the Nobel Prizes, said, "If I have a thousand ideas and only one turns out to be good, I am satisfied" (found in Weis, 2010, p.10). Inherent in this pursuit is the recognition of multiple possible answers as opposed to a single correct answer. The alternative ideas may not immediately be recognized as useful without additional effort. Creative people consistently have the ability to accept ambiguity and to hold competing or even contradictory ideas in their consciousness. When seeking a creative answer, the only wrong answer is one single answer.

Development Occurs Through Practice and Divergent Habits

While creativity is a complex set of behaviors and beliefs (Guilford et al., 1958), aspects of creativity can be developed as individual skills. Repeated and directed practice can help build the skills needed to generate multiple and diverse answers. With intentional practice, people can become more fluid in generating multiple ideas, and more accepting of ambiguous thoughts. Practicing a challenge such as seen in the Alternative Use Test can be used as a simple drill, and repeated practice at the task can build one's fluency in divergent thinking. The ability… the need... to generate multiple solutions and answers to any challenge is a threshold concept in the field of creativity.

The ability to withhold judgment in editing and selecting ideas is also critical in examining and advancing original ideas. People often reject novel or original ideas as unfeasible, embarrassing, or unconventional. In terms of creativity, however, it is important to defy the crowd in finding ideas that are untried, unusual, and original (Sternberg & Lubart, 1995). While divergent thinking is the ability to general multiple and original ideas to a given challenge, a mirrored aspect is *convergent thinking*, the ability to select and improve a chosen idea or solution. Convergent thinking is well developed in our educational system, and its focus on a single answer is both its strength and limitation. These paired aspects of creative thinking, with divergent thinking seeking new and original ideas, and convergent thinking making ideas that are useful and applicable, form the basis of the definition of creativity. As divergent thinking seeks the new and original, convergent thinking seeks the useful and applicable, and is the primary application of domain expertise and knowledge.

Learning through the most common educational processes is seen to be detrimental to the development or maintenance of creativity in children. Being "done" or completing work in the objectively correct manner is often more valued than examining alternatives and more innovative solutions. As people mature and are socialized through our educational system, they are implicitly or explicitly trained to seek a single right answer and to conform to the practices of others. The effects of this focus on creativity are well demonstrated in research on students, illustrating the decline in creative skills since 1991 (Kim, 2011). Torrance (1974) referred to it as the "fourth grade slump." Other research showed eighth graders being scored as more creative than eleventh graders in the same school district (Bart, Hokanson, Sahin, & Abdelsamea, 2015).

Current educational research encourages richer and more complex modes of instruction. The old, highly focused, didactic models of instruction are generally viewed as less effective for learning in all fields. Current trends in education recognize the value of solving complex problems and developing higher order thinking. As creativity is a complex thought process, creative skills can be seen to benefit from this parallel path for the development of higher order learning. Creative skills are challenged and developed through problem-based learning and in other pedagogical methods that are complex and messy. These are learning processes that challenge thinking processes and which do not seek single answers. More complex learning activities are comparable to a craftsperson solving a myriad of problems in completing their work (Glăveanu, 2012).

Creativity often builds from a store of existing ideas and experiences in the brain. Increasing an individual's mental repertoire can come through challenging oneself in new endeavors, gaining exposure to different social and cultural experiences, and seeking new experiences. Ideas often develop from varied exposure to different environments, events, contexts, and people through ways remote from our current context. Having a habit to vary our experiences, both large and small, builds a base for new ideas and directions.

Creativity Is Both General and Domain Specific

Creativity can be seen as existing both in a general sense and within a given domain. Although there is controversy over this issue, creativity is probably both domain-general and domain-specific (Baer & Kaufman, 2005). As noted earlier, people can be creative at both the professional and pedestrian levels. There are considerable evidence supporting the idea that creativity has both specific and general components, and that the level of specificity or generality changes with the social context and as one develops through childhood into adulthood (Plucker & Beghetto, 2004).

Creativity can be developed in both areas: One can learn to be more personally creative every day and, in our work, lives, generally in everything we do, and specifically in our professional domains.

Everyday creativity is a general skill, and it is applicable to many areas. Creativity in advanced areas of a profession is more domain specific. "Some traits and aptitudes are arguably general and relevant to any domains (e.g., openness), whereas others are more useful for certain domains only (e.g., extraversion for performance arts)" (Fürst & Grin, 2018, p. 18). While training for creativity is generally more effective when applied in a domain-specific manner, transfer of the skill between the general and the specific domain is possible. In other words, people who are generally creative are able to apply their creativity in professional practice as they develop a deeper understanding of the field (Plucker & Beghetto, 2004). On the other hand, it is important to explicitly develop creativity within the domains. Unfortunately, in many domains, best practices or known problem solutions are often commonly applied. Advanced domain knowledge is often well structured and codified, which limits the opportunity for creative output. Expertise often comes with blinders. Changing the focus on education from declarative knowledge to the development of skills and abilities is a worthwhile choice, and would help in the development of creativity in the domains.

Beyond the Individual

While we can build our own experiences and continue to explore and expand our individual skills, engagement with others through teamwork, collaboration, and interaction can increase the quantity, value, and impact of our ideas. One needs to share ideas and work with others. Group collaborative models do work well with supportive work environments (Amabile, 1998). The structure of research labs can be a good, productive model, including shared lab books, common lab gatherings, and environmentally encouraged personal interactions (Truran, 2016). Many famous innovation sites, including Building 20 at MIT, Bell Labs, and the new Apple headquarters encourage serendipitous interactions (Gertner, 2013; Howland, 2014).

This interaction can occur through informal group interactions or through one of the many structured forms often termed "brainstorming" (Al-Samarraie & Hurmuzan 2018; Markov, 2018; Parnes & Meadow, 1959). Formal brainstorming, developed by Parnes in the 1950s, involves groups of individuals each sharing ideas by turns in response to a given challenge. Judgment is curtailed and ideas are recorded for less than an hour.

Since its inception, the general form of "brainstorming" has evolved from this simple group structure for sharing ideas to more structured and layered methods.

Research beginning in the 1950s found better results from brainstorming were achieved with modest modifications of the process. (Al-Samarraie & Hurmuzan, 2018). The most positive modification was to have individuals record their own ideas prior to group interaction. Group methods incorporating isolated individual idea development along with the open and nonjudgmental interaction with others can exist in many forms. Research is also ongoing as to the effective use of electronic media in group idea development.

While creativity training and group techniques have proved effective (Scott et al., 2004), changing the context of work and school environments may have a larger effect on creativity than individual or incidental changes. Work environments can enhance or constrain creativity (Amabile, 1998). Workers acting as cogs in an industrial system are often not creative. With the advent of more robotic capabilities, human workers are often replaced with mechanized processes or globally outsourced (Friedman, 2009). Human workers are valued for their creativity as the world moves to more and more knowledge work. Knowledge work requires critical thinking and creativity, particularly as rote work declines.

Similarly, educational systems based on an industrial model focused on the distribution of information must evolve as well. Creative teachers are more effective than noncreative teachers as a model for their students in higher-order thinking. Active and complex learning is valuable both for effective learning and for the development of learner creativity.

Potential Means for Developing Creativity Through Digital Technology

Creativity is understood to be a human trait that can be encouraged and developed, or constrained and limited. It has also been described as the ultimate difference between digital artificial intelligence and human potential.

Developing the potential for human creativity through the use of technology should be viewed as an extension of our earlier use of cognitive tools as aids, hints, and encouragement. We can make ourselves more creative, and potential models are evident in current uses of digital technology which can extend our capabilities. For example, many people use an exercise wristband to record steps, to check heart rates, or to check sleeping habits. Most can also serve as reminder systems, encouraging the user to get up and move around after sitting for a certain period of time or to sit up straight when slumped. A comparable digital system could encourage one to think about different stimuli and to combine them with their current task. This would allow users to diversify their attention in a way that is helpful and creative.

A slightly more complex digital tool could be used to help increase creative habits such as journaling, exploring new ideas, challenging oneself, and being reminded to develop multiple ideas for any challenge. If digital devices have the capability to see if someone is moving or not after a certain period of time, they should also have the capability to encourage users to seek new environments and experiences. Changing locations has been shown to increase creative output and this is well within current digital capability.

Enhanced by artificial intelligence, technology could encourage people through coaching or other forms of engagement (Keenan-Lechel, Henriksen, Mishra, & Deep-Play Research Group, 2018). A digital device with artificial intelligence could manage a social calendar and encourage users to reach out and interact with other people… the ultimate nerd fix. Artificial intelligence even might encourage them to walk about at work, encouraging serendipitous meetings with other colleagues. An app could build the habits of creativity within all users.

References

Al-Samarraie, H., & Hurmuzan, S. (2018). A review of brainstorming techniques in higher education. *Thinking Skills and Creativity, 27*, 78–91.

Amabile, T. M. (1998). *How to kill creativity* (Vol. 87). Boston, MA: Harvard Business School Publishing.

Baer, J., & Kaufman, J. C. (2005). Theoretical and Interdisciplinary Perspectives: Bridging generality and specificity: The amusement park theoretical (APT) model of creativity. *Roeper review, 27*(3), 158–163.

Bart, W. M., Hokanson, B., Sahin, I., & Abdelsamea, M. A. (2015). An investigation of the gender differences in creative thinking abilities among 8th and 11th grade students. *Thinking Skills and Creativity, 17*, 17–24.

Craft, A. (2005). *Creativity in schools: Tensions and dilemmas*. Routledge.

Friedman, T. (2009). The New Untouchables, New York Times, Retrieved 8/9/18 from http://www.nytimes.com/2009/10/21/opinion/21friedman.html?ref=thomaslfriedman

Fürst, G., & Grin, F. (2018). A comprehensive method for the measurement of everyday creativity. *Thinking Skills and Creativity, 28*, 84–97.

Gertner, J. (2013). *The idea factory: Bell Labs and the great age of American innovation*. Penguin.

Glăveanu, V. P. (2012). What can be done with an egg? Creativity, material objects, and the theory of affordances. *The Journal of Creative Behavior, 46*(3), 192–208.

Guilford, J. P., Merrifield, P. R., & Wilson, R. C. (1958). *Unusual uses test*. Orange, CA: Sheridan Psychological Services.

Howland, B. (2014). *MIT Building 20: Short Stories*. Xlibris Corporation.

Kaufman, J. C., & Beghetto, R. A. (2009). Beyond big and little: The four c model of creativity. *Review of general psychology, 13*(1), 1.

Keenan-Lechel, S. F., Henriksen, D., Mishra, P., & Deep-Play Research Group. (2018). Creativity as a Sliding Maze: an Interview with Dr. James C. Kaufman. *TechTrends*, 1-6.

Kim, K. H. (2011). The creativity crisis: The decrease in creative thinking scores on the Torrance Tests of Creative Thinking. *Creativity Research Journal, 23*(4), 285–295.

Markov, S. (2018). *Base types of Brainstorming*. In geniusrevive.com. Retrieved July 6, 2018, from https://geniusrevive.com/en/series/base-types-of-brainstorming/.

Parnes, S. J., & Meadow, A. (1959). Effects of brainstorming instructions on creative problem solving by trained and untrained subjects. *Journal of Educational Psychology, 50*(4), 171.

Pauling, L. (1960). *The nature of the chemical bond and the structure of molecules and crystals: An introduction to modern structural chemistry*. Ithaca, NY: Cornell University Press.

Peterson, C., & Seligman, M. E. P. (2004). *Character strengths and virtues: A handbook and classification*. American Psychological Association; Oxford University Press.

Plucker, J. A., & Beghetto, R. A. (2004). Why Creativity Is Domain General, Why It Looks Domain Specific, and Why the Distinction Does Not Matter. In R. J. Sternberg, E. L. Grigorenko, & J. L. Singer (Eds.), *Creativity: From Potential to Realization*. American Psychological Association.

Plucker, J. A., Beghetto, R. A., & Dow, G. T. (2004). Why Isn't Creativity More Important to Educational Psychologists? Potentials, Pitfalls, and Future Directions in Creativity Research. *Educational Psychologist, 39*(2), 83–96.

Robinson, K. (2011). *Out of our minds: Learning to be creative*. Wiley.

Sawyer, R. K. (2011). *Explaining creativity: The science of human innovation*. Oxford University Press.

Scott, G., Leritz, L. E., & Mumford, M. D. (2004). Types of creativity training: Approaches and their effectiveness. *The Journal of Creative Behavior, 38*(3), 149–179.

Sternberg, R. J., & Lubart, T. I. (1995). *Defying the crowd: Cultivating creativity in a culture of conformity*. Free Press.

Torrance, E. P. (1974). *Torrance Tests of Creative Thinking: Norms-Technical Manual*. Princeton, NJ: Personnel Press/Ginn.

Truran, P. (2016). The Development of Creative Thinking in Graduate Students Doing Scientific Research. *Educational Technology*, 41–46.

Weis, D. (2010). *Everlasting wisdom*. Chicago: Paragon Publishing.

Dr. Brad Hokanson is a professor in Graphic Design at the University of Minnesota and serves as Director of Graduate Studies for Design. He has taught an ongoing course on Creative Problem Solving at the University of Minnesota since 2000 and it remains the focus of his academic work.

Smart Learning in Support of Critical Thinking: Lessons Learned and a Theoretically and Research-Based Framework

Shanshan Ma, J. Michael Spector, Dejian Liu, Kaushal Kumar Bhagat, Dawit Tiruneh, Jonah Mancini, Lin Lin, Rodney Nielsen, and Kinshuk

Introduction

Technology advancements can lead to changes in teaching approaches and instructional methods and learning environments. Based on the potential, some have predicted revolutionary improvements in education, which have seldom occurred and seldom as quickly as predicted. Although, the printing press led to many revolutionary changes in

---

The original version of this chapter was revised. The correction to this chapter is available at https://doi.org/10.1007/978-3-030-84729-6_25

S. Ma (✉) · J. M. Spector · R. Nielsen
University of North Texas, Denton, TX, USA
e-mail: shanshanma@my.unt.edu; mike.spector@unt.edu; Rodney.Nielsen@UNT.edu;
https://sites.google.com/site/jmspector007/; http://www.cse.unt.edu/~nielsen/

D. Liu
Netdragon Websoft, Fuzhou, China; http://ir.nd.com.cn/en/staff/liu-dejian

K. K. Bhagat
Advanced Technology Development Centre, Indian Institute of Technology, Kharagpur, India

D. Tiruneh
The Faculty of Education, University of Cambridge, Cambridge, UK

J. Mancini
University of North Texas, Denton, TX, USA

Private Consultant, Round Rock, TX, USA

L. Lin
Texas Center for Educational Technology, University of North Texas, Denton, TX, USA

Kinshuk
College of Information, University of North Texas, Denton, TX, USA
e-mail: Kinshuk@unt.edu; http://www.kinshuk.info/

M. V. Albert et al. (eds.), *Bridging Human Intelligence and Artificial Intelligence*, Educational Communications and Technology: Issues and Innovations, https://doi.org/10.1007/978-3-030-84729-6_22

education. A transformative change because of the printing press that took place over decades and centuries brought learning and instruction to the masses rather than to a small, privileged class. However, there have been a few efforts that were potentially transformative, including efforts attributed to Confucius, Socrates, Dewey, Vygotsky, Piaget, Skinner, Merrill, and others. Yet, those efforts have failed to scale up and be widely embraced and sustained, unlike efforts resulting from the printing press.

Recent rapidly changing technologies have led many to contemplate how the so-called intelligent technologies can transform learning and instruction. To date there now are at least four main approaches to teaching and learning: (a) traditional classroom activities, including lectures as well as accessing resources on the Internet, (b) Internet-facilitated tutoring and instruction, (c) learning anywhere and anytime with mobile applications, many of which access Internet resources, and (d) context-aware ubiquitous applications that make use of mobile devices, sensing technology, the Internet and direct instructional methods used in the previous approaches.

Context-aware ubiquitous learning is seen in association with the emergence of smart learning. A smart learning environment can enable individual learners to learn with rather than learn from technology, as proposed years ago by David Jonassen (1999). Current learning environments are in transition toward smart learning environments (Kinshuk et al., 2016). Hwang (2014) argued that "New learning modes will raise new pedagogic issues" (p. 11), which is consistent with the current emphasis on TPACK (technological pedagogical content knowledge) (Mishra & Koehler, 2006). The new concept of smart learning prompts the examination of existing pedagogical theories, instructional approaches, and the use of technology.

Against such a background, a historical examination is taken for the existing critical thinking teaching methods, such as inquiry learning and questioning, as the roots of critical thinking teaching lie in the Socratic method (Jowett, 1982). We argue for the transition from current critical thinking teaching methods that are typically limited to one subject area, high school, and college students, and of relative short duration (e.g., a unit of instruction or a few lessons) to a smarter one that cuts across subject areas, aims at developing habits of inquiry, and reasoning across years. The goal of this historical review is to find the advantages and limitations of previous approaches and use those to construct a new approach aiming at developing productive thinking habits in young children.

A Review of Critical Thinking Teaching

Socrates

Critical thinking teaching can be traced to Socrates (469– 399 BCE) (Jowett, 1982). He encouraged his students to think critically about the common-sense beliefs and accepted facts through dialogue or conversation rather than to take those beliefs for granted. What is called Socratic questioning or the Socratic method (a.k.a., the *elenchus*) is arguably an effective way to promote critical thinking. Generally, the Socratic method refers to using guided and systematic questions and responses to prompt learners to think critically and eventually draw the truth out of what they already believe to be true, which often runs counter to a popular concept such as "might makes right." The method "usually focuses on foundational concepts, principles, theories, issues, or problems" (Paul & Elder, 2006, p. 2). The Socratic method and critical thinking share the same goal (Paul & Elder, 2006) – namely, uncovering a hidden truth. Not surprisingly the Socratic method has been often applied for promoting students' critical thinking (e.g., Yang et al., 2005).

Socrates, as represented in Plato's early dialogues, and Plato both focus primarily on issues concerned with the nature of virtue and what constitutes goodness (Jowett, 1982; see also https://plato.stanford.edu/entries/plato/). This point is noteworthy in that direct instruction (e.g., lecturing) as practiced by the sophists was not appropriate because issues pertaining to virtue and goodness are complex and subject to individual situations and perceptions. As a result, Socrates engaged interlocutors in a dialogue aimed at exploring the complexities and consequences of alternative perspectives. The dialogical aspect of Socrates' questioning will be carried forward into the framework to be presented toward the end of this review. However, a major point is worth noting. Socrates was keen to point out contradictions in a particular line of reasoning offered by an interlocutor. In the early phases of inquiry and critical reasoning, the emphasis is on probing for more information and evidence rather than on indicating that a response was wrongheaded. The point was to eventually get the interlocutor to realize the response offered was in some way deficient. Rather than say, "that is confused or mistaken," Socrates wanted the interlocutor to come to the conclusion that what had been said could not be correct, as in "I must be confused or mistaken." Reflective thinking of that sort will be carried forward into the framework.

Dewey

Another earlier phase of interest in critical thinking comes from the inclusion of inquiry in K-12 science education encouraged by Dewey (1910a, b, 1916, 1938, 1944). Dewey believed that students should be encouraged to develop critical thinking through experiential learning activities, including failed attempts to do something, rather than emphasize the facts and dates without scientific reasoning and direct experience.

The early scientific method developed by Descartes (1637); an earlier form can also be traced back in history to Aristotle (350BCE) focused on dividing problems into many parts and addressing each part in order, making frequent observations and reviews to ensure that all aspects of the problem had been covered adequately. A more familiar version of the scientific method is called the hypothetico-deductive model and involves proceeding from experience and observation to formulating a tentative hypothesis, then deducing predictions based on that hypothesis and determining by observation if the hypothesis is confirmed or refuted (Godfrey-Smith, 2003). Popper (1963) emphasized that scientific claims needed to be refutable, and that progress occurred when a hypothesis had been refuted. The notion that progresses occur through being mistaken is embraced in the framework to be presented through a dialogue aimed at getting a student to keep exploring and explaining when an explanation falls short, which is consistent with Socrates' elenchus and with Dewey's notions about experiential learning. Dewey's (1910a, b, 1938) approach to developing critical thinking skills consisted of six steps: (a) sensing perplexing situations, (b) clarifying the problem, (c) formulating a tentative hypothesis, (d) testing the hypothesis, (e) revising and retesting, and (f) acting on the solution. Subsequently, Dewey modified that method to include reflective thinking, which has been embraced by those proposing problem-based learning (Barrows & Tamblyn, 1980) as well as by those proposing reflective thinking (Schön, 1983). Dewey's modified framework includes presenting problem(s), forming a hypothesis, collecting data during the experiment, and formulating a conclusion (see Barrow, 2006). In Dewey's (1910a, b, 1938) approaches, students are actively engaged, while instructors play the roles of facilitators (often by asking probing questions) and guides (often by encouraging further inquiry and investigation); these roles are embedded in the framework to be presented later in this chapter.

Recent Development

Renewed interest in critical thinking occurred in the late 1980s. Inquiry is accepted as a good way of critical thinking development (Garrison et al., 1999; King, 1995; Ikuenobe, 2001). Practicing inquiry could help learners develop critical thinking abilities and scientific reasoning while leading to deep learning (National Research Council, 2000). Note that how educators and learning scientists talk about deep learning is somewhat different from how artificial intelligence (AI) researchers talk about deep learning. The educational view stresses a deep understanding of the complexities of a challenging problem, unlike the AI view that emphasizes finding patterns in disparate sets of data.

Although inquiry was recommended in K-12 science education, the teaching typically emphasizes students' acquisition of products of inquiry rather than students' participation in inquiry and the development of understanding. In addition, there are some other barriers that have prevented teachers from promoting critical thinking and the adoption of inquiry, such as the goal of broad content coverage, large class sizes, time constraints, limited professional training programs, teachers' own lack of knowledge about teaching critical thinking, teachers' personal beliefs and values about students, teaching and the purpose of education, the quality of supplementary materials, limited instructional materials that emphasize thinking, the degree of commitment to textbook, and so on (Anderson, 2002; Onosko, 1991). Along with the development of technology and pedagogy, alternative teaching methods were explored that now include the flipped classroom.

Generally, three approaches have been established by previous research for critical thinking development: (a) pedagogy-focused, (b) technology-focused, and (c) technology-enhanced. A pedagogy-focused approach refers to the methods of using different pedagogical strategies to promote critical thinking with few technologies including accessing digital resources, like the Socratic method, problem-solving, role play, storytelling (e.g., Allen, 2018; Espey, 2018; Gold et al., 2002; Rashid & Qaisar, 2017). This approach emphasizes the value of pedagogy, and it characterizes the deeper interactions between the instructor and students.

A technology-focused approach involves using technology to improve critical thinking without paying much attention to pedagogy, such as using mind mapping, sketch noting, and digital media (e.g., Huang et al., 2017; Jahn & Kenner, 2018; Paepcke-Hjeltness et al., 2017). This approach assumes that desired learning outcomes can be achieved just by using technology, such as an interactive simulation or a management flight simulator. However, the problem with such an approach is that it overemphasizes the effect of technology and neglects how learning occurs in such an environment. Technology alone cannot be able to develop students' critical thinking systematically, its function is more like a tool.

Technology-enhanced approaches are those methods that are powered by technology to construct learning activities, such as learning through games, online platforms, multiplayer interactive simulations, and virtual realities (e.g., Chiu, 2009; Halpern et al., 2012; Shailey et al., 2018). This approach combines the advantages of the prior two approaches, technology functions as amplification as well as transformation, namely amplifying the learning effect while transforming students' learning method, learning process, learning content, or learning behaviors. Pedagogy is integrated with technology properly often achieving a balance between technology and pedagogy consistent with the advocates of TPACK (technological pedagogical content knowledge) (Mishra & Koehler, 2006). The approaches often emphasize a small group reflection on the results of a particular interaction with the technology, which is reflected in the framework to be presented below.

. Recently, owing to the emergence of wireless communication, mobile and sensing technology such as Radio Frequency Identification (RFID), the Global Positioning System (GPS) and quick response (QR) code, etc., a new version of technology-enhanced learning method called "context-aware ubiquitous learning" is growing to be the trend (Hwang et al., 2008). In such a case, learners' real-world status could be detected or recognized. It to some degree allows learners to interact with the real world while accessing learning resources without the limit of location and time. Some researchers have tried to use such a method to encourage critical thinking and corresponding skills. For example, Lee et al. (2016) utilize a mobile learning game designed with cooperative reciprocity to encourage children's critical thinking skills. It uses mixed reality resources to lead the players through a realistic scenario, providing them with physical, cognitive, and collaborative challenges. In this study, it emphasizes the application of pedagogy, the collaboration between learners rather than technologies it adopts.

The emergence of context-aware ubiquitous learning indicates a need for an intelligent, humanized, personalized, and adaptive teaching method. It is also seen as the emergence of smart learning environments (Kinshuk et al., 2016). Smart learning is a form of ideal technology-enhanced learning (Hwang, 2014). Hwang et al. (2008) defined a smart learning environment as a technology-supported learning environment that adapts to and provides appropriate support based on learners' real-world status (including time and place) and their individual learners' needs which are determined by the analysis of their learning styles, preferences, learning behavior or performance, etc. Currently, there is no unified definition of smart learning environment. But there are some characteristics of smart learning environments specified in previous studies. For example, Kinshuk et al. (2016) interpreted smart learning environments from a perspective of technology, he believed that full context awareness, big data and learning analytics, and autonomous decision making are the three key features of smart learning environment. Hwang (2014) took context awareness, adaptive and instant support, adaptive user interface, and adaptive learning as the basic features. According to Spector (2014), a smart learning environment should be capable of adapting to a wide variety of learners with different backgrounds and different interests, providing personalized instruction and learning support on a large sustainable scale. Therefore, three levels are stated, the first level consists of the following necessary features, namely effectiveness, efficiency, scalable, and autonomy. Beyond the first level, the following features are highly desirable, namely engaging, flexible, adaptive, and personalized. Further, the third level considers being conversational, reflective, innovative, self-organizing.

As Hwang (2014) pointed out, most smart learning environments currently defined are minimally smart. Kinshuk et al. (2016) and Hwang (2014) deconstructed smart learning environments from a technology view. Spector (2014) portrayed a blueprint from a pedagogy view expecting a conversational, reflective, scalable, and autonomous learning environment. Spector's expectations are somewhat humanized, which simulates an effective and natural way of human learning. Currently, the application of educational technology for smart learning is not stable, few applications are transformative enough to enable a more intelligent learning environment. A glimpse of smart learning environments through the definitions above might provide some references to its future research and development.

Given the current state of critical thinking development and the gap between the innovative technology application in practice and the ideal expectations for smart learning, we argue for a smarter method that integrates and also goes beyond all the advantages of previous approaches that enable critical thinking into habits of mind (Elder & Paul, 1998). For this purpose, we propose a framework that aims at developing critical thinking systematically from children's early childhood, especially promoting continuing inquiry and reasoning. This framework absorbed the concept of smart learning and embedded a systematic development method for the development of critical thinking. Before presenting the framework, we next review similar efforts for further reference, such as intelligent tutoring systems.

Previous Relevant Efforts: Intelligent Tutoring Systems

Intelligent tutoring systems (ITSs) could be traced to the early 1970s. An ITS is an extension of computer-assisted instruction (CAI). SCHOLAR developed by Carbonell (1970) is believed to be the first intelligent tutoring system, although it claimed to be a new and powerful type of CAI at that time. The system is characterized by engaging students in writing dialogues (mixed-initiative dialogues) on South American geography.

Intelligent tutoring systems now are also called adaptive learning systems (Hwang, 2014). Adaptive learning systems are a new form of intelligent tutoring system. They are defined as educational programs that use intelligent technologies to provide learners with individualized instruction (Nwana, 1990). The new adaptive learning systems are more intelligent than the ITSs of the 1980s and 1990s. Early ITSs had a rather static knowledge of the domain, a limited set of misunderstandings, and a view of the learner limited to performance in a particular learning environment.

Traditional intelligent tutoring systems initially deliver information to individuals and provide immediate feedback indicating if the answer is correct or wrong. Further, it prompts individuals to probe knowledge by leading questions and inducing answers. An ITS is usually seen as an information delivery system (Graesser et al., 2001). For example, ANDES (Vanlehn et al., 2005) is a physics tutoring system that does not use natural language. Known as model-tracing tutors, ANDES and similar tutoring systems follow the learner's reasoning by comparing it to a trace of the model's reasoning, such an approach is called immediate feedback (Graesser et al., 2001).

During the earlier development of ITSs, it is worth noting that there was a shift from focusing on technology to focusing on pedagogy. For example, an ITS called PAT (which stands for PUMP Algebra Tutor or Practical Algebra Tutor) was created for solving practical algebra problems with a series of technologies like spreadsheets, graphs, and symbolic calculators (Koedinger et al., 1997). The notion of pedagogy and designing increasingly challenging problems entered the world of ITSs, as a result.

Subsequently, with the advancement of technology and pedagogy, more interactive factors were introduced to some traditional intelligent tutoring systems. Many intelligent tutoring systems were developed with conversational agents like AutoTutor, Why2-Atlas, and ITSPOKE. They were all designed for physics, via simulating human tutor, some of them also employed 3-D simulation, animated conversational agent, affect sensor, and spoken dialogue system, etc. (Graesser et al., 2005; Heffernan & Koedinger, 2002; Litman & Silliman, 2004; Sidney et al., 2005; VanLehn et al., 2002). The notion of a conversational interface is carried forward into the framework as a specific kind of pedagogical agent that has been shown to potentially impact learning.

The traditional intelligent systems had learners simply observe previously recorded interactive sessions as vicarious observers (Craig et al., 2004). Learners were not immediately engaged and, as a result, learner discrepancies and misunderstandings were not considered. The immediate feedback and hints were criticized for not being able to encourage deep learning (Graesser et al., 2001). Many studies therefore started to consider students' missteps along with learning styles and learning characteristics. Learning styles diagnosis and learning preferences detection were integrated and used to analyze and diagnose learners' behaviors (Cha et al.,

2006; Kelly & Tangney, 2002). With those attempts and efforts, ITSs have been increasingly adaptive. Meanwhile, enabled by mobile technologies, some mobile intelligent tutoring systems emerged (Kazi, 2005; Stockwell, 2007). Those adaptive learning systems thus adapt to not only a variety of learners but also multiagents in a wide variety of contexts and situations.

Nowadays thanks to the maturity of technologies, many efforts are focusing on the update or facilitation of technologies used for the realization of advanced pedagogical strategies (which might have been used before) and deep learning, such as intelligent conversational agent, adaptive support (Diziol et al., 2010), adaptive learning, personalized learning and affective consideration, autonomous data-driven decision-making (Koedinger et al., 2013; Latham et al., 2012). Besides, more innovative pedagogy is integrated in the systems as well, such as gaming (Millis et al., 2017).

Meanwhile, many countries have added twenty-first-century skills to their national education plans (e.g., China and the USA). One of those skills is critical thinking. The learning content intelligent tutoring systems involve changes as well. The learning content about higher level abilities especially focusing on deep learning is increasing, such as promoting children's strategic memory of expository texts and comprehension (e.g., Wijekumar et al., 2017), developing children's emotional intelligence (e.g., Fomichova & Fomichov, 2017), teaching children self-regulation strategies (e.g., Serrano et al., 2018), detecting learners' deep understanding (e.g., Sales & Pane, 2017), and so forth.

Owing to big data and neural network development, intelligent tutoring is moving to more intelligent adaptation to learners on a larger and broader scale (Aleven et al., 2018; Fenza et al., 2017; Kolchinski et al., 2018). Smart learning environments consist of two main components: (a) an intelligent tutoring system, and (b) context-aware technologies, including a conversational interface (Hwang, 2014). A smart learning environment must be able to adapt to a wide variety of learners providing them adaptive learning and personalized learning on a large sustainable scale (Spector, 2014).

Based on the review of previous efforts on intelligent tutoring systems, we propose a framework for developing critical thinking smart and systematically, especially on continuing inquiry and reasoning.

A Framework for a Smart Learning Environment

The framework (shown in Fig. 1) absorbed the concept of smart learning and embedded systematic development methods of critical thinking. It is conversational and characterized by personalized learning, adaptive learning, emotional support and is seamlessly interwoven with the real world. It provides children with critical thinking training in a series of steps internalizing critical thinking into a habit. The framework presents a conversational and interactive learning environment.

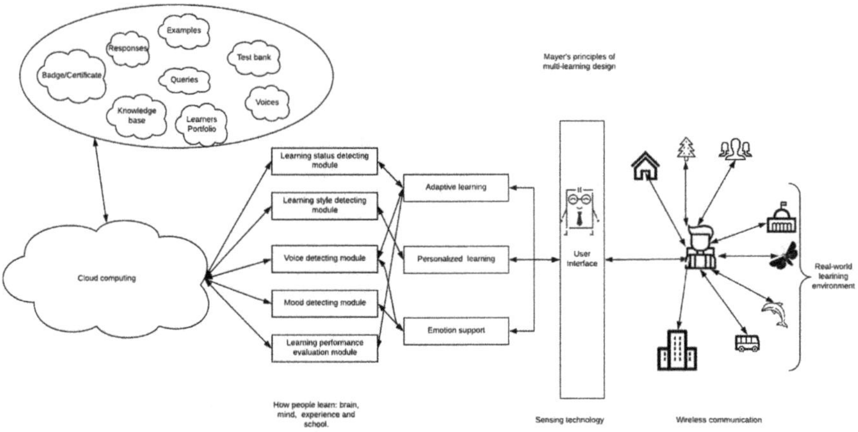

Fig. 1 Framework for a smart learning environment

For developing critical thinking systematically and effectively, the activities inside the framework are gamified and designed based on Spector's Nine phases for critical thinking development, which was first presented in a discussion paper at the 2018 International Big History Conference (Spector, 2018). Those principles are (1) Inquiry, observation, and puzzlement; (2) Exploration and hypothesis formation; (3) Evidence and hypothesis testing; (4) Influence and causality; (5) Explanation, communication, and collaboration; (6) Coherence and consistency; (7) Assumptions and biases; (8) Perspectives and alternatives; and (9) Reflection, refinement, and self-regulation. Each phase has its themes. The themes are across domains. Each phase indicates a level of critical thinking development. For motivating learners, incentive mechanisms are also employed. Once learners pass all the activities in one phase, they will be awarded with a badge or a certificate to congratulate them for reaching a new level.

However, for the purpose of this chapter, we mainly present one part, namely its technical system. For the success of learning, this framework requires innovative technologies, such as sensing technologies, wireless communication, learning analytics, cloud computing, speech identification, mood-detecting, etc.

One idea of this framework is to provide a companion for school children starting at least 1st grade (around 6 years old), provoking learners to think critically and develop their corresponding skills. The companion could be either a tutor or a tutee or a friend, which will be adapted based on learners' performance and their learning style or their own setting. The learner is also allowed to manually select which role to be a companion. But if the system is set on auto mode, acting as a tutor, a tutee, or a friend can be interchanged based on students' needs which is calculated through learning style, learning performance, and learning status (learning process). The system will adapt to learners at different ages for an appropriate companion and a proper learning mode, a default companion might be assigned. Whether the companion is male or female, young or old, child or adult, depends on learner's choice.

However, basically, for reaching an authentic level of smart learning, five modules are provided. That is, (1) Voice detecting module. This module is designed to identify learners' voice, age, and understand learners' queries. (2) Learning style detecting module. This module allows two ways of adjusting learner's learning style. One is to identify learner's learning style through a standardized test. If learners do not prefer to do a test, and the system can identify learner's learning style through human-technology interaction (e.g., queries and responses) with reference to learner's learning status and learning performance evaluation (Data-driven decision making). (3) Learning status detecting module. It monitors learners' engagement (active or inactive), learning stage of the learner (which level of critical thinking students is in). (4) Learning performance evaluation module. This module is designed for providing formative and summative evaluation. Learning performance in this app will be mainly decided by participation and progress learners made (e.g., levels or phases they finished, and time they spent). (5) Mood-detecting module (mood-detecting sensor). This module is designed to provide emotional support. First, this module is to identify learner's mood, initiate emotional support if the learner wants to talk, respond to children taking learners' mood into account. For example, If the learner sounds like he or she is in a depressed mood, the system's mode might change to emotional support by asking "Are you ok?" or "What happened?" or "You don't sound right." If the learner responses with "Nothing" or "I'm fine," then the system will continue the learning process. Otherwise, the system will initiate emotional support such as inviting children to talk and listen, under such a mode, the system helps the learner think from a different perspective (e.g., the opposite standing from his or hers).

Besides, the function mechanism of this framework is shown as follows: (1) Adaptive learning. Adaptive learning here specially means adjusting learning process with adjustable learning support and learning content for learners based on data-driven decision-making regarding learners' learning status, learning performance and mood detected. For example, adjusting responses based on learners' learning and mood situation. More hints or scaffoldings will be provided if learners continuously fail to solve problems in the learning activities. (2) Personalized learning. Personalized learning means providing learners with a proper theme and learning activities at a proper difficulty level based on learners "characteristics," such as learning style, age, and grade level. (3) Emotional support. Emotional support refers to leading learners to think positively and differently while they are in a low mood by listening, asking questions, or distracting them with interesting exploratory stories. Responses might vary in mood.

The framework proposed herein can result in multiple applications. Several are now already in prototype form as a result of a collaboration between the University of North Texas and NetDragon at the UNT NetDragon Digital Research Centre. The design of applications using this framework can be based on Mayer's twelve principles of multimedia learning design (Mayer, 2014), such as the personalization principle – "people learn better from multimedia lessons when words are in conversational style rather than formal style" (p. 394).

The applications now under development using this framework start with the early phases of observation inquiry indicated by Spector (2018). For example, the learner can be presented with a small collection of very different rocks including some gemstones and one with an embedded fossil. The learner is asked to pick two that are similar. Whichever ones the learner selects, the system simply asks, "Why did you pick those?" Any answer is acceptable and not probed further unless it is unclear. The learner is then prompted to pick two more that are somewhat similar. Again, whatever is selected is fine and the learner is asked why he or she picked those. Again, any answer is acceptable. At some point, the learner is asked to pick one that is different than the others. As before, the learner is asked how that one is different, and any answer is okay. Eventually, the learner will pick the rock with the fossil. This time the interaction is more challenging as the learner may not know what a fossil is or how it became embedded in the rock. At that point, the system becomes a more knowledgeable other (see Vygotsky, 1978). The system can tell the learner that it is a fossil of a sea creature that died, and the remains became embedded in the rock over a long period of time. Moreover, that rock with the embedded sea creature was found about several thousand meters above sea level (Gould, 1989). The system can then ask a very challenging question, such as "How do you suppose this rock with the embedded sea creature came to be thousands of meters above sea level?" That question can take the learner to higher levels in the nine-phase model, such as explanation and a search for evidence and eventually hypothesis formulation and testing.

An existing prototype created by NetDragon uses virtual reality to engage the learner as an observer watching a game being played in India. The observer does not speak the language of the players and is wondering how the winner is determined. The observer can ask a friend who has a book of games but the game being observed is not in the book. The observer can ask another friend for an opinion on how the winner is determined. No luck with that query either. The learner is then prompted to walk around the players and get an alternative perspective. Eventually, the learner is prompted to sit down in the circle with the players and happens to see a fly land on one player's coin and that play yells "Hai" and is determined to be the winner (Nielsen, 1972). More applications are under development, as is a game to test critical thinking skills based on a subset of Cornell Critical Thinking Test (Ennis, 1985).

Conclusion

This study reviewed the early development of critical thinking teaching and its theories. Three approaches of teaching, pedagogy-focused, technology-focused, and technology-enhanced, to some extent, represent the evolution of technology. Many empirical studies have proven that technology-enhanced instruction is more effective and is superior to traditional instruction in terms of cost-effectiveness, flexibility, and personalization (Dodds & Fletcher, 2004). The emergence of context-aware ubiquitous learning indicates another revolution of teaching and learning methods.

It brings the attention of education back to previous effective teaching methods advocated by Confucius, Socrates, Dewey, Piaget, etc. It can maximize human beings' learning potential. It provides learners with more opportunities to practice and learn in real-world situations while still enjoy the convenience and flexibility brought by technology. Learners could apply their knowledge in real time.

Although smart learning is enabled by innovative technology, the teaching and learning methods might need to concern that how technology is used rather than what technology is used per se. The relationship between technology and pedagogy should be appropriately addressed. Technology should serve for the pedagogy of the subjects or topics it's employed for.

Different from other subjects or topics, critical thinking is not about facts or obvious knowledge, it is a collection of thinking skills and dispositions (Facione, 1998; Paul & Elder, 2005). It leads to the mastery of content and deep learning. Its development takes time and effort. Technologies, including new devices and sophisticated software, are tools that have the potential to support learning and help young people develop productive habits of mind.

In this chapter, a basic perspective includes the belief that what matters is not the technology but the learning; what matters is not the technology but the use of technology in support of learning.

References

Aleven, V., Sewall, J., Andres, J. M., Sottilare, R., Long, R., & Baker, R. (2018, June). Towards adapting to learners at scale: Integrating MOOC and intelligent tutoring frameworks. *Proceedings of the Fifth Annual ACM Conference on Learning at Scale*. Retrieved from http://www.upenn.edu/learninganalytics/ryanbaker/LS2018GIFT.pdf

Allen, A. (2018). Teach like Socrates: Encouraging critical thinking in elementary social studies. *Social Studies and the Young Learner, 31*(1), 4–10.

Anderson, R. D. (2002). Reforming science teaching: What research says about inquiry. *Journal of science teacher education, 13*(1), 1–12.

Aristotle (350BCE). *Posterior analytics*. Retrieved from http://classics.mit.edu/Aristotle/posterior.html

Barrow, L. H. (2006). A brief history of inquiry: From Dewey to standards. *Journal of Science Teacher Education, 17*(3), 265–278.

Barrows, H. S., & Tamblyn, R. (1980). *Problem-based learning: An approach to medical education*. Springer.

Carbonell, J. R. (1970). AI in CAI: An artificial-intelligence approach to computer-assisted instruction. *IEEE transactions on man-machine systems, 11*(4), 190–202.

Cha, H. J., Kim, Y. S., Park, S. H., Yoon, T. B., Jung, Y. M., & Lee, J. H. (2006, June). Learning styles diagnosis based on user interface behaviors for the customization of learning interfaces in an intelligent tutoring system. In *International Conference on Intelligent Tutoring Systems* (pp. 513–524). Springer. Retrieved from https://www.researchgate.net/publication/221413956_Learning_Styles_Diagnosis_Based_on_User_Interface_Behaviors_for_the_Customization_of_Learning_Interfaces_in_an_Intelligent_Tutoring_System

Chiu, Y. C. J. (2009). Facilitating Asian students' critical thinking in online discussions. *British Journal of Educational Technology, 40*(1), 42–57. https://doi.org/10.1111/j.1467-8535.2008.00898.x

Craig, S. D., Driscoll, D. M., & Gholson, B. (2004). Constructing knowledge from dialog in an intelligent tutoring system: Interactive learning, vicarious learning, and pedagogical agents. *Journal of Educational Multimedia and Hypermedia, 13*(2), 163–183.

Descartes, R. (1637). *Discourse on the method of rightly conducting the reason, and seeking truth in the sciences*. Retrieved from https://www.gutenberg.org/files/59/59-h/59-h.htm

Dewey, J. (1910a). Science as subject-matter and as method. *Science, 31*, 121–127.

Dewey, J. (1910b). *How we think*. Retrieved from http://www.gutenberg.org/files/37423/37423-h/37423-h.htm

Dewey, J. (1916). Method in science teaching. *The Science Quarterly, 1*, 3–9.

Dewey, J. (1938). *Experience and education*. Collier Books.

Dewey, J. (1944). *Democracy and education*. Free Press.

Diziol, D., Walker, E., Rummel, N., & Koedinger, K. R. (2010). Using intelligent tutor technology to implement adaptive support for student collaboration. *Educational Psychology Review, 22*(1), 89–102.

Dodds, P., & Fletcher, J. D. (2004). Opportunities for new "smart" learning environments enabled by next-generation web capabilities. *Journal of Educational Multimedia and Hypermedia, 13*(4), 391–404. Norfolk, VA: Association for the Advancement of Computing in Education (AACE). Retrieved from https://www.learntechlib.org/primary/p/6583/

Elder, L., & Paul, R. (1998). Critical thinking: Developing intellectual traits. *Journal of developmental education, 21*(3), 34.

Ennis, R. H. (1985). A logical basis for measuring critical thinking skills. *Educational leadership, 43*(2), 44–48. Retrieved from https://jgregorymcverry.com/readings/ennis1985assessingcriticalthinking.pdf

Espey, M. (2018). Enhancing critical thinking using team-based learning. *Higher Education Research & Development, 37*(1), 15–29. https://doi.org/10.1080/07294360.2017.1344196

Facione, P. A. (1998). *Critical thinking: What it is and why it counts. Insight assessment*. Retrieved September 9, 2020 from https://www.insightassessment.com/Resources/Importance-of-Critical-Thinking/Critical-Thinking-What-It-Is-and-Why-It-Counts

Fenza, G., Orciuoli, F., & Sampson, D. G. (2017, July). Building adaptive tutoring model using artificial neural networks and reinforcement learning. In *Advanced Learning Technologies (ICALT)*, 2017 IEEE 17th International Conference on (pp. 460-462). IEEE. July 3-7, 2017, Timisoara, Romania. Retrieved from https://ieeexplore.ieee.org/document/8001832

Fomichova, O. S., & Fomichov, V. A. (2017). The Methods of cognitonics as the basis for designing intelligent tutoring systems developing emotional intelligence of the learners. In Informacijska druzba-IS 2017. *Proceedings of the 20th International Multiconference-IS 2017*, Edited by VA Fomichov, OS Fomichova. Vol. Kognitonika/Cognitonics. October 9-10, 2017, Ljubljana, Slovenia.

Garrison, D. R., Anderson, T., & Archer, W. (1999). Critical inquiry in a text-based environment: Computer conferencing in higher education. *The internet and higher education, 2*(2-3), 87–105. https://doi.org/10.1016/S1096-7516(00)00016-6

Gould, S. J. (1989). *Wonderful life. The Burgess shale and the nature of history*. W. W. Noryton.

Godfrey-Smith, P. (2003). *Theory and reality: An introduction to the philosophy of science*. Chicago University Press.

Gold, J., Holman, D., & Thorpe, R. (2002). The role of argument analysis and story telling in facilitating critical thinking. *Management Learning, 33*(3), 371–388. https://doi.org/10.1177/1350507602333005

Graesser, A. C., Chipman, P., Haynes, B. C., & Olney, A. (2005). AutoTutor: An intelligent tutoring system with mixed-initiative dialogue. *IEEE Transactions on Education, 48*(4), 612–618. https://doi.org/10.1109/TE.2005.856149

Graesser, A. C., VanLehn, K., Rosé, C. P., Jordan, P. W., & Harter, D. (2001). Intelligent tutoring systems with conversational dialogue. *AI magazine, 22*(4), 39. https://doi.org/10.1609/aimag.v22i4.1591

Halpern, D. F., Millis, K., Graesser, A. C., Butler, H., Forsyth, C., & Cai, Z. (2012). Operation ARA: A computerized learning game that teaches critical thinking and scientific reasoning. *Thinking Skills and Creativity, 7*(2), 93–100. https://doi.org/10.1016/j.tsc.2012.03.006

Heffernan, N. T., & Koedinger, K. R. (2002, June). An intelligent tutoring system incorporating a model of an experienced human tutor. In *International Conference on Intelligent Tutoring Systems* (pp. 596–608). Springer.

Huang, M. Y., Tu, H. Y., Wang, W. Y., Chen, J. F., Yu, Y. T., & Chou, C. C. (2017). Effects of cooperative learning and concept mapping intervention on critical thinking and basketball skills in elementary school. *Thinking Skills and Creativity, 23*, 207–216. https://doi.org/10.1016/j.tsc.2017.01.002

Hwang, G. J. (2014). Definition, framework and research issues of smart learning environments-a context-aware ubiquitous learning perspective. *Smart Learning Environments, 1*(4) Retrieved from https://slejournal.springeropen.com/articles/10.1186/s40561-014-0004-5

Hwang, G. J., Tsai, C. C., & Yang, S. J. (2008). Criteria, strategies and research issues of context-aware ubiquitous learning. *Journal of Educational Technology & Society, 11*(2), 81–91. Retrieved from http://citeseerx.ist.psu.edu/viewdoc/download?doi=10.1.1.525.5729&rep=rep1&type=pdf

Ikuenobe, P. (2001). Questioning as an epistemic process of critical thinking. *Educational Philosophy and Theory, 33*(3-4), 325–341. https://doi.org/10.1111/j.1469-5812.2001.tb00274.x

Jahn, D., & Kenner, A. (2018). Critical thinking in higher education: How to foster it using digital media. In *The digital turn in higher education* (pp. 81–109). Springer.

Jonassen, D. H. (1999). *Computers as mindtools for schools, engaging critical thinking*. Prentice Hall. Retrieved from https://itlab.us/forgetting/learning_mindtools.pdf

Jowett, B. (1982). *The dialogues of Plato* [Tr. B. Jowett]. Oxford Clarendon Press.

Kazi, S. A. (2005). *VocaTest: An intelligent tutoring system for vocabulary learning using the "mLearning" approach.* Retrieved from http://hdl.handle.net/10497/217

Kelly, D., & Tangney, B. (2002, June). Incorporating learning characteristics into an intelligent tutor. In *International Conference on Intelligent Tutoring Systems* (pp. 729–738). Springer.

King, A. (1995). Inquiring minds really do want to know: Using questioning to teach critical thinking. *Teaching of Psychology, 22*(1), 13–17. https://doi.org/10.1207/s15328023top2201_5

Kinshuk, D., Chen, N. S., Cheng, I. L., & Chew, S. W. (2016). Evolution is not enough: Revolutionizing current learning environments to smart learning environments. *International Journal of Artificial Intelligence in Education, 26*(2), 561–581. Retrieved from https://link.springer.com/content/pdf/10.1007/s40593-016-0108-x.pdf

Koedinger, K. R., Anderson, J. R., Hadley, W. H., & Mark, M. A. (1997). Intelligent tutoring goes to school in the big city. *International Journal of Artificial Intelligence in Education, 8*, 30–43.

Koedinger, K. R., Brunskill, E., Baker, R. S., McLaughlin, E. A., & Stamper, J. (2013). New potentials for data-driven intelligent tutoring system development and optimization. *AI Magazine, 34*(3), 27–41. https://doi.org/10.1609/aimag.v34i3.2484

Kolchinski, Y. A., Ruan, S., Schwartz, D., & Brunskill, E. (2018, June). Adaptive natural-language targeting for student feedback. In *Proceedings of the Fifth Annual ACM Conference on Learning at Scale* (p. 26), June 26-28, 2018. ACM. Retrieved from https://cs.stanford.edu/people/ebrun/papers/las_2018_nlp_bandits.pdf

Latham, A., Crockett, K., McLean, D., & Edmonds, B. (2012). A conversational intelligent tutoring system to automatically predict learning styles. *Computers & Education, 59*(1), 95–109. https://doi.org/10.1016/j.compedu.2011.11.001

Lee, H., Parsons, D., Kwon, G., Kim, J., Petrova, K., Jeong, E., & Ryu, H. (2016). Cooperation begins: encouraging critical thinking skills through cooperative reciprocity using a mobile learning game. *Computers & Education, 97*, 97–115. https://doi.org/10.1016/j.compedu.2016.03.006

Litman, D. J., & Silliman, S. (2004, May). ITSPOKE: An intelligent tutoring spoken dialogue system. In *Demonstration papers at HLT-NAACL* 2004 (pp. 5–8). Association for Computational Linguistics. Retrieved from https://

pdfs.semanticscholar.org/31d0/bd925fb2e517456edf03d9fa8cc20f73e9e7.pdf?_ga=2.160933822.2068405420.1560433439-540057680.1560433439

Mayer, R. E. (2014). Multimedia instruction. In J. M. Spector, M. D. Merrill, J. Elen, & M. J. Bishop (Eds.), *Handbook of research on educational communications and technology* (pp. 385–399). Springer. Retrieved from https://link.springer.com/chapter/10.1007/978-1-4614-3185-5_31

Millis, K., Forsyth, C., Wallace, P., Graesser, A. C., & Timmins, G. (2017). The impact of game-like features on learning from an intelligent tutoring system. *Technology, Knowledge and Learning, 22*(1), 1–22.

Mishra, P., & Koehler, M. J. (2006). Technological pedagogical content knowledge: A new framework for teacher knowledge. *Teachers College Record., 108*(6), 1017–1054.

National Research Council. (2000). *Inquiry and the national science education standards: A guide for teaching and learning*. National Academies Press.

Nielsen, H. A. (1972). A game of India. *Michigan Quarterly Review, 36*, 111–115. Retrieved from https://quod.lib.umich.edu/m/mqrarchive/act2080.0011.002/44:7?g=mqrg;rgn=full+text;view=image;xc=1;q1=game+of+india

Nwana, H. S. (1990). Intelligent tutoring systems: an overview. *Artificial Intelligence Review, 4*(4), 251–277. Retrieved from http://www.inf.ufpr.br/andrey/ci304/ITS_overview.pdf

Onosko, J. J. (1991). Barriers to the promotion of higher-order thinking in social studies. *Theory & Research in Social Education, 19*(4), 341–366.

Paepcke-Hjeltness, V., Mina, M., & Cyamani, A. (2017, October). Sketchnoting: A new approach to developing visual communication ability, improving critical thinking and creative confidence for engineering and design students. In *IEEE Frontiers in Education Conference (FIE)* (pp. 1-5). Retrieved from https://www.researchgate.net/publication/321170475_Sketchnoting_A_new_approach_to_developing_visual_communication_ability_improving_critical_thinking_and_creative_confidence_for_engineering_and_design_students

Paul, R., & Elder, L. (2005). *Critical thinking competency standards*. Foundation for Critical Thinking.

Paul, R., & Elder, L. (2006). *The thinker's guide to the art of Socratic questioning*. Foundation for Critical Thinking.

Popper, K. R. (1963). *Conjectures and refutations: The growth of scientific knowledge*. Routledge & Kegan Paul.

Rashid, S., & Qaisar, S. (2017). Role play: A productive teaching strategy to promote critical thinking. *Bulletin of Education and Research, 39*(2).

Sales, A. C., & Pane, J. F. (2017). The role of mastery learning in intelligent tutoring systems: Principal stratification on a latent variable. *The Annals of Applied Statistics, 13*(1), 420–433.

Schön, D. A. (1983). *The reflective practitioner: How professionals think in action*. Basic Books.

Serrano, M. Á., Vidal-Abarca, E., & Ferrer, A. (2018). Teaching self-regulation strategies via an intelligent tutoring system (TuinLECweb): Effects for low-skilled comprehenders. *Journal of Computer Assisted Learning, 34*(5) Retrieved from https://onlinelibrary.wiley.com/doi/full/10.1111/jcal.12256

Sidney, K. D., Craig, S. D., Gholson, B., Franklin, S., Picard, R., & Graesser, A. C. (2005). Integrating affect sensors in an intelligent tutoring system. In *Affective interactions: The computer in the affective loop workshop at the international conference on intelligent user interfaces*. Retrieved from http://people.cs.pitt.edu/~litman/courses/ads/readings/iui-sdmello2.pdf

Shailey, M., Steve, T. & Ana-Despina, T. (2018). Role of virtual reality in geography and science fieldwork education. In: *Knowledge* Exchange Seminar Series, Learning from New Technology, 25 Apr 2018, Belfast. Retrieved from http://oro.open.ac.uk/55876/1/ORO-KESS-Paper-in-Template-25April2018-FINAL-Submitted.pdf

Spector, J. M. (2018, July). *Thinking and learning in the Anthropocene: The new 3 Rs*. Discussion paper presented at the International Big History Association Conference, Philadelphia, PA, July 29, 2018. Retrieved from http://learndev.org/dl/HLA-IBHA2018/Spector%2C%20J.%20M.%20(2018).%20Thinking%20and%20Learning%20in%20the%20Anthropocene.pdf

Spector, J. M. (2014). Conceptualizing the emerging field of smart learning environments. *Smart learning environments, 1*(1), 2.
Stockwell, G. (2007). Vocabulary on the move: Investigating an intelligent mobile phone-based vocabulary tutor. *Computer Assisted Language Learning, 20*(4), 365–383. https://doi.org/10.1080/09588220701745817
VanLehn, K., Jordan, P. W., Rosé, C. P., Bhembe, D., Böttner, M., Gaydos, A., ... & Siler, S. (2002, June). The architecture of Why2-Atlas: A coach for qualitative physics essay writing. *International conference on intelligent tutoring systems* (pp. 158-167). Springer. Retrieved from https://link.springer.com/content/pdf/10.1007%2F3-540-47987-2.pdf
Vanlehn, K., Lynch, C., Schulze, K., Shapiro, J. A., Shelby, R., Taylor, L., ... Wintersgill, M. (2005). The Andes physics tutoring system: Lessons learned. *International Journal of Artificial Intelligence in Education, 15*(3), 147–204.
Vygotsky, L. (1978). *Mind in society: The development of higher psychological processes*. Harvard University Press. Retrieved from http://ouleft.org/wp-content/uploads/Vygotsky-Mind-in-Society.pdf
Wijekumar, K., Meyer, B. J., Lei, P., Cheng, W., Ji, X., & Joshi, R. M. (2017). Evidence of an intelligent tutoring system as a mindtool to promote strategic memory of expository texts and comprehension with children in grades 4 and 5. *Journal of Educational Computing Research, 55*(7), 1022–1048.
Yang, Y. T. C., Newby, T. J., & Bill, R. L. (2005). Using Socratic questioning to promote critical thinking skills through asynchronous discussion forums in distance learning environments. *The American Journal of Distance Education, 19*(3), 163–181. https://doi.org/10.1207/s15389286ajde1903_4

Shanshan MA, a doctoral graduate at University of North Texas with abundant experience in international cooperation. She is a Learning Technology Consultant at the San Diego State University. She has been cooperating with professors and research associates with different backgrounds from several countries (e.g., the USA, China, India, and the UK). Her research interests include technology-supported teaching and learning strategies, educational technology design, learning technology integration theory, game-based learning, and instructional design. Her recent research focuses on critical thinking development in K-12 education and critical thinking teaching integration competence in teachers. She is a reviewer for several research journals, such as the Journal of Smart Learning Environments, Computers in Human Behavior, and Contemporary Issues in Technology and Teacher Education (Science), and she is also a member of several professional associations including Association for Education Communication Technology (AECT) and American Education Research Association (AERA), and Texas Center Education Technology (TCET). She presented at several international conferences and one workshop funded by NSF, held and co-held several seminars, published several research articles.

J. Michael Spector, Professor at UNT, was previously Professor of Educational Psychology at the University of Georgia, Associate Director of the Learning Systems Institute at Florida State University, Chair of Instructional Design, Development and Evaluation at Syracuse University, and Director of the Educational Information Science and Technology Research Program at the University of Bergen. He earned a Ph.D. from The University of Texas. He is a visiting research professor at Beijing Normal University, at East China Normal University, and the Indian Institute of Technology Kharagpur. His research focuses on assessing learning in complex domains, inquiry and critical thinking skills, and program evaluation. He was Executive Director of the International Board of Standards for Training, Performance and Instruction and a Past-president of the Association for Educational and Communications Technology. He is Editor Emeritus of *Educational Technology Research & Development*; he edited two editions of the *Handbook of Research on Educational Communications and Technology* and the *SAGE Encyclopedia of Educational Technology* and more that 150 publications to his credit.

Dejian Liu is the inventor of Disciplined Design Methodology. He is the founder of NetDragon Websoft Holding Ltd., one of the most successful online gaming companies in China. NetDragon Websoft was listed on Hong Kong Stock Exchange in 2007. In 2015, Liu awarded the Special Allowance Expert in China's State Council. Under his leadership, NetDragon has brought its products to more than 180 countries in ten languages, enjoying over 65 million registered oversea users. In 2013, NetDragon announced the sale of its 91 Weireless to Baidu for 1.9 billion USD, which is the largest M&A transaction in China's Internet history at the time. In 2010, Liu founded Huayu Education, a wholly owned subsidiary of NetDragon. Huayu integrates worldwide cutting-edge education resources with leading mobile internet technology. Huayu specializes in K-12 and lifelong education for learners all over the world. Huayu Education recently earned a Smart Media Award from Academics' Choice for producing a top-quality product, 101 Education, which improves teachers' experience in preparing lessons. Liu is certified as a senior engineer by the China Association of Science and Technology, the highest level of proficiency awarded. He is co-dean and chair of the Council for the Smart Learning Institute at Beijing Normal University, and he is also invited as Adjunct Lecturer of Harvard Graduate School of Education, co-teaching a course on Next Generation Design: Methods and Heuristics with Professor Chris Dede.

Kaushal Kumar Bhagat is an Assistant Professor in the Centre for Educational Technology at Indian Institute of Technology Kharagpur, India. He received his PhD in educational technology from National Taiwan Normal University. He has published several highly cited journal articles and book chapters. Dr. Bhagat was presented NTNU International Outstanding Achievement Award. He was awarded 2018 IEEE TCLT Young Researcher award. His research areas of interest include online learning, augmented reality, virtual reality, mathematics education, flipped classroom, formative assessment, and technology-enhanced learning. He is an associate editor for British Journal of Educational Technology (https://onlinelibrary.wiley.com/journal/14678535) and the Editor-in-Chief for Contemporary Educational Technology (https://www.cedtech.net/).

Dawit Tibebu Tiruneh is a Research Associate in the Faculty of Education at the University of Cambridge. He is a member of the RISE Ethiopia research program and collaborates with an interdisciplinary and international team of researchers to understand how Ethiopia's nationwide quality education form is designed and implemented to improve learning outcomes for the marginalised. He completed his PhD at the Faculty of Psychology and Educational Sciences of the University of Leuven, Belgium. His main research interests include educational access and equity, school effectiveness, and instructional design. He publishes in renowned international journals in the field of instructional design and technology. Before joining the University of Cambridge, he was a lecture in the Faculty of Education at Bahir Dar University, Ethiopia.

Jonah Mancini is a private consultant in digital application design and development at Round Rock, US.

Lin Lin is a Professor at the Department of Learning Technologies at the University of North Texas, and the Director of Texas Center for Educational Technology. She completed her EdD at the Columbia University. Dr. Lin's research looks into intersections of mind, brain, technology and learning. Specifically, she has published in areas including creativity, virtual reality, media multitasking, multimedia design, CSCL, critical thinking, computational thinking, and learning in virtual spaces. Lin currently serves as the Director for the Texas Center for Educational Technology (TCET), and as the Development Editor-in-Chief of the journal Educational Technology Research and Development (ETR&D, http://www.springer.com/11423). She also plays several other leadership roles in affiliated professional associations. Lin is passionate about helping people develop and maintain curious minds and life-long learning with cognitive exercises and new technologies.

Rodney Nielsen is an Associate Professor at the College of Engineering at the University of North Texas. Dr. Nielsen's research is primarily in the areas of Natural Language Processing, Machine Learning, and Cognitive Science, with an emphasis on Educational Technology, Health & Clinical Informatics, and their confluence – Educational Health & Wellbeing Companion Robots. He is currently researching emotive, perceptive, spoken-dialogue companion robots, in the form of stuffed animals, to assist the elderly and isolated in need of special care. Such Companionbots might help seniors maintain their independence and continue to live in their homes. Dr. Nielsen is also inventing the future of classroom education with human language technology that facilitates a teacher's real-time understanding of the students' ongoing subject comprehension. He has developed machine learning algorithms to recognize elementary school students' understanding of science concepts when interacting with Intelligent Tutoring Systems, and is developing an end-to-end question answering and data mining system for clinical informatics. He has researched computational models for recognizing textual entailment, labeling semantic roles (predicate argument structure) in text, and estimating class probabilities in machine learning, among other things. He also has an extensive background in software engineering, including research in the areas of software re-engineering environments, operations research, automated software testing, and automatic code generation.

Dr. Kinshuk is the Dean of the College of Information at the University of North Texas. Prior to that, he held the NSERC/CNRL/Xerox/McGraw Hill Research Chair for Adaptivity and Personalization in Informatics, funded by the Federal government of Canada, Provincial government of Alberta, and by national and international industries. He was also Full Professor in the School of Computing and Information Systems and Associate Dean of the Faculty of Science and Technology, at Athabasca University, Canada. After completing his first degree from India, he earned his Masters' degree from Strathclyde University (Glasgow) and PhD from De Montfort University (Leicester), United Kingdom. His work has been dedicated to advancing research on the innovative paradigms, architectures, and implementations of online and distance learning systems for individualized and adaptive learning in increasingly global environments. Areas of his research interests include learning analytics; learning technologies; mobile, ubiquitous and location aware learning systems; cognitive profiling; and interactive technologies.

A Corpus of Biology Analogy Questions as a Challenge for Explainable AI

Vinay K. Chaudhri, Justin Xu, Han Lin Aung, and Sajana Weerawardhena

Introduction

Classical artificial intelligence systems that use rule-based knowledge representation exhibit strengths in their ability to explain their computations (Chaudhri et al., 2014a). The rule-based representation is multifunctional as the same representation can be used for multiple tasks such as question answering and question generation. *KB Bio 101* is a rule-based knowledge base curated from a biology textbook (Chaudhri et al., 2014b).

One objection to *KB Bio 101* is that it was hand crafted through knowledge engineering by biology experts, which was an enormous and expensive undertaking. To better understand the strengths and weaknesses of a hand-crafted knowledge base, we consider the task of answering analogy questions of the form "A is to B as C is to what?" The task of answering such questions has also been known as the *relational similarity* task (Gentner, 1983; Turney, 2008). The relational similarity task is of much broader interest in many different fields, such as psychology, linguistics, and cognitive science. In biology, there are many relationships between different concepts and relational similarity questions enable student learning.

The relational similarity task has also been used for evaluating the performance of word embeddings (Pennington et al., 2014). Our work on the analogy questions with *KB Bio 101* has frequently faced the criticism that such questions can be easily answered using word embeddings that can be computed by automatically processing the text. A standard example to illustrate the questions answerable using word embeddings is: A king is to a man as a queen is to what? The answer to this question is "woman." This question fits the template of the analogy questions leading many

V. K. Chaudhri (✉) · J. Xu · H. L. Aung · S. Weerawardhena
Computer Science, Stanford University, Stanford, CA, USA
e-mail: vinayc@stanford.edu

M. V. Albert et al. (eds.), *Bridging Human Intelligence and Artificial Intelligence*, Educational Communications and Technology: Issues and Innovations, https://doi.org/10.1007/978-3-030-84729-6_23

to believe that answering such questions is a solved problem. As no data currently exist to prove or disprove such a claim, in this chapter, we compare the performance of a relational similarity reasoning method operating on *KB Bio 101* to several methods to perform the same task that are based on word embeddings. We evaluate several off-the-shelf word embedding methods such as `GloVe` (Pennington et al., 2014), fastText (Bojanowski et al., 2016), and `ELMo` (Peters et al., 2018a). As some of the relational similarity examples have multiword phrases, we also investigate the use of `Seq2Seq` and `Seq2Vec` models (Kim et al., 2015; Peters et al. 2018b). Our results provide a baseline comparison between the performance of a hand-crafted knowledge base and automatically built word embeddings for the relational similarity task. We believe this to be one of the first insightful comparisons to better understand the strengths and weaknesses of hand-built knowledge representations in relation to automatically computed word embeddings on the same task.

As none of the current methods based on word embeddings can explain its answers, the corpus of questions that we provide here can serve as a data set for developing explainable methods. We are driven by the belief that any representation that can be built automatically should be built automatically, and yet, we need to better understand the limits of such representations. Automatically built representations have limits because, in many cases, the relevant knowledge is implicit and is not made explicit by the authors of the text. Such knowledge can be made explicit only during knowledge engineering. We hope to shed some light on the tradeoff between automatically built representations and curated *KB Bio 101*.

A Corpus of Biology Analogy Questions

We created a corpus of analogy questions by crawling different semantic relationships in *KB Bio 101*. Consider an example of an analogy based on *subclass of* relationship: phospholipid is to lipid as margarine is to what? Here phospholipid is a *subclass of* lipid, and as margarine is a *subclass of* fat, fat is one possible correct answer. The range of questions covered in the first release of our corpus is shown in Fig. 1. Each analogy question was generated by following the semantic relationship shown in the first column. The number of questions generated for each category is somewhat arbitrary at this stage and is based on a parameter given to the question generator. The parameter was chosen based on the number of relationships of each kind available in *KB Bio 101*. We hope to adjust this parameter depending on the feedback we get from any users of this question corpus.

Let us consider the definition of the semantic relationships considered for each type of analogy. A more detailed discussion on the meaning of these relationships can be found elsewhere (Chaudhri et al., 2013) (Table 1).

Given an entity *X* and another entity *Y* such that *Y* is considered a structure of *X*, we say that (1) *X has-region Y* if *Y* is a region of space or a *Spatial-Entity* defined in relation to *X*. (2) *X material Y* if *Y* is an *Entity* and is pervasive in *X*. *Y* is usually a mass term in this case. (3) *X* is an *element of Y* if *Y* is a set of similar entities that *Y*

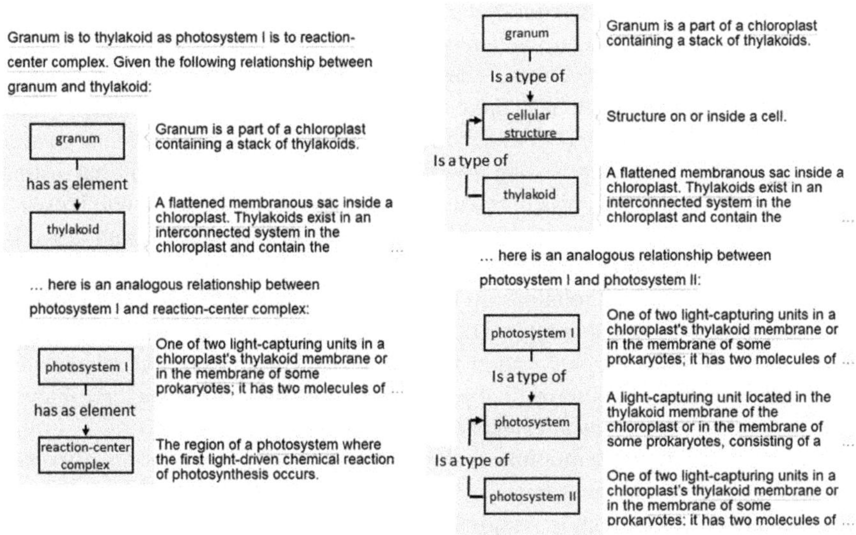

Fig. 1 An example question with answer in two different analogy categories

Table 1 Questions covered in the Biology Analogy Corpus

Type of Analogy	Count	Example Question	Answer
subclass-of	19999	Phospholipid is to a lipid as margarine is to what?	Fat
has-part	19995	Chloroplast is to a granum as mitochondrion is to what?	Ribosome
has-region	20001	Phospholipid is to a fatty acid tail as polar amino acid is to what?	polar side chain
possesses	20000	ATP synthase is to a peptide linkage as oligosaccharide is to what?	glycosidic linkage
element	4989	Granum is to a thylakoid as photo system I is to what?	Light-harvesting complex
is-inside	4999	Aquaporin is to phospholipid bilayer as stroma is to what?	Chloroplast
has-function	9986	Chloroplast is to photosynthesis as lysosome is to what?	Autophagy

is an instance of. (4) *X possesses Y* if *Y* is Energy, Bond or Gradient. (5) If none of the above applies, *X has-part Y*. *Y* must be a *Physical-Entity,* and it should be a countable noun.

The *is-inside* relationship corresponds to the well-known topological containment relationship (Bennett et al., 2013). When we say that an entity *X* is *is-inside* entity *Y*, we mean that *X* is fully contained in *Y*.

An entity *X* has a *has-function Y* if *Y* would be an answer to the question: What is the function of X? The *has-function* is a primitive relationship that is assigned by a biologist to an entity based on the consensus functions of that entity.

An analogy question can have more than one correct answer. For example, consider the question: Granum is to thylakoid as photosystem I is to what? One answer to this question is light-harvesting complex. Both thylakoid and light-harvesting complex are related by an *element* relationship to granum and photosystem I respectively. Another answer to this question is photosystem II because granum is a *subclass-of* cellular structure, and photosystem I is a *subclass-of* photosystem creating an analogous *subclass-of* relationship between the two. These analogical relationships are shown through a graphical output as seen in Fig. 1. The graphical visualization also serves as an explanation for why a particular analogical relationship was returned. Such a question will appear in both the *subclass-of* category of questions as well as in the *element* category of questions.

As another example of multiple analogous relationships, consider the question: phospholipid is to fatty acid tail as polar amino acid is to what? There is a *has-region* relationship between a phospholipid and a fatty acid tail that is analogous to the same relationship between amino acid and polar side chain. But, as seen in Fig. 2, phospholipid *has-part* a fatty acid which is *enclosed in* a fatty acid tail. Analogously, a polar amino acid *has-part* a carbon atom that is *enclosed in* a carbon skeleton. (Here, *enclosed in* is an inverse of the *is-inside* relation.) This example illustrates that the analogous relationship chains are not limited to a single relationship and can contain relationships of multiple different kinds.

The complete question set and the graphical explanations are available upon request. The current dataset has 77,654 analogy questions from which 2154 questions involve concepts with names consisting of a single word.

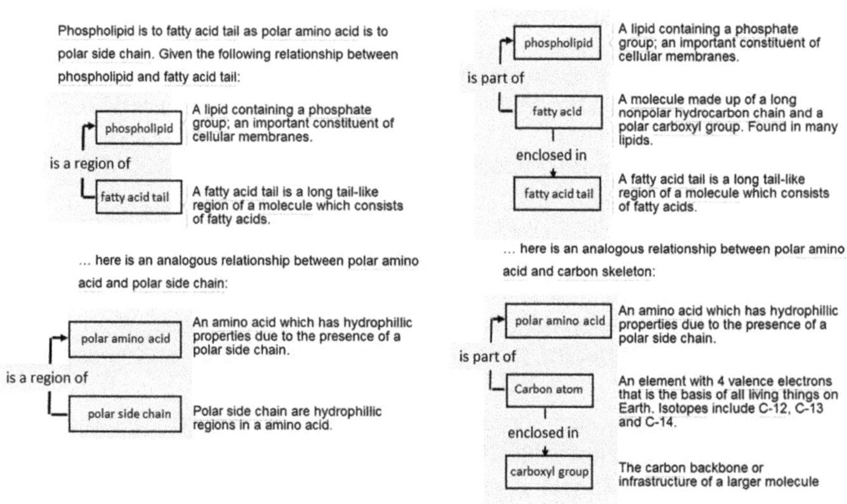

Fig. 2 An example question with analogies that contain different relationships in the explanation

For training the word embeddings, we used the raw text from the LIFE Biology textbook that has around 30,000 sentences (Sadava et al., 2017). We also incorporated several open-source biology textbooks from OpenStax (http://openstax.org). While the OpenStax textbooks are openly available, the LIFE textbook corpus is available from us under a research use license.

Approach

To solve the analogical reasoning question template, "A is to B as C is to what", we developed a model that accepts A, B, and C as input and produces the desired answer D as an output. Each of A, B, C, and D can be either a single word or a short phrase. In some cases, the predicted word D can also be unknown denoted by UNK.

Existing word embedding models such as `GloVe` and `fastText` operate only on single words, and therefore, are not capable of solving those instances of analogy questions that involve a multiword phrase. It was still interesting for us to obtain a baseline result on the performance of `GloVe` and `fastText` on the single word analogy task. Therefore, we subdivided the available analogy questions into two sets: (a) unigram analogy questions, i.e., questions that involve only a single word; and (b) n-gram analogy questions, i.e., questions that involved at least one-word phrase. To address the n-gram analogy questions, we developed `Seq2Seq` and `Seq2Vec` deep learning models that incorporate word embeddings. We will consider our results under both of these conditions.

Analogy between Concept Names that Are Single Words

In this section, we will consider model development, empirical results, and their analyses for analogies between concepts that are named by a single word. This includes questions such as "Phospholipid is to lipid as margarine is to fat."

Model Development

Using the sentence corpus available to us, we built multiple types of word vector representations as outlined below.

1. We used off-the-shelf `GloVe` vectors trained on Wikipedia. We also trained the `GloVe` vectors on the biology corpus.
2. We used the pretrained module of `ELMo` that is based on deep contextualized vectors which introduce a general approach for learning high-quality contextualized representation (Peters et al. 2018b).

3. We used off-the-shelf `fastText` word vectors and also trained a version of `fastText` on the corpus of our Biology textbook.

Our model for computing analogies between concept names that are single words was based on a straightforward application of vector offset models (Mikolov et al., 2013) as outlined below.

1. First we find the corresponding embedding vectors for each of the words *A*, *B*, *C*: x_A, x_B, x_C which are all normalized to unit norm.
2. We then compute $y = x_B - x_A + x_C$.
3. Here y is the continuous space representation of the word that is expected to be the best answer. As there is a possibility that there is no word at that exact position, we compute the greatest cosine similarity to find the word that is the closest to y. We find the greatest cosine similarity as

$$w* = argmax_w \frac{x_w y}{\|x_w\| \|y\|}$$

Experimental Results

We used two evaluation metrics for the algorithm described in the previous section: accuracy and similarity to the correct answer. We consider an answer accurate if the desired analogy word was one of the top 10 results returned by our algorithm. We report the cosine similarity between $B + C - A$ and D as a measure of how close the returned answer was to the desired answer. The number of questions we could test with each method was different because some words were missing from each of these embeddings. We show results in Table 2.

Analysis of Results

The results show that the word embeddings based on `ELMo` perform the best in accuracy. Training on the Biology corpus slightly improved the performance of the `GloVe` word embeddings, but slightly degraded the performance of the word

Table 2 Performance on analogy between concepts with names that are single words

Analaysis of Answers	Correct/Total	Top 10 Accuracy	Cosine Similarity
`ELMo` pretrained	507/2154	0.235	0.54
`GloVe` pretrained on Wikipedia	159/1510	0.105	0.42
`GloVe` pretrained on biology textbook	135/1203	0.112	0.42
`fastText` pretrained on Wikipedia	330/1931	0.171	0.55
`fastText` pretrained on biology textbook	181/1990	0.091	0.66

embeddings based on fastText. It is difficult to predict the reason for this, but one potential cause could be that the size of the Wikipedia corpus is much larger than the size of the Biology textbook. The superior performance of ELMo and fastText shows promise in using more complex embeddings instead of pure word embeddings based on GloVe.

Analogy between Concept Names that Are Multiword Phrases

In this section, we will consider model development, empirical results, and their analysis for analogies between concept names that are multiword phrases. This includes questions such as "Phospholipid is to a fatty acid tail as polar amino acid is to what?" Here, the correct answer is "polar side chain."

Model Development

We implemented the simplest possible Seq2Seq and Seq2Vec models. Each of these models takes a concatenation of A, B, and C with separation tokens' < SEP>' in between each of them as input, and predicts D as output. These models had the following structure.

1. For the Seq2Seq model, the encoder was a bidirectional LSTM (Hochreiter & Schmidhuber, 1997), and the decoder was a single LSTM cell. In the decoding process, we took multiplicative attention with respect to each word in the concatenated ABC sequence.
2. For the Seq2Vec model, we used a bi-LSTM (Schuster & Paliwal, 1997) encoder and a decoder with (dot-product) attention.

We incorporated pretrained ELMo embeddings (Peters et al., 2018a) in both Seq2Seq and Seq2Vec models. We had also experimented with BERT (Devlin et al., 2018) and BioBERT embeddings (Lee et al., 2019), but as their performance was much lower, we have omitted them from this chapter. For the Seq2Seq model, we generalized our basic multiplicative attention with a Tri-directional Attention Flow Layer (or TriDaF). This attention is a generalized version of the Bidirectional Attention Flow Layer (Seo et al., 2016). Recall that the input data to our model is a concatenation of three strings: A, B, and C. We wanted to investigate the effect of feeding each of A, B, C into three different LSTM Encoders. The TriDaF generalization helped us investigate such analogy aware input representation.

Table 3 Performance on analogy between concepts with names that are multiword phrases

	seq2Vec ELMo	Vanilla seq2seq	seq2seq TriDaF	seq2seq ELMo
Top 1 accuracy	0.51	0.5	0.48	0.5
Top 2 accuracy	0.79	0.79	0.73	0.78
Top 3 accuracy	0.93	0.93	0.85	0.93
Top 4 accuracy	0.98	0.98	0.89	0.97
Any match	0.58	0.58	0.38	0.58
BLEU	59.35	49.87	47.46	54.08

Experimental Results

Our evaluation metrics were exact-match to the top result, the number of correct results found in the top-n results, any-match to one of the correct answers, and the BLEU similarity score between the predicted answer and the set of correct answers. The number of correct results found in the top-n results takes into account that each analogy question may have more than one correct answer. The any-match metric captures the situation when any of the correct answers to the question was returned. We included the corpus BLEU score (Papineni et al., 2002) as a way of automatically calculating the similarity between two phrases using n-gram similarities. We calculated the BLEU score by taking the phrases corresponding to the correct answer for an analogy as reference sentences and the predicted answer as the hypothesis. Our results are shown in Table 3.

Analysis

`Seq2Vec` model using `ELMo` outperformed the other alternatives and its performance was very close to the Seq2Seq alternatives. The Vanilla `Seq2Seq` model performed surprisingly well. Adding the `TriDaF` refinement did not help its performance. The use of `ELMo` embeddings also did not seem to make much difference to the performance of the Vanilla `Seq2Seq` model.

`Seq2Vec` took only about one hour to train. In contrast, the `Seq2Seq` models proved to be quite a challenge to design and evaluate. It was surprising that the Vanilla `Seq2Seq` model performed better than the `TriDaF` model. A possible reason for low performance could be that the `TriDaF` model had more weights to train and we did not have sufficient training data. The relationships between each of A, B, and C which was modeled must have also either not helped or must have been a weak relationship. As the maximum length of each of A, B, and C's components was around 5 words, a complicated attention did more harm than good. Empirically a simple multiplicative attention in the Vanilla `Seq2Seq` performed much better. In fact, the Vanilla `Seq2Seq` also outperforms its `ELMo` version in some of the evaluation metrics.

Conclusion

The results reported here are the first attempt to compare the methods based on word embeddings with methods operating on a hand-crafted knowledge base for the analogical reasoning question template: A is to B as C is to what? For the domain of Biology, an immediate problem that arises is that not all concept names are single words, and the direct applicability of the word embedding methods is limited. We were, however, able to construct `Seq2Seq` and `Seq2Vec` deep learning models that leverage word embeddings, and were effective in returning the correct answer in the top four results. Obtaining the correct answer in the top four results is a useful capability, but cannot be the standard expected from a tutor or a program that claims to have an *understanding* of the subject matter.

One potential issue with the test set could be that the concept names were derived from *KB Bio 101*, and these names may not appear as explicit strings in the source text. For example, "cell communication with epinephrine in muscle cell" is a concept name in *KB Bio 101*, but this exact string does not appear in our sentence corpus. Therefore, it will be difficult for a `Seq2Seq` or `Seq2Vec` model to predict it as an answer. This points to a broader issue that many times the concepts of interest in a domain are not explicitly expressed in the text. Such concepts are important for student learning, and it is unclear how they may be exposed to automatic methods that rely on constructing word embeddings.

A bigger and more challenging issue is that the `Seq2Seq` and `Seq2Vec` do not return any explanation. From a symbolic knowledge base, it is possible to generate explanations as shown in Figs. 1 and 2. Extending the deep learning methods to explain why a particular answer was returned remains a challenge open for future work. Interpretability of neural networks has been a recent research interest, and therefore, it would be interesting to apply some of those methods in the context of analogical reasoning. Including the rationale for the output of the analogies will not only enhance the theoretical understanding of the underlying model but also increase students' understanding of how different concepts represented by these phrases are linked to each other.

The explanation and accuracy from *KB Bio 101* were achieved at a premium cost. Our hope in presenting this work is to articulate the additional capability achieved through hand-crafted knowledge. We believe that any representation or task that we can do using automatic methods should be automated, and yet we need to clearly understand the limits of that automation. We hope that the analysis presented here offers some insight into the trade-offs between the two approaches.

Acknowledgments This work has been funded by a gift award from the Wallenberg Foundation in Sweden.

References

Bennett, B., Chaudhri, V. K., & Dinesh, N. (2013, September). A vocabulary of topological and containment relations for a practical biology ontology. In *Conference on Spatial Information Theory*.

Bojanowski, P., Grave, E., Joulin, A., & Mikolov, T. (2016). Enriching word vectors with subword information. *CoRR*, abs/1607.04606.

Chaudhri, V. K., Dinesh, N. & Heller, C. (2013). Conceptual models of structure and function. In *Second Annual Conference on Advances in Cognitive Systems*.

Chaudhri, V. K., Dinesh, N., & Inclezan, D (2014a). Creating a knowledge base to enable explanation, reasoning, and dialog: Three lessons. *Advances in Cognitive Systems*, 3:183–200, 7. This is a revised version of the paper that previously appeared in the Cognitive Systems Conference 2013.

Chaudhri, V. K., Elenius, D., Hinojoza, S. & Wessel, M. (2014b). Kb bio 101: Content and challenges. In *In the Proceedings of International Conference on Formal Ontologies in Information Systems*.

Devlin, J., Chang, M-W., Lee, K., & Toutanova, K. (2018). BERT: pre-training of deep bidirectional transformers for language understanding. *CoRR*, abs/1810.04805.

Gentner, D. (1983). Structure-mapping: A theoretical framework for analogy. *Cognitive Science, 7*(2), 155–170.

Hochreiter, S., & Schmidhuber, J. (1997). Long short-term memory. *Neural Computation, 9*(8), 1735–1780.

Kim, Y., Jernite, Y., Sontag, D., & Rush, A. M. (2015). Character-aware neural language models. *CoRR*, abs/1508.06615.

Lee, J., Yoon, W., Kim, S., Kim, D., Kim, S., So, C. H. & Kang, J. (2019). Biobert: a pre-trained biomedical language representation model for biomedical text mining. *CoRR*, abs/1901.08746.

Mikolov, T., Yih, S. W., & Zweig, G. (2013, May). Linguistic regularities in continuous space word representations. In *Proceedings of the 2013 Conference of the North American Chapter of the Association for Computational Linguistics: Human Language Technologies (NAACL-HLT-2013)*. Association for Computational Linguistics.

Papineni, K., Roukos, S., Ward, T., & Zhu, W-J. (2002). Bleu: A method for automatic evaluation of machine translation. In *Proceedings of the 40th Annual Meeting on Association for Computational Linguistics*, ACL '02, (pp 311–318). USA. Association for Computational Linguistics.

Pennington, J., Socher, R., & Manning, C. D. (2014). Glove: Global vectors for word representation. In *In EMNLP*.

Peters, M. E., Neumann, M., Iyyer, M., Gardner, M., Clark, C., Lee, K., & Zettlemoyer, L. (2018a). Deep contextualized word representations. In *Proc. of NAACL*.

Peters, M. E., Neumann, M., Iyyer, M., Gardner, M., Clark, C., Lee, K., & Zettlemoyer, L. (2018b). Deep contextualized word representations. *CoRR*, abs/1802.05365.

Sadava, D. E., Hillis, D. M., Heller, H. C., & Hacker, S. D. (2017). *Life: The science of biology*. Macmillan.

Schuster, M., & Paliwal, K. K. (1997). Bidirectional recurrent neural networks. *IEEE Transactions on Signal Processing, 45*(11), 2673–2681.

Seo, M. J., Kembhavi, A., Farhadi, A., & Hajishirzi, H. (2016). Bidirectional attention flow for machine comprehension. *CoRR*, abs/1611.01603.

Turney, P. D. (2008). The latent relation mapping engine: Algorithm and experiments. *Journal of Artificial Intelligence Research, 33*, 615–655.

Dr. Vinay K. Chaudhri was formerly a Program Director in the Artificial Intelligence Center of SRI International. His research focuses on the science and engineering of large knowledge base systems and spans knowledge representation and reasoning, deductive question answering, knowledge acquisition, and innovative applications. His work on intelligent textbooks won the best video award at AAAI and the best demonstration award at the European Knowledge Acquisition Conference. His work at SRI on ontologies and query manager for intelligent assistants was part of a spinoff that later became Apple's SIRI. He is currently collaborating with Stanford University and Rice University for creating an Intelligent Textbook product. He is also involved in promoting Logic Education for high schools, in formulating new projects on computable contracts and in advising the financial services industry. He has coauthored a textbook on Logic Programming, and has taught courses on knowledge graphs, logic programming, and knowledge representation. Dr. Chaudhri holds a PhD from the University of Toronto (Canada), an MS from IIT Kanpur (India), and a BS from NIT Kurukshetra (India).

Justin Xu graduated with a Master's degree in Computer Science from Stanford University in 2021. He is currently a data scientist with Klaviyou.

Han Lin Aung is a software engineer at Facebook and graduated from Stanford University with a Master's in Computer Science specializing in Artificial Intelligence. He is passionate about the intersection of technology and social good. He was part of the Code the Change chapter at Stanford University, in which he served as a team lead to provide technical assistance for nonprofits that work on issues such as homelessness and access to computer science education around the globe. His research interests include improvements in education access and medical imaging. He was a part of several interdisciplinary AI labs at Stanford and worked in domains such as satellite imagery, intelligent biology textbook, and prostate cancer detection.

Sajana Weerawardhena is a software engineer at Confluent.Inc. and graduated from Stanford University with a Bachelor's and Master's in Computer Science in Artificial Intelligence. While in college, he worked as a research assistant for the Neural Dynamics and Computation lab where he worked on studying single directions in Neural Networks. Additionally, he spent his time teaching a Design Studio class for Stanford's Computer Science and Social Good club. At Confluent, Sajana works on Kafka Connect, a framework for writing data into and out of Apache Kafka, following principles of Distributed systems. He also works on making Kafka Connect, cloud native: building out cloud infrastructure for managing Kafka Connectors.

Uses of Artificial Intelligence in Healthcare: A Structured Literature Review

Amy Collinsworth and Destiny Benjamin

Introduction

Although a precise, universally accepted definition of artificial intelligence (AI) does not exist yet, AI is typically associated with a branch of computer science focused on building algorithm-based machines capable of performing tasks that generally require human decision-making and intelligence (Stone et al., 2016). AI can be categorized based on its capabilities and functionalities. Based on capabilities, AI can be classified as Narrow AI, General AI, or Super AI. Narrow AI, sometimes also called weak AI, focuses on a single or predefined subset of cognitive abilities, and cannot perform outside of these limitations (Kaplan & Haenlein, 2019). Narrow AI enables virtual assistants such as Siri and Alexa to understand human speech and respond when queries are within their breadth of abilities. Narrow AI is also the basis of services such as Google Translate, Facebook's facial recognition abilities, and Tesla's self-driving capabilities. General AI, also known as Strong AI, is the second generation of AI in development that allows machines to apply knowledge and skills within contexts within which they were not designed to function. Such systems can reason, plan, and solve problems independently for tasks that extend beyond their planned uses. Finally, Super AI refers to machine-based systems that are truly self-aware and capable of social skills, scientific creativity, and general wisdom (Kaplan & Haenlein, 2019). Through singularity, these systems can surpass human intelligence and have the ability to perform any task.

Several subfields exist under the umbrella of AI. Machine learning involves giving computers the ability to learn without being programmed and adapt based on previous experiences (Jordan & Mitchell, 2015). Neural networks are a branch of AI that

A. Collinsworth (✉) · D. Benjamin
University of North Texas, Denton, TX, USA
e-mail: amycollinsworth@my.unt.edu; destinybenjamin@my.unt.edu

M. V. Albert et al. (eds.), *Bridging Human Intelligence and Artificial Intelligence*, Educational Communications and Technology: Issues and Innovations, https://doi.org/10.1007/978-3-030-84729-6_24

attempts to replicate the human brain by using algorithms to discern elemental relationships across copious amounts of data. Robotics focuses on designing and constructing robots that can be deployed for tasks that may be laborious for humans to perform steadily. Finally, natural language processing facilitates the communication between computers and humans by natural language. This subfield enables computers to read and understand data by mimicking human language (Nadkarni et al., 2011).

This paper focuses specifically on the uses of AI in the field of healthcare. Applications of artificial intelligence in healthcare can be categorized as virtual or physical (Hamet & Tremblay, 2017). The virtual branch includes mathematically based algorithms that enable the systems to develop and learn through experience and use. In contrast, the physical branch of AI includes medical devices and sophisticated robots such as the da Vinci Surgical System capable of performing surgery or carebots that serve as companions for elderly individuals with limited mobility or with cognitive decline.

Methods

For this literature review, refereed online journals and other academic resources were searched for publications that described artificial intelligence applications in healthcare settings. This paper used the method of structured review to arrive at a comprehensive and reliable overview of research on artificial intelligence in the healthcare field. The selected articles were found by searching multiple academic databases, including EBSCO, ERIC, and Google Scholar, using one of the following keywords: Artificial Intelligence, Machine Learning, Neural Learning, in conjunction with the keyword, Healthcare or Patient Care. The criteria for articles included in the literature was being published in a peer-reviewed journal between 1950 and 2021, written in English, having online full-text accessibility, and searched keywords appearing in the title. This literature review used document analysis to screen articles and collect initial data. Content analysis was then used to identify research patterns and trends.

Discussion

Timeline of AI in Healthcare

1950s–1960s Although storing digital information had its start in the early 1940s with large computer systems such as Vannevar Bush's Memex, the drive of multimedia in the 1950s would also lead to significant developments in the creation and storage of digital information. During this time, the focus was on creating machines that could make human decisions as accurate as a human could. This interest included multiple areas of science, including medicine. It was during the 1950s that early experimentations of AI were being fabricated. In 1950 Alan Turing created a machine to test whether computers could be designed to think and referred to his creation as the imitation game (Turing, 1950). The goal of the experiment was to test humans to see if they could distinguish between computers and humans based on conversation text, and eventually became known as the Turing Test (Amisha et al., 2019). Since the mere mention of the term AI by John McCarthy in 1956, the world has looked into artificial intelligence and machine learning to not only solve human problems but also predict outcomes before problems occur.

The mid-1950s and 1960s were known for major advancements during the information explosion age due to the innovations in the computer and mechanical industries (Hiagh, 2009). Creating accompanying software to talk to the machines was led by pioneers like Grace Hopper, who is widely accredited for codeveloping the standardized computer language COBOL (Abbate, 2011). The developments of programming languages were considered just as important as the hardware developments; one simply did not advance without the other. It was because of the synchronicity of the advancements that the auto industry could capitalize on AI. In 1961, General Motors built a system named Unimate, which was able to automate die casting steps by following a series of instructions (Kaul Enslin, & Gross, 2020). Soon after, in 1964, Dr. Joseph Weizenbaum used natural language processing (NLP) to create what was considered the first chatterbot named ELIZA, which was designed to simulate conversions between humans in the field of psychology and communication (Kaul et al., 2020). Two years later, in 1966, what was referred to as the "first electronic person" was created by a team at the Stanford Research Institute (now known as SRI International). The robot was nick-named Shakey and was primarily programmed to solve problems on its own by mapping out its surroundings and completing mobile-based tasks. The hope was that Shakey would lead to robots carrying out and improving complicated tasks in factories (Szondy, 2015).

1970s–1980s In 1970, William B. Schwartz published an article titled "Medicine and the Computer: The Promise and Problems of Change" (Swartz, 1970). Schwartz was a medical doctor with great interest in using computers in healthcare. He documented his views on future healthcare system developments and the benefits from such advances in technology. His team developed their own computer program that would consult with a physician by attempting to diagnose a patient based on details provided by the user in what he referred to as "branching of the decision tree" (Schwartz, 1970, p. 1259). Schwartz also issued warnings over some problems that are of concern in our current healthcare system, including high costs, social economics, legal demands, and technical considerations.

As with most technological advancements in history, there were years in which progress lacked technological developments. In the world of artificial intelligence and machine learning, these are known as "Winters." The First AI Winter that occurred in the mid-1970s continued through most of the 1980s. Exceptions to this Winter included William Clancey and Edward Shortliffe, who brought to light the uses of AI applications in multiple healthcare settings. Their 1984 publication (Clancey & Shortliffe, 1984) defined what medical AI meant and considered the potentials of AI applications with the needs of healthcare professionals to improve overall documentation and communication in medicine.

1990s–2000s The Second AI Winter occurred in the late 1980s and early 1990s where the main goals were to improve medical data online accessibility. But by the late 1990s there was regained interest in part due to the American National Library of Medicine awarding contracts to medical institutions to explore new ways to incorporate AI into healthcare, improving overall infrastructures (Kaul et al., 2020). AI took shape in the form of electronic medical records (EMRs), telemedicine, and other areas of information sharing.

2010–present Mintz and Brodie (2019) define several focuses of AI in healthcare: image processing, computer vision, artificial neural network (ANN), machine learning (ML), convolutional neural network (CNN), and deep learning (DL). Deep learning is a subset of machine learning that is constructed to process the information on multiple levels, like the human brain (Mintz & Brodie, 2019). It was first investigated in the 1950s but had limitations mainly due to the absence of computer technology. It took many years, but technology finally advanced enough that DL could be re-investigated and built on. Cardiology, gastroenterology, oncology, radiology, and surgery are a few areas in healthcare exploring the uses of AI, ML, and DL (Kaul et al., 2020).

Jiang et al. (2017) performed a literature review on the topic of AI in healthcare. Their focus was to identify specific specialties in medicine utilizing artificial intelligence to improve clinical practices. They reviewed articles published during the time period 2013–2016 covering medical specialties, healthcare data, and AI categories (ML and NLP). Once the review was completed, the team found diagnostic imaging data to be the main interest in publication content, followed by genetics and electrodiagnosis. The top four diseases that resulted in publications during 2013–2016 included neoplasms, nervous, cardiovascular, and urogenital. A similar search of publications during late 2019–2020 yielded a dramatic shift of focus to the SARS-CoV-2, the novel coronavirus that causes COVID-19 (Bansal et al., 2020).

Healthcare Education and AI

Developments in artificial intelligence have also impacted medical schools and how future medical professionals are trained. The following section reviews common uses of AI in medical schools, and how students and instructors respond to the use of this technology.

Current Applications of AI in Medical Schools

Authors such as Wartman and Combs (2019) have suggested that the system for educating medical professionals requires a revolution because the amount of available medical knowledge exceeds the human mind's organizing capacity and can lead to stress-induced mental illness among learners. Wartman and Combs (2019) suggest remediating this problem by re-engineering the medical school curricula so that it shifts from a "focus on information acquisition to an emphasis on knowledge management and communication" (p. 147). AI applications can aggregate vast amounts of data, generate diagnostic and treatment options, and assign confidence ratings to those recommendations that clinicians can then interpret and communicate to patients. Training in understanding AI systems' recommendations can enable medical students to personalize treatment to the individual characteristics of each patient. Utilizing AI systems also reduces cognitive and information overload that medical students can experience earlier in their careers.

Some researchers such as Masters (2019) believe that AI will eventually affect every aspect of human life, including medicine and medical education. Masters (2019) asserts that surgical robotics, for instance, will continue to evolve until intelligent robots with AI software can perform surgery without humans. He cautions that medical schools that have not integrated AI into their curriculum and are not teaching robotic surgery will quickly fall behind this potential standard. Earlier researchers such as Moles et al. (2009) developed a program to teach and assess the development of otolaryngologic residents' basic robotic surgical skills. Moles et al. (2009) suggest AI and robotic surgery training programs be formally established in residency programs because the skill will eventually become an integral part of surgical practice. Alonso-Silverio et al. (2018) conducted a similar study focusing on the laparoscopic surgical skills of ten medical students and six residents. They found that laparoscopic box training systems based on open-source hardware and artificial intelligence improved the learning curve and dexterity of the 16 participants.

Medical schools are increasing their use of artificial intelligence in simulation-based training designed to assess and train the psychomotor skills involved in the surgery. Mirchi et al. (2020) piloted their Virtual Operative Assistant, an educational platform that automatically assesses and provides user feedback, with 28 skilled participants and 22 novice participants who were required to perform a virtual reality-based subpial brain tumor resection task using the NeuroVR simulator. The Virtual Operative Assistant successfully classified novice and skilled participants with an accuracy of 92%, specificity of 82%, and sensitivity of 100%. The researchers concluded that the AI-based system was advantageous over traditional teaching methods because it enabled instructors to identify individual components of psychomotor expertise in tasks too multifaceted for instructors to observe normally. The system mimics real life by using an apprenticeship model with auditory feedback in natural human language in a clinical or operating environment.

Medical Student Attitudes Toward AI

Sit et al. (2020) surveyed medical students (n = 484) at 19 UK medical schools and found most medical school students surveyed (88%) believed that AI would play an essential role in healthcare. However, the students surveyed did not feel adequately prepared to work alongside AI and would find training on the subject beneficial. Some participants (n = 45) experienced AI training in their medical programs, but this group still reported a lack of confidence and understanding required for the critical use of healthcare AI tools.

Discussion of AI in healthcare in the news and lay media often express the concern that AI is replacing radiologists. Park et al. (2020) administered a web-based survey to American medical students (n = 152) to understand their perceptions about radiology and determine if such reports negatively impact medical students' perceptions of radiology as a viable specialty. After analyzing results from the six-question survey, the authors concluded that more than 75% of participants believed AI would significantly impact medicine, with 66% believing the field of diagnostic radiology would be the most heavily influenced. Regarding radiology being a viable career, nearly half (44%) of those surveyed reported that AI made them less enthusiastic about radiology. Gong et al. (2019) conducted a similar study but focused on medical students (n = 322) at all 17 Canadian medical schools. In this study, 67.7% of participants believed AI would reduce the demand for radiologists, and 48.6% responded that AI caused anxiety when considering the radiology specialty. Pinto dos Santos et al. (2019) explored undergraduate medical students' attitudes (n = 263) toward artificial Intelligence (AI) in radiology and medicine at three German universities. Participants in this study had more positive opinions about AI improving radiology and not making the profession obsolete. Results showed 77% agreed that AI would improve radiology, and 83% disagreed that AI technology will eventually replace human radiologists. A total of 77 percent of those surveyed indicated that AI training should be part of the radiology curriculum.

Instructor Attitudes Toward AI in Medical Curriculum

Much of the research on instructor attitudes toward AI in medical education has focused on the assessment of medical students. Gierl et al. (2014) explored the use of AI software to grade essays written by postgraduate medical students and found that scores generated by the AI systems aligned consistently with those of human scorers at a high level. Gierl et al. (2014) concluded that AI-based grading systems could improve medical education by providing consistency in scoring, reducing the time and cost required for assessment, and providing students with immediate feedback on constructed-response tasks. Kintsch (2002) addressed the use of latent semantic analysis (LSA), which is a form of machine learning, to compare student-constructed responses to a target or model essay. Medical school students are frequently assessed using standardized patients. This involves requiring students to compose a full-text written account of the encounter with the patient that is then evaluated using a rubric. Kintsch (2002) suggests that this practice is an effective teaching method, but grading these responses is challenging. LSA, however, could be used to devise automatic grading that could be supplemented with feedback from the instructor.

Promising AI Applications in Medicine

The following section explores several applications of AI in healthcare that are used by patients and healthcare professionals. This section represents a small selection of the AI tools that are currently available or in development.

Chatbots

AI-powered chatbots simulate human conversation with a patient to help assess their symptoms and determine the next steps for care. These automated systems are important in healthcare because they provide information to help patients cure some common illnesses without the intervention of a healthcare professional. Approximately 60% of doctor visits are due to simple health concerns, and 80% of these can be cured with home remedies, simple lifestyle changes, or over-the-counter medication (Bhirud et al., 2019). If additional medical help is needed, the chatbots can provide guidance.

One example of a widely used text-based chatbot is the Centers for Disease Control and Prevention's (CDC) coronavirus self-checker. This AI-based program is designed for use by patients rather than medical professionals. After the user agrees to the terms of service and inputs demographic information relating to age, gender, race, and location, the chatbot proceeds to list potentially life-threatening symptoms. The user must respond using the on-screen "yes" or "no" buttons. Based on the response, the chatbot will either encourage the user to seek immediate medical attention or will continue asking more specific questions to gather more information. The chatbot can provide general recommendations for avoiding getting sick as well as help users determine if they should see a doctor. The AI-based software provides immediate information to the user from the comfort of their home.

Medical Imaging

Since the onset of the COVID-19 pandemic in 2019, researchers have been looking for ways to help track, diagnose and prevent the spread of the virus. Bansal et al. (2020) reviewed the potential ways in which AI and ML could be utilized to develop predictive models in the battle against COVID-19. Key highlights from their article outline how DL, NLP, sentiment analysis, and machine vision can help with predicting COVID-19 outbreaks. Diagnostic imaging can also harness the power of AI and ML for predicting COVID-19 by using algorithms to detect the virus on lung x-rays. Minaee et al. (2020) developed a deep learning algorithm that used a dataset containing 5000 chest x-rays to teach the program how to identify COVID-19 on the images. The results of the experiment were considered promising by showing a sensitivity rate of 98% and specificity of 90%. The researchers were so impressed with the outcomes that they made the dataset of 5000 chest images publicly available for other researchers.

Several other areas in medicine are currently exploring the potential uses of artificial intelligence to detect and predict the disease. For example, AI is being used to detect different types of cancers. Medical imaging such as computed tomography (CT) colonography can identify the location and size of polyps, but it lacks the ability to help radiologists always differentiate between precancerous and noncancerous tissue. Grosu et al. (2021) demonstrated the ability of ML to distinguish between benign and premalignant colorectal polyps by identifying their differences on CT images with an area under the curve (AUC) of 0.91. In Costa Rica, scientists used AI to create an automated process of reviewing cervical images for the detection of cancerous tissue. Although image quality was a limitation in the study, Hu et al. (2019) proved the algorithm showed promise by having higher accuracy when compared to the traditional cervigram interpretations or conventional cytology (Fig. 1). Dermatology studies for leveraging AI for the identification of cancerous lesions on the skin are also being investigated. Soenksen et al. (2021) used deep convolutional neural networks (DCNN) in their study to distinguish between suspicious pigmented lesions and nonsuspicious lesions on photographs of patient's backs. The results were considered promising by the researchers in that the algorithm could be used by physicians for providing rapid assessment of patient skin lesions.

Innovative uses of AI are also being used in the field of cardiology. Taylor et al. (2013) are leveraging DL and computational fluid dynamics (CFD) to create

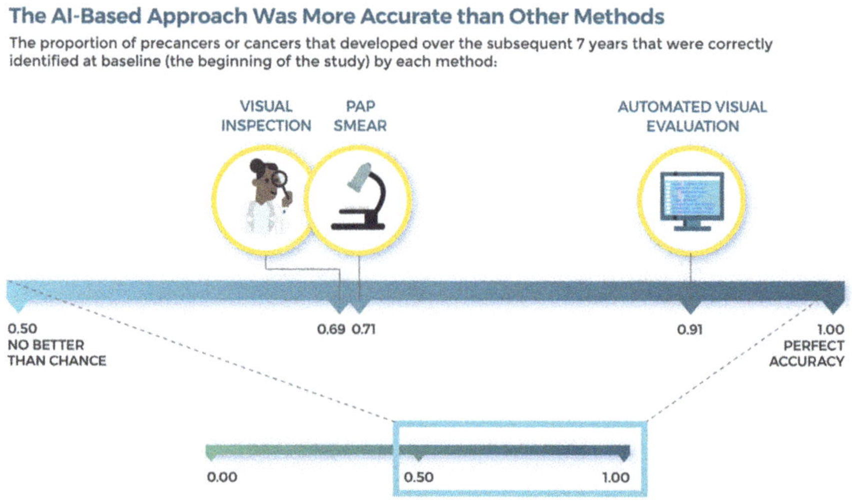

Fig. 1 Infographic demonstrating the accuracy of AI used to detect cervical cancer
Note: From "An Observational Study of Deep Learning and Automated Evaluation of Cervical Images for Cancer Screening" by Hu et al., (2019). *Journal of the National Cancer Institute, 111*(9), 923–932. https://doi.org/10.1093/jnci/djy225. Copyright 2019 by the National Cancer Institute (NCI). In the public domain

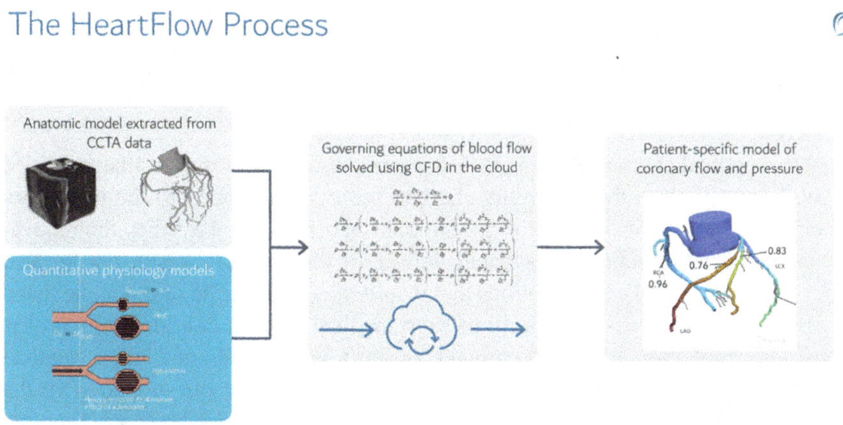

Fig. 2 Sample image of an FFRct analysis demonstrating blood flow simulation of the coronary arteries of a patient
Note: Adapted image from "Computational fluid dynamics applied to cardiac computed tomography for noninvasive quantification of fractional flow reserve: scientific basis" by C. A. Taylor, T. A. Fonte, and J. K. Min, 2013, *Journal of the American College of Cardiology*, *61*(22), 2233–2241. Copyright 2021 by HeartFlow., Inc. Reprinted with permission

simulated models of the blood flow of the coronary arteries derived from coronary CT images. Physicians are then able to review 3D models and measurements of the coronary blood flow specific to each patient. The 3D representations also give doctors a communication tool to discuss coronary artery disease diagnosis with their patients. An overview of this simulation process can be seen in Fig. 2.

Han et al. (2021), Schock et al. (2020), and York et al. (2020) are all pioneering ways to use AI to aid in the area of skeletal radiology. Han et al. (2021) explored using neural symbolic learning (NSL) and deep neural learning (DNL) to help create autogenerated reports on spinal structures identified on magnetic resonance images (MRI). The team developed a two-step framework for autocreating reports with a system demonstrating 95.8% pixel accuracy. Schock et al. (2020) developed a convolutional neural network (CNN) to aid radiologists by automatically segmenting and measuring anatomy on long-leg radiographs (n = 225). The experimental AI system showed to be faster than radiologists at measuring anatomy by 33 seconds. Lastly, York et al. (2020) wanted to gain insight into how patients felt about the use of AI in diagnostic imaging of bones and joints. The team sent questionnaires to patients (n = 300) with a 72.2% completion rate (n = 216). Overall findings from the study suggest that patients prefer a human doctor to read and assess their medical images instead of AI-based systems.

Ethics with AI in Medicine

Ethical Concerns

In 1970, medical doctor Willaim B. Schwartz published an article that provided valuable insights into the upcoming changes that would happen to the healthcare system due to advances in technology. Dr. Schwartz not only described the innovative uses that new technologies could deliver to the medical world, but he also understood the ethical considerations that would likely arise. The first item he listed as a potential threat was the ability to keep medical records confidential with the soon-to-be implementation of computer systems in hospitals and other medical institutions (Schwartz, 1970). The next issues that Schwartz questioned were the legal and liability of such things as data breaches and incorrect record keeping. Today, over 50 years later, some of those very worries are still a large concern for ethical, legal, privacy, and security reasons. As we bring AI and ML into the world of medicine, these concerns also need to be addressed with firm leadership.

To investigate these issues in today's healthcare world, Hochheiser and Valdez (2020) reviewed articles published between 2017 and 2019 with a focus on biomedical informatics and ethics in research. The authors discovered three themes among the articles selected: current systems, system designs, and research conduct. They also highlighted the important role newer technologies such as social media could have on patient recruitment for research purposes, but responsible use is needed to maintain study integrity.

Patient Privacy

To protect patients' medical records, the Health Insurance Portability and Accountability Act (HIPAA) of 1996 was introduced (U.S. Department of Health and Human Services, 2013). HIPAA provides a set of standards for medical institutions to follow in order to protect patient information. Prior to this act, the healthcare industry did not have a national set of requirements to adhere to. Most of the privacy protections addressed under HIPAA cover multiple forms of patient data. The use of AI in healthcare presents newer concerns that will need to be addressed properly even as new technology continues to emerge. Biosensors are one of such newer technologies in which the protection of patient data is causing alarm. Wearable biosensors are sensing devices attached to the human body that recognizes, measures, and/or records a biological element of that person (Kim et al., 2019). Examples of wearable biosensors documented by Kim et al. (2019) include contact lenses, watches, finger clips, and patches designed for blood glucose monitoring. Many of these sensors are approved by the Food and Drug Administration (FDA) and are contributing to patient care. However, the area of patient data and who has access is of great concern. Kim et al. (2019) highlighted the importance of designing information collection infrastructures with strict security and privacy while maintaining proper data management.

It is also important to understand that different countries comply with unique rules and regulations regarding protecting patient health information. Most nations have their own government entities that are responsible for data safety and compliance. Schönberger (2019) reviewed 300 articles covering legal and ethical issues on the topic of AI in healthcare in Europe and the United Kingdom. He concluded that current laws could be applied to AI technology in healthcare or could be adjusted to accommodate issues with modern technologies. This is a similar viewpoint shared by Vayena et al. (2018) as in their article, it was noted that the European General Data Protection Regulation (GDPR) imposes restrictions regarding the creation, storage, and communication of patient data.

Cyber Security

The important role of cyber security becomes very apparent when discussing the safeguarding of patient health information (PHI). Health information technology (IT) has the complex task of preventing data breaches and ensuring patient information is safe and used properly. In 2018, a team from Western Michigan University investigated cyber security threats in healthcare. Ronquillo et al. (2018) reviewed data breaches during the years of 2013–2017 and found there to have been 128 medical record breaches and 363 hacking occurrences reported in the United States. The team noted that because of the increased use of EMRs (electronic medical records), medical institutions had become targets for hackers to obtain private patient information illegally. The authors concluded that informatics and cyber security infrastructure in healthcare will have to evolve in order to maintain secure environments.

Limitations in AI

The greatest weakness of artificial intelligence and machine learning is the process in which the learning result is underspecified because data points outnumber the parameters and are known as underspecification (D'Amour et al., 2020). Another term for this complicated issue is called overfitting and occurs when the ML algorithm is too focused. Reliability and credibility can then become problematic in machine learning because results may be incorrect due to the algorithm overlooking certain data or focusing only on certain data points. The team at Google decided to research this weakness in several areas, including computer vision, radiology images, NLP, clinical risk predictions, and medical genomics (D'Amour et al., 2020). The result of their deep dive into each category helped them conclude that creating training models with more trusted biases may help prevent inaccurate solutions produced by some ML algorithms.

Conclusion

In conclusion, the past few decades have shown fascinating new developments using AI in healthcare to improve patients' health. Advances in AI show the potential for creating innovative solutions in the field of medicine. Both innovative and powerful, AI can be a turning point in solving medical problems and predicting outcomes. However, ethical, privacy, and security measures must be taken under thoughtful consideration when integrating AI into the healthcare setting. With proper and responsible use, AI can change the field of medicine by giving medical professionals an opportunity to learn and develop new pathways.

Although the intention of this literature review was to introduce and offer a historical overview of applications of AI in healthcare for those outside of the field, our study has some limitations that could be addressed by more in-depth future studies. First, the study was limited to articles written in English and with full-text accessibility, which may have excluded promising research. Second, our literature review took a broad approach to reviewing literature on AI in healthcare. Future studies could explore AI-based tools in specific areas of healthcare to produce results and strategies that can be implemented by healthcare professionals.

References

Abbate, J. (2011). Software's founding mother. *Metascience, 20*, 215–218. https://doi.org/10.1007/s11016-010-9418-z

Alonso-Silverio, G. A., Pérez-Escamirosa, F., Bruno-Sanchez, R., Ortiz-Simon, J. L., Muñoz-Guerrero, R., Minor-Martinez, A., & Alarcón-Paredes, A. (2018). Development of a laparoscopic box trainer based on open source hardware and artificial intelligence for objective assessment of surgical psychomotor skills. *Surgical Innovation, 25*(4), 380–388. https://doi.org/10.1177/1553350618777045

Amisha, P. M., Pathania, M., & Rathaur, V. K. (2019). Overview of artificial intelligence in medicine. *Journal of Family Medicine and Primary Care, 8*(7), 2328.

Bansal, A., Padappayil, R. P., Garg, C., Singal, A., Gupta, M., & Klein, A. (2020). Utility of artificial Intelligence amidst the COVID 19 pandemic: A review. *Journal of Medical Systems, 44*(9), 1–6.

Bhirud, N., Tataale, S., Randive, S., & Nahar, S. (2019). A literature review on chatbots in healthcare domain. *International Journal of Scientific & Technology Research, 8*(7), 225–231.

Clancey, W., & Shortliffe, E. (1984). *Readings in medical artificial intelligence: The first decade*. Addison Wesley.

D'Amour, A., Heller, K., Moldovan, D., Adlam, B., Alipanahi, B., Beutel, A., ... & Sculley, D. (2020). Underspecification presents challenges for credibility in modern machine learning. *arXiv preprint arXiv:2011.03395*.

Gierl, M. J., Latifi, S., Lai, H., Boulais, A.-P., & Champlain, A. D. (2014). Automated essay scoring and the future of educational assessment in medical education. *Medical Education, 48*(10), 950–962. https://doi.org/10.1111/medu.12517

Gong, B., Nugent, J. P., Guest, W., Parker, W., Chang, P. J., Khosa, F., & Nicolaou, S. (2019). Influence of artificial intelligence on Canadian medical students' preference for radiology specialty: A national survey study. *Academic Radiology, 26*(4), 566–577. https://doi.org/10.1016/j.acra.2018.10.007

Grosu, S., Wesp, P., Graser, A., Maurus, S., Schulz, C., Knösel, T., … Kazmierczak, P. M. (2021). Machine Learning–based differentiation of benign and premalignant colorectal polyps detected with CT colonography in an asymptomatic screening population: A proof-of-concept study. *Radiology*, 202363.

Hamet, P., & Tremblay, J. (2017). Artificial intelligence in medicine. *Metabolism, 69*, S36–S40. https://doi.org/10.1016/j.metabol.2017.01.011

Haigh, T. (2009). How data got its base: Information storage software in the 1950s and 1960s. *IEEE Annals of the History of Computing, 31*(4), 6–25.

Han, Z., Wei, B., Xi, X., Chen, B., Yin, Y., & Li, S. (2021). Unifying neural learning and symbolic reasoning for spinal medical report generation. *Medical Image Analysis, 67*, 101872.

Hochheiser, H., & Valdez, R. S. (2020). Human-computer interaction, ethics, and biomedical informatics. *Yearbook of Medical Informatics, 29*(1), 93–98. https://doi.org/10.1055/s-0040-1701990. (Links to an external site.) Retrieved from: https://www.ncbi.nlm.nih.gov/pmc/articles/PMC7442500/

Hu, L., Bell, D., Antani, S., Xue, Z., Yu, K., Horning, M. P., Gachuhi, N., Wilson, B., Jaiswal, M. S., Befano, B., Long, L. R., Herrero, R., Einstein, M. H., Burk, R. D., Demarco, M., Gage, J. C., Rodriguez, A. C., Wentzensen, N., & Schiffman, M. (2019). An observational study of deep learning and automated evaluation of cervical images for cancer screening. *Journal of the National Cancer Institute, 111*(9), 923–932. https://doi.org/10.1093/jnci/djy225

Jiang, F., Jiang, Y., Zhi, H., Dong, Y., Li, H., Ma, S., Wang, Y., Dong, Q., Shen, H., & Wang, Y. (2017). Artificial Intelligence in healthcare: Past, present and future. Stroke and Vascular. *Neurology, 2*(4), 230–243. https://doi.org/10.1136/svn-2017-000101

Jordan, M. I., & Mitchell, T. M. (2015). Machine learning: Trends, perspectives, and prospects. *Science, 349*(6245), 255–260. https://doi.org/10.1126/science.aaa8415

Kaplan, A., & Haenlein, M. (2019). Siri, Siri, in my hand: Who's the fairest in the land? On the interpretations, illustrations, and implications of artificial intelligence. *Business Horizons, 62*(1), 15–25. https://doi.org/10.1016/j.bushor.2018.08.004

Kaul, V., Enslin, S., & Gross, S. A. (2020). The history of artificial intelligence in medicine. *Gastrointestinal Endoscopy, 92*(4), 807–812.

Kim, J., Campbell, A. S., de Ávila, B. E. F., & Wang, J. (2019). Wearable biosensors for healthcare monitoring. *Nature Biotechnology, 37*(4), 389–406.

Kintsch, W. (2002). The potential of latent semantic analysis for machine grading of clinical case summaries. *Journal of Biomedical Informatics, 35*(1), 3–7. https://doi.org/10.1016/S1532-0464(02)00004-7

Masters, K. (2019). Artificial Intelligence in medical education. *Medical Teacher, 41*(9), 976–980. https://doi.org/10.1080/0142159X.2019.1595557

Minaee, S., Kafieh, R., Sonka, M., Yazdani, S., & Soufi, G. J. (2020). Deep-covid: Predicting covid-19 from chest x-ray images using deep transfer learning. *Medical Image Analysis, 65*, 101794.

Mintz, Y., & Brodie, R. (2019). Introduction to artificial intelligence in medicine. *Minimally Invasive Therapy & Allied Technologies, 28*(2), 73–81.

Mirchi, N., Bissonnette, V., Yilmaz, R., Ledwos, N., Winkler-Schwartz, A., & Maestro, R. F. D. (2020). The Virtual Operative Assistant: An explainable artificial intelligence tool for simulation-based training in surgery and medicine. *PLoS One, 15*(2), e0229596. https://doi.org/10.1371/journal.pone.0229596

Moles, J. J., Connelly, P. E., Sarti, E. E., & Baredes, S. (2009). Establishing a training program for residents in robotic surgery. *The Laryngoscope, 119*(10), 1927–1931. https://doi.org/10.1002/lary.20508

Nadkarni, P. M., Ohno-Machado, L., & Chapman, W. W. (2011). Natural language processing: An introduction. *Journal of the American Medical Informatics Association, 18*(5), 544–551. https://doi.org/10.1136/amiajnl-2011-000464

Park, C. J., Yi, P. H., & Siegel, E. L. (2020). Medical student perspectives on the impact of artificial intelligence on the practice of medicine. *Current Problems in Diagnostic Radiology*. https://doi.org/10.1067/j.cpradiol.2020.06.011

Pinto dos Santos, D., Giese, D., Brodehl, S., Chon, S. H., Staab, W., Kleinert, R., Maintz, D., & Baeßler, B. (2019). Medical students' attitude towards artificial Intelligence: A multicentre survey. *European Radiology, 29*(4), 1640–1646. http://dx.doi.org.libproxy.library.unt.edu/10.1007/s00330-018-5601-1

Ronquillo, J. G., Erik Winterholler, J., Cwikla, K., Szymanski, R., & Levy, C. (2018). Health IT, hacking, and cybersecurity: national trends in data breaches of protected health information. *JAMIA Open, 1*(1), 15–19.

Schock, J., Truhn, D., Abrar, D. B., Merhof, D., Conrad, S., Post, M., ... & Nebelung, S. (2020). Automated analysis of alignment in long-leg radiographs using a fully automated support system based on artificial intelligence. *Radiology: Artificial Intelligence*, e200198.

Schönberger, D. (2019). Artificial Intelligence in healthcare: A critical analysis of the legal and ethical implications. *International Journal of Law and Information Technology, 27*(2), 171–203.

Schwartz, W. B. (1970). Medicine and the computer: The promise and problems of change. In *Use and impact of computers in clinical medicine* (pp. 321–335). Springer.

Sit, C., Srinivasan, R., Amlani, A., Muthuswamy, K., Azam, A., Monzon, L., & Poon, D. S. (2020). Attitudes and perceptions of UK medical students towards artificial intelligence and radiology: A multicentre survey. *Insights Into Imaging, 11*(1), 14. https://doi.org/10.1186/s13244-019-0830-7

Soenksen, L. R., Kassis, T., Conover, S. T., Marti-Fuster, B., Birkenfeld, J. S., Tucker-Schwartz, J., … Gray, M. L. (2021). Using deep learning for dermatologist-level detection of suspicious pigmented skin lesions from wide-field images. *Science Translational Medicine, 13*(581).

Stone, P., Brooks, R., Brynjolfsson, E., Calo, R., Etzioni, O., Hager, G., Hirschberg, J., Kalyanakrishnan, S., Kamar, E., Kraus, S., Leyton-Brown, K., Parkes, D., Press, W., Saxenian, A., Shah, J., Tambe, M., & Teller, A. (2016). *Artificial intelligence and life in 2030: The one hundred year study on artificial Intelligence* [Report]. Stanford University. https://apo.org.au/node/210721

Szondy, D. (2015). Fifty years of Shakey, the "world's first electronic person". *New Atlas*. Retrieved from: https://newatlas.com/shakey-robot-sri-fiftieth-anniversary/37668/

Taylor, C. A., Fonte, T. A., & Min, J. K. (2013). Computational fluid dynamics applied to cardiac computed tomography for noninvasive quantification of fractional flow reserve: scientific basis. *Journal of the American College of Cardiology, 61*(22), 2233–2241.

Turing, A. M. (1950). I.—Computing machinery and Intelligence. *Mind, 59*(236), 433–460. https://doi.org/10.1093/mind/LIX.236.433

US Department of Health and Human Services. (2013). Summary of the HIPAA security rule. *Health Insurance Portability and Accountability*.

Vayena, E., Blasimme, A., & Cohen, I. G. (2018). Machine learning in medicine: Addressing ethical challenges. *PLoS Medicine, 15*(11), 1–4. https://doi.org/10.1371/journal.pmed.1002689(EBSCOhost)

Wartman, S. A., & Combs, C. D. (2019). Reimagining Medical Education in the Age of AI. *AMA Journal of Ethics, 21*(2), 146–152. https://doi.org/10.1001/amajethics.2019.146

York, T., Jenney, H., & Jones, G. (2020). Clinician and computer: a study on patient perceptions of artificial intelligence in skeletal radiography. *BMJ Health & Care Informatics, 27*(3), e100233. https://doi.org/10.1136/bmjhci-2020-100233

Amy Collinsworth is a doctoral student in the Learning Technologies program at the University of North Texas. She has a background in medical imaging and clinical trials. Her interests include AI in healthcare, technology in the medical field, and educational simulations. She has licenses in radiography and computed tomography with the American Registry of Radiologic Technologists (ARRT) and is a member of the American Society of Radiologic Technologists (ASRT).

Destiny Benjamin is a learning technologies doctoral student at the University of North Texas and a K-12 special education teacher. Her research interests include technology-supported teaching and learning strategies for students with disabilities, game-based learning, and artificial intelligence applications in education. She is a member of the Association for Education Communication Technology (AECT). She has presented at several international conferences such as PPTELL 2020, SITE 2021, MIRS 2021, and EDIL.

Correction to: Smart Learning in Support of Critical Thinking: Lessons Learned and a Theoretically and Research-Based Framework

Shanshan Ma, J. Michael Spector, Dejian Liu, Kaushal Kumar Bhagat, Dawit Tiruneh, Jonah Mancini, Lin Lin, Rodney Nielsen, and Kinshuk

Correction to:
Chapter 22 in: M. V. Albert et al. (eds.), *Bridging Human Intelligence and Artificial Intelligence*, Educational Communications and Technology: Issues and Innovations, https://doi.org/10.1007/978-3-030-84729-6_22

The affiliation of the author "K. K. Bhagat" was inadvertently published incorrectly. This has now been corrected throughout the book as "Advanced Technology Development Centre, Indian Institute of Technology, Kharagpur, India".

The updated version of this chapter can be found at:
https://doi.org/10.1007/978-3-030-84729-6_22

M. V. Albert et al. (eds.), *Bridging Human Intelligence and Artificial Intelligence*, Educational Communications and Technology: Issues and Innovations, https://doi.org/10.1007/978-3-030-84729-6_25

Index

M. V. Albert et al. (eds.), *Bridging Human Intelligence and Artificial Intelligence*, Educational Communications and Technology: Issues and Innovations, https://doi.org/10.1007/978-3-030-84729-6

B

C

D

Q

R

S

W

Y

Z

www.ingramcontent.com/pod-product-compliance
Ingram Content Group UK Ltd.
Pitfield, Milton Keynes, MK11 3LW, UK
UKHW021410091026
15624UKWH00009B/174
* 9 7 8 3 0 3 0 8 4 7 2 8 9 *